DIRTY MONEY:

THE EVOLUTION OF MONEY LAUNDERING COUNTERMEASURES

Second edition
Revised and expanded

William C. Gilmore

Council of Europe Publishing

Cover design: Graphic Design Workshop, Council of Europe

Council of Europe Publishing
F-67075 Strasbourg Cedex

ISBN 92-871-3854-0
© Council of Europe, May 1999
Printed in Belgium

Dedicated to the memory of
John R. Gilmore (1909-69)

TABLE OF CONTENTS

ACKNOWLEDGEMENTS

Such is the pace of developments as the international community seeks to counter money laundering, and so numerous the fora which are contributing to that process, that I have found it necessary on many occasions to request assistance from those involved. Almost without exception such pleas have elicited positive and constructive responses. Particular thanks are due to Ms D. Stafford in London, Mr H. Nilsson and Mr A. Beverly in Brussels, and Mr P. Csonka, Mr J. Ringguth and Mr L. Aigrot in Strasbourg. I would also like to take this opportunity to acknowledge the research assistance provided by Mr V. Mitsilegas of the University of Edinburgh in relation to the human rights issues addressed in Chapter V and the financial support received from both the Faculty of Law of the University of Edinburgh and the trustees of the Russell Trust. Finally, I would like to express my thanks to Ms B. Zatlokal of Council of Europe Publishing for her kindness and support, and to Miss L. Lawson of the University of Edinburgh whose secretarial skills and exceptional tolerance were relied upon throughout.

The views contained in the pages which follow are mine alone and are not intended to represent the perceptions of the Council of Europe or of any other institution or government with which I am associated. I am, of course, responsible for any deficiencies of style or substance which remain. The text seeks to represent the position as of 31 December 1998 although I have made use of materials of a more recent vintage where possible.

Old College   William C. Gilmore
Edinburgh

19 March 1999

FOREWORD

Money laundering is not a new phenomenon - criminals have always tried to hide their bounty - but it is taking on new forms. Long considered a marginal problem, the explosion of drug trafficking has made it an important part of any serious criminal enterprise. The proceeds of crime, particularly cash, must be laundered for reinvestment. This involves a series of complicated financial operations (deposits, withdrawals, bank transfers, etc.) which ultimately results in criminal money becoming "clean" and acceptable for legitimate business purposes.

The problem of money laundering has grown in recent years, to keep pace with the magnitude of the funds involved. According to some estimates, several hundreds of billions of American dollars are available for laundering every year, mostly gained from illicit drug trafficking but also from corruption, fraud and organised crime. This laundered criminal money is recycled through normal businesses and thus may penetrate legitimate markets and corrupt entire economies.

The Council of Europe was well ahead of its time in 1980 when it adopted the first international instrument against money laundering (Recommendation No. R (80) 10 on measures against the transfer and the safekeeping of funds of criminal origin). In 1988, faced with the threats posed by drugs and drug money, the international community reacted firmly by adopting the United Nations Convention on Illicit Drugs and Psychotropic Substances. This convention was the first to require states to consider money laundering a criminal offence in their national legislation. In 1990 the Council of Europe adopted the Convention on Laundering, Search, Seizure and Confiscation of the Proceeds from Crime, the first and so far only international treaty dealing comprehensively with money laundering, which goes beyond the UN treaty. Its significance was highlighted by the heads of state and government of Council of Europe member states, who launched an appeal for its ratification at their 2nd Summit in October 1997.

However, the implementation of legal norms is even more important than their adoption. Such considerations led the G7 countries to create the Financial Action Task Force on Money Laundering (FATF) in 1989. By means of its forty recommendations and effective review mechanism, based on mutual evaluations and peer pressure, it has become the world's leading body in combating money laundering. Today, the FATF is 'the reference' for any national anti-money laundering policy; its review mechanism is seen as a model for regional anti-laundering initiatives. In 1997, when creating its own review mechanism in the form of an Expert Committee (PC-R-EV), the Council of Europe took the FATF mechanism as a model. The Council of Europe's new anti-corruption structure, Greco (Group of States against Corruption), is also largely inspired by the same model.

The fight against money laundering is a top political priority: various international organisations place it high on their agenda, political action plans have been adopted to step up legal and other actions to prevent and prosecute money launderers and many governments have made considerable efforts to address this issue at both national and international level. There has been noticeable progress in the last ten years in this area but money laundering is a "moving target"; launderers invent new techniques, such as cyber-laundering; they use new non-financial laundering channels and they penetrate new sectors or markets such as real estate, securities and antiques.

Professor Gilmore's book is a milestone in the international literature on money laundering. It not only captures the spirit of international effort developed over the last decade, giving an excellent account of all international norms, instruments and structures relating to the problem of money laundering, but it also clearly demonstrates that money laundering is a changing, multi-faceted phenomenon to which only an adaptable policy can respond.

Daniel Tarschys,
Secretary General of the Council of Europe

CHAPTER I – INTERNATIONAL AND ORGANISED CRIME: THE CONTOURS OF THE PROBLEM

The context

In the course of the past twenty-five years there has been ever-growing public anxiety and political concern with the threat posed by modern and sophisticated forms of transnational criminal activity. In stark contrast with the nineteenth century when issues of criminal justice policy were thought of in almost exclusively national terms, the need for enhanced international co-operation and co-ordination in this sphere now occupies an important position on the political agenda. This represents an inevitable recognition of the fact that reliance on unilateral domestic legislative and law enforcement measures is no longer sufficient. As Peter Wilkitzki has aptly remarked, "no domestic criminal legislator can afford to treat crime merely as a national phenomenon".[1]

Among the factors which have contributed to the growth of cross-border criminal activity pride of place must go to the technological revolution witnessed since the end of the second world war.[2] While this has brought about countless benefits of an economic and social nature, such as with the growth in world trade and in international travel, it has also provided the criminal entrepreneur with new opportunities and wider geographic horizons. As has been noted elsewhere: "Modern technology has provided new impetus not only to legitimate trade and commerce, but also to criminal business enterprises. Thus, mass communications have facilitated contacts with associates in other countries and continents, modern banking has facilitated international criminal transactions, and the modern revolution in electronics has given criminal groups access to new tools enabling them to steal millions and to launder the huge illicit profits".[3]

Wider opportunities to engage in transborder illicit conduct are also emerging in several parts of the world as a consequence of the enhanced mobility of individuals and the decreasing significance of national frontiers brought about by economic integration movements and similar factors. This is perhaps most obviously the case for the member states of the European Union (EU) as they give effect to their commitment to create a single internal market comprising an area without internal borders in which the free movement of goods, people, services and capital is ensured.

Notwithstanding the absence of comprehensive data on the scale of trans-frontier crime in the EU, and the widely acknowledged difficulty of quantifying the contribution of border controls to law enforcement and crime deterrence, the member states have accepted the need to take action to minimise the possibilities of abuse in a Europe without internal borders by criminal elements.[4] Indeed, Title VI of the Treaty of the European Union (the Maastricht Treaty) has highlighted the importance of this dimension of the integration movement by specifically acknowledging that justice and home affairs are to be treated as matters of common concern.[5] Concrete expression has been given to this commitment to improve co-operation and co-ordination in a number of ways including the creation of a law enforcement body, known as Europol, charged with co-ordinating the exchange and analysis of police intelligence. As will be seen in greater detail in Chapter VI, while the initial mandate of Europol was restricted to drug trafficking and related money laundering it has since been broadened to include a number of other areas of serious crime possessing a transnational dimension. Further significant compensatory law enforcement measures have been agreed between the so-called "Schengen" states. These include, among others, according the police limited rights of hot pursuit of criminal suspects across international borders and the sharing of important categories of police data through a computer network known as the Schengen Information System.[6] While the criminal justice dimension to regional economic integration is at its most advanced within the EU it is not, however, an exclusively European issue. Its wider significance can, for example, be seen in the acceptance of the need for greater co-operation in criminal matters to compensate for increased freedom of movement within the Economic Community of West African States.[7]

This is not to say that the concept of international co-operation in criminal matters is itself new. For example, the nineteenth century witnessed the beginnings of the modern system of extradition which continues to provide the basic international mechanism for the return of fugitives who have sought refuge abroad to face justice in the territory where the crime was in fact committed. At much the same time the international community started, on a modest scale, to negotiate agreements designed to combat crimes of particular concern. To early examples of treaty-based action to counter such abuses as the slave trade and forgery of currency have been add(particularly since 1945, a growing list of international instruments de=ling with such diverse subjects as terrorist offences, genocide and apartheid. There are, in addition, well established structures for co-operation among law enforcement authorities. These include, among others, the International Criminal Police Organisation (ICPO/Interpol) with its headquarters in Lyon, France[9] and the Brussels-based World Customs Organisation (formerly the Customs Co-operation Council (CCC)).[10] However, the high political priority currently accorded to the subject is of relatively recent origin. This change can be attributed in large measure to the enhanced level of appreciation of the magnitude and complexity of the problem which emerged in the early 1980s when international concern came to focus on the threat posed by the international drugs trade.

That international drugs trafficking emerged as a central issue of concern for the world community was not merely a result of the escalating nature of the problem of drug abuse. It was also, and importantly, a reflection of an enhanced understanding of its negative social impact, its distortive effects on economies, and its implications for domestic political stability. The extent of the societal threat posed by trafficking syndicates has been clearly demonstrated in Colombia and seen most vividly in the murder, at the behest of the powerful cocaine cartels, of some of that country's leading politicians, judges and journalists. Less visible, but equally serious, have been the efforts to penetrate and corrupt the central organs of state power. In its most extreme form, as evidenced by the US invasion of Panama, undertaken to remove General Noriega from power, the drugs trade can even pose an indirect threat to the maintenance of international peace and security.

In addition, drugs trafficking is by its nature global in character requiring the international movement of products from producer countries to the major drug consumer nations. For example, cocaine produced mainly in South America must be shipped through the transit countries of the Caribbean and Central America to reach its major market in the United States. Similarly, heroin, originating primarily in the "Golden Triangle" of Southeast Asia and the "Golden Crescent" of Southwest Asia must be moved, by land, air or sea, to meet demand in North America and western Europe. In the case of the latter most of the product has traditionally been exported by road via the so-called "Balkan route". Originating from Turkey this transits through Bulgaria and the former Yugoslavia. With the advent of hostilities in Bosnia and elsewhere in the region, however, diversionary routing proved to be necessary posing major problems for the emerging democracies of central and eastern Europe.

It would, however, be unduly simplistic to think merely in terms of a movement from producer countries in the developing world to consumers located in the advanced industrialised economies. Producer and transit countries have their own, increasingly serious, problem of drug abuse. Furthermore, Europe is a major exporter of psychotropic substances to other regions of the world including Africa.[11] A further illustration of the geographical complexity of the situation is the dependence of developing country drug producers on the chemicals, manufactured primarily in the industrialised world, which are essential to the process of converting the coca leaf into refined cocaine and raw opium into heroin. For example, a kind of "reverse Balkan route" exists to facilitate the transfer of precursor and essential chemicals, particularly acetic anhydride, from western Europe, through the southern borders of Turkey to the Persian Gulf states and the nations of Southwest Asia.

For these reasons, among others, the drugs trade is now universally recognised as a global problem requiring a global solution. Given this fact, major emphasis throughout the 1980s was placed on the need to improve the effectiveness and extend the scope of international co-operation in this area. One major achievement in this regard was the conclusion in Vienna in December 1988 of the United Nations Convention Against Illicit Traffic in Narcotic Drugs and Psychotropic Substances. This important international agreement, which is examined in Chapter III of this study, has attracted the participation of nearly 150 states including some of the most important source, transit and consumer countries.

More recently the members of the world community have expanded their area of concern to encompass other forms of transnational criminal activity, especially organised crime. A major stimulus in this regard was provided by developments in central and eastern Europe. The end of the cold war, the dissolution of the Warsaw Pact, and the disintegration of the Soviet Union have been events of major global significance. They have also brought about unparalleled opportunities and challenges for the states concerned and their people as domestic political structures have moved swiftly to embrace both liberal democracy and entrepreneurial capitalism.[12] Of the many problems confronted by these states in the period of transition one of the most serious, least wanted, and most heavily publicised, has to do with crime. In essence, the traumatic economic and political changes had the unintended but perhaps inevitable effect of increasing the potential for crime, opportunities which have been enthusiastically seized by criminal elements.

In the overall context of this work one of the most alarming features of this rise in levels of criminality has been the emergence (in some cases the resurgence) of powerful organised crime groups which have exploited the opportunities presented by the decline of existing structures of authority and legitimacy to further their own ends. Nowhere is the severity of this threat more obvious than in the Russian Federation. As a 1994 UN report was to explain: "Perhaps the most striking recent example of the way in which transnational criminal organisations can thrive in an environment of political, social and economic upheaval can be seen in the states of the former Soviet Union. Russian criminal organisations are not new, but the demise of the Communist Party, the disintegration of the Soviet Union, and the collapse of the criminal justice system clearly produced conditions that

were highly conducive to the consolidation of existing criminal organisations and the emergence of new ones".[13]

The growing importance attached by governments to this issue was well
illustrated in November 1994 by the convening, under the auspices of the
UN, of the World Ministerial Conference on Organised Transnational Crime
in Naples, Italy. There the threat posed by the activities of such crime
groups was regarded as both serious and increasing. It was perceived to
pose a threat to sovereignty, to national authority and state control, to
democratic values and public institutions as well as to national economies,
financial institutions and individuals. All states, including developing countries and nations in transition from communist rule to democratic gover-
nance, were seen to be vulnerable.[14]

In spite of such shared perceptions of the nature of the problem the conference was unable to resolve one fundamental issue; namely, the absence
of a universally agreed definition of organised crime.[15] This difficulty stems
not only from differences in national legal approaches and traditions but
also from the considerable variations which exist among the groups themselves. There is no single model. As has been pointed out elsewhere: "The
groups vary in shape and size and in skills and specialisations. They operate
in different geographical domains and different product markets and use a
variety of tactics and mechanisms for circumventing restrictions and avoiding law enforcement. Transnational criminal organisations range from highly structured organisations to more fluid and dynamic networks".[16]

In the absence of an agreed definition it has become the norm to approach
the issue in terms of the possession of certain common characteristics. For
instance, at a 1988 Interpol symposium participants from forty-six countries agreed to the following working definition: "Any enterprise or group
of persons engaged in continuing illegal activity which has as its primary
purpose the generation of profits irrespective of national boundaries".[17]
Among the national law enforcement agencies which have based their
approach to organised crime on this definition is the British National
Criminal Intelligence Service (NCIS). In the UK four explicit and three
implicit characteristics have been seen to be derived from it; namely, that it
is a group activity; its primary purpose is financial profit; it is a criminal
activity which is long term and continuing; it is carried out irrespective of
national boundaries; it is large scale; it generates proceeds which are often
made available for licit use; and, it is carried out by groups that have some
form of discipline and structure.[18] As the Home Office has noted: "The
seven characteristics reflected in the NCIS definition are evident in the
working definitions (...) that have been adopted by other European police
and intelligence agencies ".[19]

While some forms of organised crime groups, such as the Colombian cartels, are involved primarily in one form of criminal activity, others engage in diverse activities. These range from traditional fields such as gambling, extortion, prostitution, counterfeiting and arms trafficking, to emerging areas like environmental crime, computer-related crime, the theft of technology, industrial espionage, and copyright infringement.[20] A particular concern for the world community is the involvement of a number of crime groups in criminal activities which have a major international dimension such as the smuggling of illegal migrants, the theft and smuggling of vehicles, and money laundering.[21]

In addition to a highly diversified "product" base the most mature of these criminal syndicates have developed extremely complex organisational structures, reminiscent of multinational corporations, which are designed to maximise profits and minimise risks. This analogy with international businesses can greatly assist an understanding of the forces which have assisted the growth of this form of criminality. As two leading Australian scholars have stated:

> Just as the move to corporate identity allowed capitalism to flourish, the move to organised crime allows crime to flourish. Economies of scale and limited liability operate within criminal organisations just as they operate in corporate organisations such as General Motors. Both systems reward entrepreneurship, and profit maximisation is the ultimate goal of both enterprises. Costs are internalised, and the possibility of monopolistic pricing is ever present.[22]

While the absence of an agreed definition can be the source of difficulties, among which is the blurring of distinctions with other types of serious criminality such as "white collar" crime, this has not prevented the gradual emergence of a consensus among governments as to the organisations which are most deserving of international attention. Selected because of their involvement in operations which cross national boundaries, this priority group includes long established networks such as the Chinese Triads, the Colombian cartels, the Japanese Yakuza, and the Sicilian Mafia. Also of concern are newer groups with home bases in the Caribbean, West Africa and, most recently, central and eastern Europe.[23]

Although the threat posed by these organisations is greatest in their home countries, an increasing ability and willingness to operate across international frontiers in the pursuit of profit means that few states, if any, are completely unaffected by their activities. By way of illustration, "[g]roups like the Sicilian Mafia are spreading their activity into both western and eastern Europe, in addition to maintaining their traditional connections in the Americas".[24] Similar concerns are attached to the increasing internationalisation of the activities of Russian and other central and eastern European organised crime groups. For example, it is widely accepted in law enforcement circles that "Russian criminal organisations have extended their activities to other countries of the Commonwealth of Independent States (US) and to the countries of eastern Europe".[25] In a January 1994 report on criminal activities in Europe, the Committee on Civil Liberties and Internal Affairs of the European Parliament took note of the presence of Russian and Ukrainian groups in Poland and in the Czech and Slovak Republics.[26] In addition there is clear evidence of an increasing impact on crime elsewhere and especially in western Europe.

One illustration of such east-west linkages is to be seen in the area of drug trafficking. As was noted above, with the outbreak of hostilities in the Balkans the trans-shipment route for Southwest Asian heroin and other drugs was displaced and now transits through a number of central and eastern European countries *en route* to major western European markets. Furthermore, "[s]ome of this heroin is being produced from the opium poppy fields found in parts of the former USSR. Also South American drugs gangs are routing cocaine into western Europe via eastern European entry points and borders".[27] Other aspects of the east-west crime flow relate to involvement in a range of activities including the smuggling of illegal migrants and transborder prostitution.

Some of the crime opportunities which have been exploited, however, go in the reverse direction. This is reflected in the west-east movement of luxury cars stolen in Germany and other western European countries. A 1998 study has described this aspect of their activities as follows:

> Beside drug and migrants trafficking, also the traffic in stolen cars organised by, among others, Russian and Ukrainian criminal groups is increasing noticeably. In fact, Russia, the Baltic states and, to a lesser extent, Ukraine rank as the most promising markets for stolen cars. Three main routes pass through eastern European countries. Through the Balkan route, stolen vehicles are driven from west European countries towards the Middle East. Otherwise, stolen cars are driven from western European countries via Poland, the Czech Republic and Hungary to the CIS countries. The northern route, finally, brings cars by ferry from the Nordic states and Germany directly or through Finland to the Baltic countries and Russia.

> The problem with foreign cars in Russia (including stolen ones) is that they are usually stolen again, this time from the new owners to be sold once again in the republics of Central Asia or the Caucasus. Sometimes it is the same syndicate that sold a stolen car to a Russian which steals it again and transports it further into the ex-Soviet hinterland.[28]

Available evidence also suggests an increasing degree of co-ordination and co-operation between such groups. As the Naples Conference was informed: "Like transnational corporations, transnational criminal organisations are entering more and more frequently into strategic alliances. (...)

Strategic alliances permit them to co-operate with, rather than compete against, indigenous entrenched criminal organisations, enhance their capacity to circumvent law enforcement, facilitate risk sharing, make it possible to use existing distribution channels, and enable criminal organisations to exploit differential profit margins in different markets".[29] This phenomenon was clearly illustrated by Operation Green Ice. This was an undercover police operation which "revealed evidence of collusion between the Colombian cocaine cartels and organised crime groups in Italy for the importation and distribution of cocaine into Europe".[30] It was brought to a conclusion in late September 1992 with co-ordinated police raids in the United States, Italy, Spain, the United Kingdom, Canada, the Cayman Islands, Costa Rica and Colombia. In the words of the US Department of State: "The raids resulted in seizures of US$ 47.7 million, and the freezing of 140 bank accounts containing US$ 7.3 million, and dozens of arrests (...)".[31] That this is not an isolated example of co-operation is clear. For instance, an early 1999 report of the Financial Action Task Force on Money Laundering (FATF) noted the formation of new alliances between Colombian drug traffickers and Russian organised crime groups.[32]

A clear indication of the perceived magnitude of the problem came in October 1995 when, in Presidential Decision Directive 42, it was declared that international crime was a threat to the national security interests of the United States. As the Department of State has noted the President ordered "the Departments of Justice, State and Treasury, the Coast Guard, National Security Council, intelligence community, and other federal agencies to increase and integrate their efforts against international crime syndicates and money laundering". Similarly, in the United Kingdom the demise of the cold war has permitted the security services to divert significant resources to the effort to combat the drugs trade, organised crime and money laundering.[33] As the Foreign Secretary was to remark in November 1998: "The work of the agencies is of major importance in fighting the menace of the drugs trade. The intelligence that they provide to the law enforcement agencies help us to go further up the supply chain, targeting the barons rather than the underlings".[34]

A final issue worthy of note in this context is the increasing recognition of the close relationship between organised crime and corruption. At the 21st Conference of European Ministers of Justice, held in Prague in June 1997, the Minister of Justice of the Czech Republic articulated the link between them as follows:

In many cases (...) corruption is indeed one of the basic accompanying phenomena of organised crime. Organised crime tries, through corruption, to obtain the information it seeks, to minimise the risk of being subject to law enforcement measures and to acquire decisive influence in society. Organised crime has at its disposal considerable financial means, thus giving uncontrolled dimensions to corruption. If these phenomena are not effectively tackled and if, rather to the contrary, conditions are created – even if inadvertently – for their growth, the forms of corruption stemming from organised crime may endanger the very foundations of society, and official government structures may become mere puppets in the hands of the criminals.[35]

The strategy

The drugs trade and organised crime are not only international in character, they are also exorbitantly profitable.[36] While it is notoriously difficult to estimate with any precision the sums generated by such activities all indications are that they are enormous.[37] As the Director General of the UN Office in Vienna noted in opening the 1988 Conference for the Adoption of a Convention Against Illicit Traffic in Narcotic Drugs and Psychotropic Substances: "The amount of money involved in illicit drug trafficking was staggering. A single drug, cocaine, was worth billions of dollars on the illicit market. (…) In some cases, the astronomical profits of the drug trade were used to create alternative economies and to undermine legislative and political systems".[38] Recent estimates within the United Nations put the retail value of the world trade in illicit drugs at about US$ 400 billion per year. Although a large number of individuals are involved at the many differing levels of this illicit trade, "most of the gains go to a rich, small elite that has come to wield impressive economic and political power. Some members are believed to have a personal worth that exceeds their country's national debt".[39]

The difficulties in seeking to make estimates in the context of organised crime more generally are even greater. As a June 1996 expert report explained:

> The Italian Mafia, the Japanese Yakuza, the Colombian cartels, Russian and eastern European criminal enterprises, American ethnic groups and other, similarly structured groups are involved in a wide range of criminal activities. In addition to drug trafficking, these enterprises generate funds from loan sharking, illegal gambling, fraud, embezzlement, extortion, prostitution, illegal trafficking in arms and human beings, and a host of other offences.[40]

Increasingly, domestic and international law enforcement strategies have come to emphasise the need to focus on the financial aspects of these forms of crime; that is to target the huge profits which have been aptly described as "the lifeblood of organised and transnational crime".[41] Somewhat surprisingly, however, even in the early 1980s the necessary legal framework to permit effective action against organised crime through "financial devastation" was found to be lacking in most domestic legal systems. It was totally absent at the international level. Two central tools are now widely acknowledged to be required in order to give effect to this strategy. First, the criminal justice system must make provision for an efficient and effective method of tracing, freezing and eventually confiscating the proceeds derived from criminal activity. While some countries, including Switzerland and Italy, have had at least a limited ability to take such action for some time, legislation to permit the confiscation of criminal proceeds became popular only in the course of the last decade.[42]

The second basic requirement is that modern legislation must be enacted which both criminalises and counters the process known as money laundering. The term money laundering is one of fairly recent vintage. It appears to have first been coined by American law enforcement officials and to have entered popular usage during the Watergate inquiry in the United States in the mid-1970s.[43] The expression seems to have been used in a judicial or legal context for the first time, again in the United States, only in 1982 in the case of US v. $4 255 625.39.[44] Since then it has become widely accepted as a term of art at both the international and domestic level, being extensively utilised, for example, in the 1990 European Convention on Laundering, Search, Seizure and Confiscation of the Proceeds from Crime – an important initiative examined in Chapter V. As Tom Sherman, the then Chairperson of the Australian National Crime Authority, has explained: "Money laundering is the process of converting or "cleansing" property knowing that such property is derived from serious crime for the purpose of disguising its origin. The concept of money laundering generally covers those who assist that process and ought reasonably to be aware that they are assisting such a process".[45] Here again the vast majority of the members of the international community lacked appropriate domestic legal remedies. For instance, in the United States the phenomenon of money laundering was addressed for the first time in the Bank Secrecy Act of 1970 and was criminalised as such only in October 1986 with the enactment of the Money Laundering Control Act. Similarly in the United Kingdom a modern legal framework for drug related money laundering had to await the passage of the Drug Trafficking Offences Act 1986 and the Criminal Justice (Scotland) Act 1987.

Over the last decade, and largely as a result of the 1988 UN convention, the need for a modern anti-money laundering strategy has become widely accepted in both law enforcement and policy-making circles; so much so that it has been characterised as "the white collar crime of the 1990s (...)".[46] As Nadelmann has pointed out: "It was perceived as essential both to identifying and prosecuting the higher-level drug traffickers who rarely if ever came into contact with their illicit goods, and to tracing, seizing and forfeiting their assets".[47] Progress in this area is also seen to be a critical element in the fight against organised crime and, increasingly, as crucial in efforts to combat corruption. Consequently money laundering countermeasures have been afforded a central position in both European and global programmes and political declarations.

A further impetus for action has come from the increasing recognition of the negative impact which vast flows of "dirty money" can have on the financial sector. Here we are also confronted with serious difficulties in formulating estimates of any reliability and all such efforts must be regarded with caution.[48] However, the common perception in governmental circles is that the amounts in question are very substantial. For instance, in 1990 the FATF, the work of which is examined in Chapter IV, estimated that as much as US$ 85 billion could be available annually for laundering and investment from the proceeds of drug trafficking in the US and Europe.[49] A March 1998 report released by the US State Department's Bureau for International Narcotics and Law Enforcement Affairs placed the annual value of laundered funds derived from all crimes at between US$ 300 and US$ 500 billion. Similarly, in a February 1998 speech in Paris the Managing Director of the International Monetary Fund (IMF) underlined the magnitude of the issue of criminal profits in these words: "While we cannot guarantee the accuracy of our figures (...) the estimates of the present scale of money laundering transactions are almost beyond imagination – 2% to 5% of global GDP would probably be a consensus range".[50]

It is widely acknowledged that these are but rough estimates and efforts are underway in various fora, including the FATF, to develop a methodologically sound method for calculating the magnitude of money laundering.[51] However, for present purposes such uncertainty is not fatal. As Evans has remarked: "Fortunately there is no particularly compelling reason to spend much time on estimates. It is abundantly clear that the proceeds of crime have reached unacceptable levels and that action must be taken to contain criminal profits".[52]

The apparent magnitude of the sums involved has stimulated a growing concern about the adverse consequences which flow from the investment of the substantial profits derived from crime in the legitimate economy and the degree of power and control which results. As Lamberto Dini, the then Italian Minister of the Treasury, remarked in June 1994: "The social danger of money laundering consists in the consolidation of the economic power of criminal organisations, enabling them to penetrate the legitimate economy".[53] It is, for instance, a commonly expressed view that the Mafia in Italy derives more income from its "legitimate" business interests than from its criminal activities. Although such businesses will, like any other, create wealth and employment, their control by criminal elements pose a number of difficulties and dangers. As one leading law enforcement official has remarked: "There are clear signs that when organised crime invests in legitimate business activity it will attempt to dominate that market and engage in predatory pricing, extortion and corruption. In other words, the organised criminal is not content simply with legitimate profit but to maximise profit, by fair means or foul".[54]

Also of interest in this context is the fact that increasing attention is now being paid to the impact of money laundering activities on the world financial system. As Pino Arlacchi, the Executive Director of the UN Office for Drug Control and Crime Prevention remarked in mid-1998: "Globalisation has turned the international financial system into a money launderer's dream, and this criminal process siphons away billions of dollars per year from economic growth at a time when the financial health of every country affects the stability of the global marketplace".[55] Here the lead has been taken by the IMF.[56] As Vito Tanzi was to explain in an influential 1996 IMF working paper:

> The international laundering of money has the potential to impose significant costs on the world economy by (a) harming the effective operations of the national economies and by promoting poorer economic policies, especially in some countries; (b) slowly corrupting the financial market and reducing the public's confidence in the international financial system, thus increasing risks and the instability of that system; and (c) as a consequence (... reducing the rate of growth of the world economy.[57]

A final, and critical, element of the strategy to counter money laundering flows from the international nature of the crimes in question and the extent to which criminals resort to the use of the global financial system in an effort to launder their funds and protect them from possible confiscation by law enforcement. Thus close international co-operation is recognised as essential. The ultimate overall goals of such international action "are to make the environment for transnational criminal organisations hostile and inhospitable, to infiltrate, disrupt, and destroy the network structures on which many of these organisations are based, and to make continued transnational criminal activities as difficult and as costly as possible".[58]

Notes: I

1. Wilkitzki, P., "Development of an Effective International Crime and Justice Programme – a European View", in Eser, A., and Lagodny, O., (eds.), *Principles and Procedures for a New Transnational Criminal Law*, Freiburg, 1992, p. 267, at p. 270.

2. "Problems and Dangers Posed by Organized Transnational Crime in the Various Regions of the World". UN Doc. E/CONF. 88/2; 18 August 1994, p. 8.

3. "The Impact of Organized Criminal Activities Upon Society at Large: Report of the Secretary General". UN Doc. E/CN.15/1993/3; 11 January 1993, p. 4.

4. See, e.g., Bruggeman, W., "Transnational Crime: Recent Trends and Future Prospects", in Cullen, P. and Gilmore, W., (eds.), *Crime Sans Frontières: International and European Legal Approaches*, Edinburgh, 1998, p. 85.

5. See generally, Anderson, M., et al, *Policing the European Union*, Oxford, 1995.

6. See, e.g., den Boer, M., and Walker, N., "European Policing After 1992", *Journal of Common Market Studies*, 1993, pp. 3-28.

7. See, e.g., Gilmore, W., (ed.), *Mutual Assistance in Criminal and Business Regulatory Matters*, Cambridge, 1994, at pp. ix-x.

8. See Clark, R., "Offences of International Concern: Multilateral State Treaty Practice in the Forty Years Since Nuremberg", *Nordic Journal of International Law*, 1988, pp. 49-119.

9. See generally, Anderson M., *Policing the World: Interpol and the Politics of International Police Co-operation*, Oxford, 1989.

10. See Rigdon, A., "Aspects of International Police and Customs Co-operation", in *Action Against Transnational Criminality: Papers from the 1992 Oxford Conference on International and White Collar Crime*, London, 1993, pp. 83-88.

11. See, e.g., Council of Europe, Doc. P-PG/Psychotropes (93) 3; 22 March 1993.

12. Joutsen, M., "Crime Trends in central and eastern Europe". Council of Europe Doc. PC-TP (94) 13, p. 1.

13. *Supra*, note 2, p. 10.

14. See id., at pp. 24-29.

15. See UN Doc. E.CONF. 88/L.3/Add.1, 23 November 1994, at pp. 3-4. See also, European Parliament, "Report of the Committee on Civil Liberties and Internal Affairs on Criminal Activities in Europe". Doc. EN/RR/244/244371; 27 January 1994, p. 9.

16. *Supra*, note 2, at pp. 10-11.

17. See memorandum submitted by Interpol and reproduced in House of Commons, Home Affairs Committee, *Organised Crime*, H.C. Paper 18-II, 1994-95 (hereafter Select Committee), at p. 150. See also, Anderson, M.,

"Control of Organised Crime in the European Community", Working Paper IX, A System of European Police Co-operation after 1992, Department of Politics, University of Edinburgh, 1993, p. 6; *supra,* note 3, at pp. 2-3; and, Nilsson, H., "Future Corruption Control in Europe". Paper presented at the Fifth International Anti-Corruption Conference, Amsterdam, 7-12 March 1992, (typescript), p. 3.

18. See Select Committee, op. cit., at pp. 77-78.

19. Id., p. 78.

20. See, id., at p. 143.

21. See, *supra,* note 2, at pp. 16-22.

22. Fisse, B., and Fraser, D., "Some Antipodean Scepticisms About Forfeiture, Confiscation of Proceeds of Crimes, and Money Laundering Offences", *Alabama Law Review,* 1993, p. 737, at p. 738.

23. See Savona, E., and De Feo, M., "Money Trails: International Money Laundering Trends and Prevention/Control Policies". Paper presented to the International Conference on Preventing and Controlling Money Laundering and the Use of the Proceeds of Crime: A Global Approach, Courmayeur Mont Blanc, Italy, 18-20 June 1994 (hereafter the 1994 Conference) (typescript), at pp. 10-16. Since reproduced in Savona, E.U., (ed.), *Responding to Money Laundering: International Perspectives,* Amsterdam, 1997. Subsequent references are to the original.

24. Id., p. 90.

25. "Appropriate Modalities and Guidelines for the Prevention and Control of Organised Transnational Crime at the Regional and International Levels". UN Doc. E/CONF.88/5; 19 September 1994, p. 14.

26. "Report of the Committee on Civil Liberties and Internal Affairs on Criminal Activities in Europe", *supra,* note 15, p. 11.

27. See Gregory, F., "Unprecedented Partnerships in Crime Control: Law Enforcement Issues and Linkages Between Eastern and western Europe Since 1989", in Anderson, M., and den Boer, M., (eds.), *Policing Across National Boundaries,* London, 1994, p. 85, at p. 96.

28. Adamoli, S. et al., *Organised Crime Around the World,* Helsinki, 1998, pp. 51-52.

29. *Supra,* note 2, p. 23.

30. Sherman, T., "The Internationalisation of Crime and the World Community's Response", in *Action Against Transnational Criminality: Papers from the 1993 Oxford Conference on International and White Collar Crime,* London, 1994, p. 1, at p. 5.

31. US Department of State, *International Narcotics Control Strategy Report: Executive Summary* Washington, D.C., 1993, p. 111. See also, Wilson, G., "The Changing Game: The United States Evolving Supply-Side Approach to

Narcotics Trafficking", *Vanderbilt Journal of Transnational Law*, 1994, p. 1163, at pp. 1204-1206.

32. See "Financial Action Task Force on Money Laundering: 1998-99 Report on Money Laundering Typologies", p. 16.

33. See, e.g., *supra*, note 5, at pp. 172-175.

34. Parl. Deb., House of Commons, 2/11/1998, col. 579.

35. Council of Europe Doc. MJU-21 (97) 1, p. 3.

36. See Fisse and Fraser, op. cit., at p. 739.

37. See, e.g., Vetere, E., "Introductory Statement", to the 1994 Conference, (typescript), at p. 3.

38. UN Doc. E/CONF.82/SR. 1, p. 3.

39. "International Narcotics Control", US Department of State Dispatch (10 September 1990) p. 83, at p. 85.

40. "Financial Action Task Force on Money Laundering: Annual Report 1995-1996", Annex 3, p. 2.

41. "Control of Proceeds of Crime: Report of the Secretary General". UN Doc. E/CN.15/1993/4; 25 January 1993, p. 6.

42. See, id., at p. 18.

43. See Vallance, P., "Money Laundering: The Situation in the United Kingdom". Paper presented to the Council of Europe Money Laundering Conference, Strasbourg, France, 18-30 September 1992, (typescript), p. 1.

44. (1982) 551 F Supp. 314.

45. Sherman, T., "International Efforts to Combat Money Laundering: The Role of the Financial Action Task Force", in MacQueen, H.L., (ed.), *Money Laundering*, Edinburgh, 1993, p. 12, at p. 13.

46. UN Office for Drug Control and Crime Prevention, *Financial Havens, Banking Secrecy and Money-Laundering*, New York, 1998, p. 34.

47. Nadelmann, E., *Cops Across Borders: The Internationalization of US Criminal Law Enforcement*, University Park, Pennsylvania, 1994, p. 388.

48. See, e.g., Gold, M., and Levi, M., *Money Laundering in the U.K.: an appraisal of suspicion-based reporting*, London, 1994, at pp. 39-49.

49. See Gilmore, W., (ed.), *International Efforts to Combat Money Laundering*, Cambridge, 1992, p. 4, at p. 6.

50. "Financial Action Task Force on Money Laundering: Annual Report 1997-98", Annex A, p. 37.

51. See, e.g., id., at p. 27 for progress to date within the FATF on this matter.

52. Evans, J., "The Proceeds of Crime: Problems of Investigations and Prosecution". Paper presented to the 1994 Conference (typescript), p. 1. Since reproduced in Savona, E.U. (ed.), op. cit.

53. Dini, L., "Opening Remarks" to the 1994 Conference, (typescript), p. 2.

54. Sherman, *supra*, note 45, at p. 13.

55. UN Office for Drug Control and Crime Prevention, *Attacking the Profits of Crime: Drugs, Money and Laundering*, Vienna, 1998, p. 5.

56. See, *supra*, note 50, Annex A. See also, Quirk, P., "Macroeconomic Implications of Money Laundering", IMF Working Paper, WP/96/66, June 1996.

57. Tanzi, V., "Money Laundering and the International Financial System", IMF Working Paper, WP/96/55, May 1996, p. 2.

58. "The Feasibility of Elaborating International Instruments, Including Conventions, Against Organised Transnational Crime". UN Doc. E/CONF. 88/6, 29 September 1994, p. 2.

CHAPTER II – MONEY LAUNDERING: AN OVERVIEW OF THE PROCESS

Introduction

Governmental interest in seeking to combat money laundering is, as we have seen, of relatively recent origin. Similarly, the term itself has entered the accepted vocabulary of diplomacy and legislative drafting only in the course of the last decade. Although the terminology may be relatively recent, the concept is one of very long standing in relation to financially motivated criminal conduct. As McClean has stated:

> From the point of view of the criminal, it is no use making a large profit out of criminal activity if that profit cannot be put to use. (..). Putting the proceeds to use is not as simple as it may sound. Although a proportion of the proceeds of crime will be kept as capital for further criminal ventures, the sophisticated offender will wish to use the rest for other purposes. (...) If this is to be done without running an unacceptable risk of detection, the money which represents the proceeds of the original crime must be "laundered"; put into a state in which it appears to have an entirely respectable provenance.[1]

This is not to say that all criminals will have the need to resort to elaborate schemes in order to create the perception of legitimacy of the source and ownership of wealth and property. Small-time criminals will rarely do so. As Evans has pointed out: "They deal in cash and avoid financial institutions as much as possible. Their criminal associates and suppliers expect cash and they pay cash for most living expenses".[2] Even in more significant ventures the perception of the need to engage in laundering activity will differ widely from country to country. Here the judgement of those involved as to the effectiveness of the local criminal justice system and the associated level of risk of detection and prosecution will be central considerations. For example, in jurisdictions which have embraced modern law enforcement strategies in which the confiscation of the proceeds of crime is utilised both as a deterrent and as a form of punishment money laundering schemes are likely to be resorted to with greater frequency than elsewhere. As has been pointed out:

> As financial investigative and prosecutorial activity becomes more professional and effective, the more resources the criminal organisation tends to devote to lowering the risk of being traced and apprehended through the money trail and the risk of losing the criminal proceeds. (...) Increased sophistication in prevention and control methods tends to be matched by increased sophistication in

money laundering activities, until one side or the other reaches the point of diminishing returns.[3]

In much the same way considerable variations exist, both between countries and among sectors of criminality, as to the scope, complexity and sophistication of the money laundering schemes which are in fact resorted to. In this regard the situation prevailing in Australia is likely to be reflective of the general position elsewhere. As the National Crime Authority of that country was to note in a December 1991 report:

> Money laundering schemes uncovered so far are generally unsophisticated but some of the very large cases involve the use of complex corporate structures and trusts as part of the laundering process. Most money laundering activity is carried out by the primary offender, not by "professional" launderers, although the use of corrupt or complicit individuals is often crucial to the success of money laundering schemes.[4]

On the other hand, organised crime groups, such as the Colombian cartels, have created diverse and sophisticated systems with a global reach in order to protect and legitimise the vast profits which are generated by their activities. One Colombian cocaine "kingpin", Rodriguez Gacha, is reputed to have laundered approximately US$ 130 million using eighty-two company and other accounts in sixteen countries located in Central and South America, the Caribbean, Asia and Europe. As a 1993 UN report noted: "The basic characteristics of the laundering of the proceeds of crime, which to a large extent also mark the operations of organised and transnational crime, are its global nature, the flexibility and adaptability of its operations, the use of the latest technological means and professional assistance, the ingenuity of the operators and the vast resources at their disposal. In addition, a characteristic that should not be overlooked is the constant pursuit of profits and the expansion into new areas of criminal activity".[5]

It should be stressed, however, that while the international movement of criminal proceeds is a hallmark of laundering activities carried out by or on behalf of such powerful organised groups it is by no means restricted to them. Indeed, the transnational movement of funds is a common feature of sophisticated laundering activities. For example, a 1990 report carried out by the Ministry of the Solicitor General of Canada, based on an examination of actual police files, revealed that an international dimension was present in over 80% of those cases.[6] While the evidence suggests that the Canadian figures may be higher, for a variety of reasons, than in some other jurisdictions, including the United States, they do underline the fact "that crime, like much else, is increasingly international".[7]

There are sound reasons for resorting to such an international strategy. At one level, as the European Commission has noted, "[i]nternationalisation of economies and financial services are opportunities which are seized upon by money launderers to carry out their criminal activities, since the origin of funds can be better disguised in an international context".[8] In addition, such mechanisms take advantage of the delays and inefficiencies which confront regulators and the law enforcement community arising from such factors as differences in language and criminal justice systems. Finally, cross-border strategies reflect a natural displacement of activity from jurisdictions which have been active in addressing the issue to countries and territories which possess no or insufficient anti-money laundering measures. As Savona and De Feo have remarked, launderers are motivated by the desire "to find and to take advantage of the weakest link in the global regulatory and enforcement chain, by shifting transactions, communications or assets to the country which has the weakest or most corruptible regulatory or police and prosecution authorities, the most restrictive bank and professional secrecy, or extradition, or asset seizure law, the most ineffective bank supervision, etc."[9]

The money laundering process

The stages of the process

It is important to bear in mind that money laundering is a process, often a highly complex one, rather than a single act. Furthermore launderers, as will be seen in greater detail below, make use of a wide variety of techniques in order to accomplish their ends.

In an effort to assist in the exposition and analysis of this phenomenon it has become common to utilise a three-part framework which seeks to encompass an ideal money laundering scheme. In the words of the 1991 Australian National Crime Authority report: "Such a scheme would take raw proceeds of crime, held by the offender, manoeuvre them through a process that would conceal their source and confuse or break the money trail, and then return them to the offender legitimised and ready for further safe use".[10] This model can, in turn, be expressed by reference to the following three stages:

- *Placement stage* – where cash derived directly from criminal activity (e.g. from sales of drugs) is first placed either in a financial institution or used to purchase an asset.

- *Layering stage* – the stage at which there is the first attempt at concealment or disguise of the source of the ownership of the funds.

- *Integration stage* – the stage at which the money is integrated into the legitimate economic and financial system and is assimilated with all other assets in the system.[11]

In many instances all three of these stages will be clearly discernible. Take the following illustration of an actual, and fairly typical, money laundering scheme:

> Cash collected in the US from street sales of drugs was smuggled across the border to Canada where some was taken to currency exchanges to increase the denomination of the notes and reduce the bulk. Couriers were organised to hand carry the cash by air to London where it was paid into a branch of a financial institution in Jersey.

> Enquiries in London by HM Customs and Excise revealed that internal bank transfers had been made from the UK to Jersey where fourteen accounts had been opened in company names using local nominee directors. The funds were repatriated to North America with the origin disguised, on occasions in the form of sham loans to property companies owned by the principals, either using the Jersey deposits as collateral or transferring it back to North America.[12]

In other cases, however, the basic steps "may occur simultaneously or, more commonly, they may overlap. How the basic steps are used depends on the available laundering mechanisms and the requirements of the criminal organisations".[13]

Money laundering techniques

The context

Money laundering techniques "are innumerable, diverse, complex, subtle and secret".[14] All, however, contain three common features in order to meet the normal requirements of those involved:

- launderers need to conceal the true ownership and origin of the proceeds;
- launderers need to maintain control of the proceeds; and,
- launderers need to change the form of the proceeds.

Taking these requirements, as well as the three-phased ideal of the process, into consideration, policy makers and agencies charged with the task of devising appropriate countermeasures have sought to identify those points where the launderer is most vulnerable to detection. Given the fact that drug trafficking was, as noted in the previous chapter, the original catalyst for concerted international action in this area it was inevitable that the initial focus would be on the placement stage. This flowed from the fact that drug trafficking, as with certain other forms of profit- generating criminal activity, is highly cash intensive. Indeed, "in the case of heroin and cocaine, the physical volume of notes received from street dealing is much larger than the volume of the drugs themselves".[15] The drug criminal is therefore faced with the problem of physically disposing of a significant volume of small denomination bank notes.

Deposit-taking institutions

As a senior Bank of England official has explained: "Because of the money launderer's need to get rid of cash, deposit-taking institutions are particularly vulnerable to being used. Hence, many of the efforts to combat money laundering have concentrated on the procedures adopted by deposit-takers".[16] As will be seen in our examination of the work of the Financial Action Task Force in Chapter IV and of the European Union Directive in Chapter VI, among other initiatives, it has become common practice to impose significant obligations on banks, building societies and other deposit-taking institutions in the fight against money laundering. Requirements for customer identification, the imposition of comprehensive record-keeping rules, and the need to report suspicious transactions are but some of the means used to ensure, through the creation of an "audit" or "paper" trail for use by law enforcement authorities and otherwise, that the risks for the criminal are maximised at the placement stage. This policy also recognises the wider attractiveness of deposit-taking institutions, as providers of an extensive range of services, to launderers at the layering and integration stages.

The imposition of obstacles to placement have generated a range of innovative responses from criminal money managers. For example, in the United States it has become common practice for criminals to engage the services of numerous individuals to convert cash in small denominations into larger bills – a process sometimes known as the "refining" of dirty money.[17] A similar *modus operandi* has been utilised in an effort to evade the US legal requirements for the mandatory reporting of all cash transactions over a specified threshold. Known as "smurfing", this involves the structuring of transactions in such a way as to avoid the automatic triggering of the system. As a law enforcement official has explained, this "involves the employment of 'smurfs', money couriers of innocuous appearance who make large numbers of small transactions, always under US$ 10 000, at various financial institutions. In this manner, large quantities of cash can enter the banking system without attracting undue attention".[18]

The task of the launderer is, of course, greatly eased if the integrity of bank employees can be compromised. In a small minority of cases banks themselves come to acquire a corrupt culture which lends itself to involvement as a willing partner in laundering operations. This was most strikingly the case with the Bank of Credit and Commerce International (BCCI).[19] The involvement of BCCI in facilitating the international movement of criminal proceeds first came to public attention in late 1988 with the culmination of a US Customs undercover investigation known as operation "C-Chase". This identified some US$ 32 million of laundered funds and resulted in the arrest of a substantial number of individuals including nine high ranking BCCI employees. In addition to the subsequent conviction of staff members in both the United States and the United Kingdom, the bank itself was proceeded against. As the US Department of State noted: "BCCI Ltd plead guilty to one count of conspiracy and twenty-eight counts of money laundering. BCCI SA plead guilty to one count of conspiracy and two counts of money laundering. BCCI's convictions resulted in the forfeiture of approximately US$ 15.3 million in criminal penalties to the US Government".[20] "C-Chase" was, as Ehrenfeld has noted, "the beginning of the end for BCCI"[21] and it was eventually closed down by co-ordinated international regulatory action in July 1991 leaving an estimated 530 000 creditors worldwide and a substantial "black hole" in its accounts.[22] In a 1993 report prepared on behalf of the UN Secretary General it is alleged that this rogue bank was responsible for laundering some US$ 20 billion.[23]

In the vast majority of cases, however, launderers are confronted by non-corrupt deposit-taking institutions seeking to give effect to an increasingly sophisticated package of countermeasures. In these circumstances it was inevitable that there would be increased efforts by criminal money managers to shift the placement stage to less well-regulated, or totally unregulated, jurisdictions. This can be accomplished in various ways including currency smuggling. As the International Criminal Police Organisation (ICPO/Interpol) has noted: "The money courier fills suitcases with cash, hides cash in cargo, or sends cash in an international express package. The money is physically transported to a foreign country that has no currency controls and preferably has bank secrecy laws. (...) In the tax haven country the cash will be deposited into a bank or other financial institution and from there it can be moved at will. The money is now indistinguishable from the legitimate funds that are routinely transferred throughout the world's financial systems".[24]

Resort to such a strategy of geographic displacement is not without risk. At a practical level the launderer must weigh both the possibility of loss or theft as well as the risk of detection and subsequent action by law enforcement. In so far as the latter is concerned, a growing number of countries have put in place legal structures which permit action to be taken to interdict certain categories of cross-border cash shipments.[25] Three basic systems have been utilised. Some countries, including Australia and the United States, have imposed mandatory reporting of the import, or export (or both) of international currency transfers above a stipulated threshold. Failure to comply with such requirements can result in the imposition of penalties and the forfeiture of the currency. For example, US Customs in

Operation Buckstop targeted outbound currency and monetary instrument flows to narcotics source and money laundering countries. In the 1992 fiscal year this resulted in 862 seizures totalling over US$ 42 million.[26] In other jurisdictions, such as Ireland and the United Kingdom, the legislature has given the relevant law enforcement authorities the right to seize large sums of cash which are being imported or exported in circumstances which give rise to reasonable grounds to believe that it represents the proceeds of drug trafficking.[27] Yet other jurisdictions are able to invoke provisions of their exchange control or other similar legislation.

In the event that cash placement, at home or abroad, is successful, the "layering" process can commence. Although a range of possibilities exist, in recent years particular concern has been expressed about the abuse of electronic fund or "wire" transfers. As Savona and De Feo have remarked: "wire transfers are probably the most important layering method available to money launderers. They offer criminals many advantages as they seek to cover their trail. Speed, distance, minimal audit trail, and increased anonymity amid the enormous daily volume of electronic fund transfers are all major benefits".[28] Although there are numerous ways for launderers to abuse the system "the objective for most money launderers is to aggregate funds from different accounts and move those funds through accounts at different banks until the origins of the funds cannot be traced. Most often this involves moving the funds out of the country, through a bank account in a country with strict bank secrecy laws, and possibly back. (...)".[29] At this stage detection becomes extremely difficult and full integration relatively straightforward.

While the major policy focus has been on the use of banks and other deposit-taking institutions for the purposes of laundering, it is clear that a wide range of other mechanisms, either alone or in combination, can be used for the same purpose. As Tom Sherman, a former president of the FATF, has stated: "experience shows that money launderers will utilise almost any form of corporate and trust activity to launder their profits. The mainstream and underground financial systems in all their varieties are susceptible".[30] It is to this wider panorama that this study now turns.

Non-bank financial institutions

The introduction of measures to prevent banks being readily used for the purposes of money laundering has, without doubt, made life more difficult by increasing the costs and the risks for those involved. However, launderers have proved to be adept in identifying and exploiting weaknesses in such structures. This has been manifested not only in a resort to more complex techniques such as "smurfing" but also, and increasingly, in a diversion of activities from better to less well regulated sectors of the economy.

As the US Department of State has noted: "In too many countries, the governments have concentrated on identifying cash deposits at the teller's window, and have failed to mount a total programme against money laundering that takes into account all of the traditional and non-traditional resources used today to convert illicit proceeds. Traffickers are all too familiar with traditional customer identification procedures used by banks, so they have adopted new strategies".[31]

In recent years launderers have proved to be particularly innovative in the way in which they utilise non-bank financial institutions and systems. This term will be used, for present purposes, to encompass "those businesses which provide bank-like services (...) but which are historically less closely supervised than traditional financial institutions".[32] The activities most commonly mentioned within the FATF and other expert groups include, among others, *bureaux de change*; cheque cashers and money transmission services; securities and commodities brokers; life insurance companies; and, underground and parallel banking systems.

Some of these activities, as with cheque cashers and *bureaux de change*, have a singular utility and significance in the cash placement stage of the process. Others, such as the life insurance industry, can be used for placement but are particularly associated with layering and integration. By way of example, cash could be utilised for the purchase of a single premium life insurance policy. With placement secured it could subsequently be sold or switched to other forms of investment. The final, or integration, stage would be represented by the redemption of the contract or by a switch to other forms of investment.[33] Resort to substantial cash transactions in this sector is, in many jurisdictions, sufficiently unusual as to generate suspicion. Accordingly use at the placement stage is infrequent save with the complicity of an employee.

Somewhat similar considerations apply when the launderer seeks to engage in a strategy which involves investment in stocks and bonds. In an era characterised by the ever increasing integration of financial markets and global trading the securities sector holds an obvious attraction for the sophisticated money launderer. As a June 1996 report has explained:

> A number of features make this business an attractive target. First, it is by its nature international. Brokerage firms frequently have offices all over the world, and it is ordinary for transactions to be conducted by wire transfer from, to or through multiple jurisdictions. Second, the securities markets are highly liquid. Purchases and sales can be made and settlements consummated within a very short period of time. Third, securities brokers operate in a competitive environment. Because their compensation is often based primarily on sales commissions, there is ample incentive to disregard the source of client funds. Finally, in some

countries, securities accounts can be maintained by brokerage firms as nominees or trustees, thus permitting the identities of true beneficiaries to be concealed."[34]

While there have been reported instances of the proceeds of drug trafficking, insider dealing and market manipulation, being laundered through securities investments, evidence suggests that its use is restricted to the more sophisticated and professional operations. A number of factors account for this. First, and most importantly, "in many jurisdictions, securities and futures brokers that are authorised to receive and hold customer funds do not, in most cases, accept such funds in the form of cash. For this reason, the securities and futures markets may not lend themselves to the "placement" phase of money laundering".[35] In other words the use of cash as a means of settlement of securities transactions is likely, in most financial centre jurisdictions, to attract suspicion and thus greatly increase the risk of detection. Consequently, it is again only with the complicity of employees that launderers can readily avoid the need to convert cash into negotiable instruments, through a bank or otherwise, before seeking to access the securities markets.

The resulting emphasis on the layering and integration stages of the process acts as a further disincentive to the popularisation of its use. As has been pointed out elsewhere: "It is unlikely that this area will often be used as few people understand the workings of securities and futures markets. International experience seems to indicate that the securities and futures markets are only used in money laundering schemes by persons who are thoroughly familiar with the system".[36] For those able to access the markets for these purposes, its attractive features can be brought fully into play in order to break or confuse the audit trail. In such circumstances detection becomes difficult though not impossible. One method utilised to improve the prospects for detection has been to impose on market participants the obligation to report suspicious transactions to the authorities. In some jurisdictions, such as the United Kingdom, official guidance has been provided to assist brokers and others to more readily identify the kinds of dealing patterns and settlement methods which might be indicative of money laundering. In so far as the former is concerned these include such things as entering into "a large number of securities transactions across a number of jurisdictions" and "buying and selling of a security with no discernible purpose or in circumstances which appear unusual, e.g. churning at the clients" request".[37] A somewhat similar effort has been undertaken by the Montreal-based International Organisation of Securities Commissions (Iosco).[38]

In some countries, money launderers may also have the option of utilising long established though informal systems which are closely identified with specific ethnic groups. ICPO/Interpol research indicates that there are two primary forms of underground or parallel banking; namely, the

Hundi/Hawala, and Chop Shop/Chitti systems. The former, which is primarily associated with the states of the Indian sub-continent, extends to Southeast Asia, the Middle East, Europe, North America and Africa. The latter, normally identified with China and Hong Kong, is reported to extend to, among others, the countries of Southeast Asia and North America.

Although the historical origins[39] of both are closely associated with trade and, in more recent times, with facilitating capital flight from developing countries, it is widely believed in law enforcement circles that they are extensively utilised in the international transfer of funds of criminal origin. As a member of the Drug Enforcement Directorate of the Royal Canadian Mounted Police was to note in February 1988, the Chinese underground banking system was "felt to be responsible for the transfer of a great deal of the heroin money in Southeast Asia".[40] These informal channels are also reputed to have been utilised in connection with other offences ranging from advance fee frauds to the financing of "terrorist" activities in the Indian sub-continent.

One of the principal advantages of such systems from the point of view of the money launderer is that transactions which are processed through them do not leave a "paper" or "audit" trail of the orthodox kind. As a specialist with the German Bundeskriminalamt was to explain to a Council of Europe conference in Strasbourg in September 1992, these systems "are based on trust and/or family connections. The money launderer will deposit funds with an underground banker. This banker will notify an associate in the receiving country that the funds have been delivered and/or will give the depositor a special receipt such as a piece of paper money torn in half or a special mark or chop. The depositor will present this receipt in the foreign country and receive the funds in the local currency less a fee or commission".[41]

As with mainstream international commercial banking, and in stark contrast to currency smuggling, the cash in question is not physically transported across international boundaries. In addition, these informal processes have a reputation for efficiency and have proved to be extremely difficult for western law enforcement agencies to penetrate. Such advantages, when combined with the threat posed by the introduction of money laundering countermeasures, seems likely to generate increasing demand for such services, and to result in their possible geographic spread in the future.[42]

Non-financial institutions

As Ronald Noble, then a Vice-President of the FATF, put it in a paper prepared for a 1994 UN conference held in Courmayeur, Italy: "Money laundering is not simply a problem faced by the banking community and other mainstream financial institutions".[43] Non-financial businesses of various kinds have been identified as being of ever-increasing importance as vehicles for carrying out laundering operations.

Perhaps best known in this regard are the attractions offered by the use of companies in laundering schemes. As Beare and Schneider have noted: "the incorporation, financing and operation of companies satisfies the three prime objectives of a laundering vehicle. It allows criminals to convert illicit cash into other assets, create a perception of a legitimate source of funds, all the while effectively concealing the true beneficial owner – the criminal enterprise".[44] Law enforcement experience has demonstrated that both active businesses and so-called "shell" companies are frequently used.

It is common for those involved in laundering operations to either establish or purchase a business of a highly cash-intensive type. These include, among others, retail shops, car washes, vending machine enterprises, restaurants and bars. It is then relatively simple to commingle illicit funds with those generated by the legitimate activities of the company. As has been pointed out elsewhere: "While the excess profits are subject to tax, the trafficker is now free to spend his profits since he has a legitimate source of income".[45] While such methods provide the launderer with both legitimacy and respectability they do present certain limitations. In the words of the Australian National Crime authority report: "Smaller-cash businesses may be unattractive to some money launderers because they do not offer large scale laundering opportunities".[46] Highly unrealistic revenue figures for the type of business concerned may attract suspicion and the consequent attention of investigators. This is well illustrated by a Canadian case in which a launderer established two retail outlets and then opened a corporate bank account locally. Thereafter, substantial funds moved through the account. Surveillance conducted on the stores revealed clearly insufficient business to generate the quantities of cash being deposited.[47] Such difficulties can be minimised. The criminal enterprise concerned can, for instance, extend the range and number of the businesses concerned. It can also resort to the use of other corporate techniques.

Of significance in this regard has been the establishment of "shell corporations" and similar entities such as "ghost" or "front" companies. As Beare and Schneider have noted: "They are legally incorporated and registered by the criminal organisation but have no real business apart from the manipulation of business and financial transactions for laundering purposes".[48] The evidence suggests that these are commonly established in offshore "tax havens'. There is, however, no universally recognised definition of this term and efforts to arrive at one have found the task to be a difficult one. For example, in a 1987 OECD study entitled "Tax Havens: Measures to Prevent Abuse by Taxpayers" the highly relative nature of the concept was noted. Indeed, the study contains the admission that: "It can be argued that the "tax haven" concept is such a relative one that it would serve no useful purpose to make further attempts to define it".[49] That perspective notwithstanding the 1987 study went on to identify what it regarded as the main characteristics of "classical" tax havens. Drawing its inspiration from the 1981 Gordon Report in the United States it described these as including "relatively low rates of tax; high levels of bank or commercial secrecy which the government is generally unwilling to breach; a disproportionally large financial sector; modern communications facilities; the absence of currency controls on foreign deposits of foreign currencies; and self promotion as an offshore financial sector".[50] More recently the OECD has sought to develop a working definition for the purposes of its efforts to combat "harmful tax competition".[51] Furthermore, in a highly controversial move it has set in motion a procedure through which it intends to determine, by October 1999, a list of countries and territories which are to be regarded as tax havens for these purposes.

The number of jurisdictions which are popularly perceived to be tax havens continues to expand. Particular concentrations are to be found in the Caribbean, Europe, and increasingly among the small island states of the Pacific. As will be seen in subsequent chapters there have been increasing calls within the international community for radical reforms to be introduced in respect of these financial havens.[52] However, for present purposes it will suffice to note that, from the perspective of the money launderer, several of the services often offered by such jurisdictions are highly attractive. Such features include "[e]ase of incorporation, especially where ownership can be held through nominees or bearer shares, or where off-the-shelf corporations can be acquired".[53] Such offshore shell corporations have a special utility at the placement and layering stages of the operation. In the latter context it is not uncommon for several such companies in different jurisdictions to be used in an effort to eliminate the audit trail. In many cases, however, the overall needs of the criminal will require that the funds are eventually "repatriated in such a way that it appears [they] have been legitimately acquired from abroad".[54]

There are a number of methods by which this goal can be achieved. One is by direct investment. Here funds held offshore are invested in legitimate businesses in the criminal's own country with the foreign company shown as the purchaser. An interesting variant of this is the "loan back method". As a 1997 United Natons International Drug Control Programme (UNDCP) study has explained, in this situation a criminal "with illicit funds in a foreign account decides to make an investment, which he secures with a down payment of legitimate funds. To pay the balance, he takes out two loans, one, legitimate, and the second from the foreign bank holding his illicit funds (probably offshore). He then repays the loans plus interest as if they were both legitimate. In some cases these repayments may be tax deductible. The income from the initial investment is sufficiently documented to appear entirely legitimate, and the trafficker is free to use it in any way he chooses. As he repays the loan of his initial illicit funds, they are again available for him to "borrow" and the cycle can be repeated".[55]

A further technique is to resort to some form of invoice manipulation. This can involve entirely fictitious transactions as when an offshore shell company pays its domestic counterpart in full upon presentation of a false invoice. Alternatively, where the launderers own ostensibly legitimate businesses in both the country where the criminal proceeds are generated and in the jurisdiction where the money is to be placed, the transfer of funds can be disguised by the inflation of invoices relating to actual trading activities. Just such a method was utilised in the undercover operation known as "Operation Green Ice" which was discussed in the previous chapter. In that instance American law enforcement officials, representing themselves as money launderers, established a chain of leather goods stores. As the then Chief of the Money Laundering Section of the US Department of Justice explained: "The leather stores were used by the money launderers as a means of shipping leather goods to the United States and padding the invoices to show more merchandise than actually was shipped. This enabled them to legitimise the export businesses and to justify the United States currency deposits in their bank accounts in Colombia".[56] It has been reported that in this case twenty tonnes of imported leather goods were listed for each tonne actually shipped.[57] Research in the United States has indicated that such practices are widespread.[58]

In all of the examples given so far launderers exploit corporate techniques based on ownership and control to further their ends. However, there are also various ways in which legitimate non-financial institutions can be exploited by launderers without their knowledge or consent. Those that deal extensively in cash are particularly vulnerable. As Noble has remarked: "Such businesses range from casinos and other gambling operations to vendors of luxury goods of all kinds".[59]

In many jurisdictions gambling is legal. It is also often less well regulated than banking. Perhaps less fully appreciated among the general public is that many modern casinos offer a wide range of banking-type services to their customers. These include the sale and cashing of cheques, foreign currency exchange, the hiring of safety deposit boxes, and international wire transfers. Furthermore, the gambling industry is highly cash intensive thus affording an unusual degree of anonymity to an individual involved in the placement stage of a laundering scheme. At its most basic level, the casino may be used for little more than the "refining" of small denomination banknotes. Another common practice is to seek to represent criminal proceeds

as winnings thus both concealing the true origin of the funds and legitimising them. The simple process involved has been described by
ICPO/Interpol thus: "This method is accomplished by the money launderer when casino chips in large amounts are purchased for cash or when cash
is deposited with the casino for alleged further gaming activity. The money
launderer then redeems his chips or closes his account and requests a
cheque either in his name or a third party name. The cheque is then
deposited in the money launderer's account. If there are any questions
about the source of the deposit it is explained as gambling winnings".[60] In
one case reported by the Royal Hong Kong Police to the FATF, some
US$ 8 million, representing cash from street drug sales in that jurisdiction,
was processed in this way through casinos in the United States. The
cheques were then deposited in accounts in Hong Kong being subsequently transferred to Australia for use in real estate purchases.[61] Such high
volume and value transactions are, however, the exception. Unwanted suspicion is likely to be aroused by large scale operations unless the complicity of the casino management has been arranged in advance or the enterprise itself has come to be controlled by organised crime. The attractiveness
of such methods will, of course, differ widely from country to country
depending on a range of factors including the size and nature of the industry and the degree of regulation to which it is subject.

A number of other types of non-financial institutions have also been identified by the law enforcement community as being vulnerable to abuse.
Many of these, such as art and antique dealers, auction houses, and sellers
of luxury goods and precious metals, deal in high value items in an environment where the use of cash is by no means uncommon. These business
sectors are also largely unregulated. The potential for abuse is well illustrated by the following example:

> The Royal Hong Kong Police reports that a money launderer was employed to
> cleanse cash from the street sale of heroin in Australia. The hired money laun-
> derer utilised the cash to purchase krugerrands and kilogram gold bars, which he
> then carried into Hong Kong and placed in safety deposit boxes. The gold was
> sold a few kilograms at a time over the counter in a Hong Kong bank. The pro-
> ceeds from the sale of the gold were wire transferred to shell company accounts
> in the Channel Islands, Zurich, New York and Vanuatu. The money launderer
> requested that the proceeds of one particular sale be paid in the form of a num-
> ber of demand drafts, which were traced to Manila where they had been cashed
> by the bearer. A total of HK$ 13 812 000 in drug proceeds was remitted from
> Hong Kong.[62]

The emergence of new challenges

Given the range and complexity of money laundering methods, it has
come to be recognised that it is essential for law enforcement officials and

regulators with a mandate in this area to have regular discussions with their counterparts abroad concerning trends, identified variations in methods and emerging threats. Within the FATF, the nature and activities of which are examined in Chapter IV, this has assumed the form of an annual money laundering typologies exercise. The perceived value of this forum for the exchange of insights into enforcement issues has been such as to persuade other specialist anti-money laundering bodies, including the Caribbean Financial Action Task Force (CFATF) and the Asia-Pacific Group (APG) (as to which see Chapter VII), to take similar steps.

At the most recent FATF typologies meeting, held in London in November 1998, a broad range of issues was discussed. Topics extended from the abuse of offshore financial centres to the vulnerability of the derivatives market for money laundering purposes. In addition, it turned its consideration to the money laundering implications which flow from two new developments.[63]

The first of these relates to the phased introduction of a common currency for eleven European Union member countries. It will be recalled that the euro came into being on 1 January 1999. This marked the commencement of a transitional phase during which the new currency will not be issued in physical form. However, "[o]n 1 January 2002, euro coins and banknotes will be introduced, and, the existing national currencies of the participating members will then be withdrawn as legal currency by 30 June 2002 at the latest".[64]

The actual physical conversion of existing national currencies into euro denominated notes and coins will be a major undertaking and attention has turned to the question of how best to ensure that the resulting pressure on financial institutions does not provide an opportunity for criminals to evade anti-money laundering controls. As the European Commission has noted: "It is anticipated that a vast amount of dormant cash will emerge held by people who do not have bank accounts. By definition these people will not be known to the banks when they seek to change their money. (…) [i]t will be more difficult for banks to identify suspicious transactions (…) given the pressure they will be under and the appearance at their counters of large numbers of unknown customers".[65] This issue was given further consideration at the November 1998 FATF meeting, at which time several additional concerns were also addressed. These included the potential problems posed by the proposed introduction of a 500 euro note. As criminal proceeds converted into such a high denomination note would be significantly less bulky than the equivalent in US$ 100 bills or £50 notes this has implications for the ease with which cross-border transportation of cash will be able to take place. For this and other reasons the majority of FATF experts were of the view "that the potential legitimate and illicit uses of large denomination banknotes ought to be thoroughly examined by the European Central Bank".[66]

A further issue which has come to attract increasing attention in specialist anti-money laundering circles in recent years is the challenge posed by the development of new payments technologies. The seriousness with which the matter is viewed was underlined in 1996 when the FATF elaborated a new recommendation which calls upon its members to "pay special attention to money laundering threats inherent in new or developing technologies that might favour anonymity, and take measures, if needed, to prevent their use in money laundering schemes".

Two aspects of developing cyberpayments technology have attracted particular attention in specialist circles to date; namely, "smart cards" and network based systems. As has been noted elsewhere, "smart cards" are "credit-card like devices containing a microchip on which value is encoded. The cards can be read by vending machines or terminals that deduct the amount of each transaction from the total stored value. When the card's value is used up, it may be re-loaded via ATM (automated telling machine), telephone, "electronic wallet" or personal computer, or it may be discarded".[67] One aspect of this developing technology which has been a source of concern is the so-called peer-to-peer variant which would permit electronic cash to be transferred from card to card without recourse to a financial intermediary. Other features which present acute actual or potential challenges relate to the capacity of smart cards to operate in multiple currencies and without limits as to the value which can be stored. Taken together, for example, stored value card technology could significantly reduce the need for, or the vulnerability to detection associated with, the bulk smuggling of currency thus rendering efforts to detect cross-border flows difficult if not impossible.

The second aspect of this technological revolution of relevance in this context concerns those systems which utilise the Internet as a means of transfer of electronic or "e-money". Perhaps the most firmly entrenched manifestation of this dimension of the issue is represented by on-line banking. As has been pointed out elsewhere, this "has increasingly come to mean the method whereby certain types of financial transactions may be performed through the Internet website of those banks that offer this service. (...) In its most basic form, the service provided includes verification of cheque accounts balances and transfers among accounts at the same institution. In those systems that allow payments or transfers to be made, the customer is often restricted in the amount of transaction or the identity of the beneficiary".[68] The provision of such services is growing very rapidly in certain industrialised countries. Other network-based systems "contemplate the use of digital value or tokens, where the value is purchased from an issuer then stored on the computer rather than held in an account".[69]

A further element of complexity is presented by the potential to marry these sophisticated technologies in so-called hybrid systems. As one report on the subject has noted: "The interrelationship of the different features and the rapid move toward system interoperability (where stored value cards and/or network-based systems are compatible and accepted by each other) makes it difficult to identify distinct categories. Systems are now being developed that would allow stored value cards to be used inter-changeably, regardless of issuer. Other developing systems would permit cards to be used in connection with network-based systems".[70]

Over recent years the FATF, among others, has sought both to develop a better understanding of the possible law enforcement and regulatory impli-cations of these innovations and to enter into a dialogue with the leading private sector developers and providers of these technologies and products. From the former there has emerged an enhanced appreciation of the potential risks when viewed from the perspective of the efficacy of existing anti-money laundering programmes. These include:

- inability to identify and authenticate parties that use the new technolo-gies;
- level of transparency of the transaction;
- lack or inadequacy of audit trails, record keeping, or suspicious transac-tion reporting by the technology provider;
- use of higher levels of encryption (thus blocking out law enforcement access); and
- transactions that fall outside current legislative or regulatory definition.[71]

It is hoped that dialogue with the private sector will permit governments and industry to determine what steps they can "take together to ensure that these systems are developed in ways that minimize their potential abuse by criminals".[72] Among the countermeasures currently under active consideration are:

- limiting the functions and capacity of smart cards (including maximum value and turnover limits, as well as number of smart cards per cus-tomer);
- linking new payment technology to financial institutions and bank accounts;
- requiring standard record keeping procedures for these systems to enable the examination, documentation, and seizure of relevant records by investigating authorities; and
- establishing international standards for these measures.[73]

Conclusions

From the overview of money laundering techniques provided in this chapter some appreciation will have been gained of the range of options which are provided by a modern economic system to those who are intent on legitimising the proceeds derived from criminal activity. There is an obvious truth in the contention of Beare and Schneider that the available methods "are limited only by the imagination of the criminal enterprise".[74]

While recourse to relatively simple schemes carried out by the perpetrator of the profit-generating offence is still the norm in most jurisdictions, there is a clear trend towards greater complexity, sophistication and internationalisation of activities. This is especially so for powerful organised crime groups such as the Colombian cartels and the Sicilian Mafia which are increasingly able to call upon the expertise of accountants, lawyers and other professionals.[75] In addition to the greater internal professionalism of these criminal enterprises, recent years have witnessed the emergence of a specialist money laundering industry; one in which expert services are offered to more than one criminal organisation. "These professionals once acted as brokers, charging a commission for handling cash and other transactions; today they increasingly buy the entire proceeds at a discount and control its disposition, reaping profits beyond the discount by investing in legal businesses".[76]

It is against this background that the problems confronted by the law enforcement community must be seen and the adequacy of the evolving programme of money laundering countermeasures must be assessed. It is to these issues that this study now turns.

Notes: II

1. McClean, J.D., *International Judicial Assistance*, Oxford, 1992, at p. 184.

2. Evans, J.L., "The Proceeds of Crime: Problems of Investigation and Prosecution". Paper presented at the International Conference on Preventing and Controlling Money Laundering and the Use of the Proceeds of Crime: A Global Approach, Courmayeur Mont Blanc, Italy, 18-20 June 1994 (hereafter 1994 Conference), (typescript), p. 2. Since reproduced in Savona, E.U., (ed.), *Responding to Money Laundering: International Perspectives*, Amsterdam, 1997. Subsequent references are to the original. For a somewhat broader view of the categories of offenders who, based on UK experience, do not launder the proceeds of their crimes in any systematic way see, the evidence of Professor M. Levi reproduced in, House of Commons, Home Affairs Committee, *Organised Crime*, H.C. Paper 18-II, 1994-95 (hereafter Select Committee), at p. 187.

3. Savona, E.U., and De Feo, M.A., "Money Trails: International Money Laundering Trends and Prevention/Control Policies". Paper presented at the 1994 Conference, (typescript), p. 84. Since reproduced in Savona, E.U., (ed.), id. Subsequent references are to the original.

4. National Crime Authority, *Taken to the Cleaners: Money Laundering in Australia*, Canberra, 1991, Vol. I, p. vii.

5. "Control of Proceeds of Crime: Report of the Secretary General", UN Doc. E/CN.15/1993/4; 25 January 1993, p. 11.

6. See, Beare, M.E., and Schneider, S., *Tracing of Illicit Funds: Money Laundering in Canada*, Ottawa, 1990, at p. 304.

7. Evans, op. cit., p. 14.

8. Reproduced in Gilmore, W., (ed.), *International Efforts to Combat Money Laundering*, Cambridge, 1992, at p. 243.

9. Savona and De Feo, op. cit., at p. 93.

10. *Supra*, note 4, p. 31.

11. Drage, J., "Countering Money Laundering", *Bank of England Quarterly Bulletin*, November 1992, p. 418, at p. 420. For an interesting variant on this classic approach see, UN Office for Drug Control and Crime Prevention, *Financial Havens, Banking Secrecy and Money Laundering*, New York, 1998, pp. 4-5.

12. *Money Laundering: Guidance Notes for Banks and Building Societies*, London, 1990, Appendix A.

13. *Money Laundering: Guidance Notes for Mainstream Banking, Lending and Deposit Taking Activities*, London, 1993, para. 8.

14. US Department of State, *International Narcotics Control Strategy Report*, Washington, D.C., 1988, p. 46.

15. "Financial Action Task Force on Money Laundering: Report of 6 February 1990", reproduced in Gilmore, W., (ed.), op. cit., p. 4, at p. 7.

16. Drage, J., "Countering Money Laundering: The Response of the Financial Sector", in MacQueen, H.L., (ed.), *Money Laundering*, Edinburgh, 1993, p. 60, at p. 61.

17. See, Chaikin, D.A., "Money Laundering: An Investigatory Perspective", *Criminal Law Forum*, 1991, p. 467, at pp. 478-479.

18. Bowie, B.W., "Money Laundering Techniques" (typescript: Drug Enforcement Directorate, Royal Canadian Mounted Police, February 1988), p. 3.

19. See generally, Adams, J.R., and Frantz, D., *A Full Service Bank*, New York, 1992.

20. US Department of State, *International Narcotics Control Strategy Report*, Washington, D.C., 1991, p. 347. In December 1993 a second deposit-taking institution, the Bank Leu (Luxembourg), was convicted of money laundering in the US In addition to a US$ 60 000 fine it agreed to forfeit US$ 2.3 million, representing tainted funds, to the US. It also agreed to submit special audit reports in the US for three years and to publish and distribute to other financial institutions and regulatory bodies a document on the subject of money laundering.

21. Ehrenfeld, R., *Evil Money: Encounters Along the Money Trail*, New York, 1992, p. 70.

22. See, e.g., "Prison for Naqvi over BCCI fraud", *The Times*, London, 20 October 1994.

23. See "The Impact of Organised Criminal Activities Upon Society at Large: Report of the Secretary General". UN Doc. E/CN.15/1993/3; 11 January 1993, at p. 12.

24. *FOPAC Bulletin*, No. 6, 1991, p. 3.

25. For the revised stance of the FATF on this issue see, "Financial Action Task Force on Money Laundering: Annual Report 1995-96", at p. 8.

26. See Greenberg, T.S., "Anti-Money Laundering Activities in the United States", in *Action Against Transnational Criminality: Papers from the 1993 Oxford Conference on International and White Collar Crime*, London, 1994, p. 3, at p. 61.

27. For the position in the UK see Organised and International Crime Directorate, Home Office, *Confiscation and Money Laundering: Law and Practice – A Guide for Enforcement Authorities*, London, 1997, pp. 61-63.

28. Savona and De Feo, op. cit., p. 21.

29. Paper (untitled) presented by R.A. Small of the US Federal Reserve System to the Financial Action Task Force Money Laundering Symposium, Singapore, 21-23 April 1993 (typescript), p. 76.

30. Sherman, T., "International Efforts to Combat Money Laundering: The Role of the Financial Action Task Force", in MacQueen, H.L., (ed.), op. cit., p. 12, at p. 14.

31. See US Department of State, *International Narcotics Control Strategy Report*, Washington, D.C., 1994, at p. 472.

32. Savona and De Feo, op. cit., p. 19.

33. See *Money Laundering: Guidance Notes for Insurance and Retail Investment Products*, London, 1993, at para. 8.

34. *Supra*, note 25, Annex 3, p. 7.

35. "International Organisation of Securities Commissions, Working Party Number 4, Report on Money Laundering" (typescript: 1992), at p. 4.

36. *Supra*, note 4, p. 43.

37. *Money Laundering Guidance Notes for the Financial Sector [Revised and Consolidated June 1997]*, 1997, London, Appendix I.

38. See, *supra*, note 35, at p. 8.

39. See, e.g., Cassidy, W.L., "Fei-Ch'ien, Flying Money: A Study of Chinese Underground Banking". Paper presented at the 12th International Asian Organised Crime Conference, Fort Lauderdale, Florida, USA, 26 June 1990 (typescript).

40. *Supra*, note 18, p. 8.

41. Mobius, M., "Laundering Methods". Paper presented at the Council of Europe Money Laundering Conference, Strasbourg, France, 28-30 September 1992 (typescript), p. 8.

42. See, *supra*, note 4, at p. 36.

43. Noble, R., "The Financial Action Task Force Recommendations and their Implementation". Paper presented to the 1994 Conference (typescript), para. 28.

44. Beare and Schneider, op. cit., p. 183.

45. *Supra*, note 18, p. 4.

46. *Supra*, note 4, p. 47.

47. Beare and Schneider, op. cit., p. 188.

48. *Id.*, p. 186.

49. *International Tax Avoidance and Evasion: Four Related Studies*, Paris, 1987, p. 21.

50. Id., p. 22.

51. *Harmful Tax Competition: An Emerging Global Issue*, Paris, 1998.

52. See, e.g., the 1998 UN study at *supra*, note 11.

53. *Supra*, note 31, p. 477.

54. Chaikin, op. cit., p. 488.

55. UNDCP, *World Drug Report*, Oxford, 1997, p. 39.

56. Greenberg, op. cit., pp. 64-65.

57. See Robinson, J., *The Laundrymen*, London, 1994, at p. 227.

58. See, e.g., "Cash at any price", *The Economist*, 9 May 1992.

59. Noble, op. cit., para. 28.

60. *Supra*, note 24, p. 6.

61. See "Typology of Money Laundering", in "Financial Action Task Force on Money Laundering: Annexes to the Report, 1990-91", at pp. 26-27.

62. Savona and De Feo, op. cit., p. 24. For a discussion of the increased use of jewellery companies and bullion dealers for money laundering see, Hill, C., "Money laundering methodology", in Parlour, R., (ed.), *Butterworths International Guide to Money Laundering Law and Practice*, London, 1994, Ch. 1.

63. See generally, "Financial Action Task Force on Money Laundering: 1998-99 Report on Money Laundering Typologies".

64. Id., p. 2.

65. *Second Commission Report to the European Parliament and the Council on the Implementation of the Money Laundering Directive*. Commission of the European Communities, COM (1998) 401, final, 01.07.1998, p. 17.

66. *Supra*, note 63, p. 5. Similar concerns have been expressed by the European Parliament. See Committee on Legal Affairs and Citizen's Rights "Report on the Second Commission Report to the European Parliament and the Council on the implementation of the Money Laundering Directive", European Parliament doc. A4-0093/99, 26 February 1999, at p. 6.

67. *Supra*, note 34, p. 5.

68. *Supra*, note 63, p. 8.

69. "Financial Action Task Force on Money Laundering: Annual Report 1996-97", Annex A, p. 18.

70. Id.

71. *Supra*, note 63, p. 7.

72. *Supra*, note 69, p. 16.

73. *Supra*, note 63, p. 9. The European Parliament has also called for action to be taken by the Commission and the member states in this area of concern. See *supra*, note 66, at p. 6, p. 15 and pp. 17-18.

74. Beare and Schneider, op. cit., p. xi.

75. See, e.g., *supra*, note 55, at p. 141.

76. *Supra*, note 31, p. 469.

CHAPTER III – GLOBAL RESPONSES TO MONEY LAUNDERING

The United Nations

Introduction

The initial impetus for co-ordinated international action to combat money laundering arose, as has been seen, out of a growing concern within the world community about the problems of drug abuse and illicit trafficking. These subjects have for long been recognised as being particularly suited for action at the global level. Indeed, the first international agreements which sought to regulate these matters, such as the International Opium Convention of 1912 and the 1931 Convention for Limiting the Manufacture and Regulating the Distribution of Narcotic Drugs, predate the creation of the United Nations.[1] In the years since 1945 the UN has built extensively upon these foundations. Its broad mandate in this area has provided the basis for the creation of a comprehensive and multifaceted strategy with initiatives linked to, among others, prevention, demand reduction, and the treatment and rehabilitation of offenders. It is, however, the actions taken on the supply side which are of the greatest interest in the present context.

Prior to 1988 there were two central pillars which supported that effort. The first was the 1961 UN Single Convention on Narcotic Drugs, as amended by a 1972 protocol, which has attracted substantial support from the international community. This "provides for international controls over the production and availability of opium and its derivatives, synthetic drugs having similar effects, cocaine and cannabis".[2] By 31 October 1998 some 153 states were parties to the convention and the protocol while a further 13 were bound only by the former. The second major plank of the supply-side system took the form of the 1971 UN Convention on Psychotropic Substances, with 158 state parties, which extends the concept of international control to a wide range of synthetic drugs.[3]

While these international treaties have made a highly positive contribution in controlling the production of drugs and seeking to prevent their diversion into the illicit market place, it gradually became apparent that they were inadequate to the task of dealing with the range of complex issues raised by modern international drug trafficking. As Donnelly has remarked: "An international drug control regime based primarily on controlling the production of and regulating legal trade in dangerous drugs has proved valuable in safeguarding medical and scientific uses. It has increased the costs and difficulties of illegal trafficking. It also provides a firm basis for further forms of international co-operation. Alone, however, it is completely inadequate to the problem – in large part because of its conceptual narrowness".[4]

A new initiative at the global level to supplement existing arrangements was clearly necessary. It was widely accepted that this would need to focus on transnational drug trafficking operations and make provision for greatly enhanced co-operation in law enforcement. The underlying philosophy was well articulated in the Comprehensive Multidisciplinary Outline of Future Activities in Drug Abuse Control, adopted by the 1987 UN Conference on Drug Abuse and Illicit Trafficking:

> (...) it is necessary to ensure vigorous enforcement of the law in order to reduce the illicit availability of drugs, deter drug-related crime, and contribute to drug abuse prevention by creating an environment favourable to efforts for reducing illicit supply and demand. (...) Co-ordination of activities and co-operation among national agencies within each country and between countries are vital for the achievement of the objective.[5]

Following an initiative taken by the Government of Venezuela, the UN General Assembly, on 14 December 1984, unanimously adopted a resolution in which it expressed the conviction that "the wide scope of the illicit traffic in narcotic drugs and its consequences make it necessary to prepare a convention which considers the various aspects of the problem as a whole and, in particular, those not envisaged in existing international instruments". The Assembly requested the UN Economic and Social Council to instruct the Commission on Narcotic Drugs to prepare a draft convention "as a matter of priority".[6] Acting on that mandate the Commission adopted, by consensus, on 14 February 1986 a resolution in which it identified fourteen elements for inclusion in a draft convention. This set in motion a detailed process of consultation, study and review which culminated in the holding in Vienna, from 25 November to 20 December 1988, of the UN Conference for the Adoption of a Convention Against Illicit Traffic in Narcotic Drugs and Psychotropic Substances. This important gathering, attended by 106 countries, succeeded in adopting, again by consensus, a detailed treaty text consisting of thirty-four articles and one annex.

In spite of its scope and ambition this instrument, described by the then US President George Bush as "of fundamental importance to effective international co-operation to combat drugs",[7] it entered into force on 11 November 1990 – a near record in terms of time for an instrument of this kind. By October 1998 it had attracted 148 states parties as well as the formal participation of the European Community. It is of interest to note in this regard that the United Kingdom, which embraced the convention regime in 1991, has since acted to extend its application to a number of jurisdictions for which it has responsibility in the foreign affairs sphere, several of which are significant offshore financial centres. Such extension took effect for Bermuda and the remaining British Overseas Territories in the Caribbean (which include both the Cayman Islands and the British Virgin Islands) with effect from February 1995. In 1997 the convention was extended to the Bailiwick of Jersey and similar action in relation to Guernsey is anticipated in the near future.

In addition to this impressive numerical total the quality of participation has also been very encouraging. In addition to the major consumer nations of North America and western Europe, it has attracted the support of key transit states in central and eastern Europe, the Caribbean and Central America. Of even greater significance a growing number of the world's major drug producers have accepted its obligations. These include, among others, Afghanistan, Bolivia, Colombia, India, Iran, Lebanon, Mexico, Morocco, Myanmar, Nepal, and Pakistan. Such has been its reception that it is now widely regarded as constituting the essential "foundation" of the international legal regime in this important area of concern.[8] As Savona and De Feo have remarked: "Ratification of the Vienna drug convention is becoming virtually an indicator of responsible membership in the anti-drug and anti-money laundering world community".[9]

Major provisions of the 1988 UN convention

Money laundering and confiscation

At the very heart of an effective strategy to counter modern international drug trafficking is the need to provide the law enforcement community with the necessary tools to undermine the financial power of the cartels and other groups; and to do so in a way which is sensitive to the requirements of international co-operation. As was seen in Chapter I, throughout the 1980s a broad consensus emerged that the criminalisation of money laundering and providing for the confiscation of criminal proceeds were the essential components of such a strategy. The 1988 convention addressed both of these issues – the first time that a convention of global reach had done so.

Critical to the approach adopted to the issue of money laundering was the imposition, in Article 3 (1) (a), of a strict obligation for each participating country to criminalise a fairly comprehensive list of activities concerning drug trafficking which have a major international impact. These range from production and cultivation through to the organisation, management, and financing of trafficking operations. The latter was believed to be a particularly important component of the effort to reach those involved at the highest levels of the drugs trade. As Bassiouni has remarked: "The organisers of the international illicit traffic do not in most cases physically handle any drugs themselves, but instigate, finance and direct these operations which are carried out by underlings (...)".[10] Sub-paragraph (b) then requires that drug-related money laundering be established as a criminal offence. The actual term was not (due to its novelty and for translation reasons) used in the text. Rather the concept was expressed in these words:

i. the conversion or transfer of property, knowing that such property is derived from any offence or offences established in accordance with sub-paragraph (a) of this paragraph, or from an act of participation in such offence or offences, for the purpose of concealing or disguising the illicit origin of the property or of assisting any person who is involved in the commission of such an offence or offences to evade the legal consequences of his actions;

ii. the concealment or disguise of the true nature, source, location, disposition, movement, rights with respect to, or ownership of property, knowing that such property is derived from an offence or offences established in accordance with sub-paragraph (a) of this paragraph or from an act of participation in such an offence or offences.

In addition, the same article of the 1988 convention requires each party, to the extent that it is not contrary to its constitutional principles and the basic concepts of its legal system, to criminalise "the acquisition, possession or use of property, knowing, at the time of receipt" that it was derived from drug trafficking (Article 3 (1) (c) (i)) as well as conspiracy, aiding and abetting, and facilitating the commission of drug trafficking offences including money laundering (Article 3 (1) (c) (iv)). The important issue of the appropriate burden of proof in relation to all such offences is addressed in Article 3 (3) which provides that knowledge, intent or purpose "may be inferred from objective factual circumstances".

Many of the remaining provisions of this lengthy and complex article are designed to ensure that money laundering and other trafficking offences are treated with appropriate seriousness by the judiciary and the prosecutorial authorities of each participating state. By way of illustration, paragraph 5 requires that each party ensure that "their courts or other competent authorities" can take into account a non-exhaustive list of factors which make these offences particularly grave. Those specifically mentioned, and of obvious relevance to the world of money laundering, include the involvement of organised criminal groups, the use of violence, and "[t]he fact that the offender holds a public office and that the offence is connected with the office in question".

The significance of the approach adopted in Article 3 to drug-related money laundering for the future of international co-operation should not be underestimated. By requiring its criminalisation and treating it as a serious offence in paragraph 1 the drafters have sought to ensure that co-operation in respect of confiscation, mutual legal assistance and extradition will be forthcoming. For example, the United States delegation hailed the achievement of the convention in relation to extradition, a subject addressed in detail in Article 6, in these words:

> Because all parties are obligated to establish Article 3, paragraph 1, offences as criminal offences in their domestic law, any requirements of dual criminality, that is that the offence is criminal in both jurisdictions, in a party's extradition law should be met. Although there has been almost universal recognition that illicit drug trafficking offences are extraditable offences, narcotics-related money laundering is a new criminal offence for many states and has not been traditionally recognised as an extraditable offence. The universal recognition of narcotics related money laundering as an extraditable offence is one of the most important aspects of this article.[11]

A further indication of the sensitivity of the drafters of this convention to the transnational dimension of the problem is to be seen in Article 3 (10) which seeks to restrict the possibility that narco-terrorists, money launderers and others involved in the drugs trade could take advantage of two traditional restrictions on international co-operation. It will be recalled that the concept that individuals who have been accused or convicted of offences of a political character should not be subject to extradition has a lengthy history and continues to find frequent expression in domestic extradition laws and international treaty practice. Similarly, many arrangements for international co-operation do not extend to fiscal offences. The provision in question restricts, but does not entirely eliminate, the possibility of invoking such grounds in this context.

At a practical level, the mandatory wording of the convention in relation to money laundering and other serious offences means that many states wishing to become parties to this significant international instrument will be faced with the need to enact complex implementing legislation in order to ensure that they can act in full compliance with its terms. Indeed, experience demonstrates that even states which possess relatively modern legislative instruments governing money laundering may have to introduce amendments in order to bring the law into line with convention requirements. Thus, the United Kingdom Parliament had to include specific provisions in the Criminal Justice (International Co-operation) Act of 1990 in order to bridge the gap between section 24 of the Drug Trafficking Offences Act 1986 (the relevant statute at that time) and the money laundering requirements of Article 3.

A second major feature of the approach adopted in Vienna relates to the subject of the confiscation of the proceeds derived from, and the instrumentalities used in, drug trafficking. This is treated in detail in Article 5 which addresses both the measures to be taken at the national level and the necessary mechanisms to give effect to international co-operation in this vital area. It is of importance because confiscation measures aim "to incapacitate, by depriving a person of the physical or financial ability, power, or opportunity to continue to engage in proscribed conduct, to prevent offenders from unjustly enriching themselves, by eliminating the advantages and benefits which the offender has gained through his or her illegality, to deter the offender and others from crime by undermining the ultimate profitability of the venture and to protect the community by curbing the circulation of prohibited items".[12]

The first three paragraphs of Article 5 treat the issue of confiscation at the level of domestic law and practice. They impose a series of broad obligations which are free from any limitations or safeguard clauses. Paragraph 1 reads:

1. Each Party shall adopt such measures as may be necessary to enable confiscation of:

a. Proceeds derived from offences established in accordance with Article 3, paragraph 1, or property the value of which corresponds to that of such proceeds;

b. Narcotic drugs and psychotropic substances, materials and equipment or other instrumentalities used in or intended for use in any manner in offences established in accordance with Article 3, paragraph 1.

It should be noted that, whilst framed in mandatory terms, this paragraph was deliberately worded so as to leave to each state a wide measure of discretion as to how best to achieve the desired result. This emphasis on flexibility also permitted due account to be taken of the differing approaches to confiscation which had evolved in domestic legislation. As the United States delegation pointed out, the wording "allows the option of forfeiting either the proceeds of the offence or, in their place, property which has a corresponding value".[13] In order to ensure the effectiveness of the confiscation procedure, paragraph 2 makes provision for necessary preliminary steps to be taken to "identify, trace, and freeze or seize proceeds, property, instrumentalities or any other thing referred to in paragraph 1 (...)". The text, however, provides no guidance on how states are to handle a broad range of practical issues which arise in giving effect to these obligations. By way of illustration, experience has "demonstrated the pressing need to provide a coherent and adequately financed asset-management regime to deal with property subject to provisional measures and with confiscated property. It will be necessary for the appropriate authority to have the necessary power to take possession and control of, and to manage or otherwise deal with, the property in question. This might include the need, for example, to run restrained businesses, ranging from restaurants to ski resorts, to dispose of perishable or rapidly depreciating property, and to compensate innocent creditors".[14]

The Vienna Conference also acted to ensure that the concept of bank secrecy did not needlessly hinder the search for and the eventual confiscation of the assets derived from this form of criminal activity. As was seen in Chapter II, complex laundering schemes typically incorporate some aspect of the protection afforded by strict rules of customer confidentiality. Experience had shown that "existing bank secrecy laws are being used in many instances to obstruct co-operation and the provision of information needed for the investigation of allegations of drug-related offences".[15]

The solution which commends itself to the drafters of the convention, now reflected in paragraph 3, was to require that each state party empower its courts or other relevant authorities to order that bank, financial or commercial records be made available. Most importantly it is specifically provided that: "A party shall not decline to act under the provisions of this paragraph on the ground of bank secrecy". The inclusion of this affirmative obligation has been widely characterised as a major breakthrough. In the words of Sproule and Saint-Denis: "The exclusion of bank secrecy as a justification to decline to act may prove to be one of the most important measures in combating drug money laundering operations".[16]

The centrality of this issue (which, as noted below, also arises in the context of mutual legal assistance under Article 7) was highlighted when, in March 1996, the instrument of accession deposited by the Government of the Lebanon included reservations to these bank secrecy provisions. In its 1996 report the International Narcotics Control Board expressed concern over what it regarded as these "far-reaching reservations". It also expressed the view that: "the validity of reservations going to the core of the 1988 convention, for example, by excluding important provisions on money laundering, is questionable from both the legal and policy perspectives".[17] It also drew attention to the relevant provisions of the Vienna Convention on the Law of Treaties which, in the absence of specific coverage of reservations in the 1988 text, are deemed to govern this issue.[18] In the course of the following year eight states formally objected to the reservations made by the Lebanon. While Austria and Germany regarded them as "problematic" the remainder went further in that they considered them to be contrary to the object and purpose of the 1988 convention and thus inadmissible. As Sweden noted in March 1997: "The convention establishes that bank secrecy shall not be a ground for a failure to act or for a failure to render mutual assistance. The Government of Sweden considers that these reservations therefore undermine the object and purpose of the convention as stated in Article 2, paragraph 1, (i) (e), to promote co-operation among the parties in order to effectively address the international dimension of illicit traffic in drugs".

While there is no doubt that the bank secrecy provision in paragraph 3 is of profound significance to the effectiveness of confiscation as a criminal justice measure, it has been argued that it does not go far enough. There has been a growing perception that the removal of such secrecy provides only an illusory benefit where additional layers of protection, such as anonymous trusts and shell companies, are available.[19] In this context particular concern has been expressed about the range of services provided in the ever growing number of offshore financial centres. A detailed and hard-hitting 1998 study published by the UN expressed the following view:

> The common denominator in money laundering and a variety of financial crimes is the enabling machinery which has been created in the financial havens. The effectiveness of these centres in helping people and companies to hide assets is not the result of any single device. Changing bank secrecy rules alone will not help. Rather the centres have created a tool kit composed of new corporate instruments, foundations, trusts, trust companies, banks and bank accounts. The tools are mixed and matched with jurisdictions that have made a point of non-co-operation with the rest of the international community in criminal and tax investigations. What started as a business to service the needs of a privileged few has become an enormous hole in the international legal and fiscal system.[20]

As will be seen in Chapter IV, one of the long-standing priorities of the Financial Action Task Force on Money Laundering (FATF) has been to secure further progress in this sphere; an interest which was reinforced in a significant fashion by G-7 finance ministers at their meeting held in London in May 1998.

It was also widely accepted by the drafters of the 1988 convention that action in the confiscation sphere when undertaken on a unilateral basis at the level of domestic law was unlikely to be fully effective in combating an activity, such as drug trafficking, which has conspicuous transnational features. As McClean has pointed out: "The facility with which assets, particularly in the form of financial credits of some sort, can be passed across national boundaries means that an order enforceable only in the country of origin may be of limited value".[21] The need for effective international co-operation in this context was therefore viewed as being critical. It too is treated in Article 5 of the 1988 text.

Here a mandatory framework is provided which, nonetheless, recognises the need for a substantial element of flexibility for national legislatures. Paragraph 4 (a) is central to the approach adopted and reads, in full, as follows:

4.a. Following a request made pursuant to this article by another party having jurisdiction over an offence established in accordance with Article 3, paragraph 1, the party in whose territory proceeds, property, instrumentalities or any other thing referred to in paragraph 1 of this article are situated shall:

i. Submit the request to its competent authorities for the purpose of obtaining an order of confiscation and, if such order is granted, give effect to it; or

ii. Submit to its competent authorities, with a view to giving effect to it to the extent requested, an order of confiscation issued by the requesting party in accordance with paragraph 1 of this article, in so far as it relates to proceeds, property, instrumentalities or any other things referred to in paragraph 1 situated in the territory of the requested party.

Two different approaches to securing the co-operation of other states are thus contemplated. In the words of the chairman of the relevant conference committee: "Sub-paragraph (a) (i) dealt with the case of confiscation in a state where the proceeds were found. The order in that case would be issued by the local authorities of the requested state. It was immaterial whether an order by the requesting state had been issued or not. In sub-paragraph (a) (ii) an order by the requesting state was essential".[22] In adopting this approach it was recognised that the former procedure was more in keeping with the traditional disinclination of members of the international community to directly enforce foreign criminal judgements. However, this was an area in which some countries, including the United Kingdom, had enacted legislation to permit them "under certain circumstances to recognise and enforce a foreign forfeiture judgement"[23] and it was thought appropriate that the convention reflect that fact. Provision is also made to ensure that a requested party shall take effective preliminary measures, including tracing and freezing proceeds and property, "for the purpose of eventual confiscation to be ordered either by the requesting party or, pursuant to a request under sub-paragraph (a) of this paragraph, by the requested party" (Article 5 (4) (b)).

Two further points deserve emphasis at this point. First, although these actions take place according to the domestic laws and procedures of the requested state, its legal system must permit such assistance to be granted. Second, no further international action is required to perfect this obligation although states parties are encouraged to enter into detailed bilateral and multilateral agreements in order to make their confiscation arrangements as effective as possible. In the absence of such agreements the parties to the 1988 convention are obliged to regard it as sufficient.

The unparalleled ambition and intrusiveness of this new form of co-operation was bound to give rise to both difficulties and inefficiencies. To some extent the emphasis on flexibility has been an unintended source of problems at the practical level. Take, for example, the decision not to impose a single confiscation system, thus permitting the two principal approaches which had evolved in domestic legislation (property and value confiscation) to continue. As we have seen, states parties to the 1988 convention may select either (although there is nothing to prevent the adoption of both).

Problems will arise when a request emerges from a country with one system and is directed at a state utilising the other unless the domestic law of the requested state has been framed in such a way as to permit it to respond to either type of request. Just such a degree of responsiveness is to be found in the legislation of a number of jurisdictions including the United Kingdom and Australia. Subsequent international initiatives, such as the 1990 Council of Europe money laundering convention, reviewed in Chapter V, have learned from and sought to improve upon this UN precedent in this and other areas in order to maximise the effectiveness of confiscation assistance.

This convention article also requires states to provide the UN Secretary General with the texts of relevant laws and regulations as well as any subsequent amendments. This enables the UN Secretariat to act as an effective clearing house for information. Article 5 goes on to treat the important issue of the final disposition of the proceeds and property which are eventually confiscated. The basic rule is that such matters are to be determined in accordance with the domestic law of the state which gives effect to the confiscation. In many countries confiscated profits are simply used to supplement general government revenues. In others, such as the United States, the fruits of forfeiture are reinvested in federal, state, local and international law enforcement. In yet others, such as the United Kingdom, a distinction is made in terms of the eventual disposition of confiscated proceeds based on whether or not the case possessed an international element. It has created a specific fund which can be drawn upon to support identified priorities. However, as has been pointed out elsewhere: "The United Kingdom only deposits monies received from international cases into its fund, i.e., those obtained when a foreign confiscation order is registered or enforced or gifts from overseas countries in connection with joint investigations where confiscation has resulted".[24] In all other instances, resulting monies are paid into the Consolidated Fund.

In so far as confiscations resulting from international co-operation are concerned, paragraph 5 (b) invites parties to give special consideration to contributing such funds to intergovernmental bodies specialising in efforts to counter trafficking or drug abuse or to concluding agreements for sharing the same with other states. "Since 1988, practice has tended to focus on the latter".[25] Indeed, to date only Luxembourg has opted for the alternative approach. It has contributed substantial sums to the UN International Drug Control Programme (UNDCP).

Particularly in recent years considerable emphasis has been placed on the practical benefits to be derived from asset-sharing among states which have contributed to a successful confiscation. It is the view of the US Justice Department "that asset-sharing among nations enhances international forfeiture co-operation by creating an incentive for countries to work together, regardless of where the assets are located or which jurisdiction will ultimately enforce the forfeiture order".[26] The sums in question can be substantial. By December 1998 transfers of approximately US$ 173 million to other countries had been approved by the American authorities (primarily the Justice Department). This attitude towards asset-sharing at the international level is but an extension of a well-established practice in relation to purely domestic cases.

While in some states it has been possible to utilise existing laws and administrative procedures as a basis for entering into the international asset-sharing arena, in others new legislation has been required. In the case of Canada, for example, "the Seized Property Management Act creates a statutory regime for international asset-sharing based on prior reciprocal agreements. The terms of the subsequent Forfeited Property Sharing Regulations of 1995 provide the necessary detail to make the scheme operational. This includes coverage of such matters as the determination of the amount available for sharing, the time at which any sharing will take place, and the rules by which, and the grounds upon which, the respective contributions of the jurisdictions in question will be assessed".[27]

The concept that confiscation of criminal proceeds is "a good way to make law enforcement pay for itself"[28] has an obvious attraction. Similarly, there is no doubt that such funding, whether resulting from national or international cases, can both reinforce the effectiveness of existing programmes and permit initiatives to take place which might not otherwise have been possible. In 1994, for instance, the FATF established a small Asian secretariat. Based in Sydney it was paid for primarily out of the Australian confiscated assets fund. There are, however, obvious dangers which can flow from lax management of this new revenue source. As has been pointed out elsewhere: "Poetic justice is not necessarily suitable justice. If the primary purpose of asset seizure becomes the maximisation of government profit or equipping enforcement agencies, there is the possibility that enforcement discretions will be exercised not on the basis of the seriousness of the offence or the dangerousness of the offender but on the wealth of the offender or what the agency sees as desirable to retain".[29]

Another provision particularly worthy of note in the context of money laundering is that contained in paragraph 6. This has as its focus the need to "ensure that proceeds derived from and instrumentalities used in illegal trafficking could not escape forfeiture simply because their form had been changed or they had been commingled with other property".[30] Here again the convention uses mandatory language – a decision of great practical importance given "the skill and speed with which large-scale traffickers are able to launder their profits."[31] Given this issue, and the nature of Article 5 as a whole, it was felt necessary to provide that its provisions "shall not be construed as prejudicing the rights of bona fide third parties". (Article 5 (8)).

Finally, it should be noted that, pursuant to paragraph 7, each party may give consideration to reversing the burden of proof in regard to the lawful origin of the alleged proceeds of trafficking and a minority of countries, including Cyprus, have done so.[32] It is, however, clear from both the wording of this provision and from its drafting history that there is absolutely no requirement to so act.

From the above overview of this highly complex and innovative article it is easy to see why it has attracted great praise from commentators. In the words of Sproule and Saint-Denis:

> The provisions now contained in this article are clear, specific, and in most cases, mandatory. They can be properly viewed as a major breakthrough in attacking the benefits derived from drug trafficking activities and are a forceful endorsement of the notion that attacking the profit motive is essential if the struggle against drug trafficking is to be effective.[33]

Other important provisions

The precedents established by the Vienna convention in the fields of money laundering and confiscation are supported by a range of other important mechanisms designed to promote international co-operation. Of these perhaps the most significant is Article 7 dealing with the provision, on an interstate basis, of mutual legal assistance in investigations, prosecutions and judicial proceedings relating to money laundering and other serious convention offences.

In contrast with confiscation, the drafters of the 1988 text were able to build upon an established and developing international practice in this area in relation to which the Council of Europe had played a major role. It envisages the provision of assistance in a number of highly practical areas. A non-exhaustive list includes: the taking of evidence or statements; effecting service of judicial documents; executing searches and seizures; examining objects and sites; providing information and evidentiary items; providing relevant documents and records including bank, financial, corporate or business records; and identifying or tracing proceeds and instrumentalities for evidential purposes. As one leading commentator has stressed: "Obtaining evidence from abroad (...) is as essential to the success of prosecutions as collecting intelligence and obtaining the offender. It is also the most dependent upon legal formalities and affords the least latitude for the sorts of informal measures and understandings upon which the police normally rely in their international dealings".[34]

In the course of the conference at Vienna, a number of delegations pressed for the specific inclusion of a statement to the effect that requests for assistance could not be refused on the grounds of bank secrecy. Such concerns find reflection in the clear wording of paragraph 5 of the final text. The extent of the obligation so imposed was described by the United States Attorney General as follows:

> First, it is an obligation to enact implementing legislation, if necessary, to modify domestic bank secrecy laws to permit execution of requests for bank records under the Convention. Second, with respect to an individual request for bank records under the Convention, it obliges a requested Party to grant the request, if the only basis for refusing would be bank secrecy laws.[35]

The authorised grounds for the refusal of a request are set out, in broadly worded fashion, in such a way as to ensure the protection of the essential interests of the requested state. Similarly, and in common with pre-existing practice, Article 7 imposes restrictions on the use to which the assistance obtained may be put and places certain obligations on the requested state.

In spite of the detail contained in these and other substantive and procedural provisions in this article, it was clearly recognised that the complexity of this subject area is such that states might well wish to conclude further agreements of a bilateral or multilateral nature in order to more adequately address issues of importance. Account also had to be taken of the fact that a substantial number of such agreements already existed. The solution adopted has been summarised by the United Kingdom Home Office in the following way: "By paragraph 20, the Parties are to consider the possibilities of bilateral or multilateral agreements to give effect to or enhance the provisions of the article, and if such an agreement is in force the procedures specified therein shall prevail over the normative procedures specified in Article 7".[36]

By embracing the concept of mutual legal assistance the UN convention has made a major contribution towards increasing its availability in areas of the world, and within legal traditions, where it was underdeveloped or unknown. It has, in addition, provided a critical level of support for those charged with prosecuting money laundering offences containing a substantial international dimension. As Kriz has pointed out: "mutual legal assistance can assist with attacking each of the basic steps in the money laundering process. Indeed, if the proceeds derived from a drug trafficking operation are physically carried out of country A in which it was obtained and deposited into a financial institution in country B (placement); transferred from that financial institution through various other financial institutions in various countries to another financial institution in country C (layering); and finally paid into a number of corporations in various countries in purported payments of share transfers (integration), then the investigators/prosecutors in country A would not have much hope in tracing, let alone confiscating, the proceeds of drug trafficking without using mutual legal assistance".[37]

Less innovative though equally important is the attention paid to the oldest and most firmly established method of co-operation; namely, extradition. This is the formal procedure governing the return of persons who have been accused or convicted of criminal offences in order that they may face prosecution or the execution of a sentence in a third country. It lies at the very heart of both the 1961 UN Single Convention on Narcotic Drugs, as amended, and the 1971 Convention on Psychotropic Substances and continues to occupy a position of significance in the 1988 arrangements.

The basic approach adopted in this regard is similar to that found in other multilateral instruments dealing with criminal activity of international concern. First, as is common, Article 6 requires that the domestic criminal offences which give effect to the obligations of this convention shall be deemed to be extraditable offences in any existing extradition treaty between the parties. This obligation is restricted to the more serious offences, including money laundering, provided for in Article 3 (1). Similarly, the parties "undertake to include such offences as extraditable offences in every extradition treaty to be concluded between them". (Article 6 (2)).

The second common element of practice reflected in the 1988 convention was summarised by Earl Ferrers, on behalf of the UK Government, in January 1990 in these words: "(…) where a party's extradition law depends on the existence of a treaty and there is no such treaty with another party, the convention may serve as a legal basis for extradition in respect of offences covered by it".[38] In the course of the Vienna Conference a number of delegations pressed for the inclusion of a mandatory provision in this regard. However, a majority favoured the use of permissive wording and it is this approach which finds reflection in the final treaty text. A number of States have utilised the option in a positive sense. For example, the United Kingdom has since legislated to add this convention to the list of international instruments, contained in section 22 of the Extradition Act 1989, which may be used in UK law for this purpose. By way of contrast America, which faces particular domestic law constraints in this regard, subjected its ratification of the convention to the specific understanding that: "The United States shall not consider this convention as a legal basis for extradition of citizens to any country with which the United States has no bilateral extradition treaty in force".

The third element common to international criminal conventions is to provide that "a party in whose territory an alleged offender is found shall itself either extradite or prosecute".[39] Though applicable in a number of different situations its greatest relevance is where extradition is refused because the individual concerned is a national of the requested state. Both prior to and during the Vienna Conference a major effort was made to secure the inclusion of a provision which would have obliged states to extradite their own nationals. However, this particular innovation was resisted by a clear majority of delegations. As has been pointed out elsewhere "there was overwhelming opposition from countries which, for either political or legal reasons, would not accept any provision on the extradition of their nationals, even a hortatory provision".[40] For such countries, which include many from the civil law tradition, when extradition is refused on the ground of nationality the requirement is to submit the case to the competent authorities for the purpose of prosecution "unless otherwise agreed with the requesting party". (Article 6 (9) (a)).

While a full review of the convention's treatment of extradition lies beyond the scope of the present study it is fair to say that it does not, when taken as a whole, constitute a particularly radical departure from the traditional approach to this subject as reflected in international practice. None the less, in the words of Stewart, Article 6 makes it somewhat easier "for prosecuting states to obtain the extradition of narcotics traffickers and cartel chiefs from overseas".[41]

Finally, it should be stressed that the formal procedures for mutual assistance in the administration of justice contained in this important international instrument are intended to supplement, rather than to replace, existing channels of police-to-police co-operation. This subject is separately addressed in Article 9 which is entitled "Other Forms of Co-operation and Training". As has been pointed out elsewhere: "This Article is designed to preserve and enhance forms of co-operation which may exist on a less formal basis than the mutual legal assistance referred to in Article 7. It provides that parties shall co-operate more closely with each other in matters of intelligence in investigating offences. It also calls on them to facilitate co-ordination of the work of their competent agencies and promote exchanges of staff, to carry out suitable training programmes and to assist one another in their training and research programmes".[42]

Conclusions

From this brief overview of some of the central features of this multilateral treaty one can readily appreciate why it has been so widely characterised by those involved in the efforts to combat money laundering as a major achievement. In particular it has responded to many of the challenges faced by the law enforcement community in their efforts to address the traditional fragmentation of legal arrangements which are so frequently exploited by sophisticated money launderers. As the FATF stated in 1990: "Many of the current difficulties in international co-operation in drug money laundering cases are directly or indirectly linked with a strict application of bank secrecy rules, with the fact that, in many countries, money laundering is not today an offence, and with insufficiencies in multilateral co-operation and mutual legal assistance".[43] The 1988 convention has addressed each of these concerns and, in so doing, has made an important contribution to future progress in this vital area of concern.

Supportive UN activities

The centrality of international legal instruments in the fight against drug abuse continues to be widely accepted by the member states of the UN. It is appreciated, however, that it is one thing to have reached agreement on paper and quite another to secure its effective operation in practice. Indeed, to date the results – as indicated by the raw and incomplete statistics which are available – tell a rather disappointing story even among the world's richest industrialised countries. For example, money laundering convictions have proved to be very difficult to secure in most jurisdictions.[44] As the 1997 UNDCP *World Drug Report* has explained: "Most legislation requires evidence of three specific elements in order to bring a successful money laundering prosecution – the predicate crime (...), the awareness of the launderer of the illegal source of the proceeds, and the action of removing or concealing the funds".[45]

A somewhat similar picture presents itself at the level of the confiscation of criminal proceeds. In a July 1998 report to the European Parliament, the Commission of the European Communities reflected upon the results achieved by its fifteen member states thus: "It does not appear that large amounts are being confiscated and there are indications, from certain member states, that much of the money seized or frozen ultimately has to be returned or released".[46] In so far as international co-operation is concerned a review of the practice of FATF members published in 1997 acknowledged that "there has been relatively limited mutual assistance experience (...) in the confiscation field, and asset-sharing and co-ordinating seizure and confiscation proceedings are also in their infancy at present".[47]

While the reasons for this state of affairs are many, complex and varied the experience of EU and FATF members helps, for present purposes, to underline the magnitude of the challenge facing developing countries and states in transition. Consequently one of the priorities for the UN system has been to provide such states with both encouragement and technical and other forms of assistance in order to convert political momentum into practical reality.

While various agencies have a mandate in this area the primary responsibility has been given to the Vienna-based UNDCP which became operational in 1991. "It provides leadership in international drug control, monitors trends in drug production, consumption and trafficking, and promotes the implementation of drug control treaties".[48]

Among a myriad of other activities, UNDCP provides vital assistance in the legal field including help to those jurisdictions faced with the challenge of enacting often highly complex legislation required to give domestic effect to the numerous obligations contained in the 1988 convention. This is a particular area of difficulty for small developing countries which suffer from a chronic shortage of appropriately trained professionals including legislative drafters. One development of importance was the elaboration by the UNDCP in November 1993 of a "model law" on money laundering. Specially adapted to the needs of civil law countries it is available in English, French, Spanish, Russian and Arabic. It is of interest to note that, unlike the 1988 convention, this measure is not restricted to the simple criminalisation of drug-related money laundering. It has drawn on other major initiatives, such as the recommendations of the FATF, in order to provide a text which seeks to reflect current best international practice in this area. A heavy emphasis is accordingly placed on measures to prevent the use of financial institutions (and certain non-financial businesses such as casinos) for the purposes of drug-related laundering. In 1995 a further model law was developed for common law jurisdictions. Both are updated from time to time.

It is of importance to stress that, particularly in recent years, UN-based consideration of money laundering and related issues has gone well beyond the confines of the 1988 convention. Increasingly, emphasis has been placed upon the need to have resort to preventative strategies which fully engage the banking and financial sectors in the anti-money laundering effort as well as the desirability of extending the scope of money laundering predicate offences beyond drug trafficking. This is well illustrated by Resolution 5 (XXXIX) adopted by the UN Commission on Narcotic Drugs on 24 April 1996. This provides, among other matters, encouragement to states to require the establishment of customer identification, record keeping and other preventative strategies by banks and other financial institutions. It also urges countries to "broaden money-laundering countermeasures (...) to include the transit, conversion or other disposition of illegal proceeds from serious crime". The resolution, importantly, notes that the forty recommendations of the FATF "remain the standard by which the anti-money-laundering measures adopted by concerned states should be judged".

This trend was consolidated by the UN General Assembly Special Session on the World Drug Problem which was held in New York from 8 to 10 June

1998. This high-level event was convened to mark the tenth anniversary of the 1988 convention and to provide an opportunity to develop a forward-looking strategy for the twenty-first century. One of the specific objectives set for the Special Session was to adopt further measures to prevent and sanction money laundering. To this end the Assembly embraced the need to tackle the laundering of profits derived both from drugs trafficking and other serious crimes, stressed the centrality of the preventative strategy and emphasised the importance of the implementation of law enforcement measures including information-sharing mechanisms.

Although UNDCP has played a key role a valuable contribution has also been made by others. For example the Centre for International Crime Prevention (formerly known as the Crime Prevention and Criminal Justice Branch) is also based in Vienna. It has been responsible for the preparation of various studies which have raised the awareness of governments about such matters as the extent of non-drug-related money laundering and the threat posed by the growth of organised crime. It is also involved in efforts to promote the use of UN model treaties, on such matters as mutual assistance in criminal matters and extradition, which have been adopted by the United Nations Congresses on the Prevention of Crime and the Treatment of Offenders.[49] The model on mutual assistance in criminal matters, for example, was adopted by the eighth Congress held in Havana, Cuba, in 1990 and approved by the UN General Assembly later the same year. Designed to popularise this important form of co-operation and to facilitate the negotiation of bilateral agreements between interested states it is, unlike the 1988 convention, not restricted to drug trafficking offences. In its original formulation it contains an "optional protocol" on the subject of co-operation in the confiscation of the proceeds of crime.[50] However, in 1998 it was decided to amend the model so as to insert the proceeds of crime provisions into the main body of the text.[51] It does not, however, directly treat the issue of laundering. As has been pointed out elsewhere: "If all countries criminalize money laundering (...) then in so far as the granting of assistance is governed by the principle of dual criminality, the protocol would be available in respect of such conduct".[52]

Importantly, for present purposes, the Centre for International Crime Prevention is, in conjunction with UNDCP, jointly responsible for the implementation of the Global Programme Against Money Laundering. This is a three year initiative (1997-99) which aims to increase the effectiveness of international action in this sphere through the provision to governments of technical co-operation, support to financial investigation units and the development of research. Under the research and analysis arm, for example, the UN has created (in a joint effort with other international bodies) an Internet-based information system known as the International Money Laundering Information Network (IMOLIN).[53] It contains a database of

anti-money laundering laws and regulations, an electronic money laundering "library", a calendar of forthcoming events in the anti-money laundering field, and a secure news forum.

The Global Programme also facilitates the conduct of original research on
central issues of concern and publishes the results. It was within this context that the UN commissioned four experts to prepare an extensive report
entitled *Financial Havens, Banking Secrecy and Money Laundering*. The
preliminary report, prepared by Mr J. A. Blum (USA), Professor M. Levi
(UK), Professor R. T. Naylor (Canada) and Professor P. Williams (USA), was
published by the UN Office for Drug Control and Crime Prevention on
29 May 1998.

It is of interest to note that this study was the subject of a panel discussion
held at the UN in New York at the time of the Special Session of the UN
General Assembly on 10 June 1998. In his contribution to that session, UN
Under Secretary General Pino Arlacchi, Executive Director of the Office for
Drug Control and Crime Prevention, stressed the need "to promote greater
transparency and oversight of the financial world" and his belief that it is
no longer possible to tolerate that the concept of banking privacy "should
offer immunity to criminals and their money". In relation to possible future
developments he remarked:

> The international community could also consider new international agreements
> that address the issue of financial and banking secrecy head on. The changing
> priorities of financial law enforcement should be taken into consideration when
> the international convention against organised transnational crime is considered.
> I favour a special protocol to complement the convention, devoted to counter-
> ing money laundering and, in particular, to strengthening transparency in finan-
> cial businesses.[54]

This UN initiative has its origins in the Political Declaration and Global
Action Plan adopted at the World Ministerial Conference on Organised
Transnational Crime held in Naples, Italy in 1994. The formal product of
this high-level meeting, subsequently approved by the General Assembly in
resolution 49/59 of 23 December 1994, was designed to strengthen and
improve "national capabilities and international co-operation against
organised transnational crime and [to] laying the foundations for concerted and effective global action against organised transnational crime and the
prevention of its further expansion".[55] It should be noted here that action
to combat organised crime has also formed a regular part of the G-7/8
agenda since the Halifax Summit of June 1995.[56] Similarly the topic has
taken on a position of some importance within the European Union, especially in the work of the so-called "Third Pillar" which is devoted to justice
and home affairs. This is evidenced by, *inter alia*, the ambitious June 1997
Action Plan to Combat Organised Crime.[57]

In December 1996 the UN General Assembly set in motion a process for consideration of the possible elaboration of a multilateral convention to address the issue of transnational organised crime and provided the Commission on Crime Prevention and Criminal Justice with a mandate to this end. The initiative was also afforded priority status. Subsequent discussions have revealed broad support in the international community for such a convention. Indeed, at the April 1998 meeting of the Commission there was unanimity on this point. A target date of the year 2000 for the finalisation of the convention also received substantial backing. However, in order to meet this goal much progress will have to be achieved. This is well illustrated by the report of the group of experts which met in Warsaw, Poland, in February 1998.[58] It is apparent that in determining the rate of progress which can in fact be achieved much will depend on reaching agreement on the all important question of the scope of application of the proposed text: an issue which raises particular difficulties given the absence of a generally accepted definition of "organised transnational crime". Nonetheless there is growing political support at a high level which should help to pave the way for progress. For instance the G-8 summit communiqué of May 1998 expressed full support for bringing this initiative to a conclusion within two years.

There does appear to be a broad consensus over some aspects of the package. According to the Commission: "The convention should constitute a legal framework for concerted action against organised crime and a basis for the harmonization of national legislation. (...) It should also contain detailed provisions on international co-operation, such as mutual legal assistance, extradition, law enforcement co-operation, confiscation and seizure of proceeds from crime and transfer of criminal proceedings".[59] There is no doubt that any such instrument would also contain detailed provisions on money laundering. It has also been suggested that specific topics of relevance might be addressed in additional protocols to the proposed convention and it appears to be this possibility that the Under Secretary General favoured in his June 1998 remarks in the panel discussion in New York.

It is apparent from the work undertaken to date that the experts have been drawing heavily on the 1998 UN drugs convention and the 1990 Council of Europe money laundering convention for inspiration. However, at the Warsaw meeting the concept of "prevention" emerged as a new and strong theme. In the words of paragraph 62 of the official report:

> Measures to ensure the transparency and accountability of financial institutions were particularly important preventative measures. The new convention should include provisions that would promote such measures, as well as transparency of flows of capital, reporting suspicious transactions, establishing mandatory record-keeping systems and applying the "know-your-customer" rule. It was

suggested that those measures should be expanded to apply to all business transactions and not be restricted only to financial institutions.

Global law enforcement co-operation

The UN is not the only institution with a global constituency which has an interest in countering money laundering and promoting the tracing, seizing and confiscation of the proceeds of crime. These aims are shared by those charged with servicing the needs of the world's law enforcement community; namely, the International Criminal Police Organisation (ICPO/Interpol) and the World Customs Organisation (WCO) (formerly the Customs Co-operation Council (CCC)).

Interpol, the successor to the International Criminal Police Commission which was founded in 1923, is the principal facilitator of police-to-police co-operation on a global scale. With its headquarters in Lyon, France, to which it moved in 1989, it has a worldwide membership. Staffed by a mix of serving police officers and civilian employees, it has four official working languages (English, French, Spanish and Arabic). Its major aims, as expressed in Article 2 of its constitution, are to promote the widest possible co-operation between police authorities in the spirit of the Universal Declaration of Human Rights, and to contribute to the "prevention and suppression of ordinary law crimes".[60]

It is of importance to stress that, contrary to popular belief, Interpol has no operational policing mandate. One of its two major functions is to facilitate communication between its members through the provision of a modern, safe and secure communications network. For this purpose each member has a National Central Bureau (NCB) which acts as the focal point for liaison with both the General Secretariat in Lyon and the NCB's of other members. This communications system processes over one million police messages each year. Concern about its efficiency has greatly abated since the introduction, in 1987, of the Automated Message Switching System. This is a fully computerised process, to which the majority of members are linked, which automatically relays messages without the need for manual intervention.[61] The second major function performed by Interpol is to act as a source of information on criminals and on developing trends and patterns of criminality. In so far as the former is concerned the computerised Criminal Information System provides a database consisting of a significant number of criminal files. A new automated search facility permits NCBs to have instant access to certain important categories of information.

A major priority of the organisation is the fight against illicit drug trafficking. Approximately 20% of its annual budget is devoted to this activity and in excess of 50% of the total message traffic is drugs related. In the General

Secretariat in Lyon the collection, collation, analysis and dissemination of drug-related information is carried out by the Drugs Sub-Division – the most active part of a wider Police Division. It is the Police Division which has special responsibility for laundering and related issues through its FOPAC group; an acronym derived from the French *Fonds Provenant des Activités Criminelles*.

Established as a working group in 1983 and given permanent status in January 1990, FOPAC has a variety of functions and responsibilities. A substantial part of the effort of its modestly sized staff is devoted to providing information on money laundering to national law enforcement agencies. One vehicle used is the FOPAC *Bulletin*. This contains details on such matters as new, significant or unusual cases; developments, changes, trends and patterns; and countermeasures initiated by member countries.[62] A further valuable information service is FOPAC's *Financial Assets Encyclopaedia*. Since 1992 this has taken the form of a loose-leaf publication the contents of which can be readily updated. It contains information on the status of money laundering and confiscation legislation in member countries; a listing of contact points for national police units that specialise in money laundering and financial investigations; the texts of relevant international conventions of a multilateral character; and model legislation.

It is also charged with maintaining contact with specialists in the field. Although these are primarily national policing experts and the WCO, FOPAC reaches out to relevant groups within international organisations (such as UNDCP and the Commercial Crime Unit of the London-based Commonwealth Secretariat) as well as to the FATF. It also has contact with the private sector. It enjoys, for example, a close working relationship with the International Banking Security Association (IBSA) which is an umbrella group representing the security and compliance officers of the major international banks.[63] By way of illustration, the Commonwealth Secretariat and IBSA were involved in the 1991 discussions of a working group, convened by FOPAC, on the problems associated with underground and parallel banking systems. Its staff is concerned with raising the awareness of the problem of money laundering more generally and contributes speakers with commendable frequency to conferences and seminars devoted to the topic.

Furthermore, FOPAC has an intelligence gathering and dissemination role. As Hogarth has noted: "Its intelligence function is limited to what reporting agencies choose to pass on. That data is fed into Interpol's computer and link analysis is employed to identify trends, patterns and personalities involved in money laundering and related activities".[64] Of special interest is "financial information connected with, arising from, related to or resulting from narcotics transactions and other crimes, including suspicious and large currency transactions and large currency exchanges involving domestic and/or foreign currency".[65] One of its major activities at present is to seek to supplement sources of information on laundering activities in regions of the world where such data are scarce. For example, in conjunction with the US Financial Crimes Enforcement Network (FINCEN) it has produced a series of country specific reports on money laundering in central and eastern Europe. These contain information on such matters as the general nature and extent of the local crime problem, the composition of the banking and financial services sector, legislation in place or in contemplation, and the division of responsibilities within national law enforcement bodies and the scope of their authority for international law enforcement co-operation.[66] The same partnership is presently affording a high priority to a similar initiative dealing with Asian countries.[67]

As mentioned earlier, the Brussels-based WCO shares Interpol's concern with money laundering and has close links with Lyon on this and other matters of common concern. This includes the routine sharing of information and intelligence. Established in 1952 to meet the specialist international needs of customs administrations, it has a somewhat smaller membership and staff than its policing counterpart. Its two central missions are "[t]o promote the simplification and harmonisation of customs procedures and to promote effective customs controls".[68]

In the discharge of its enforcement responsibilities the WCO provides its members with somewhat similar services to those offered by Interpol. It too has no operational powers. In terms of subject areas there are, as with drugs, areas of overlap between them which can be the source of difficulties. In the specific instance of money laundering the involvement of the WCO flows from the fact that in some jurisdictions the enforcement of the relevant legislation "is the responsibility of customs administrations or the finance ministries to whom they report".[69] Specific activities have included the provision of information and training and the promotion of appropriate legislation, the creation of a list of national customs contact points for money laundering issues, and a central database on actual and suspected cases. It has also been active in promoting international co-operation. As Mitsilegas has noted: "International co-operation is further enhanced with the signature of bilateral agreements between customs agencies, and a series of memoranda of understanding with the private sector and international organisations, such as the one signed with the International Banking Security Association in 1995".[70]

The Egmont Group

While Interpol and the WCO are long established and formally structured international bodies in which the money laundering issue forms but a part of the overall mandate, the Egmont Group is an informal international grouping which has emerged in a specific anti-money laundering context. It is named after the Egmont-Arenberg Palace in Brussels where, in June 1995, the first meeting took place following a joint Belgian/US initiative. Since that time this grouping has met on a regular basis and has, in the words of the European Commission, "become a genuine international forum and, though having no official status, has become an essential element in the international fight against money laundering".[71]

Its origins are to be found in the challenges posed for national authorities in securing the effective implementation of agreed anti-money laundering measures. Of particular importance in this regard has been the creation of often extensive new, and potentially valuable, sources of financial information available to national authorities arising out of the elaboration of those aspects of the evolving strategy which embrace the private sector. For example, both the recommendations of the FATF[72] and the 1991 EC directive on money laundering[73] call for the mandatory reporting of suspicious transactions to the relevant national authorities. However, in neither case is it specified what form such national authorities should take.

In consequence there has been little in the way of harmonisation of approach to this matter although the majority of countries have seen a need for some centralisation of this task.[74] These disclosure-receiving bodies, commonly known as Financial Intelligence Units (FIUs), tend to be of any one of four types.[75] In the police model – as used, for instance, in the United Kingdom (NCIS) and Slovakia (OFIS) – such suspicious transaction reports are made directly to law enforcement for investigation. In the judicial model, as used in Iceland and Portugal, among others, disclosures are addressed to the office of the public prosecutor. In a few instances reports are transmitted to a joint police/judicial unit. This mixed system has been favoured, for example, in Norway and Denmark. Finally, there is the intermediary or administrative model, variants of which have been created in a wide variety of jurisdictions including Slovenia (OMLP), the USA (FINCEN) and Australia (AUSTRAC). These act as a buffer between the private sector and the police and prosecutorial authorities. As Verhelst, the Deputy Director of the Belgian unit (CTIF/CFI), which falls into this category, has remarked: "Reports are made to a specifically designated (and mostly newly created) administrative authority to be analysed and processed before being passed on for investigations and prosecution".[76]

This highly diverse institutional architecture has, in turn, been the source of some difficulties in achieving a further goal of the anti-money laundering system; namely, international co-operation. For example FATF Recommendation 32 calls upon its members to "make efforts to improve a spontaneous or 'upon request' international information exchange relating to suspicious transactions, persons and co-operations involved in those trans-actions between competent authorities". The Egmont Group has emerged as the major international forum devoted to maximising co-operation between such national units.

At its meeting in Rome in November 1996 it adopted a definition of a Financial Intelligence Unit. It reads thus:

A central, national agency responsible for receiving (and, as permitted, request-ing), analysing and disseminating to the competent authorities, disclosures of financial information:

i. concerning suspected proceeds of crime, or

ii. required by national legislation or regulation in order to counter money laun-dering.

By the time of its meeting in Argentina in mid-1998 some thirty-eight national bodies had been deemed to meet that definition.

In June 1997, at its meeting in Madrid, the group reaffirmed this definition and formally adopted a "Statement of Purpose". Here priority was afford-ed to the enhancement of international information exchange and other measures to improve co-operation between participating jurisdictions. One highly practical manifestation of its approach to the latter is the creation of the Egmont Secure Website. This permits members "to access information on FIUs, money laundering trends, financial analysis tools, and technologi-cal developments. The website is not accessible to the public; therefore, members are able to share this information in a protected environment".[77] It is understood that by mid-1998 twenty-one FIUs had been connected to it. Other priorities include the provision of training and fostering the devel-opment of similar units in further countries around the world.

As will be seen in subsequent chapters of this work, the potential for enhanced international co-operation through the creation of national FIUs on the basis of the Egmont Group definition is now widely recognised. Initiatives are being taken in an increasing number of institutional contexts, including the European Union and the Organisation of American States, to further this process. The prospects for the gradual emergence of the Egmont Group as a genuinely global forum thus appear to be good.

Notes: III

1. See Bassiouni, M.C., "The International Narcotics Control Scheme", in Bassiouni, M.C., (ed.), *International Criminal Law*, Dobbs Ferry, New York, 1986, Vol. I, at pp. 507-524.

2. "Home Office Memorandum of December 1984" reproduced in House of Commons, Home Affairs Committee, *Misuse of Hard Drugs*, H.C. Paper No. 66, Minutes of Evidence (27 March 1985) (1985-86).

3. See Chatterjee, S.K., *A Guide to the International Drugs Conventions*, London, 1988, at pp. 17-19.

4. Donnelly, J., "The United Nations and the Global Drug Control Regime", in Smith, P.H., (ed.), *Drug Policy in the Americas*, 1991, p. 282, at p. 287.

5. (1987) 26, *International Legal Materials*, p. 1637, at p. 1686.

6. UN General Assembly Resolution 39/141.

7. *National Drug Control Strategy*, Washington, D.C., 1989, p. 67.

8. US Department of Justice, *Manual for Compliance with the United Nations Convention Against Illicit Traffic in Narcotic Drugs and Psychotropic Substances*, Washington, D.C., 1992, p. I.

9. Savona, E.U., and De Feo, M.A., "Money Trails: International Money Laundering Trends and Prevention/Control Policies". Paper presented at the International Conference on Preventing and Controlling Money Laundering and the Use of the Proceeds of Crime: A Global Approach, Courmayeur Mont Blanc, Italy, 18-20 June 1994 (hereafter 1994 Conference), (typescript) p. 96. Subsequently published in Savona, E.U., (ed.), *Responding to Money Laundering: International Perspectives*, Amsterdam, 1997. References in this work are to the original.

10. Bassiouni, op. cit., p. 521.

11. Reproduced in Gilmore, W., (ed.), *International Efforts to Combat Money Laundering*, Cambridge, 1992, p. 98, at p. 120. There is evidence to suggest that the manner in which some countries have given effect to this obligation has resulted in a continuing element of difficulty with the dual criminality concept. See, Woltring, H.F., "Money Laundering: Impediments to Effective International Co-operation". Paper presented at the 1994 Conference, (typescript), at pp. 8-9.

12. Freiberg, A., "Criminal Confiscation, Profit and Liberty", *Australian and New Zealand Journal of Criminology*, 1992, p. 44, at pp. 45-46.

13. Gilmore, W. (ed.), op. cit., p. 112.

14. *Commentary on the United Nations Convention Against Illicit Traffic in Narcotic Drugs and Psychotropic Substances 1988*, New York, 1998 (hereafter Commentary), p. 141.

15. *Supra*, note 5, at p. 1692.

16. Sproule, D.W., and Saint-Denis, P., "The UN Drug Trafficking Convention: An Ambitious Step", *Canadian Yearbook of International Law*, 1989, p. 263, at pp. 281-282.

17. *Report of the International Narcotics Control Board for 1997*, New York, 1997, p. 5.

18. See Gilmore, W.C., *Combating International Drugs Trafficking: The 1988 United Nations Convention Against Illicit Traffic in Narcotic Drugs and Psychotropic Substances*, London, 1991, at pp. 40-41.

19. "Money Laundering and Associated Issues: The Need for International Co-operation". UN Doc., E/CN.15/1992/4/Add.5; 23 March 1992, p. 22.

20. UN Office for Drug Control and Crime Prevention, *Financial Havens, Banking Secrecy and Money Laundering*, New York, 1998 (Preliminary Report of 29 May), p. v.

21. McClean, J.D., "Seizing the Proceeds of Crime: The State of the Art", *International and Comparative Law Quarterly*, 1989, p. 334, at p. 339.

22. UN Doc., E/CONF.82/C.1/SR.7, at p. 2.

23. Gilmore, W. (ed.), op. cit., p. 114.

24. "Financial Action Task Force on Money Laundering: Annual Report 1996-97" (hereafter Report VIII), Annex B, p. 10.

25. *Commentary*, p. 150.

26. Greenberg, T.S., "Anti-Money Laundering Activities in the United States", in *Action Against Transnational Criminality: Papers from the 1993 Oxford Conference on International and White Collar Crime*, 1994, p. 53, at p. 58.

27. *Commentary*, p. 151.

28. Nadelmann, E., "Unlaundering Dirty Money Abroad: US Foreign Policy and Financial Secrecy Jurisdictions", *Inter-American Law Review*, 1986, p. 33, at p. 34.

29. Freiberg, op. cit., p. 68.

30. Gilmore, W. (ed.), op. cit., p. 118.

31. Sproule and Saint-Denis, op. cit., p. 284.

32. See s.7 of the Prevention and Suppression of Money Laundering Activities Law, 1996. See also, Ministry of Foreign Affairs, Republic of Cyprus, *Measures Taken by the Republic of Cyprus on Preventing and Combating Money Laundering*, Nicosia, 1998. The significance of the easing or reversal of the burden of proof to the creation of an effective confiscation system is increasingly acknowledged in specialist circles. See, e.g., Report VIII, at p. 19.

33. Sproule and Saint-Denis, op. cit., p. 281.

34. Nadelmann, E.A., Cops Across Borders: *The Internationalization of US Criminal Law Enforcement*, University Park, Pennsylvania, 1993, p. 313.

35. *United Nations Convention Against Illicit Traffic in Narcotic Drugs and Psychotropic Substances*, 101st Congress, 1st Session, Senate, Exec. Rept. 101-15, at p. 185.

36. *Criminal Justice (International Co-operation) Bill: Explanatory Memorandum on the Proposals to Implement the Vienna Convention Against Illicit Traffic in Narcotic Drugs and Psychotropic Substances*, London, 1989, at p. 29.

37. Kriz, G., "International Co-operation to Combat Money Laundering: The Nature and Role of Mutual Legal Assistance Treaties", *Commonwealth Law Bulletin*, 1992, p. 723, at p. 726.

38. Parl. Deb., H.L., Vol. 514, No. 24, 22 January 1990, col. 896.

39. Id.

40. Gilmore, W. (ed.), op. cit., pp. 119-120.

41. Stewart, D., "Internationalising the War on Drugs: The UN Convention Against Illicit Traffic in Narcotic Drugs and Psychotropic Substances", *Denver Journal of International Law and Policy*, 1990, p. 387, at p. 397.

42. *Supra*, note 36, p. 29.

43. Reproduced in Gilmore, W. (ed.), op. cit., p. 4, at p. 14.

44. For details concerning the fifteen member states of the European Union see, "Second Commission Report to the European Parliament and the Council on the Implementation of the Money Laundering Directive", Brussels 1/7/1998. COM (1998) 401, final, at Annex 9, pp. 43-44.

45. Oxford, 1997, p. 137.

46. *Supra*, note 44, p. 21.

47. Report VIII, p. 20.

48. "United Nations General Assembly Special Session on the World Drug Problem, New York, 8-10 June 1998: Information Sheet No. 1".

49. See, Clark, R.S., "Crime: The UN Agenda on International Co-operation in the Criminal Process", *Nova Law Review*, 1991, pp. 475-500.

50. See, id., at pp. 490-493.

51. See "Commission on Crime Prevention and Criminal Justice: Report on the Seventh Session (21-30 April 1998)". UN Doc. E/CN.15/1998/11, p. 11.

52. *Supra*, note 19, p. 20.

53. At the time of writing the website address was: https:www.imolin.org

54. UN Global Programme Against Money Laundering, *Attacking the Profits of Crime: Drugs, Money and Laundering*, Vienna, 1998, p. 13.

55. (1995) *UN Crime Prevention and Criminal Justice Newsletter*, Nos. 26/27, p. 17.

56. See, Wrench, P., "The G8 and Transnational Organised Crime", in Gilmore, W., and Cullen, P. (eds.), *Crime Sans Frontières: International and European Legal Approaches*, Edinburgh, 1998, pp. 39-43.

57. This and other elements of EU activities directed at organised crime are outlined in Chapter VI below.

58. See generally, UN Doc. E/CN.15/1998/5.

59. *Supra*, note 51, p. 56.

60. See generally, Anderson, M., *Policing the World: Interpol and the Politics of International Police Co-operation*, Oxford, 1989.

61. See Kendall, R., "Drug Trafficking and Related Serious Crime: The International Dimension", in *Action Against Transnational Criminality: Papers from the 1991 Oxford Conference on International and White Collar Crime*, London, 1992, p. 3, at p. 8.

62. See *FOPAC Bulletin*, No. 13, 1994, p. 1.

63. See Chaikin, D.A., "Money Laundering: An Investigatory Perspective", *Criminal Law Forum*, 1991, p. 467, at p. 509.

64. Hogarth, J., "Beyond the Vienna Convention: International Efforts to Suppress Money Laundering". Paper presented at the 1994 Conference, (typescript), p. 25.

65. "ICPO/Interpol General Assembly Resolution on Money Laundering and Related Matters, November 1989". Reproduced in Gilmore, W. (ed.), op. cit., p. 278.

66. See, e.g., Interpol/FOPAC, *Situation Report on Money Laundering in Estonia*, Lyon, 1997.

67. See "Financial Action Task Force on Money Laundering: Annual Report 1997-98", p. 56.

68. Rigdon, A.M., "Aspects of International Police and Customs Co-operation", in *Action Against Transnational Criminality: Papers from the 1992 Oxford Conference on International and White Collar Crime*, London, 1993, p. 83, at p. 83.

69. Id., p. 84.

70. Mitsilegas, V., "International and Regional Initiatives", forthcoming in Rider, B., and Nakajima, V. (eds.), *CCH Money Laundering Service*. Typescript, p. 37.

71. "Second Commission Report to the European Parliament and the Council on the Implementation of the Money Laundering Directive". COM (1998) 401 final, Brussels 1 July 1998, p. 14.

72. See Appendix III, Recommendation 16.

73. See Appendix VI, Art. 6.

74. See generally, Thony, J.-F., "Processing Financial Information in Money Laundering Matters: The Financial Intelligence Units", *European Journal of Crime, Criminal Law and Criminal Justice*, 1996, p. 257.

75. See Verhelst, B., "The Organisation of a Financial Intelligence Unit". Paper presented to a training Seminar for Council of Europe Evaluators, Brussels, 25 March 1998 (typescript).

76. Id.

77. US General Accounting Office, "Money Laundering: FINCEN's Law Enforcement Support, Regulatory, and International Roles". GAO/T-GGD-98-83, Appendix III, p. 19.

Chapter IV – The Financial Action Task Force

The background

In any assessment of efforts at the international level to ensure the utility and effectiveness of money laundering countermeasures, pride of place must be given to the work of the Financial Action Task Force (FATF).[1] Best known for its forty recommendations, it has become the single most important international body in terms of the formulation of anti-money laundering policy and in the mobilisation of global awareness of the complex issues involved in countering this sophisticated form of criminality.[2]

The origins of FATF are firmly rooted in the growing concern, evident particularly in the 1980s, with the increasing extent of the problem of drug abuse and heightened sensitivity to the associated issue of the financial power of drug trafficking syndicates and other organised crime groups. When these matters arose for discussion at the July 1989 Paris Summit Meeting of the Heads of State or Government of the seven major industrial nations (Group of Seven, or G-7), joined by the President of the Commission of the European Communities, it was concluded that there was an "urgent need for decisive action, both on a national and international basis" to counter drug production, consumption and trafficking as well as "the laundering of its proceeds".[3] In this context the decision was taken to create the Task Force. Its initial mandate was: "to assess the results of co-operation already undertaken in order to prevent the utilisation of the banking system and financial institutions for the purpose of money laundering, and to consider additional preventative efforts in this field, including the adaptation of the legal and regulatory systems so as to enhance multilateral judicial assistance".[4]

In addition to the summit participants (Canada, France, Germany, Italy, Japan, the United Kingdom, the United States and the Commission of the European Communities), eight other states (Australia, Austria, Belgium, Luxembourg, the Netherlands, Spain, Sweden and Switzerland) were invited to take part in this initiative which was convened under French chairmanship. This expansion of the Task Force was undertaken "in order to enlarge its expertise and also to reflect the views of other countries particularly concerned by, or having particular experience in the fight against money laundering, at the national or international level".[5]

In the months which followed "[m]ore than one hundred and thirty experts from various ministries, law enforcement authorities, and bank supervisory and regulatory agencies, met and worked together".[6] The fruits of these labours are to be found in an impressive report of 6 February 1990. This contains an analysis of the extent and nature of the money laundering process, an overview of international instruments and national programmes then in place to counter the problem and, most importantly, forty separate recommendations for action. These recommendations are reproduced in full in Appendix II.

Building on the firm foundations established by the 1988 UN convention, and the Statement of Principles for the guidance of bank supervisors issued on 12 December 1988 by the Basle Committee on Banking Regulations and Supervisory Practices, which is outlined below, the 1990 FATF recommendations were to focus on three central areas: (i) improvements to national legal systems; (ii) the enhancement of the role of the financial system; and (iii) the strengthening of international co-operation.[7]

This report was endorsed at the ministerial level by all participating countries in May 1990 and submitted to the Group of Seven summit in Houston in July. There it was agreed that FATF would be reconvened for a further year "to assess and facilitate the implementation of the forty recommendations and to complement them where appropriate. It was agreed that all OECD and financial centre countries that would subscribe to the recommendations of the Task Force should be invited to participate in this exercise".[8]

Strengthened by the addition of eight further OECD countries (Denmark, Finland, Greece, Ireland, New Zealand, Norway, Portugal and Turkey) as well as Hong Kong and the Gulf Co-operation Council to its list of members,[9] several meetings were held in Paris, again under French presidency, and a second report was issued on 13 May 1991. Importantly this recorded an agreement "to continue FATF for a period of five years, with a decision to review progress after three years (...)".[10] The decision taken to extend the lifespan of FATF was but one of a number of measures designed to ensure the coherence, flexibility and efficiency of this initiative. Of these one of the most significant was that "membership should not be further widened".[11] An exception was, however, agreed in respect of those who had been invited to participate in FATF II but who had yet to accept the recommendations. It was on this basis that Iceland and Singapore joined in the course of the FATF III session[12] bringing the membership to its present total of twenty-six countries and territories and two international organisations.

The promised mid-term review in turn took place during the 1993-94 round (FATF V) at which time it was unanimously agreed that the group should remain in being until 1998-99.[13] At that time the possibility of accommodating "a very limited expansion" was signalled but did not, in fact, take place.[14]

The issue of the future of the FATF was revisited in the course of the 1997-98 session (FATF IX) and again the conclusion was reached that there remained "an obvious need for continued mobilisation at the international level to deepen and widen anti-money laundering action".[15] Consequently a ministerial meeting of members held in Paris in April 1998 extended its life, though with a somewhat revised mandate, until 2004. This decision swiftly gained the support of OECD ministers, G-7 finance ministers, and the heads of state and government of the G-8. On 17 May 1998 the latter "welcomed the FATF decision to continue and enlarge its work to combat money laundering in partnership with regional groupings".[16] While the nature and extent of the new mandate will be discussed at a later stage of this chapter, it is of importance to note at this stage that it does envisage this long-awaited increase in numbers. The June 1998 report anticipates "an adequate expansion of the FATF membership to strategically important countries which already have key anti-money laundering measures in place (...), and which are politically determined to make a full commitment towards the implementation of the forty recommendations, and which could play a major role in their regions in the process of combating money laundering".[17]

The structure and purpose of the FATF

Steps were agreed in the course of FATF II to strengthen the institutional structure of the grouping and to regularise its methods of operation. Of particular importance in this context was the decision to institute a rotating presidency involving a one year term of office. "The president would be chosen by the FATF, taking into account as much as possible geographical locations and membership of various international groupings".[18] Since that time this position has been held by Switzerland, Australia, the United Kingdom, the United States, Italy, the Netherlands and Belgium. Japan assumed this role for FATF X on 1 July 1998.[19]

The nature of the internal working structure of the FATF has not been characterised by excessive rigidity and has been permitted to evolve and mature. For example, initially working groups played a significant part in its work. This was made possible by the multidisciplinary character of many national delegations which remains a major strength of this body. As a senior delegate explained, the FATF "brings together policy makers and experts from a wide range of disciplines, finance and justice ministries, banking and other financial regulators, as well as law enforcement and legal agencies. This multidisciplinary approach is essential to the

FATF's work and indeed to the effectiveness of action to combat money laundering".[20]

The strength of the working group structure was, however, bound to have an impact on the nature of the role and contribution of the plenary meetings. The issue of working practices was consequently examined in the course of FATF V and it was decided "that following the completion of their current work programmes, the committee structure should be discontinued and the functions of the plenary strengthened (...) However, ad hoc groups might be created to carry out specific tasks in line with specific terms of reference approved by the plenary".[21]

The Task Force meets several times each year. Normally one meeting is held in the country of the presidency with the remainder being convened at the headquarters of the OECD in Paris. The latter houses a modest FATF secretariat. This was established following FATF II and services the regular meetings and facilitates other aspects of the ongoing work programme including the processes for the evaluation of the progress of the membership in implementing the forty recommendations, and arranging an ambitious range of external relations activities.

Though located within the OECD it is important to note that FATF is not formally a part of that or any other international organisation. Similarly, as the Head of the Financial Affairs Division of the OECD has remarked: "It is not a permanent international organisation nor a body managing a legally-binding convention".[22] It is, rather, an ad hoc grouping of governments and others with a complex single issue agenda. As has been pointed out elsewhere: "Their common purpose is, and will remain, their determination to pursue convergent and comprehensive money laundering strategies based on international co-operation while preserving both the efficiency of the financial system and the freedom to engage in legitimate financial transactions".[23] Central to the achievement of that ambition is the package of recommended countermeasures which was first elaborated in the February 1990 report.

The 1990 recommendations of the FATF

The context

The major goal of the Task Force when first established in 1989 was "the establishment of standards in the form of recommendations that could be endorsed by national authorities and applied internationally in a consistent manner".[24] As was noted above, this effort to formulate a comprehensive anti-money laundering programme was to be based on a prior study of the nature and extent of the problem and a critical examination of existing domestic and international countermeasures.[25]

Out of the above, a multi-track approach to the problem gradually emerged. First, it calls for the strengthening of the criminal law with a particular emphasis on the development of legislative and enforcement techniques, such as the confiscation of the proceeds of crime, designed to undermine the financial power of trafficking networks and organised crime groups. Thus, as with the 1988 UN convention, there is a clear recognition that in the fight against money laundering major reliance must be placed on criminal justice mechanisms. In the words of the 1994 Courmayeur conference: "As a credible deterrent, the criminal law will continue to play an essential role".[26] However, in contrast to that UN precedent, the FATF recognised that sole reliance on such measures would be insufficient. As one commentator has stated: "The criminal law cannot by itself carry the burden of reducing, or even containing, money laundering. A broad range of measures is required".[27]

This perception resulted in the inclusion of a second and more highly innovative element in the FATF programme. It is reflected in the decision to involve, in an unprecedented fashion, participants in financial sector activity in the strategy to combat money laundering. This decision flowed from the analysis of money laundering techniques and the identification of the stages in the process where the launderer was most vulnerable to detection. As the February 1990 report noted: "Key stages for the detection of money laundering operations are those where cash enters into the domestic financial system, either formally or informally, where it is sent abroad to be integrated into the financial systems of regulatory havens, and where it is repatriated in the form of transfers of legitimate appearance".[28]

However, the decision of the FATF to place banks and other financial institutions "in the front line against laundering"[29] was not based exclusively on an assessment of the key role that they could play in the detection process. A further important factor was the enhanced appreciation of the negative impact which "dirty money" can have on the credit and financial institutions through which it passes or in which it is deposited or invested in the course of laundering operations.[30] As Tom Sherman, the then Australian President of FATF, was to state in September 1992: "Combating money laundering is not just a matter of fighting crime but of preserving the integrity of financial institutions and ultimately the financial system as a whole".[31]

While "[c]riminal and regulatory, or control and preventative, policies are necessarily connected"[32] they are not, when conceived of in traditional national terms, sufficient to deal with this complex problem. Modern money laundering techniques, as was demonstrated in Chapter II, commonly, and increasingly, include a transnational dimension. The FATF recognised from the outset that the possibilities of success for any strategy which sought to combat laundering depended in a critical way on the range, scope and quality of the mechanisms of international co-operation.[33] This was, accordingly, made the third central feature of its programme of action.

The nature of the 1990 recommendations

The package of countermeasures formulated by FATF I, which is repro-duced in Appendix II, consisted of forty separate recommendations for action. Although viewed as constituting "a minimal standard in the fight against money laundering"[34] it should be noted that some failed at the time to attract unanimous support. As the 1990 report admits "the minimal standard we recommend can be viewed as rather ambitious".[35] It should also be stressed that, following normal international practice, these recom-mendations have no binding force as a matter of international law; cus-tomary or conventional.[36] A number are, however, also embodied or reflected in the provisions of existing multilateral conventions and are, to that extent, binding on the parties *inter se*. Beyond that their force and authority derive from their endorsement by member governments and their practical implementation.[37]

A minority of the forty "action steps" in essence call only for further study or consideration to be given to particular matters or articulate alternative approaches. Even those of a more mandatory character are commonly, and deliberately, formulated in a fairly open-textured manner.[38] As has been pointed out elsewhere, it was recognised "that there can be significant dif-ferences between the legal systems, financial systems and, indeed, the money laundering situations of different countries. So the recommenda-tions allow considerable flexibility in how they are applied and concentrate on laying down the general principles for combating money laundering rather than prescribing in great detail what should be done".[39] It is also of relevance to note that individual member countries of the FATF are permit-ted to adopt stricter measures should they so wish[40] and a number have, in fact, done so.[41]

The general framework of the 1990 recommendations

The 1990 FATF report identifies three measures which were unanimously regarded as constituting the overall general framework for its many specific proposals. All were intended to cure major difficulties and inefficiencies in international co-operation. The specific recommendations were as follows:

1. Each country should, without further delay, take steps to fully implement the Vienna Convention and proceed to ratify it;

2. Financial institutions secrecy laws should be conceived so as not to inhibit implementation of the recommendations; and,

3. An effective money laundering enforcement programme should include increased multilateral co-operation and mutual legal assistance in money laundering investigations and prosecutions and extradition in money laundering cases where possible.[42]

In formulating the specific elements for inclusion in the general framework, delegates were conscious of the fact that at that stage no FATF member country had become a party to the 1988 UN convention (which is referred to throughout as the Vienna Convention) and that it had yet to enter into force. Indeed, it was feared that, given the ambition and complexity of that international instrument, "some countries could have difficulties in ratifying and implementing it for reasons that are not related to the issue of money laundering".[43]

Given the need to make rapid and specific progress on money laundering, the decision was taken to include in the recommendations "important steps which are implied by this Convention".[44] For example, at least in so far as drug-related money laundering is concerned, Recommendation 2 on financial secrecy finds reflection, as was seen in the previous chapter, in Article 5 (3) and Article 7 (5) of the Vienna Convention. In addition, the concerns of Recommendation 3 relating to improved international legal co-operation are addressed by a number of central provisions of that instrument including Articles 5 to 11.

The drafters of the FATF programme did not, however, feel constrained by the Vienna Convention which, as has been seen, since its entry into force on 11 November 1990, has come increasingly to represent a minimum standard of responsible international behaviour in this area. In this regard they were prepared to recommend a "reinforcement of its provisions applicable to money laundering issues"[45] and to venture into areas, as with the enhancement of the role of the financial sector, which fell entirely outside the scope of the Vienna exercise.

Improvement of national legal systems

The first of three distinct sets of specific recommendations (4 to 8) were directed towards securing improvements in national legal systems. A number of these, for reasons given above, represented primarily a reaffirmation of the principles contained in the 1988 text. This was explicitly the case, for example, in the call to criminalise drug-related money laundering (Recommendations 4 and 6) and to make appropriate provision for the confiscation of proceeds and related provisional measures (Recommendation 8).

Two of the recommendations, however, sought to broaden the approach adopted in Vienna. Thus, Recommendation 5 encouraged member countries to "consider extending the offence of drug money laundering to any other crimes for which there is a link to narcotics; an alternative approach is to criminalise money laundering based on all serious offences, and/or on all offences that generate a significant amount of proceeds, or on certain serious offences".[46] Similarly, Recommendation 7 concerning the possible extension of corporate criminal liability to this area of concern has no parallel in the 1988 UN text.

Enhancement of the role of the financial system

The second set of area-specific measures (Recommendations 9 to 29) articulated a strategy to engage the financial system in the effort to combat laundering while, at the same time, seeking to ensure the retention of the conditions necessary for its efficient operation. As Pecchioli has stated: "The common thread underlying these recommendations is the view that financial institutions are the key element in the detection of illicit transactions given their unique function in a country"s payments system and in the collection and transfer of financial assets".[47]

In approaching this matter the Task Force decided to build upon the precedent established by the December 1988 Statement on Prevention of Criminal Use of the Banking System for the Purpose of Money Laundering issued by the Basle Committee on Banking Regulations and Supervisory Practices. Its basic purpose is to encourage, through "a general statement of ethical principles", the banking sector to adopt a common position in order to ensure that banks are not used to hide or launder funds acquired through criminal activities and, in particular, through drug trafficking. The key principles which it enunciates have been summarised by a senior official of the Bank of England as follows:

- *Know your customer*: banks should make reasonable efforts to determine the customer's true identity, and have effective procedures for verifying the bona fides of new customers (whether on the asset or liability side of the balance sheet).

- *Compliance with laws*: bank management should ensure that business is conducted in conformity with high ethical standards, that laws and regulations are adhered to and that a service is not provided where there is good reason to suppose that transactions are associated with laundering activities.

- *Co-operation with law enforcement agencies*: within any constraints imposed by rules relating to customer confidentiality, banks should co-operate fully with national law enforcement agencies including, where there are reasonable grounds for suspecting money laundering, taking appropriate measures which are consistent with the law.

- *Policies, procedures and training:* all banks should formally adopt policies consistent with the principles set out in the statement and should ensure that all members of their staff concerned, wherever located, are informed of the bank's policy. Attention should be given to staff training in matters covered by the statement. To promote adherence to these principles banks should implement specific procedures for customer identification and for retaining internal records of transactions. Arrangements for internal audits may need to be extended in order to establish an effective means of testing for general compliance with the statement.[48]

In an effort to increase the impact of this statement the Committee took the step of commending it to supervisory authorities in other countries. It has since been endorsed by, among others, the Offshore Group of Banking Supervisors (OGBS) the membership of which includes, *inter alia*, the principal offshore banking and financial services "havens" in the Caribbean and elsewhere.

It is important to note that the Basle statement, unlike the UN convention, is not a treaty in terms of public international law. Similarly it has no direct legal effect in the domestic law of any country. An exclusive concentration on the formal status of the text would, however, be extremely misleading. As was pointed out in the 1990 report: "Although it is not itself a legally binding document, various formulas have been used to make its principles an obligation, notably a formal agreement among banks that commits them explicitly (Austria, Italy, Switzerland), a formal indication by bank regulators that failure to comply with these principles could lead to administrative sanctions (France, United Kingdom), or legally binding texts with a reference to these principles (Luxembourg)".[49]

The influence of that 1988 initiative can be clearly discerned in the more detailed FATF treatment of customer identification, compliance with local law, co-operation with law enforcement agencies, and the establishment by appropriate institutions of anti-money laundering policies, procedures and training. However, while the FATF approach owed much to the Basle statement it is, without doubt, a far more ambitious undertaking. This is so both in terms of the areas common to both texts, and in the willingness of the 1990 report to break new ground. By way of illustration of the former, while both address the critical question of customer identification the FATF reached out to the closely related issues of obtaining information on the beneficial ownership of funds (Recommendation 13) and the retention of records, for a period of at least five years, "sufficient to permit reconstruction of individual transactions (...) so as to provide, if necessary, evidence for prosecution of criminal behaviour" (Recommendation 14).

Among the measures with no obvious counterparts in the 1988 statement one might mention the FATF effort to cope with the problem of countries with no or insufficient anti-money laundering measures (Recommendations 21 and 22), its treatment of the monitoring of cross-border flows of cash (Recommendation 23), and suggestions made as to the role of regulatory and other administrative authorities in order to ensure effective implementation (Recommendations 26 to 29). Most importantly, while the financial recommendations "appear to have been developed primarily with deposit-taking institutions in mind"[50] they were specifically extended to non-bank financial institutions (Recommendation 9). They also have an impact on "certain other professions dealing with cash, which are unregulated or virtually unregulated in many countries".[51] While this expansion of the reach of the countermeasures in question has been the source of considerable difficulty it was, as underlined by the analysis of money laundering methods in Chapter II, an innovation of great practical importance. As a past president of the FATF has explained: "Much of the pre-occupation of anti-money laundering activity has been with the banking system. But experience shows that money launderers will utilise almost any form of corporate and trust activity to launder their profits".[52]

As was to be expected, however, it was not possible to achieve a consensus on all central issues in this sensitive sphere. This is well illustrated by the divergence of views as to the effectiveness of a system of mandatory and routine reporting of domestic and international currency transactions above a fixed threshold. The two member countries which had opted to establish such a system, the US and Australia, viewed it as a vital part of any comprehensive package of countermeasures. The majority, however, were not convinced.[53] Accordingly, Recommendation 24 merely called upon FATF participants to "consider the feasibility and utility" of this approach.

Strengthening of international co-operation

As emphasised in Chapter II, modern money laundering techniques contain conspicuous transnational features. While national countermeasures, such as criminalisation, confiscation, and the institution of comprehensive preventative strategies, are a precondition for making substantial progress, it has been accepted from the outset that "[w]ithout appropriate international co-operation, all these efforts could yield few results while incurring large costs".[54] The facilitation of international interaction between law enforcement and prosecutorial authorities and financial regulators and supervisors was the central thrust of Recommendations 30 to 40 inclusive. The majority of the proposals to enhance co-operation between legal authorities (Recommendations 33 to 40) reaffirmed the processes and sought to consolidate the progress achieved in the 1988 UN convention. This was particularly so in respect of such areas as co-operation in the seizure and confiscation of the proceeds of crime, mutual assistance in criminal matters, and extradition.

As with the Vienna Convention, the Task Force gave explicit recognition to the fact that "international co-operation should be supported by a network of bilateral and multilateral agreements and arrangements based on generally shared legal concepts with the aim of providing practical measures to affect the widest possible range of mutual assistance".[55] The work then being done within the Council of Europe, which was to result in the conclusion later the same year of the European Convention on Laundering, Search, Seizure and Confiscation of the Proceeds from Crime received positive support. This highly significant European initiative is examined in Chapter V.

The 1990 report also sought to pave the way for the improved exchange of information relating to suspicious transactions (Recommendation 32), and to enhance "the knowledge of international flows of drug money, noticeably cash flows, and the knowledge of money laundering methods, to enable a better focus of international and national efforts to combat this phenomenon".[56]

The revised recommendations of 1996

The context

In the years since its creation the FATF has consistently demonstrated an awareness of the need to take action to ensure the continuing relevance and utility of its programme of action. In particular, it was anticipated from the outset that the process would be a dynamic one and that changes in strategy would be brought about by, among other factors, an enhanced understanding of the techniques used by criminals and the impact thereon of the increasingly effective countermeasures of FATF members. Consequently it was recognised in the 1990 report that "our recommendations will probably need periodic re-evaluation".[57] In this regard, however, the conscious decision was taken "not to amend the recommendations before the completion of the first round of mutual evaluations of FATF members so that they could all be assessed against the same standard".[58] This highly innovative process of "peer review", designed to facilitate the international monitoring of the implementation of the recommendations by members, is discussed in section 5b of this chapter.

Until the end of the first mutual evaluation period was reached, the grouping had to content itself with adopting what are known as "interpretative notes" to the original recommendations. Griffiths explained the formal position thus: "These do not change the scope or substance of the recommendations but clarify or provide supplementary guidance on their application".[59] A significant number of such clarifications were issued.[60] Of these the great majority related specifically to one or more of the original recommendations. For example, Recommendation 23 was a rather weakly worded measure directed at the detection and monitoring of cross-border flows of cash. Following further consideration of this important point of vulnerability in actual money laundering operations, a specific interpretative note was formulated in the course of FATF III. This recorded agreement that, in spite of its wording, "this recommendation is not limited to currency, but also covers cash equivalent monetary instruments and other highly liquid valuables (e.g. precious metals and gems)".[61] A minority, however, as with those adopted during FATF III on shell corporations, and on the issue of deferred arrests and seizures,[62] were not tied to particular recommendations in this way.

The nature of the process is well illustrated by the active consideration in various early rounds of problems associated with the use of shell companies. Such entities, particularly those registered in "offshore" jurisdictions, as has been seen earlier in this work, have been widely used in complex international money laundering schemes. Initial consideration of this matter resulted in the formulation, during FATF III, of an interpretative note. This urged members to take heed of the potential for abuse which they represented and to "consider measures to prohibit unlawful use of such entities".[63] The issue was returned to in the following year. It was concluded that "[a] key factor which makes shell corporations attractive to money launderers is the ability in many jurisdictions to conceal or obfuscate the true beneficial ownership of the entity".[64] However, as the study progressed into FATF V "the importance of applying the principle of transparency of ownership to corporate bodies in general was emphasised since not only shell corporations but virtually any legal entity could be used in money laundering schemes".[65] These insights in turn provided the basis for a further interpretative note to Recommendations 12, 13 and 16 through 19 concerning the utilisation in money laundering schemes of accounts in the names of customers who are not natural persons.[66]

There was, of course, a certain artificiality associated with the notion that such notes "do not add to or change the scope or the substance" of the original recommendations.[67] With the end of the first phase of the mutual assessment process in sight, it was announced that "a stocktaking exercise will be conducted in 1995, taking in (sic) account experience gained over the last four years, including the interpretative notes which have been developed".[68]

The 1996 revisions

The first steps in this major "stocktaking review" of the 1990 recommendations were undertaken during the Dutch Presidency. A questionnaire was circulated to members seeking views on what alterations might be made to the recommendations and the notes. The results of this survey were prepared in summary form in May 1995.[69] Most members indicated the need for caution in conducting this exercise in order, for example, not to undermine the extensive efforts to encourage the broadest possible geographic extension of the Task Force programme of action. However, initially there was less agreement on where these changes should fall. Indeed, the responses to the consultation questionnaire included suggestions for either substantive or stylistic modifications to be made to all forty of the original recommendations.

In order to facilitate progress the then FATF President, Leo Verwoerd, proposed that "the review should focus on a relatively limited number of major issues of substance which have been identified by the consultation exercise".[70] He identified eight such issues: the extension of the predicate offences for money laundering beyond drugs trafficking; the expansion of the financial recommendations to cover non-financial businesses; the expansion of treatment of customer identification; the imposition of a requirement for the mandatory reporting of suspicious transactions; the issues of cross-border currency monitoring, asset seizure and confiscation, shell corporations, and, controlled delivery. Once agreement had been achieved on issues of substance a "policy-neutral review" could be undertaken of stylistic changes and consequential amendments.

This course of action was agreed to and the detailed work commenced early in the 1995-96 round of meetings under the presidency of the United States. However, further consultations resulted in the inclusion of two further issues of importance; that is, the treatment of *bureaux de change* and the challenges posed by new technologies. The former subject had been the subject of an interpretative note and was, in addition, perceived to be a practical problem of considerable significance. Indeed, FATF experts "observed that criminal abuse of this industry is reaching epidemic proportions".[71] The latter issue, placed on the agenda by the United States, sought, in essence, to anticipate a future threat to the integrity of the anti-money laundering system.

While the changes of substance under discussion in the "stocktaking review" were thus not insignificant in numerical terms, the changes actually in contemplation were not particularly radical. As FATF President Ronald

Noble was to remark to the membership in early 1996:

Virtually all of the proposals advanced involve refinements to existing recommendations as opposed to introducing entirely new concepts. Most entail nothing more than elevating material set out in the interpretative notes to the text of the recommendations. (In this vein, members should keep in mind that the interpretative notes were designed to further clarify the recommendations and were also adopted by consensus.) A few involve strengthening the character of extremely permissive recommendations. Consequently, even if all of the proposals were adopted, members would not be confronting onerous new burdens.[72]

In the final event it proved possible to reach agreement in all of the key areas which had been identified, with the exception of the proposed incorporation of the note on asset seizure and confiscation which would have urged consideration of the establishment of domestic asset forfeiture funds and the introduction of procedures to promote international asset-sharing.

The agreed amendments, along with stylistic and consequential alterations to the 1990 recommendations and the interpretative notes, were published along with the annual report on 28 June 1996. The revised texts are reproduced in full in Appendix III and Appendix IV of this study for ease of reference. It was of some interest to note that the total number of recommendations remains the same as in 1990. This outcome was not mere happenstance. Indeed, in the course of the discussions this emerged as a separate and distinct goal. As the FATF president noted: "Whatever changes to the substance of the recommendations the membership accept, the total number of recommendations will remain at forty. The forty recommendations have become synonymous with the FATF and its mission. They have gained a measure of notoriety that has been helpful to the external relations effort. Any reduction or increase in the total might adversely affect that recognition".[73]

As we have seen, the major purposes of this "stocktaking" exercise were to bring the 1990 recommendations "fully up to date with current trends and developments and to anticipate future threats".[74] In relation to the former the most important change was, without doubt, the decision to extend money laundering predicate offences beyond narcotics trafficking. While the new position, now embodied in Recommendation 4, represents a significant departure from the hesitant approach taken in 1990 it is perhaps best viewed as an effort to bring the countermeasures into line with actual domestic and international practice. Since 1990 a firm trend had emerged in favour of decoupling money laundering from drug trafficking. This had, in turn, been increasingly reflected in domestic legislation. For example, while in 1992 the FATF stated that few of its twenty-six members had criminalised laundering beyond the narcotics predicate, its June 1996 report was able to note that "nineteen members have enacted an offence which covers the laundering of the proceeds of a wide range of crimes in addition to drug trafficking".[75] Such developments in national legislation had found increasing reflection in, and been reinforced by, a number of international instruments and political declarations. As will be noted in subsequent chapters, an early position of leadership in this sphere had been taken by the Council of Europe and thereafter by the member states of the European Union. It was thus essential for the continued credibility of the FATF programme of action that its formal stance be brought into line with this new reality.

At the other end of the spectrum is the entirely new Recommendation 13 which calls upon FATF members to "pay special attention to money laundering threats inherent in new or developing technologies that might favour anonymity, and take measures, if needed, to prevent their use in money laundering schemes". The inclusion of this hortatory provision was explicitly proactive rather than reactive. It was admitted that there was no concrete evidence of the abuse of "cyberpayments" technologies for money laundering. However, as was seen in Chapter II, it was also clear that these developing technologies have the potential to undermine the efficacy of anti-money laundering systems. Consequently it was felt to be appropriate to require "countries to note the potential threat posed by new technologies and to adopt the appropriate measures to minimise this threat".[76]

A further inducement to take account of possible future vulnerabilities in the course of the review flowed from the uncertainty which then surrounded the future of the Task Force after its mandate came to an end in 1999. As noted earlier, however, this issue was resolved in the course of discussions in the 1997-98 round where it was agreed to keep the Task Force in being for a further five years. It was acknowledged at the same time that it may prove to be necessary to undertake a further updating exercise of this kind in 2003-4. In the words of the June 1998 report, this could cover "new countermeasures as well as perhaps reviewing those recommendations which currently ask members simply to consider and decide whether action should be mandatory or not. (...) In any case, FATF must ensure that the forty recommendations remain the most effective and widely-respected international standard in the anti-money laundering area".[77]

The continuing work of the FATF

Task force priorities

The elaboration of the forty recommendations, while a major accomplishment, was not an end in itself. The Task Force has been kept in being since in order to ensure both the continuing utility of its comprehensive programme and to maximise its practical impact. To these ends it has concentrated on three priorities: (i) monitoring the implementation of the recommendations by its members; (ii) keeping track of developments in money laundering methods and examining the adequacy of its countermeasures in the light thereof; and, (iii) carrying out an ambitious "outreach" or external relations programme to promote the greatest possible mobilisation of effort in the wider international community to counter this problem. In the course of the review undertaken during FATF IX, it was resolved that these would continue to be central concerns over the next five years although there would be significant new elements in its approach to the issue of geographic expansion.

Monitoring implementation by FATF members

In the conclusion to the 1990 report it was recognised that "a regular assessment of progress realised in enforcing money laundering measures would stimulate countries to give to these issues a high priority (...)".[78] Three procedures have since been developed to this end. The first of these, established in the course of the 1990-91 round, takes the form of a process of self-assessment based on two detailed questionnaires circulated to each member country or territory. As was pointed out in the June 1997 report: "These responses are then compiled and analysed, and provide the basis for assessing to what extent the forty recommendations have been implemented by both individual countries and the group as a whole".[79]

In the years since its introduction the self-assessment process has been refined on a number of occasions. In the early years particular attention was paid to measures designed to enhance the objective nature of the exercise. More recent developments have resulted from the maturing of the FATF process. For example, the questionnaires have been revised in order to take into account the 1996 amendments to the recommendations outlined above. Other modifications, such as the introduction of a question and answer session at a plenary meeting, have been introduced in order to improve the practical utility of the process. The June 1998 report announced that an "enhanced self-assessment" procedure would continue to be afforded a place of prominence in the years up to 2004.

In a move then without precedent in international practice in the criminal law sphere, FATF II decided to supplement the process of self-assessment with a system of mutual evaluation based on existing OECD procedures.[80] As the 1991 report stated: "Individual members would be chosen for examination by the FATF with the examination carried out by selected other members of the FATF, according to an agreed protocol for examination and agreed selection criteria. The objective would be to examine every FATF member by the end of 1996".[81] In fact the initial round of mutual evaluation, the major purpose of which was to assess the degree of formal compliance with the recommendations, was completed in 1995. A second round, with a focus on the effectiveness in practice of the measures taken by members, was initiated in the following year and is due to be completed in mid-1999. The remit here also includes an assessment of "any follow-up action taken in response to the suggestions for improvement made in the first round".[82]

Mutual evaluation is, in essence, an international system of periodic peer review under which each member is subject to a form of on-site examination. As Patrick Moulette, the current FATF secretary, has pointed out: "Each evaluation team usually comprises three examiners (four for the larger countries) of different nationalities whose expertise must cover all aspects of the fight against money laundering. Each team therefore comprises a legal expert (a judge or justice ministry representative), a financial expert (from a finance ministry, central bank or regulatory authority for the financial sector), and an operational services (law enforcement) expert (from the police, the customs or an agency receiving and analysing suspicious transaction reports, such as FINCEN in the United States)".[83]

The examination team visits the country in question, normally for three days, during which time it meets those ministries and institutions (public and private) with a mandate or substantial practical involvement in the anti-money laundering sphere. The team then prepares a detailed report which is discussed in and adopted by a plenary meeting of the Task Force. Although each such report is and remains confidential, agreement was reached to make executive summaries public. These are contained in the annual reports of the work of the group which can now be accessed by the general public on the Internet.[84]

Mutual evaluation has been widely perceived as a success both by individuals who have participated in the process and, more importantly, by governments. In a public lecture delivered in Edinburgh in May 1993, Mr Tom Sherman, the then FATF president, characterised it as "a very effective mechanism indeed".[85] Five years on this remains the preponderant view. As Mr Stan Morris, until recently the Head of the Financial Crimes Enforcement Network of the US Department of the Treasury (FINCEN), stated in March 1998: "The critical role of mutual evaluation in ensuring the consistent anti-money laundering standards cannot be overstated".[86]

Perhaps the clearest illustration of the depth of this perception is to be found in the increasing resort being made to the FATF process, or variants of it, in other fora. As will be seen in subsequent chapters, mutual evaluation has been introduced as a key part of anti-money laundering efforts elsewhere (most significantly in the work of the Council of Europe and the Caribbean Financial Action Task Force). It has also started to be introduced in other contexts. It is, for example, an important feature of European Union efforts to combat organised crime and is set to play a central role in the ambitious agenda of the Council of Europe to counter corruption. It is not without interest that the concept now also finds expression in Article 12 of the 1997 OECD convention on combating bribery of foreign public officials in international business transactions.

Given the above, it was not surprising that the June 1998 Task Force report announced "a third round of simplified mutual evaluations for all FATF members starting in 2001, focusing exclusively on compliance with the revised parts of the recommendations, the areas of significant deficiencies identified in the second round and generally the effectiveness of the counter-measures".[87]

There is no doubt that, in practice, the prospect of a mutual evaluation visit frequently acts as a catalyst for governmental action. As Dilwyn Griffiths, the then FATF Secretary, noted in his address to the 1993 Oxford Conference on International and White Collar Crime: "I do not think that progress in implementing the recommendations would have been as swift and substantial without it. Countries are concerned to have a good story to tell to the examiners and there is thus an impetus to get things done which would otherwise be lacking".[88] Similarly the detailed reports indicate often quite extensive areas in which improvements in laws, regulations and practices could and should be made. As was noted above, one of the functions of the second round (which will also be a feature of the third) is to check on the measures adopted in response to the deficiencies identified in the earlier report.

While these periodic reviews have been sufficient to secure substantial improvements in many FATF members, they have not eliminated the problem of inadequate compliance by some with the forty recommendations. For this reason the Task Force has formulated a policy which reflects a graduated approach. At its most basic, and frequently invoked, level this takes the form of a requirement for the country concerned to make periodic reports. As one insider has noted: "when a country fails to comply with a large number of FATF recommendations, we initiate a follow-up procedure, a major feature of which is the obligation to submit regular progress reports on the implementation of the recommendations. (...) There would be no point in completing an evaluation and then ignoring the result".[89]

When this tactic for increasing peer pressure fails the policy on non-complying members envisages the taking of additional steps. This process is well illustrated by action taken in connection with Turkey in 1995-96. Its failure, *inter alia*, to even enact basic anti-money laundering legislation had placed it in a position of serious non-compliance with the recommendations. Accordingly, the FATF president first wrote to relevant ministers in that member country expressing concern. Subsequently a high-level mission was sent to Ankara to encourage the government to take urgent action or face the possibility of having more serious steps taken against it.[90] Finally, on 19 September 1996 the FATF issued a public statement in which it invoked its so-called Recommendation 21 procedure against a member for the first time. Recommendation 21 reads as follows:

> Financial institutions should give special attention to business relations and transactions with persons, including companies and financial institutions, from countries which do not or insufficiently apply these recommendations. Whenever these transactions have no apparent economic or visible lawful purpose, their background and purpose should, as far as possible, be examined, the findings established in writing, and be available to help supervisors, auditors and law enforcement agencies.

This seems to have had the effect of focusing the attention of policy makers and others in Ankara and in November of 1996 Turkey enacted and brought into force the Law on the Prevention of Money Laundering. The Recommendation 21 measures were then lifted.[91]

Concerns over partial non-compliance by other members have been frequently expressed. Of these the most serious to date relates to Austria which has declined to abolish anonymous passbooks for Austrian residents in spite of the fact that this is regarded as a clear breach of the requirements of Recommendation 10. As a result the FATF policy has been triggered. The president first wrote to the Austrian Government about this matter. This having failed to bring about a change of policy, it was decided to send a high level mission to Vienna.[92] Finally, given the failure of Austria to take timely action, the Task Force invoked Recommendation 21 and called on financial institutions to give special attention "to transactions with bank cheques issued by Austrian banks and denominated in Austrian schillings, as these funds might be the result of the closing of anonymous passbook savings accounts". In the FATF news release of 11 February 1999 which announced this measure it was indicated that it would continue to monitor the situation.

The self-assessment and mutual evaluation mechanisms and associated follow-up procedures were developed with the twenty-six member jurisdictions in mind. However, the Task Force also has two institutional members; namely the European Commission and the Gulf Co-operation Council. In so far as the former is concerned no problems of significance arise due to the fact that all fifteen European Union states are also FATF members. However, none of the six members of the Gulf Co-operation Council (Bahrain, Kuwait, Oman, Qatar, Saudi Arabia and the United Arab Emirates) are Task Force participants in their own right.

Over time the absence of regular monitoring procedures for these countries has emerged as a source of concern. In May 1997 agreement was reached on how to carry out an evaluation of the measures taken by them to date. The first step was to distribute self-assessment questionnaires. Unfortunately the partial and incomplete nature of the subsequent returns made it impossible to form a view as to the state of compliance. Consequently, it was agreed that a high level FATF mission would be despatched to the Council Secretariat and the United Arab Emirates to seek further information and "to discuss how to improve the implementation of effective anti-money laundering systems in the Gulf region".[93]

For the sake of completeness it should be noted that the FATF has a third mechanism through which it can seek to monitor implementation by its membership; namely, cross-country reviews. This is a little-used device intended to provide an analysis of the implementation of specific recommendations by the membership as a whole. For example, in 1996-97 such evaluations were carried out in relation to asset confiscation and provisional measures, and on measures taken to deal with customer identification.[94] While such studies have generated some interesting insights the process itself has failed to win a significant place in the thinking of the membership. It is anticipated that it will be resorted to fairly infrequently in the years ahead.

The extent of implementation of the recommendations

In each annual report the FATF has been able to report progress by its OECD and financial centre membership on the implementation of the forty recommendations. However, there remains some unevenness, both geographically and in terms of specific issues, in giving practical effect to the programme as a whole.

Perhaps the most significant progress has been recorded in securing improvements in national legal systems. This can be well illustrated by reference to the fundamental requirement, reflected in Recommendation 4 of the 1990 package, that each member should criminalise drug-related money laundering. At the time of the formulation of the 1990 report money laundering was a specific criminal offence in only seven FATF jurisdictions although legislation was pending in four others.[95] By the end of the fifth round in 1994 only three countries in a greatly expanded membership had still to take this step.[96] However, as was noted earlier it was not until late 1996 that full compliance was achieved when Turkey finally took this elementary legislative initiative.

Somewhat more surprising, however, has been the progress achieved in giving effect to the 1996 amendment in this sphere (Recommendation 4) concerning the extension of the money laundering offence beyond that of drugs. In 1992 the annual report acknowledged that very few of the participating countries had criminalised laundering beyond the narcotics predicate. However, by 1994 the FATF was able to record the fact that sixteen members had taken this step. The strong trend has accelerated since the stocktaking review and by June 1998 the Task Force was able to report that "all but three members have enacted an offence which covers the laundering of the proceeds of [a] range of crimes in addition to drug trafficking".[97] Furthermore all three delinquent members were expected to take swift action to secure compliance.

In a number of other areas, however, progress has been much less well marked. Take, for example, the important issue, addressed in Recommendation 6, that "where possible" corporations, as distinct from their employees, should be subject to criminal liability for money laundering. In spite of general agreement that such a step is an important part of an effective programme of countermeasures this has not resulted in a significant shift in domestic legislative practice to date.

This relatively poor level of progress is formally explained by reference to constitutional and other fundamental difficulties faced by a number of countries.[98] This is particularly so for European FATF members who are from the civil law tradition.[99] Indeed, as Noble has pointed out, it was for precisely such reasons that this and certain other recommendations "have a discretionary rather than a mandatory character. They are ones which call on members to consider applying the measure in question or take action to the extent possible rather than stating categorically that they should do so. And it was recognised from the outset that not all members would be able or necessarily prepared to take the action specified".[100]

However, it is possible to discern in this area a more general international trend which may well influence legislative practice in the direction of greater compliance in the future. By way of illustration, Article 18 (1) of the 1999 Criminal Law Convention on Corruption, drafted under the auspices of the Council of Europe, requires participating states to ensure that legal persons can be held liable for the criminal offences of active bribery, trading in influence and money laundering. In this instance, however, the establishment of either criminal liability or a functional equivalent will suffice. As the explanatory report states: "by virtue of this provision Contracting Parties undertake to establish some form of liability for legal persons engaging in corrupt practices, liability that could be criminal, administrative or civil in nature. Thus, criminal and non-criminal – administrative, civil – sanctions are suitable, provided that they are "effective, proportionate and dissuasive" (...)".[101]

Not all areas in which progress has been far from stellar in character can, however, be explained by reference to such a discretionary formulation. This is most strikingly, and embarrassingly, the case in relation to

Recommendation 1 whereby, as noted earlier, it was unanimously agreed that all members should "without further delay" ratify the 1988 UN convention and fully implement its provisions. In spite of the obvious centrality of this measure, progress towards formal compliance has been extremely slow and remains incomplete. The following table details the extent of formal FATF participation as of 31 October 1998 along with the year in which this was achieved:

Table I: Parties to the 1988 UN convention

USA	1990	Netherlands	1993
Canada	1990	Germany	1993
Spain	1990	Finland	1994
France	1990	Norway	1994
Italy	1990	Belgium	1995
United Kingdom	1991	Turkey	1996
Sweden	1991	Ireland	1996
Portugal	1991	Hong Kong*	1997
Denmark	1991	Austria	1997
Greece	1992	Iceland	1997
Luxembourg	1992	Singapore	1997
Japan	1992	New Zealand	N/A
Australia	1992	Switzerland	N/A

* The United Kingdom extended the application of the convention to Hong Kong with effect from July 1997. However, on 10 June 1997 it notified the UN Secretary General that it would cease to be responsible for the international rights and obligations arising from the application of the convention following its restoration to the People's Republic of China on 1 July 1997. China itself became a party in October 1989.

As was noted above, two regional organisations are also FATF participants; namely the European Commission and the Gulf Co-operation Council. All fifteen European Union countries are FATF members in their own right and all have now ratified the 1988 UN Convention. Of the six countries which are members of the Gulf Co-operation Council, only Kuwait has yet to take this basic step. Irrespective of the reasons for such a slow rate of progress, the current state of affairs, especially when viewed in the context of the extent of ratification of this instrument within the wider international community, is clearly highly unsatisfactory. Among other things, it continues to undermine the moral authority and political leverage of the FATF as it seeks to persuade non-member countries to accept its programme of action and implement it.

A somewhat similar overall picture emerges in relation to the implementation of measures related to financial issues. A major influence in securing positive advances in this regard has been the 1991 European Community directive which is examined in some detail in Chapter VI. In addition to the states of that grouping, the directive has direct relevance for the majority of European Free Trade Association (EFTA) countries by virtue of the terms of the 1992 agreement on the European Economic Area.[102]

Although considerable progress has been recorded on such key issues as customer identification, record keeping and due diligence, some areas of relative weakness remain. This is particularly so in respect of the extension of the programme to the non-bank financial sector.[103] It is of some interest to note that the 1997-98 self-assessment survey indicates that only in two areas covered by the financial recommendations (protection of financial institutions from legal liability, and the need to take notice of the potential for abuse of shell corporations) was compliance absolute.

The overall conclusion expressed in the June 1998 report of the Task Force was that "a large majority of members have reached an acceptable level of compliance with the 1996 forty recommendations". It went on to warn, however, that there was a need for some countries to take further steps and that it was of importance "that these changes be brought in as soon as possible"[104]

Reviewing developments in money laundering methods and countermeasures

One of the major tasks of the FATF has been, and will continue to be, to monitor developments in money laundering methods. This annual review, known as a "typologies" exercise, draws upon both the expertise of the delegates and specific case histories of money laundering investigations. It has charted the increasing sophistication, complexity and professionalism of the process. Particular attention has been paid to such questions as the use of shell companies, wire transfers, non-bank financial institutions, non-financial professional activities, the development of "cyberpayments" technologies, and, most recently, the implications flowing from the introduction of the euro. While these discussions focus primarily on developments taking place within its own membership, an effort is also made to keep abreast of money laundering patterns and trends in other countries and geographic regions. Given their nature these typologies exercises are mainly attended by law enforcement officials and regulators with increasingly frequent participation from international institutions with observer status such as Interpol, the World Customs Organisation and UNDCP.

On occasion, as during the 1995-96 round, experts drawn from the financial sector have also been invited to attend. This is but one illustration of a wider goal; namely to establish strong links between the Task Force and the financial services industry with a view to working "in partnership with the private sector on combating money laundering".[105] To this end the FATF has organised two major meetings with private sector representatives. The first such "Forum" was held in January 1996 with a second taking place in Brussels during FATF IX. As the June 1998 report noted: "The purpose of this event was to discuss with the private sector areas of common interest and ways to best develop measures to prevent and detect money laundering through the financial community".[106]

A major function of the typologies exercises and related dialogue has been to provide a basis upon which to judge the continuing relevance and coherence of the package of countermeasures which it has put in place. As was noted above, this process has resulted in the formulation of numerous interpretative notes and also contributed to the stocktaking process which culminated in the 1996 amendments to the recommendations.

However, not all of the lessons learned from the ongoing evaluation of laundering methods have required formal change before action could be taken. This was so, for example, with the important issue of the use of wire transfers in laundering schemes. Study within the FATF had highlighted the need to take additional steps to lessen the possibility that the audit trail could be broken by having resort to such systems. A particular problem was that "payment orders (...) frequently omit the name of the true originator and beneficiary of the payment".[107] In the search for a practical solution the FATF mandated, in 1992, the creation of an *ad hoc* group to study this issue. It, in turn, initiated discussions with the Society for Worldwide Interbank Financial Telecommunications (Swift) which is the primary carrier of wire payment messages. Swift was a natural choice. It has a presence in most jurisdictions. In addition, its "membership base is very broad and includes commercial banks, investment banks, securities brokers/dealers, and other financial institutions".[108] As a consequence the Chairman of Swift asked, in July 1992, "all users of its system to ensure that when sending Swift MT 100 messages (customer transfers), the fields for the ordering and beneficiary customers should be completed with their respective names and addresses".[109] In addition, "national authorities have also taken steps to encourage users of the Swift system, within their respective jurisdictions, to follow the advice contained in the Swift broadcast".[110] Following further discussions between the FATF and Swift the latter officially brought the 1992 broadcast to the attention of both the Basle Committee and the Offshore Group of Banking Supervisors.[111] Notwithstanding increased compliance some difficulties remained. Consequently further discussions involving Swift took place, during the 1996-97 round. These also had a positive and practical outcome.[112]

The external relations activities of the FATF

It has been emphasised on a number of occasions that modern money laundering is highly sophisticated in nature and money managers have proved to be adept in identifying loopholes and exploiting weaknesses in the structures, both national and international, which have been constructed to combat their operations. Internationally this has involved displacement from jurisdictions which have been active in securing improvements to countries and territories which possess no or insufficient anti-money laundering measures. Given its restricted membership base the need to tackle the problem of geographic displacement has been a priority of the FATF from the outset and is addressed in a number of its recommendations. For instance, Recommendation 21 stipulates that, among other things, financial institutions "should give special attention to business relations and transactions with persons, including companies and financial institutions, which do not or insufficiently apply these recommendations". Recommendation 20 calls upon FATF member country financial institutions to apply certain principles to their branches and majority-owned subsidiaries located abroad to the extent that the laws of the host state permit. This applies "especially in countries which do not or insufficiently apply these recommendations (...)". In spite of the difficulties which flow from the disinclination of the FATF to establish a common definitive list of such jurisdictions, an issue to which this study will return, progress has been recorded. As of 1998, banks in twenty-two of the twenty-six members reported paying special attention, pursuant to Recommendation 21, to transactions involving countries which do not or insufficiently apply the FATF package of countermeasures. In a further three countries partial compliance by banks with this recommendation was reported. The position was only slightly less satisfactory in relation to non-bank financial institutions. Similarly, the vast majority of members have reported positively on compliance with the obligations set out in Recommendation 20.[113]

Although the absence of a common "black list" of non-co-operative jurisdictions makes the application of the above measures difficult, practice has demonstrated that, at least in extreme cases, they can be activated. For example, the first use of Recommendation 21 by the FATF in relation to a non-member took place in early 1996 in relation to developments in the small Indian Ocean island state of the Seychelles. In November 1995 its National Assembly enacted the Economic Development Act, the stated purpose of which was "to ensure a very high level of sustainable economic development for Seychelles and its people".[114] In order to do so, however, it was deemed necessary to offer certain highly controversial "comforts and guarantees" to investors.

Among the concessions granted under section 5 of the 1995 Act are the following:

7. For the purposes of this section a concession or incentive includes –

a. immunity from prosecution for all criminal proceedings whatsoever except criminal proceedings in respect of offences involving acts of violence and drug trafficking in Seychelles;

b. immunity from compulsory acquisition or sequestration of the assets belonging to an investor other than a confiscation or forfeiture made by the court in relation to a criminal proceeding which is excepted under paragraph (a).

Furthermore, to set the minds of potential investors at rest, the legislation sought to ensure that these concessions, among others, could not readily be retracted or withdrawn. To this end, the decision was taken to afford the 1995 Act a high level of constitutional entrenchment. In the words of the Attorney General of the Seychelles, any future law seeking to amend or repeal the Economic Development Act 1995 "will need to be first of all approved by 60% of the votes at a referendum and must be passed by a two-thirds majority".[115]

These developments were considered by the FATF in February 1996. Its then president characterised the enactment as being clearly designed "to attract capital by permitting international criminal enterprises to shelter both themselves and their illicitly-gained wealth from pursuit by legal authorities".[116] Given the threat which it posed to the effectiveness of international money laundering countermeasures, the FATF resolved to place all available pressure on the Seychelles Government to repeal the legislation. It also invoked Recommendation 21 and "urged financial institutions worldwide to scrutinise closely business relations and transactions with persons, companies and financial institutions domiciled in the Seychelles".

Faced with the above, and other manifestations of deep diplomatic unease, the government acted. In particular, on 2 April 1996 it introduced into the National Assembly the Anti-Money Laundering Bill which was enacted shortly thereafter.

While elements of the Seychelles fiasco still remained to be resolved, the actions outlined above serve as a vivid illustration of what is possible within the Task Force, at least in the most extreme cases, where there is a perception that a member of the international community has departed in a radical way from the standards of conduct reflected in the recommendations. At an even more practical level the Economic Development Act saga is instructive. The evidence suggests that with the emergence of high profile attention those interested in taking advantage of this law quickly made themselves scarce. As The Economist noted at the time: "Nasty noises from abroad have had their effect. (…) The initial batch of interested 'investors' – some South Africans, Italians and Britons among them – have fled, many leaving high piles of large, and unpaid, hotel bills, behind them to show the height of their calibre".[117]

In order to further minimise the "diversion" problem a major effort has been made throughout to secure the active co-operation of others. At the G-7 summit in Houston, all non-members "were invited to participate in the fight against money laundering and to implement the recommendations of the FATF".[118] In the course of the 1990-91 round it was determined that the first step should involve explaining the nature of the FATF action plan in different parts of the world "with a view towards obtaining formal endorsements and, as far as possible, universal effective implementation of these recommendations".[119] This emphasis on obtaining the endorsement of and political commitment to its programme of action remains today as a central priority.

The second major element of the external relations strategy has been to reach out to non-member countries through a process of regional mobilisation.[120] Although all areas of the globe have received some attention, the FATF has concentrated its efforts on the Caribbean, central and eastern Europe, and Asia.[121] The means adopted have included, among others, the convening of regional conferences,[122] undertaking country-specific missions,[123] and co-operating closely with other organisations with a mandate in the money laundering area including the formulation of joint ventures with them. The organisational contacts which have been developed over the years are extensive. They range from global bodies such as ICPO/Interpol, the World Customs Organisation, UNDCP and international financial institutions such as the International Monetary Fund to specialised bodies with a more restricted membership such as IOSCO and the Offshore Group of Banking Supervisors (OGBS). Joint ventures are increasingly common. For example in April 1993, November 1994 and December 1995 the FATF combined with the Commercial Crime Unit of the Commonwealth Secretariat to organise major conferences in Singapore, Malaysia and Japan intended to raise the awareness of Asian and Pacific governments about the nature and extent of the money laundering threat and the evolving international response to it. In 1996 the same partnership sponsored the first Southern and Eastern African Money Laundering Conference which was convened in Cape Town in October.

Such co-operation with others is of considerable importance for a number of reasons. For example, given the small size of its Paris secretariat, co-operation is essential in order to ensure the appropriate provision of technical assistance and other follow-up activities in non-FATF member countries. It also helps to reduce, though by no means to eliminate, the problems which inevitably flow from the involvement of a number of different bodies in the same general sphere of concern. As the report of June 1993 remarked: "It is clearly important that the international community avoids overlap and duplication and draws strength from collective action. In conjunction with the other major organisations, FATF is therefore taking steps to promote a more co-ordinated approach in this area".[124] This has most frequently taken the form of co-ordination meetings held on the margins of FATF plenary meetings. More recently, however, the co-ordination function has been further strengthened with regular meetings among the international organisations with an anti-money laundering mandate. It is understood that henceforth there will be two meetings each year between such organisations and the FATF; one dealing with policy issues and the other with technical assistance, training and related matters.

Perhaps the most concrete results obtained so far through the outreach programme have been in a region which has for many years been a major source of concern to law enforcement officials and others involved in anti-laundering investigations; namely, the Caribbean.[125] It is no doubt for this reason that the FATF has been active in promoting its programme among the countries of that region since as early as June 1990 when an important conference on the subject was held in Aruba. As will be seen in Chapter VII, these efforts have since resulted in the creation of a Caribbean Financial Action Task Force. It has for long been hoped that the same path might eventually be followed by Asian countries. It is of interest to note that in 1994 a first step in that direction was taken with the establishment, by the FATF, of a small unit, based in Sydney, Australia, which was tasked with providing support for initiatives in that region. This unit was "funded by advances from Australia's Confiscated Assets Trust Fund".[126] In 1997, following a fourth and final awareness-raising seminar held in Bangkok, Thailand, agreement was reached on the establishment of an autonomous regional body known as the Asia/Pacific Group on Money Laundering (APG).[127] The APG, which currently consists of sixteen members, held its first annual meeting in Tokyo in March 1998. This development has been warmly welcomed by the Task Force. In the words of its June 1998 report: "The Tokyo meeting represented the full establishment of the APG as a cohesive regional group following on from earlier awareness-raising efforts. The Asia/Pacific Group provides an essential foundation for countering the global threat of money laundering".[128]

The above are but selected examples of the impressive progress of the FATF in achieving formal acceptance of its programme of action by non-members.[129] Recent years have also seen significant strides being taken elsewhere which mirror the emphasis of the FATF on securing effective implementation. The closeness of the resulting relationship with other international bodies is perhaps most vividly illustrated by the decisions taken by the Caribbean Financial Action Task Force (CFATF), the Offshore Group of Banking Supervisors (OGBS), and the Council of Europe, to establish

FATF-style forms of mutual evaluation. In the case of the Council of Europe this process, outlined in detail in Chapter V, applies to those of its members which are not participants in the FATF.

These developments have, in turn, required the Task Force to formulate policies and procedures for assessing these developments. In particular, it has supported the establishment of these processes and acted so as to validate them. As has been pointed out elsewhere: "the FATF assessed the CFATF, the Council of Europe and the OGBS's mutual evaluation procedures as being in conformity with its own principles. As the latter is comprised of representatives of banking supervisory authorities, the FATF has sought formal political endorsement of the procedures and the forty recommendations from those governments of the members of the OGBS which are not represented on the CFATF or the FATF".[130] These undertakings were secured from all of the jurisdictions concerned, with the exception of the Lebanon which has since moved from a full member of the OGBS to that of a country with observer status.[131]

This validation process also has an obvious relevance to the application of Recommendation 21 measures by the FATF to members of these groupings in the future. As the June 1996 annual report noted: "where a non-member has successfully gone through a mutual evaluation by an international organisation, using a methodology in line with FATF standards, and is in compliance with the FATF forty recommendations according to this evaluation, that non-member should not fall under the policy outlined in Recommendation 21".[132] Conversely, a mutual evaluation by such a body which revealed substantial non-compliance could be expected to make the imposition of this measure by the FATF even more likely.

Progress in meeting the goals of the external relations programme has also been secured through other international organisations and groupings. As will be seen in some detail in Chapter VII, the FATF recommendations have had an impact in Latin America primarily as a consequence of initiatives taken under the umbrella of the Organisation of American States.

Future challenges

Looked at in the overall, there can be no doubt that the Task Force experiment commenced by the G-7 in 1989 has been highly successful thus far. In spite of the apparent drawbacks of its limited, western-dominated membership and its informal legal status, it has become the single most important body in terms of the formulation of anti-money laundering policy and in the mobilisation of global awareness of the complex issues involved in countering this new and sophisticated form of criminality. Central to this achievement has been the comprehensive set of forty recommendations, first contained in its 1990 report which have become "an internationally accepted benchmark".[133] For the monitoring of this ambitious package of countermeasures, the Task Force has developed a willingness among member jurisdictions to accept innovative and intrusive procedures which were without precedent in the area of international co-operation in the criminal sphere. While there may be divergences of view as to whether mutual evaluation "has been able to achieve substantive as well as procedural equivalence"[134] among participants, the positive elements of this mechanism have been sufficient to induce other institutions and countries to adopt it both in the sphere of money laundering and, increasingly, in other areas of international concern such as organised crime and corruption.

A number of significant challenges, however, lie ahead as the Task Force seeks to move forward. Of these two appear to be of particular importance. First, and most immediately, there is a demanding task of giving effect to the most radical aspect of its future mission agreed to during the 1997-98 round; namely, to establish a worldwide anti-money laundering network. This, in essence, is an exercise designed to expand and strengthen the regional strategy outlined above.

Motivated, in large measure, by the recognition that in spite of the progress achieved through its external relations strategy "a large number of countries around the world still need to implement anti-money laundering systems",[135] it has been decided to place the development of regional bodies at the very centre of its future activities. This will involve both seeking to strengthen the work of those entities, such as the CFATF, the APG and the Council of Europe, which already exist, and encouraging the establishment of others. In the latter context Africa, the Middle East and Latin America are obvious priorities. It is recognised within the Task Force that this will be a difficult goal to achieve and that considerable flexibility on its part will be required. None the less, it is accepted that "the ideal model for a FATF-style regional body would be: a local group exerting peer pressure among its members and whose mutual evaluation procedures had been endorsed by the FATF, with one or several FATF members present in it, and a secretariat which would liaise regularly with the FATF. Moreover, the presidents/secretariats of each FATF-style regional body should become full members of the FATF. The FATF-style regional bodies should also be committed to the forty recommendations and to any other anti-money laundering principles they wish to endorse to reflect local problems. The main tasks of these bodies should include conducting mutual evaluations of their members and carrying out self-assessment surveys and regional typologies exercises".[136]

Closely associated with this renewed emphasis on regionalism has been the decision, noted earlier, to permit the first limited expansion of FATF membership since the early 1990s. In this regard the June 1998 report looks forward to "an adequate expansion of the FATF membership to strategically important countries which already have certain key anti-money laundering measures in place (criminalisation of money laundering; mandatory customer identification and suspicious transactions reporting by financial institutions), and which are politically determined to make a full commitment towards the implementation of the forty recommendations, and which could play a major role in their regions in the process of combating money laundering".[137] This process is being managed by the Japanese Presidency. It is anticipated that it will result in the first new members being admitted in 1999 – most probably after an interim period of observer status during which their satisfaction of the pre-conditions for membership would be subject to detailed scrutiny. Decisions will also have to be taken on various other issues which will necessarily arise; for example, how to manage cases of dual membership (of the FATF on the one hand and a regional body on the other), or instances in which existing Task Force members decide to withdraw from the FATF in favour of exclusive participation in the work of a regional group.

It is to be hoped that in the process of giving effect to this limited expansion of membership the FATF is not diverted from its intention to insist upon the satisfaction of strict and substantive criteria by candidate countries. The risk that geo-political, diplomatic and similar considerations might come to influence the process in a disproportionate way is a real one. However, the negative consequences for the integrity of the FATF process were it to admit a major regional power which lacked a genuine commitment to the anti-money laundering strategy should not be underestimated. The example of Turkey, especially in the period prior to 1997, serves to illustrate how lack of compliance with the forty recommendations can serve to undermine the credibility and influence of the Task Force.

The second major challenge confronting the FATF as it approaches the new millennium is how best to manage its agenda in order to ensure that its countermeasures remain up-to-date, comprehensive, and effective. In this regard two developments at the May 1998 meeting of G-7 finance ministers are deserving of some attention.

In their communiqué finance ministers characterised efforts to combat financial crime as "one of the major challenges of our times"; one that could "only be met if all major financial centres work together". In particular ministers identified effective international co-operation between financial regulators and law enforcement as being critical to reaching this goal. Study of this aspect of the problem had been entrusted to an expert group by the Denver summit in 1997.

Following discussion of this topic in May 1998, ministers reached agreement in a number of important areas. In particular it was decided to "review our laws and procedures concerning information exchange between financial regulators and law enforcement agencies against a common list of key elements for effective co-operation". This was to be accompanied by an effort to identify by late 1998, through reviews of existing national laws and practices of member states, what modifications were required to improve co-operation. The G-7 expert group is to report to the 1999 summit on progress.

As with efforts to counter unfair tax competition, which are outlined below, ministers envisaged the need for action to combat financial crime as extending well beyond the limited geographical confines of their own member countries. Their views on this critical matter are reflected in paragraph 9 of the communiqué which reads, in full, as follows:

> We also recognise that action must not be confined to G-7 members and we emphasise that all countries should provide effective international administrative and judicial co-operation. In particular, we are concerned at the number of countries and territories, including some financial offshore centres, which continue to offer excessive banking secrecy and allow screen companies to be used for illegal purposes. We recognise that the Financial Action Task Force (FATF) has already taken significant steps in this area and endorse FATF's efforts to support the Offshore Group of Banking Supervisors in its mutual evaluation process. We therefore call on the FATF to review the present position and make recommendations to ministers by the Cologne summit on what can be done to rectify these abuses.

This unprecedented direct referral to the FATF has been accepted by that body. It has, in particular, established a working group on non-co-operative countries and territories. It is understood that this group has concentrated thus far in canvassing views among its membership on standards with a view to the development of "objective" criteria against which the position of states and territories could be measured. It is possible that, following agreement on the "objective" criteria the FATF may proceed to draw up a list of non-co-operative jurisdictions; in essence a formal "black list". The creation of such a list would, in turn, pave the way for the consideration of the imposition of appropriate countermeasures to be deployed by the FATF membership against the countries and territories concerned.

Should discussions within the Task Force in Paris develop along the above lines it would constitute the clearest possible indication of the strength of political feeling in this area. It would also be unprecedented. Thus far, as has been seen at an earlier stage of this chapter, the FATF has deliberately refrained from attempts to create a "black list" of non-co-operative jurisdictions in relation to non-compliance with its general package of forty recommendations. Furthermore, it has to date deployed the countermeasures contained in Recommendation 21 on only two occasions; once in respect of Turkey, a member state, and once in relation to the Seychelles, which is not a member.

The second element contained in the May 1998 conclusions of G-7 finance ministers of direct relevance to the future work of the FATF relates to the subject of harmful tax competition; a matter which, in its traditional economic aspect, had featured on the agenda of the former at its 1996 and 1997 meetings in Lyon and Denver respectively. It can, for ease of analysis, be readily divided into two parts. The first consists of the expression of strong support for an ambitious OECD initiative on harmful tax competition which was agreed to in early 1998.[138] Such support, in a practical sense, is in turn reflected by two separate elements: (a) a commitment to work within the new Forum on Harmful Tax Practices to secure the effective implementation of the recommendations and to promote the OECD initiative on a global basis; and (b) to encourage the strengthening of the OECD approach to the international exchange of tax information.

The second central dimension to the tax co-operation initiative focuses on its interface with international efforts to combat money laundering. The intention of finance ministers in this area is set out in paragraph 16 of the communiqué. It is worded thus:

> 16. In addition we encourage international action to enhance the capacity of anti-money laundering systems to deal effectively with tax related crimes. Action here would both strengthen anti-money laundering systems and would also be an essential component of a coherent programme to increase the effectiveness of tax information exchange arrangements. Action could be based on furthering the following objectives:
>
> a. Effective anti-money laundering systems must ensure that obligations to report transactions relating to suspected criminal offences continue to apply even where such transactions are thought to involve tax offences.
>
> b. Money laundering authorities should be permitted to the greatest extent possible to pass information to their tax authorities to support the investigation of tax related crimes, and such information should be communicated to other jurisdictions in ways which would allow its use by their tax authorities. Such information should be used in a way which does not undermine the effectiveness of anti-money laundering systems.

Ministers at the same time announced their intention to pursue the development and implementation of the above matters in other relevant international fora including the FATF.

Since that time the subject of the "Enhancement of the Capacity of Anti-Money Laundering Systems to Deal Effectively with Tax Related Crimes" has been officially included on the work agenda of the FATF and it is currently considering how best to proceed in conjunction with the Committee on Fiscal Affairs of the OECD. It is apparent that the decision to include this matter in the plan of work for 1998-99 was not taken lightly. Indeed, it is understood that it generated more discussion and reaction than any other issue.

That this should be so is to be explained by the fact that the subjects of tax evasion and the international exchange of tax information are politically sensitive issues even for the FATF membership. This is well illustrated by the fact that none of the forty recommendations of the FATF are tax specific. For example, there is no mention of fiscal offences in Recommendation 4 on the scope of the criminal offence of money laundering or in the interpretative note which has been formulated in respect of the same. On the other hand the practical difficulties posed for anti-money laundering systems by differing perspectives and practices in the tax area has been a source of disquiet in a number of FATF governments over the years. In addition, there has been disquiet in specialist circles for some time concerning a range of difficulties which have arisen with offshore financial centres in the context of international co-operation. Although the FATF recommendations similarly do not address the "offshore" issue directly they do contain coverage of a number of matters which arise with some frequency in connection with such jurisdictions. Examples include financial institution secrecy laws (Recommendation 2), the identification of beneficial owners (Recommendation 11 and interpretative notes), and the abuse of shell corporations (Recommendation 25).

It is within this somewhat ambiguous context that the first cautious steps have been taken to respond to the G-7 finance ministers initiative. In so doing the FATF appears to have adhered to the distinction between the issue of suspicious transaction reports and that of the sharing of information which is found in paragraph 16 of the communiqué reproduced above. In so far as the former is concerned the intention is to tackle what is perceived to be a deficiency in the current package of money laundering countermeasures. This has attracted increasing attention both in the specialist literature, in the discussions of law enforcement practitioners, and in the public statements of policy makers. As a 9 May 1998 press notice issued by HM Treasury in London explained, it:

> addresses a potential weakness in international anti-money laundering systems by ensuring that financial institutions report suspicions about the movement of criminal assets regardless of whether they believe that the criminality involved is tax related. This is partly motivated by growing evidence that criminals can evade anti-money laundering systems by presenting their affairs as tax related to reassure their bankers, brokers and professional advisers.

It is likely that this part of the G-7 proposal will become the primary responsibility of the FATF.

By way of contrast, the initial response of the secretariat and the FATF membership to the second element of the G-7 proposal appears to have been more cautious. This, it will be recalled, seeks to improve the flow of information, both nationally and internationally, from money laundering to tax authorities.

At the time of writing it is too early to predict with any certainty the nature, extent or timing of future developments in this sphere, although logic would appear to dictate that it should prove to be easier for the FATF to fashion a consensus in relation to suspicious transaction reporting than on information flows. The challenge for the Task Force in the tax area, taken as a whole, is a substantial one. As mentioned above, the issue is highly sensitive even within its existing membership – a fact well illustrated by the decision of Luxembourg and Switzerland to distance themselves from the associated OECD initiative. Perhaps more significant, however, is the fact that forceful action by the FATF in this sphere could be expected to cause tensions in, among other geographic areas, the Caribbean and the Pacific which have significant numbers of offshore financial centres. These are, on the one hand, the very jurisdictions which are at the heart of the OECD initiative and yet, on the other, are important to the plans of the FATF to expand and strengthen its regional strategy. It is not without interest, for example, that the November 1998 CFATF council meeting devoted substantial attention to developments in this subject area. It will be of considerable interest to see how the Task Force rises to this and the other challenges outlined above in the years to come.

Notes: IV

1. Also known as GAFI derived from its French title; i.e., Groupe d'Action Financière sur le Blanchiment de Capitaux.

2. In an address delivered to the FATF plenary meeting in February 1998 the Managing Director of the IMF described it as "the main body for dealing with money laundering". See, "Financial Action Task Force on Money Laundering: Annual Report 1997-98" (hereafter Report IX), Annex A, p. 37.

3. Reproduced in Gilmore, W., (ed.), *International Efforts to Combat Money Laundering*, Cambridge, 1992, at p. 3. See also, Zagaris, B., and Kingma, E., "Asset Forfeiture International and Foreign Law: An Emerging Regime", *Emory International Law Review*, 1991, p. 445, at pp. 460-461.

4. Gilmore, W., (ed.), id.

5. "Financial Action Task Force on Money Laundering: Report of 6 February, 1990" (hereafter Report I), reproduced in Gilmore, W., (ed.), op. cit., p. 4, at p. 4.

6. Id.

7. See e.g., Drage, J., "Countering Money Laundering: The Response of the Financial Sector", in MacQueen, H.L., (ed.), *Money Laundering*, Edinburgh, 1993, p. 60, at p. 65.

8. "Financial Action Task Force on Money Laundering: Report 1990-91" (hereafter Report II), reproduced in Gilmore, W., (ed.), op. cit., p. 31, at p. 33.

9. See, id., at p. 44. See also, "Financial Action Task Force on Money Laundering: Annual Report 1991-92" (hereafter Report III), at p. 5, note 1.

10. Report II, p. 31.

11. Report II, p. 53.

12. See Report III, at p. 5.

13. See "Financial Action Task Force on Money Laundering: Annual Report 1993-94" (hereafter Report V), at p. 6. The length of time that FATF has remained operational is one of the main points of contrast with the 1990 G-7 initiative to create a Chemical Action Task Force (CATF). See, "Chemical Action Task Force: Final Report", Washington, D.C., June 1991. In the following year it was determined that this Task Force should not be maintained and that the necessary follow up should be "assumed by the competent UN and treaty-based bodies, as provided for under the UN Convention". "Chemical Action Task Force: Status Report for the 1992 Economic Summit", Washington, D.C., June 1992, p. 14.

14. See, Report V, at p. 7.

15. Report IX, p. 7.

16. Id., p. 9.

17. Id., p. 8.

18. Report II, p. 53.

19. The presidency is supported by a steering group consisting of the immediate past and future presidencies.

20. Noble, R., "The Financial Action Task Force Recommendations and their Implementation". Paper presented to the International Conference on Preventing and Controlling Money Laundering and the Use of the Proceeds of Crime: A Global Approach, Courmayeur, Mont Blanc, Italy, 18-20 June 1994 (hereafter 1994 Conference) (typescript), p. 2.

21. Report V, p. 8.

22. Pecchioli, R.M., "The Financial Action Task Force". Paper presented at the Council of Europe Money Laundering Conference, Strasbourg, France, 28-30 September 1992 (hereafter Strasbourg Conference) (typescript), p. 1.

23. Report III, p. 22.

24. Pecchioli, op. cit., p. 2.

25. See Report I, pp. 5-13.

26. "Report and Recommendations" of the 1994 Conference, (typescript), p. 4.

27. Evans, J.L., "The Proceeds of Crime: Problems of Investigation and Prosecution", Paper presented at the 1994 Conference, (typescript), p. 28. A revised version of this appears in Savona, E.U., (ed.), *Responding to Money Laundering: International Perspectives*, Amsterdam, 1997, p. 189.

28. Report I, p. 9.

29. Noble, op. cit., p. 3.

30. See, e.g., Hogarth, J., "Beyond the Vienna Convention: International Efforts to Suppress Money Laundering". Paper presented at the 1994 Conference (typescript), pp. 6-13.

31. Sherman, T., "Opening Session Speech", Strasbourg Conference (typescript), p. 6.

32. Savona, E.U., and De Feo, M.A., "Money Trials: International Money Laundering Trends and Prevention/Control Policies". Paper presented at the 1994 Conference (typescript), p. 28. Subsequently published in Savona, E.U., (ed.), op. cit., at p. 9. All references are to the original.

33. See Report I, at p. 14.

34. Report I, p. 15.

35. Id.

36. See, e.g., Sherman, T., "International Efforts to Combat Money Laundering: The Role of the Financial Action Task Force", in MacQueen, H.L., (ed.), op. cit., p. 12, at p. 18. Some have characterised the recommendations as "soft law". See, e.g., Zagaris, B., and Castilla, S.M., "Constructing an International

Financial Enforcement Subregime: The Implementation of Anti-Money Laundering Policy", *Brooklyn Journal of International Law*, 1993, p. 871, at p. 879.

37. See Pecchioli, op. cit., at p. 3; and Noble, op. cit., at p. 2.

38. See, e.g., Fisse, B., "Money Laundering, Regulatory Strategy and International Corporate Controls". Paper presented to the 1994 Conference, (typescript), at p. 9. Subsequently published in Savona, E.U., (ed.), op. cit., p. 283.

39. Noble, op. cit., p. 2.

40. See Report I, at p. 15.

41. See, e.g., Report V, at p. 13.

42. See Report I, at p. 14.

43. Id., p. 14.

44. Id.

45. Id.

46. Id., p. 15.

47. Pecchioli, op. cit., p. 3.

48. Drage, op. cit., p. 65. The Committee, in September 1997, formulated twenty-five core principles for effective banking supervision. Principle 15 requires banking supervisors to ensure that the banks which they supervise have adequate anti-money laundering procedures in place.

49. Report I, p. 11.

50. "International Organisation of Securities Commissions, Report on Money Laundering", Montreal, 1992, p. 5 (hereafter IOSCO Report).

51. Report I, p. 17.

52. Sherman, *supra*, note 36, p. 14.

53. See Report I, at pp. 20-21.

54. "Money Laundering and Associated Issues: The Need for International Co-operation", UN Doc. E/CN.15/1992/4/Add.5; 23 March 1992, p. 4.

55. Report I, p. 23.

56. Report I, p. 22.

57. Id., p. 15.

58. Noble, op. cit., p. 6. See also, Report III, at p. 16; "Financial Action Task Force on Money Laundering: Annual Report 1992-1993" (hereafter Report IV), at pp. 17-18; and Report V, at p. 22.

59. Griffiths, D., "International Efforts to Combat Money Laundering: Developments and Prospects", in *Action Against Transnational Criminality:*

Papers from the 1993 Oxford Conference on International and White Collar Crime, London, 1994, p. 11, at p. 12. See also, Report III, at p. 16.

60. See Report III, pp. 16-18; Report IV, pp. 18-19; and Report V, pp. 31-34.

61. Report III, at p. 17.

62. See id., at p. 18.

63. Report III, p. 18.

64. Report IV, p. 19.

65. Report V, p. 23.

66. See, id., at pp. 31-32.

67. Report III, p. 16.

68. Report V, p. 7.

69. "Stocktaking Review of the Forty FATF Recommendations: Summary of Responses to the Consultation Questionnaire". FATF VI, PLEN/40.

70. "Stocktaking Review of the Forty FATF Recommendations: Paper by the President". FATF VI, PLEN/48.

71. "Stocktaking Review of the Forty FATF Recommendations: Proposals by the President". FATF VII, PLEN/23.

72. Id.

73. Id.

74. "Financial Action Task Force on Money Laundering: Annual Report 1995-96" (hereafter Report VII), p. 6.

75. Id., p. 11.

76. Id., p. 8.

77. Report IX, p. 8.

78. Report I, p. 24.

79. "Financial Action Task Force on Money Laundering: Annual Report 1996-97" (hereafter Report VIII), p. 9.

80. See OECD Press Release, SG/PRESS (92) 52, 22/6/92, at p. 1.

81. Report II, p. 51.

82. Report VIII, p. 10.

83. Moulette, P., "The Mutual Evaluation Process of the Financial Action Task Force on Money Laundering", in Council of Europe doc. PC-R-EV (98) 1, 29 January 1998, p. 23, at p. 25.

84. At the time of writing the Website adress was: http://www.oecd.org/fatf/

85. *Supra.*, note 36, p. 19.

86. Morris, S.E., "An Introduction to Mutual Evaluation: Checklists and Question-naires". Unpublished speech delivered at the Egmont Palace, Brussels, 23 March 1998.

87. Report IX, p. 8.

88. Griffiths, op. cit., p. 13.

89. Moulette, op. cit., p. 27.

90. See Report VII, p. 15.

91. See Report VIII, at pp. 9-10.

92. See id., at p. 24.

93. Id., p. 11.

94. See Report VIII, pp. 19-20.

95. See Report I, at p. 12.

96. See Report V, at p. 9.

97. Report IX, p. 10.

98. See Report V, at p. 9.

99. See, e.g., *Liability of Enterprises for Offences: Recommendation No. R. (88) 18 adopted by the Committee of Ministers of the Council of Europe on 20 October 1988 and Explanatory Memorandum,* Strasbourg, 1990, at p. 10.

100. Noble, op. cit., p. 5.

101. Council of Europe doc. CM (98) 181, 29 October 1998, p. 44.

102. See, e.g., Articles 7, 101 and Annex IX (Financial Services), s.23. See also, Rosello Lopez, J.L., "The EC Directive on Money Laundering". Paper pre-sented at the Strasbourg Conference (typescript), at p. 12.

103. See, e.g., Report IX, at pp. 10-11.

104. Id., p. 11.

105. Report VII, p. 9.

106. Report IX, p. 28.

107. Report III, p. 15.

108. Paper (untitled) presented by R.A. Small of the US Federal Reserve System to the Financial Action Task Force Money Laundering Symposium, Singapore, 21-23 April 1993, (typescript), pp. 73-74.

109. *Money Laundering: Guidance Notes for Mainstream Banking, Lending and Deposit Taking Activities,* London, 1993, para. 104. See also, "Financial Action Task Force on Money Laundering: Annexes to the Annual Report 1992-93", Paris, 29 June 1993, (unpublished typescript) p. 11.

110. Report IV, p. 20.

111. See Report V, at p. 25.

112. See Report VIII, at pp. 7-8.

113. See Report IX, Annex D, p. 70.

114. Economic Development Bill 1995 (Bill No. 21 of 1995), Objects and Reasons.

115. Id.

116. FATF Press Release, Paris, 1 February 1996.

117. *The Economist*, London, 17 February 1996, p. 59.

118. Report II, p. 33.

119. Id., p. 44.

120. See Report III, at pp. 46-47.

121. See Report IV, at pp. 21-23; and, Report V, at p. 7. See also, Griffiths, op. cit., at p. 14.

122. See, e.g., Report III, at p. 18.

123. See, e.g., Report V, at p. 27. A more recent example was a mission to Cyprus undertaken in June 1997.

124. Report IV, p. 23.

125. See, e.g., Gilmore, W., "International Action Against Drug Trafficking: Trends in United Kingdom Law and Practice", *International Lawyer*, 1990, p. 365, at pp. 379-391.

126. Report V, p. 27.

127. For background information see, "The Asia/Pacific Group on Money Laundering: Papers by the APG Secretariat". Commonwealth Secretariat doc. SOMML (98) 6.

128. Report IX, p. 31.

129. For a partial listing of these achievements see id., Annex B, pp. 42-43.

130. Id., p. 31.

131. Id., p. 32.

132. Report VII, p. 17.

133. Report IX, p. 7.

134. UN Office for Drug Control and Crime Prevention, *Financial Havens, Banking Secrecy and Money Laundering*, Vienna, 29 May 1998 (Interim Report), p. 78.

135. Report IX, p. 7.

136. "Review of the Future of FATF: Strategic Issues". FATF IX, PLEN/12.BIS.REV1.

137. Report IX, p. 8.

138. See generally, *Harmful Tax Competition: An Emerging Global Issue*, Paris, 1998.

CHAPTER V – PAN-EUROPEAN RESPONSES TO MONEY LAUNDERING

The context

Although, as will be seen in Chapter VI, the member states of the European Union have sought to promote enhanced co-operation in criminal law matters for some time, the leading role within the European region in this area has been played by the Strasbourg-based Council of Europe. Established in 1949, its "principal aims are to promote European unity, foster social and economic progress and protect human rights".[1] Its membership was, until relatively recently, limited to the countries of western Europe (including for this purpose, both Iceland and Turkey). However, with the demise of communist rule and the end of the "cold war" it has played a key role in reaching out to embrace the countries of central and eastern Europe. The great majority of these emerging democracies have now obtained full membership. Importantly, Russia was admitted to this grouping in 1997. As the Secretary General, Daniel Tarschys, has remarked: "The recent member states have varied backgrounds: some lived under dictatorship for more than forty years, others for over seventy years; some had previously experienced democracy, while others never had; and some had never existed before as an independent state".[2] Nor has this process, which has seen the geographic area covered by membership quadrupled, come to an end. A number of further applications for admission, including those of Belarus, Georgia and Armenia, have been lodged, thus opening up the probability of it becoming the first truly pan-European organisation.

The Council of Europe has, for many years, afforded a high priority to activities in the legal sphere.[3] Its efforts to promote the modernisation of the law and closer co-operation between its members have resulted in the conclusion of an extensive network of treaties and conventions. Some of these relate to specific crimes of concern while others promote a broad range of forms of international co-operation. The most recent, concluded during 1999, relate to the protection of the environment through criminal law and to corruption. The latter, the 1999 Criminal Law Convention on Corruption, is closely tied to an ambitious agreement, concluded in the same year, which establishes the Group of States Against Corruption (Greco) which will have a critical role in monitoring compliance with commitments made by member states in an increasingly important area of interest.[4]

Among the other relevant areas of activity in recent years one might mention crime in cyberspace and organised crime. In both instances it was decided in 1997 to create committees of experts to examine the challenges which they pose. In the latter case, Committee PC-CO will, as Csonka has remarked, "analyse the characteristics of organised crime with a view, *inter alia*, to identifying lacunae in international co-operation instruments and possible solutions which could be included in new instruments".[5] The Council has also demonstrated a willingness to acknowledge the particular problems confronted by its new members and to design and execute programmes which deal exclusively with their needs. One example is afforded by a joint project between the Council of Europe and the European Commission. Initiated in 1996 and known as Octopus, its focus is on the problems of organised crime and corruption in states in transition. As has been pointed out elsewhere: "Under a first phase of this programme, which lasted until February 1998, an evaluation of the problem of corruption and organised crime and of countermeasures taken by governments of the sixteen states involved was carried out. Recommendations and guidelines were also formulated for each of these countries".[6] A second phase, to run until the end of 2000, is primarily directed towards the provision of training in these interlinked areas.

Among the most significant achievements of the Council in facilitating international co-operation in criminal matters has been the elaboration of two multilateral conventions which have come to be regarded as the central pillars of European co-operative efforts to combat crime; namely the 1957 European Convention on Extradition, and the 1959 European Convention on Mutual Assistance in Criminal Matters.[7] The former, which emerged from intensive diplomatic negotiations in the early 1950s, sets out in detail provisions governing all aspects of extradition law and practice which were then thought to be of importance. By mid-1998 it had been ratified by thirty-six member states including thirteen of the new democracies of central Europe. The 1959 instrument, which represented the first major breakthrough in fostering this highly practical form of co-operation at the multilateral level and has proved to be highly influential elsewhere, has been nearly as popular since its entry into force in 1962. Yet again there is now significant participation by the new member states.

In the years since these texts were agreed, the Council has both monitored their implementation and sought to improve upon their effectiveness in practice. This has been done, in part, through a series of recommendations issued by the Committee of Ministers. Such recommendations "although lacking any direct binding effect under international law, are of great value in applying and interpreting the conventions (...)".[8] In addition, this process of oversight and review has resulted in the conclusion of two modernising protocols to the extradition convention and one which relates to the operation of the 1959 text. The process continues.

It was thus within a well established tradition of awareness of the importance of the transnational dimension to effective crime control that the Council of Europe became, in 1977, the first international organisation to focus, in a systematic manner, on the problem of money laundering.

Money laundering initiatives

The context

Concerned over the growing number of acts of criminal violence such as kidnapping, the European Committee on Crime Problems decided, in 1977, to establish a select committee of experts to examine various aspects of this issue. As the first phase of the exercise the select committee was directed to focus on "the serious problems raised in many countries by the illicit transfer of funds of criminal origin frequently used for the perpetration of further crime".[9] This set in train a process of study and deliberation which was to conclude with the adoption by the Committee of Ministers, on 27 June 1980, of a formal recommendation entitled "Measures Against the Transfer and Safekeeping of Funds of Criminal Origin".

It is of interest to note that this recommendation fully embraces the philosophy of prevention so central to the programme of countermeasures subsequently adopted by the FATF. This stance flowed from the conviction that "the banking system can play a highly effective preventative role, while the co-operation of the banks also assists in the repression of such criminal acts by the judicial authorities and the police".[10] Within the package of measures which was recommended for consideration particular emphasis was placed on the "know your customer" rule. It was felt that all private and public banks should "as a minimum" undertake identity checks on customers whenever "an account or securities deposit is opened; safe deposits are rented; cash transactions involving sums of a certain magnitude are effected, bearing in mind the possibility of transactions in several parts; inter-bank transfers involving sums of a certain magnitude are made, bearing in mind the possibility of transactions in several parts".[11] In spite of the fact that these and certain other recommended measures, such as staff training, are now generally regarded as central aspects of any comprehensive anti-money laundering programme, the 1980 initiative failed to find a receptive audience and was not widely implemented. As Nilsson has observed, "[t]he Council of Europe was probably ahead of its time (...)".[12]

In the years which followed, work on the confiscation of the proceeds of drug trafficking was carried out under the auspices of the so-called

"Pompidou Group". Formed in 1971 at the suggestion of the then President of the French Republic, the Co-operation Group to Combat Drug Abuse and Illicit Trafficking in Drugs, to use its formal title, has operated since 1980 under the umbrella of the Council of Europe.[13]

A further impetus for progress was provided by European ministers of justice in 1986 when it was decided to request that the European Committee on Crime Problems undertake the formulation "in the light *inter alia* of the work of the United Nations, of international norms and standards to guarantee effective international co-operation between judicial (and where necessary police) authorities as regards the detection, freezing and forfeiture of the proceeds of illicit drug trafficking".[14] It, in turn, established in 1987 a select committee of experts which enjoyed fairly wide terms of reference. In particular, it was not obliged to restrict its focus to the proceeds derived from drug trafficking alone.

The 1990 convention

The select committee, which initially consisted of experts drawn from sixteen member states, was chaired by Mr G. Polimeni of Italy. Interestingly the committee also had the benefit of the direct participation of, among others, the United States, Canada, Australia and the Commission of the European Communities. Its work was to culminate, in September 1990, in the adoption by ministers of a new Convention on Laundering, Search, Seizure and Confiscation of the Proceeds from Crime. It was opened for signature in Strasbourg that November and entered into force in September 1993. While the initial pace of ratification was somewhat disappointing, recent years have witnessed a significant upsurge of activity. Consequently by January 1999 twenty-five states had become parties and it is widely expected that others will follow in the months and years ahead. While the majority of those who are parties are also members of the FATF, there is now an encouraging level of involvement by others; namely, Bulgaria, Croatia, Cyprus, the Czech Republic, Latvia, Lithuania, Slovenia and Ukraine. It is also hoped in Strasbourg that it will eventually count among the participants a broad cross-section of non-member and, indeed, non-European states. As Hans Nilsson, the secretary to the committee of experts, explained: "In order to encourage worldwide co-operation in combating money laundering, the convention does not use the word European in its title. This reflects the drafters' opinion that the instrument should from the outset be open to like-minded states outside the framework of the Council of Europe".[15] Australia is the only non-member to have taken this step to date.

In the preparation of the convention, the committee was anxious to ensure that its activities and product were sensitive to and complemented already existing Council of Europe conventions in the penal field. Following an examination of the relevant law and practice the decision was taken that the new instrument would seek "to provide a complete set of rules, covering all the stages of the procedure from the first investigations to the imposition and enforcement of confiscation sentences and to allow for flexible but effective mechanisms of international co-operation to the widest extent possible in order to deprive criminals of the instruments and fruits of their illegal activity".[16] It was primarily for this reason that the resulting text is one of considerable length and complexity. It is, however, limited in its ambition in the sense that it is, in contrast to the 1980 recommendation, essentially an international criminal law agreement. It does not, therefore, include comprehensive measures intended to enhance the role of the private sector in preventing money laundering activities.

A second major concern of the drafters was to protect the advances which had so recently been secured by the 1988 UN convention. As the official explanatory report noted:

> The relevant provisions of the United Nations convention were constantly taken into consideration: on the one hand, the experts tried as far as possible to use the terminology and the systematic approach of that convention unless changes were felt necessary for improving different solutions; on the other hand, the experts also explored the possibilities of introducing in the Council of Europe instrument stricter obligations than those of the United Nations convention on the understanding that the new convention – in spite of the fact that it is open to other states than the member states of the Council of Europe – will operate in the context of a smaller community of like-minded states.[17]

By way of illustration, the basic definition of the crime of money laundering, contained in Article 6 (1) of the text, is based on that utilised in Article 3 of the UN convention of 1988.

However, Article 6 also provides a clear example of the willingness of the Council of Europe to go beyond the 1988 precedent. Its greater ambition is revealed in a number of different ways. First, and most importantly, the obligation to criminalise money laundering is not restricted to drug trafficking offences. Instead it extends to any "predicate offence". This approach underlies the convention as a whole. As has been pointed out elsewhere: "One of the purposes of the convention is to facilitate international co-operation as regards investigative assistance, search, seizure and confiscation of the proceeds from all types of criminality, especially serious crimes, and in particular drug offences, arms dealing, terrorist offences, trafficking in children and young women (...) and other offences which generate large profits".[18] It was not felt, however, that the point had yet been reached where it would be appropriate to impose an absolute obligation to have in place domestic legislation on an "all crimes" basis. For this reason it was decided to permit the formulation of reservations as to scope. This element of flexibility is provided by Article 6 (4) which reads:

Each Party may, at the time of signature or when depositing its instrument of ratification, acceptance, approval or accession, by declaration addressed to the Secretary General of the Council of Europe declare that paragraph 1 of this article applies only to predicate offences or categories of such offences specified in such declaration.

Taken as a whole the approach adopted may best be regarded as an implicit invitation for domestic money laundering legislation to be as broad in scope as possible. This interpretation is supported by the drafting history of this provision and also that of Article 2 which deals with confiscation of proceeds and which gives expression to the same philosophy. For example, the committee of experts agreed that states which took advantage of the reservations facility in the latter context "should review their legislation periodically and expand the applicability of confiscation measures, in order to be able to restrict the reservations subsequently as much as possible. They also agreed that such measures should at least be made applicable to serious criminality and to offences which generate huge profits".[19]

While the expansion of the definition of money laundering beyond its 1988 association with drug trafficking had no precedent in a binding international agreement, it was a development which was not, even in 1990, unexpected. For example, it was a proposal which, as was seen in the previous chapter, had attracted the cautiously worded support of the FATF in the fifth of the forty recommendations contained in its February 1990 report. Furthermore, it had support in the legislative practice of a small minority of countries including Switzerland. Article 305 (*bis*) of its Penal Code, which came into effect on 1 August 1990 (the month before the convention was adopted by the Committee of Ministers of the Council of Europe), rendered money laundering in respect of all forms of crime a criminal offence.

Since 1990 a firm trend has emerged in favour of decoupling money laundering from drug trafficking and this is increasingly reflected in domestic legislation elsewhere. Indeed, many of the parties have declined to avail themselves of this limiting facility. These range from Belgium to Croatia; Slovenia to Australia. One of the early participants did take advantage of Article 6 (4) as an interim measure. The United Kingdom elected to restrict money laundering "to offences the commission of which constitutes drug trafficking as defined in its domestic legislation". The explanation for the British position is primarily historical in that its original (and pioneering) legislation, passed in 1986 and 1987, was confined to drug trafficking. Since that time, however, its scope has been expanded. Initially this was done to include proceeds relating to terrorist activities. This was followed by a further extension to cover the proceeds of all serious crimes.[20] As a consequence the UK was able to withdraw this reservation on 1 September 1995.

Some countries, such as Cyprus, have used Article 6 (4) in such a way as to limit their obligations to the range of predicate offences specified in relevant domestic legislation. Thus, as the range of those offences is progressively increased there is no need to deposit further declarations with the Council of Europe. The obvious disadvantage of this approach is that other state parties must look elsewhere to find the exact nature of legislative coverage at any given time. By way of contrast, in depositing its instrument of ratification in 1998 Latvia enumerated the fourteen categories of predicate offences contained in its 1997 legislation and utilised Article 6 (4) so as to limit the scope of its obligations to those categories.[21]

It is of particular relevance to note that some recent conventions on particular crimes of international concern elaborated under the auspices of the Council of Europe have contained specific provisions on the criminalisation of money laundering within the meaning of Article 6 of the 1990 text. This stance was, for instance, adopted in the 1999 Criminal Law Convention on Corruption.[22]

This strong trend away from drug-related definitions of money laundering mirrors a near consensus among commentators and practitioners concerning the practical and policy disadvantages of the narrow approach. As the UN secretariat has stated:

> The international community, through the adoption of the 1988 convention, has expressed its universal abhorrence of drug-related money laundering. However (...) there would seem to be little policy justification for the proscription of money laundering arising from some profit generating criminal activities and not others. Double standards, particularly in criminal law, are not conducive to the maintenance of the rule of law or to international co-operation, and there may be difficulties in proving that particular proceeds are attributable to particular predicate offences. In any event, drug trafficking may not remain – or for that matter still be – the most profitable form of transborder criminal activity.[23]

The extension of money laundering beyond the narcotics predicate is not, however, the sole difference in approach contained in the Council of Europe instrument as compared to the 1988 convention. One clear improvement is the manner in which it treats the question of jurisdiction in circumstances in which the predicate offence was committed extraterritorially. Given the transnational nature of many sophisticated money laundering operations, it is of great significance for the effective functioning of international co-operation, that a state be in a position to prosecute an individual for involvement in such activities in its jurisdiction even when the underlying criminal activity (the "predicate offence") which generated the proceeds in question took place elsewhere. For this reason it is unfortunate that the 1988 convention does not specifically require its parties to adopt legislative provisions in this area with such an extraterritorial reach. By way of contrast, Article 6 (2) (a) stipulates that for the purposes of implementing and applying the substantive provisions "it shall not matter whether the predicate offence was subject to the criminal jurisdiction of the party". Specific provision to this effect has been included in the legislation of some participating countries. For instance, in the United Kingdom "it does not matter that the conduct which generated the laundered proceeds may have taken place abroad, provided that the actual laundering took place in England and Wales (or, as the case may be, Scotland or Northern Ireland)".[24]

Also worthy of note is the fact that paragraph 3 of Article 6 of the 1990 convention permits, but does not require, the criminalisation of certain acts, including negligent laundering, in addition to those contained in the 1988 text. Such an approach to negligent behaviour in this context is compatible with Recommendation 5 of the FATF and finds expression in the domestic legislation of a number of European countries.

In addition to Article 6 on money laundering, Chapter II of the 1990 convention, which addresses the measures to be taken by participating states at the national level, contains a number of interesting and innovative provisions. Thus, Article 2 imposes "a positive obligation for states to enact legislation which would enable them to confiscate instrumentalities and proceeds".[25] As with money laundering this is done on an all crimes basis while holding out the possibility of formulating a reservation as to the categories of offences covered. For instance, the Netherlands has acted to remove the proceeds of taxation and customs and excise offences from the scope of the confiscation obligation while Ireland took steps to ensure that Article 2 (1) only applied "to drug trafficking offences as defined in its domestic legislation and other offences triable on indictment". In so far as the United Kingdom is concerned, a reservation was inserted in the 1992 instrument of ratification to restrict the obligation as it applies to Scotland to drug trafficking. This reflected the fact that in Scotland, which enjoys a separate legal system and legal tradition from that of England and Wales, there was at that time no legislation in place similar to that of the 1998 Criminal Justice Act which extended confiscation in respect of other serious offences to England and Wales. However, in September 1994 the Scottish Law Commission produced a report on confiscation and forfeiture containing proposals intended to update the law.[26] The process culminated with the enactment of legislation in 1995 which introduced a confiscation regime for the proceeds of crime more generally.[27] It is a matter of some regret that, notwithstanding this fact, significant delays in putting in place the necessary technical and detailed arrangements in relation to the enforcement of external confiscation orders have thus far prevented the UK from withdrawing this reservation. It is, however, anticipated that this difficulty will be remedied in the near future.

As with money laundering, subsequent treaty practice within the Council of Europe has sought to extend the scope of the confiscation obligation. In the course of 1998, for example, new multilateral instruments dealing with corruption[28] and the protection of the environment through criminal law[29] adopted this stance.

States parties must also be able to identify and trace property liable to confiscation and to take appropriate provisional measures to ensure that the property in question cannot be dissipated before a final confiscation order is made and implemented. In an approach similar to that utilised in the 1988 UN convention, Article 4 (1) requires appropriate steps to be taken to facilitate access to banking, financial and commercial records. It stipulates that: "A party shall not decline to act under the provisions of this article on grounds of bank secrecy". Finally, for present purposes, it is of interest to note that parties are to consider the domestic adoption of a number of special investigative techniques "which are common practice in some states but which are not yet implemented in other states".[30] Specifically mentioned in Article 4 (2) are monitoring orders, observation, interception of telecommunications, access to computer systems, and orders to produce specific documents. However, it is clear that this list was not intended to be exhaustive. The permissive wording used is sufficiently flexible to encompass other investigative tools which commend themselves to the law enforcement community because of their utility in this new and complex sphere of policing.

This would include, for example, the investigative technique, frequently used in drug trafficking cases, known as controlled delivery. In that context the "procedure involves allowing a delivery of illicit drugs, once detected, to proceed, under constant and secret surveillance, to the ultimate destination envisaged by the traffickers".[31] The purpose is to allow the investigation to proceed in order to maximise the possibility of identifying the principals in the criminal scheme rather than merely those with a lower level involvement such as drug couriers. The 1988 UN convention and the 1990 Schengen Convention both contain provisions to pave the way for the use of this technique at the international level. The potential of controlled delivery to contribute positively to the outcome of money laundering investigations has been studied by the FATF. In the course of the 1992-93 round, the conclusion was reached that controlled delivery operations should be encouraged and that appropriate steps should be taken to remove legal impediments to its use both domestically and internationally. The Task Force experts felt that the technique had an even greater utility in money laundering cases than those involving trafficking in drugs. As the original interpretive note explained:

> In the latter, it is easy to establish if the substances are illegal. However, it may not be readily apparent whether or not particular funds are the proceeds of crime. Further investigations are generally necessary to determine this and controlled delivery is a very effective method in this context. Even where it is clear that funds are of criminal origin, a controlled delivery operation (…) can be of great value in helping to identify and gather evidence against as many as possible of the criminals involved. In particular, it offers a route to the higher level criminals and the beneficial owners of the funds.[32]

It was no surprise therefore that in the course of the stocktaking exercise within the FATF, which was discussed in the previous chapter, it was agreed to amend Recommendation 36 "so as to give greater recognition to the benefits of such a technique, and to encourage countries to support its use, where possible".[33]

The drafters of the convention anticipated that any new law enforcement techniques made available in domestic law could also be used to further the process of international co-operation. It is to the removal of obstacles to such co-operation that the numerous provisions of Chapter III of the convention are directed. In the words of Article 7:

> 1. The parties shall co-operate with each other to the widest extent possible for the purposes of investigations and proceedings aiming at the confiscation of instrumentalities and proceeds.
>
> 2. Each party shall adopt such legislative or other measures as may be necessary to enable it to comply, under the conditions provided for in this chapter, with requests:
>
>> a. for confiscation of specific items of property representing proceeds or instrumentalities, as well as for confiscation of proceeds consisting in a requirement to pay a sum of money corresponding to the value of proceeds;
>>
>> b. for investigative assistance and provisional measures with a view to either form of confiscation referred to under a. above.

In order to give effect to these general principles and measures of international co-operation subsequent provisions establish, in some detail, the necessary rules and procedures. Separate sections are devoted to investigative assistance, provisional measures, confiscation, refusal and postponement of co-operation, notification and protection of third parties' rights, and procedural and other general rules. In certain respects this scheme seeks merely to reflect established and accepted forms of best practice. In other areas, however, the text seeks to improve upon and extend the co-operative mechanisms embodied in pre-existing international agreements.

By way of illustration, a number of innovations have been included to assist the law enforcement authorities in their investigative tasks. Thus, Article 8 of the money laundering convention, which requires that parties afford each other "the widest measure of assistance" at the investigative stage, goes further than the 1959 European Convention on Mutual Assistance in Criminal Matters. As the secretary to the committee of experts noted: "The paragraph is to be interpreted broadly. It allows for police co-operation that does not involve coercive action".[34] Police-to-police contact is also facilitated by other provisions. For instance, Article 24 permits direct contact between such competent authorities internationally when no use of coercive authority is contemplated. Perhaps more importantly, Article 10 permits the spontaneous provision of information relating to instrumentalities and proceeds in circumstances where it is felt that this might be of practical assistance to the authorities of another participating state. This was one of the first occasions in which a multilateral convention on criminal matters had specifically contemplated the provision of assistance without a prior request to do so.[35] The potential of these provisions to improve the speed and effectiveness of law enforcement is well reflected in the September 1993 agreement between the Netherlands and the United Kingdom, designed to supplement and facilitate the operation of the 1990 convention. Article VII reads, in relevant part, as follows:

> In the event of urgency (...) requests for investigative assistance and any immediate response thereto, as well as spontaneous information (...) may be exchanged directly between the competent law enforcement authorities of the parties or through law enforcement liaison officers which each party may have seconded in the territory of the other.

A further area, and one of crucial importance, where progress has been achieved is that of international co-operation in the confiscation of the proceeds of crime. As was seen in Chapter III, one source of difficulty under the 1988 UN convention arises out of the failure of the international community to impose a single mandatory approach to confiscation. Instead, it gives recognition to both the property and value confiscation systems which had been utilised in pre-existing domestic legislation. The Council of Europe text does likewise but goes further in requiring, in Article 7 (2) (a), that each participating state be in a position to respond to both types of request. As has been pointed out elsewhere, "if a state applies only the system of property confiscation of proceeds, it will need to take such legislative measures as would enable it to grant a request from a state that uses value confiscation".[36] In this and other provisions[37] the drafters were able to place both systems on an equal footing.[38]

As with the 1988 precedent, the Council of Europe convention recognises two basic options in giving effect to international confiscation assistance; that is, either to seek a domestic order or to give direct effect to an order made by the competent authorities of the requesting state.[39] In such cases it is necessary to focus on the status to be accorded to a final judicial order issued in the requesting state. Although it remains untreated in the UN convention the committee of experts considered it to be of crucial importance to resolve the issue specifically and in a manner which placed confidence in the standards of justice prevailing in the foreign country.[40] Article 14 (2) accordingly provides:

> The requested party shall be bound by the findings as to the facts in so far as they are stated in a conviction or judicial decision of the requesting party or in so far as such conviction or judicial decision is implicitly based on them.

Here the courts of the requested state cannot make an independent assessment of the evidence. This does not, however, apply to the legal consequences which flow from such facts, or to the hearing of new evidence if such was not available for some valid reason in the original hearings.[41]

A further issue of concern to the drafters was how most appropriately to accommodate the differences which had evolved in national legal systems. Particular problems arise when states resort to forms of confiscation which are not based on a prior conviction for a relevant criminal offence. For example, in the United States much of the emphasis in practice is on civil, *in rem*, procedures.[42] The majority of international instruments concluded to date, however, either explicitly or implicitly require a criminal conviction to trigger confiscation. A similar requirement is also evident in the domestic legislation of a number of states such as Australia. In other domestic systems a more flexible approach has been adopted. In England, for instance, although domestic measures are primarily conviction based, the definition of an external confiscation order is wide enough to permit the registration of foreign orders resulting from civil proceedings. Furthermore, the High Court can order certain provisional measures even when the proceedings which have been instituted abroad are civil proceedings *in rem*.[43]

In the view of the committee of experts there was an obvious need for an added element of flexibility in addressing this issue. Thus, in discussing the obligation to confiscate at the request of another party, contained in Article 13, the official explanatory report states: "Any type of proceedings, independently of their relationship with criminal proceedings and of applicable procedural rules, might qualify in so far as they may result in a confiscation order, provided that they are carried out by judicial authorities and that they are criminal in nature, that is, that they concern instrumentalities or proceeds".[44] Action on the basis of purely administrative procedures is, however, not covered by the terms of the 1990 text.

These are but some of the innovative features contained in an agreement which, in many respects, reflected the state of the art in what was, in 1990, a new area of international concern. In the ensuing years it has come to occupy a prominent place in anti-money laundering policy discussions and political declarations both in Europe and beyond. In the latter context the significance attached to the so-called Strasbourg Convention is well illustrated by the fact that Recommendation 35 of the FATF package of countermeasures makes specific reference to it in formulating general encouragement to states to ratify and implement relevant international conventions on money laundering. The reasons for such special treatment are not hard to identify. As we have seen, its general approach is entirely consistent with the philosophy of the Task Force. Indeed, many of its specific provisions act to reinforce – in treaty form – both the general framework recommendations as well as specific measures designed to enhance the role of national legal systems and to strengthen international co-operation.

In Europe, however, it has come to be regarded as a critical element in the fashioning of an effective stance against profit-generating crimes of international concern. Thus securing the broadest possible geographic participation has emerged as an important goal. This can, in turn, be well illustrated by two developments in 1997. In June European ministers of justice, meeting in Prague, examined the links between organised crime and corruption. The first substantive provision of the resolution which emerged from their deliberations was to call for the speedy ratification of Council of Europe instruments on international co-operation in criminal matters and, in particular, of the 1990 convention. The priority thus afforded to the 1990 text was further underlined by the heads of state and government of the member states of the Council of Europe at their second summit which was held in Strasbourg in October 1997. In that part of the resulting action plan devoted to fighting corruption and organised crime they also called upon all states to ratify.

As will be seen in greater detail in Chapter VI, a similar importance has been afforded to it by the European Union. In the 1997 action plan to combat organised crime, it is included as one of a limited number of multilateral conventions regarded as "essential to the fight against organised crime (...)".[45] Similarly, in the 1998 Pre-Accession Pact on Organised Crime between the member states of the EU and the applicant countries of central and eastern Europe and Cyprus, agreement was obtained from the latter, as recorded in Principle 2, to adopt and implement the 1990 convention, among others, as soon as possible.

Notwithstanding what has been said above, it should not be thought that the 1990 convention is a totally comprehensive let alone perfect instrument. For example, it does not impose an obligation to ensure that corporations and other legal persons can be held liable for money laundering. In this regard, it contents itself, in Article 18 (8) with provisions which seek to minimise the possibility of international co-operation being refused on the basis that the request arises out of investigations or proceedings in relation to such legal persons. As was noted in the previous chapter, the concept of corporate criminal liability poses particular difficulties for states from the civil law tradition. However, a clear trend towards the wider acceptance of it can be identified in state practice. Given this trend, the question arises as to whether it would not be advantageous to amend the convention so as to introduce more robust treatment of this matter.

Similarly, the gradual extension, outlined above, of money laundering and confiscation legislation from the initial focus on drug trafficking to a much broader range of predicate offences has conspired to call into question the adequacy of the approach adopted by the drafters to the important question of the final disposition of confiscated proceeds in international cases. At present Article 15, following the precedent set in the 1988 UN drug trafficking convention in the context of "victimless" drugs crimes, simply provides that this matter is to be dealt with in accordance with the domestic law of the country where the confiscation is, in fact, effected. Disquiet over this stance became evident at a major Council of Europe gathering in Strasbourg in late 1994 which examined the problem of money laundering in the states of central and eastern Europe. There delegates from the participating states approved the recommendation in the report of the general rapporteur, Mr L.-O. Broch of Norway, that the Council of Europe assess the possibility of drafting a protocol which would have the effect of facilitating the return of confiscated proceeds, in certain cases such as the theft of property in the course of the privatisation process, to the jurisdiction where the predicate offence was committed.[46]

It was generally acknowledged during that meeting that, unlike the position in the United States and certain other countries, drug trafficking did not constitute the major source of criminal funds within that geographic region. The accuracy of this perception has subsequently been confirmed by non-regional experts. For example, in its June 1997 report on money laundering "typologies" the FATF categorised the sources of illicit proceeds in central and eastern Europe thus: "(a) the illegal sale of natural resources such as oil, natural gas, metals, etc.; (b) the smuggling of alcohol, tobacco, arms and drugs; (c) proceeds from traditional organised crime activity such as extortion, prostitution, theft, fraud, motor vehicle theft, etc.; and (d) white collar crimes such as the embezzlement of state property and funds, income and profit declaration evasion, tax fraud, tax evasion and illegal capital flight".[47] The first "typologies" exercise carried out by the new Council of Europe Select Committee on the Evaluation of Anti-Money Laundering Measures, the mandate and activities of which are examined in greater detail below, reached somewhat similar conclusions in December 1998. In its discussion of cash money laundering it became clear that cash proceeds from drug related activity was but one of a range of profit-generating criminal activities of concern to its member countries from central and eastern Europe.[48]

The case for the establishment of a mechanism to review the adequacy of the treatment of such issues, among others, is increasingly seen as being strengthened by the fact that updating measures have already been taken by the Financial Action Task Force in relation to its package of counter-measures and, as will be seen in the following chapter, a similar process is now underway in respect of the 1991 EC money laundering directive. Perhaps even more compelling is the fact that, as will be seen in some detail at a later stage of this work, on 3 December 1998 the member states of the European Union adopted a joint action with the primary intention of enhancing the operation of the 1990 convention in their mutual relations.

Some support for such a modernising initiative has emerged in recent years within the context of the Council of Europe itself. At a general level, the 21st Conference of European Ministers of Justice, meeting in Prague in June 1997, requested the European Committee on Crime Problems (CDPC) "to submit proposals on the possible review and update of the existing conventions in the field of international co-operation in criminal matters, in order to take due account of the new demands to combat organised crime and corruption". In November 1998 a high level multilateral meeting held in Strasbourg on pan-European co-operation in the fight against organised crime and corruption concluded that the 1990 convention "should be rein-forced with new provisions to facilitate the conducting of enquiries and confiscation of unlawful proceeds at international level, with the help of measures such as the elimination of tax havens and offshore zones, the lift-ing of bank secrecy or the sharing of confiscated assets".[49]

However, the question of whether there exists at present a need for an additional protocol to the 1990 text remains somewhat contentious. Some have expressed the view that practical experience of its operation has not yet been sufficient to permit conclusions to be drawn as to its adequacy and that, consequently, it would be premature to undertake a modernising initiative of this type. At the time of writing the question of whether or not to initiate a process which would result in the elaboration of a protocol was under intense study in Strasbourg. It is expected that a decision will be taken in the course of 1999.

Mutual evaluation

From what has been said above, it is clear why the 1990 convention has been so positively viewed by both governments and commentators.[50] However, it has been appreciated within the Council of Europe from the outset that it would achieve its full potential only if it was both widely adopted and effectively implemented by the countries of Europe.

In this regard it should be noted that the 1990 convention does not contain specific provision for the creation of any mechanism through which the quality of the implementation of its obligations by participating countries could be subject to periodic review. Something of a functional equivalent did, however, exist for the European members of the FATF. This, as described in some detail in the previous chapter, takes the form of the self-assessment and mutual evaluation procedures designed to test compliance with the forty recommendations. Given the limited membership of the Task Force, this did not extend to the many non-OECD member countries of the Council of Europe including the emerging democracies of central and eastern Europe. A further cause for concern arose out of the fact that the 1990 convention does not reach out to embrace the important preventative aspects of the anti-laundering strategy articulated by the FATF. As will be seen in Chapter VI, the great majority of the relevant recommendations in this sphere have obtained concrete expression for the states of the European Union in the form of the 1991 money laundering directive. Notwithstanding the efforts of the European Commission and the Council of the EU to extend the geographic impact of that measure there have remained important gaps in its coverage.

From as early as 1991 the external relations activities of the FATF came to focus on the extent to which the states of central and eastern Europe, in particular, were willing to introduce comprehensive money laundering countermeasures. This attention was not, in the first instance, dictated by their importance in the global money laundering process. Rather, it flowed from the identification of both the problems and opportunities presented by the transition from state control to market economies in the aftermath of the collapse of communist rule. As the FATF report of 25 June 1992 was to note: "as the economies of these countries become more integrated into the world financial system and their currencies move to convertibility, they will become attractive to money launderers. At the same time, the reform and restructuring of the eastern European financial sector presents an ideal opportunity for these states to take measures which would help them to protect themselves against money laundering".[51]

In its first direct contact with the region, the FATF steering group held discussions with representatives from Hungary, Poland and Czechoslovakia (as it then was) in Paris during the third round.[52] An opportunity to build upon and extend this dialogue was provided by a major conference on money laundering which was convened by the Council of Europe in Strasbourg in late September 1992. The FATF president and other representatives of the group addressed a number of the formal sessions of this gathering. They also took the opportunity to hold "meetings with delegates from most central and eastern European countries to find out more about the money laundering situations within these countries and discuss how the FATF might assist them".[53] These contacts, in turn, paved the way for the Task Force to arrange two specialist seminars in the region (at Budapest and Warsaw) early the following year. A further such meeting was convened in Moscow in November 1993.[54]

This engagement has continued, and indeed been extended, in more recent years in a range of activities frequently undertaken in conjunction with others. For example, in the autumn of 1996 a joint mission from the Task Force, the European Commission and the Council of Europe, headed by the FATF president, visited Moscow for further discussions with the Russian authorities on the subject of money laundering.[55] Increasingly members of a FATF *ad hoc* group on central and eastern Europe, either along or in conjunction with relevant international organisations, are providing legal and technical assistance to the countries concerned. For example, "[u]nder the Phare multi-country programme to combat drugs the [European] Commission is currently involved in technical assistance efforts in the field of anti-money laundering measures in thirteen countries of central and eastern Europe".[56]

An important factor underlying this concentration is the perception, reflected in the annual "typologies" exercises conducted by the Task Force, of the extent of the laundering of funds with a central or eastern European origin. As was noted in the June 1997 report: "Large volumes of cash and other types of transfers continue to make their way from these countries into the banks and financial institutions of FATF member countries".[57] Such criminal proceeds are frequently reported to be invested in the legitimate economies in western Europe and elsewhere rather than returning to their country of origin. For instance, it has been concluded that "[g]roups tied to the former Soviet Union and eastern Europe are continuing to make extensive investments in real estate, hotels, restaurants and other businesses (...)".[58]

The focus of the FATF on this geographic area has also been facilitated by the success of the outreach programme in gaining political commitments to the implementation of its recommendations. This is well illustrated by a declaration signed in Riga in November 1996. In it "the governments of Estonia, Latvia and Lithuania made a commitment to implement the measures which are set out in the Vienna and Strasbourg conventions, the European Union directive as well as the FATF recommendations".[59]

Such developments were critical in paving the way for an unprecedented initiative within the Council of Europe to introduce a highly intrusive system of peer review based on the FATF model. As has recently been pointed out elsewhere: "In September 1997, the Committee of Ministers of the

Council of Europe established a select committee (PC-R-EV) to conduct self and mutual assessment exercises of the anti-money laundering measures in place in twenty-one Council of Europe countries, which are not members of the Financial Action Task Force (FATF). The PC-R-EV takes into account the practices and procedures of the FATF in its work. The PC-R-EV is a sub-committee of the European Committee on Crime Problems of the Council of Europe (CDPC)".[60] It is important to recall at this juncture that the Task Force has agreed to validate this process for its own purposes.

The relationship between this Council of Europe procedure and the Paris-based FATF is intended to be particularly intense. This is well illustrated by the fact that full membership of the committee is extended to the past and current presidencies of the FATF. In addition, observer status has been accorded to Council of Europe countries which are members of the FATF steering group as well as to its secretariat. In addition, the terms of reference for the PC-R-EV call upon it to structure its key activities "taking into account the procedures and practices used by the FATF". Furthermore, the secretariat of the PC-R-EV is increasingly involved in participation in the activities of the Task Force.

It should not be thought, however, that this Council of Europe committee is but a mirror of a "parent" body. FATF precedents have not been slavishly followed. Indeed, in some respects the Council of Europe exercise is more ambitious and exacting. Of special significance in this context is the fact that the process of self-assessment and mutual evaluation is undertaken against a more extensive set of anti-laundering standards. Thus, in addition to the forty recommendations, participating countries are assessed in relation to their compliance with the 1988 UN and 1990 Council of Europe conventions, and the 1991 EC directive.[61]

The PC-R-EV held its first plenary meeting in December 1997 at which time it elected Mr Klaudijo Stroligo of Slovenia as its chairman. It also paved the way for the first mutual evaluations to take place. In the course of 1998, evaluation teams visited Slovenia, Slovakia, Cyprus, the Czech Republic, Malta, Lithuania and Hungary. In the two 1998 plenary meetings, reports were adopted on all save Lithuania and Hungary, which will be subjects for discussion in June 1999. Fairly extensive summaries of these reports, which are to be made public, were also agreed to.[62] Each evaluation team consisted of three experts from the PC-R-EV membership who were assisted by two individuals drawn from FATF countries. Furthermore, "[u]nder an agreement with the FATF these evaluation teams also include a representative of the Offshore Group of Banking Supervisors (OGBS) where the country undergoing evaluation is also a member of that organisation".[63] During 1998 this arrangement was put into effect for the visits to both Cyprus and Malta.

More recently, agreement has been reached on the timetable for an ambitious programme of future evaluations due to be completed with a country visit to Albania in September 2000.[64] This programme acknowledges that a full round of evaluations cannot be undertaken within the original time frame envisaged for the work of the committee. Consequently, the December 1998 plenary formally requested that its mandate be renewed to enable this process to be completed. It is widely anticipated that the decision, due to be taken in June 1999, will be a positive one.

The committee has, as a result of strong leadership from the chair and its bureau,[65] and excellent support from its secretariat, made impressive progress in a very short period of time. It has put into place "a clear reference document which aims to bring certainty, consistency and an even-handed approach to the mutual evaluation process"[66] and, importantly, has made significant progress in putting it into practice. Few would disagree with the conclusion expressed in the first annual report: "The Council of Europe now has a solid record of achievement in mutual evaluation and has begun important work on typologies within the region".[67] It is necessary for a variety of reasons, not least in providing a substantive underpinning to the new FATF regional strategy in a critical area of concern, that this process be allowed to continue and to mature.

The human rights dimension

From what has been said in section 2 above, it is clear that the 1990 convention, like other instruments designed to combat laundering and deprive criminals of their illicitly acquired profits, is highly intrusive in nature. This is especially so in relation to the imposition of obligations which impact directly on the domestic criminal justice system of each participating state. Thus, in addition to requiring a high level of international co-operation, in which considerable trust is placed in the standards of justice prevailing in other countries, the convention requires or permits radical changes in domestic criminal law.

In an area of concern such as this, where progress is very much driven by a law enforcement and criminal policy agenda, it is imperative to ensure that human rights and civil liberties issues are not lost sight of. As Dolle has remarked: "In the efforts to stamp out the canker presented by organised crime we have to be careful not to overreact and bend the rules so far that we contribute to the destruction of the very democratic values we are trying to protect".[68]

Such concerns are of particular centrality to instruments elaborated under the auspices of the Council of Europe which, in Article 3 of its Statute, makes respect for human rights a condition of membership. Furthermore, "[t]he importance of human rights is emphasised in several other provisions of the Statute, (...) and Article 8 even provides that serious violations of human rights and fundamental freedoms are grounds for suspending or expelling a member state from the Council".[69]

It is clear from the record that Mr Polimeni and his colleagues on the committee of experts which drafted the 1990 convention were sensitive to the importance of striking an appropriate balance between the needs of crime suppression and international co-operation on the one hand and the rights of affected individuals on the other. Such concerns are most clearly reflected in those provisions which seek to afford protection to the rights of bona fide third parties. That this is a highly practical rather than a merely theoretical issue is beyond doubt. As the official explanatory report has noted: "Practice has shown that criminals often use ostensible "buyers" to acquire property. Relatives, wives, children or friends might be used as decoys. Nevertheless, the third parties might be persons who have a legitimate claim on property which has been subject to a confiscation order or a seizure".[70] In order to ensure that the latter group are adequately protected, Article 5 requires each party to the convention to have in its domestic law an effective set of legal remedies through which they can preserve their rights. The scope of this obligation has been officially described thus:

> The legal provisions required by this article should guarantee "effective" legal remedies for interested third parties. This implies that there should be a system where such parties, if known, are duly informed by the authorities of the possibilities to challenge decisions or measures taken, that such challenges may be made even if a confiscation order has already become enforceable, if the party had no earlier opportunity to do so, that such remedies should allow for a hearing in court, that the interested party has the right to be assisted or represented by a lawyer and to present witnesses and other evidence, and that the party has a right to have the court decision reviewed.[71]

Having required such measures to be taken at the national level the convention goes on to mandate complementary protection in cases involving international co-operation. In this regard Article 21 addresses the issues of the serving of judicial documents on third parties affected by provisional measures and confiscation orders which have been taken or handed down abroad. The following article then sets out the general rule that a state which receives a request from another party will recognise any judicial decision which has been made regarding rights claimed by third parties. This does not apply, however, where the matter has not been considered in the requesting state. In such cases the individual concerned has the right to invoke the protection of the law of the requested state. The general rule is subject to a number of exceptions which are specified in Article 22 (2). For example, recognition of the foreign judicial decision may be refused in instances where "third parties did not have adequate opportunity to assert their rights".

The concern of the drafters of the convention extended beyond the protection of the interests of innocent third parties. This wider effort to promote a balance between the need for effective law enforcement and the protection of the rights of the individual is reflected in Article 18 which sets out a detailed and broad range of discretionary grounds for the refusal of requests for international co-operation. For example, co-operation may be declined where "the action sought would be contrary to the fundamental principles of the legal system of the requested party". In the course of their deliberations a number of examples were given by members of the expert committee of cases which might properly trigger this provision. These included, among others, "where the proceedings on which the request are based do not meet basic procedural requirements for the protection of human rights such as the ones contained in Articles 5 and 6 of the Convention for the Protection of Human Rights and Fundamental Freedoms".[72]

The committee of experts also took the opportunity afforded by the official explanatory report to signal its conviction that certain possible interpretations of convention articles which might raise human rights and civil liberties concerns were invalid. One such example, which had provoked lively debate and controversial litigation in the United States, related to the payment of legal fees by money launderers and others subsequently convicted of relevant offences for which confiscation is either permitted or required.[73] In the words of the explanatory report:

> The question has been raised, in relation to the United Nations convention, whether it would be illegal for a lawyer's fees to be paid out of funds related to a laundering offence. Some lawyers have even suggested that the United Nations Convention would, by its wording, make it criminal to hire a lawyer or accept a fee. In the view of the experts, the wording of the present convention cannot be misinterpreted to that effect.[74]

Finally, it should be noted that the same commentary indicates that the provisions of the 1990 money laundering convention, in so far as they impact on individuals, remain subject to the requirements of the Convention for the Protection of Human Rights and Fundamental Freedoms (ECHR) which was signed on 4 November 1950 and entered into force in September 1953.[75]

Concluded with the intention of providing a system of collective guarantees for the protection of human rights in post-war Europe, the ECHR has come to be viewed as the crowning achievement of the Council of Europe. The Convention, together with a number of amending protocols concluded in later years, is primarily concerned with safeguarding a broad range of civil and political rights.[76] Relevant examples include the right to a fair and public hearing within a reasonable time by an independent and impartial tribunal established by law (Article 6), and the prohibition of retroactive criminal legislation (Article 7). Parties to the ECHR must, pursuant to Article 1, secure these rights for everyone within their jurisdiction and not merely, as with the traditional approach of international law, for foreign nationals.

In order to ensure that these important obligations are upheld in practice, the Convention created machinery for the determination of violations which constituted, at that time, a near revolutionary precedent. Among other matters, it created the European Commission of Human Rights to determine the admissibility of complaints alleging violations, to undertake the tasks of fact finding and conciliation, and where no friendly settlement could be reached, to express a view as to whether the facts disclosed a violation of the Convention. In addition to contemplating orthodox inter-state complaints, it also provided for the right of individual petition to the Commission, "provided that the state complained against has declared that it recognises the competence of the Commission to receive such petitions".[77] It is important to appreciate that, as with the orthodox approach in the international law of diplomatic protection, no such application can be entertained unless all domestic remedies have first been exhausted. An inability to satisfy this and other requirements relating to admissibility results, in practice, in a majority of applications failing to progress beyond this initial stage.

A further innovation of great significance was that the ECHR provided for the creation of a judicial body to supplement the process of political settlement available in the form of the Committee of Ministers. Known as the European Court of Human Rights, it was granted the power to hand down binding decisions concerning the interpretation and application of the Convention. This too constituted a departure from the cautious diplomatic traditions of the time and it was accordingly decided that the Court would only have jurisdiction as regards those states which had voluntarily accepted it by making a declaration to that effect under Article 46.

The intervening years have witnessed a major transformation in the way in which the states of Europe perceive both the ECHR and its control mechanisms. For example, it eventually became a *de facto* requirement of membership of the Council of Europe that a state be prepared both to become a party to the Convention and accept the jurisdiction of the Court.[78] In addition, as Finnie noted in 1994, "there has again crystallised a convention that the acceptance of individual petitions is a condition of entry to the Council of Europe".[79] In practice, resort by aggrieved individuals to the

Commission in Strasbourg has become commonplace and the case load of the Court has soared. As the office of the Registrar of the Court noted: "the number of applications registered annually with the Commission increased from 404 in 1981 to 2 037 in 1993. By 1997 that figure had more than doubled (4 750). By 1997 the number of unregistered or provisional files opened each year in the Commission had risen to over 12 000. The Court's statistics reflected a similar story, with the number of cases referred annually rising from seven in 1981 to fifty-two in 1993 and 119 in 1997".[80]

Given these factors and the additional strains expected to arise out of the continuing expansion of membership, the decision was taken to streamline and modernise these ECHR procedures. Agreement on this important matter was reached and embodied in the terms of Protocol No. 11 which entered into force on 1 November 1998. While a detailed examination of the new structure brought about by the protocol lies beyond the scope of this work, it is important to note that it significantly alters the internal structure of the Court, eliminates the Commission, and abolishes the adjudication role of the Committee of Ministers. In addition, it gives formal legal effect to certain of the practices and conventions which had evolved over the years. Particularly worthy of note in this context is the fact that "Protocol No. 11 made automatic the acceptance of both the right of individual petition and the compulsory jurisdiction of the Court (...)".[81]

The ease and immediacy with which an individual can invoke the protection of the rights set out in the ECHR differs widely from jurisdiction to jurisdiction. It depends, in large measure, on the approach which has been adopted nationally to the issue of the relevance of international legal obligations in domestic law. In many European countries, such as Germany, the process of approval of international treaties involves the legislature with the result that their terms gain the force of law unless and until amended by a subsequent inconsistent statute. Individuals can therefore invoke the ECHR before their national courts in the same manner as purely domestic legal rights. A variant of this approach is found in the Netherlands. As Schermers has stated: "The Netherlands Government is not allowed to ratify any international treaty without parliamentary approval. Once it has been ratified the treaty becomes part of domestic law and has superior rank over all domestic legislation".[82]

By way of contrast, in the United Kingdom the executive branch of government exercises the treaty-making power. International obligations contained in such instruments become part of domestic law only if subsequently incorporated by Act of Parliament. In the case of the ECHR no such statute was enacted until 1998. Consequently, the provisions of the Convention could not be directly invoked by an aggrieved individual. As has been pointed out elsewhere:

The relatively large number of complaints brought against the United Kingdom can partly be explained by the fact that the domestic courts cannot themselves apply the European Convention. This fact makes claims against Britain not only more numerous but also more difficult. The European Convention requires the exhaustion of domestic remedies before a complaint can be brought to Strasbourg. Domestic remedies are exhausted only when the applicant has invoked the violation concerned before his national court. Where the applicant is not allowed to invoke the Convention itself, he must invoke the equivalent national rule of law, though it is often difficult to establish what rule of national law is equivalent to a provision of the Convention. This complication makes the exhaustion of domestic remedies more difficult and therefore also more expensive for the individual concerned.[83]

A profound change in this regard will be brought about when the 1998 Human Rights Act fully enters into force; a development which is unlikely to take place before the year 2000. This measure, part of an ambitious programme of constitutional reform initiated by the Labour Government following its election in 1997, incorporates specific provisions of the Convention and its protocols into British law for the first time. Although this is accomplished in a manner which reflects the somewhat idiosyncratic nature of the constitution, including procedures and norms which attempt to reconcile this measure with the principle of the sovereignty of the Westminster Parliament, it holds out the prospect of eventually minimising the number of instances in which the United Kingdom is subject to adverse rulings from the Strasbourg Court.

When faced with the need to formulate legislation in new fields such as money laundering and confiscation of proceeds, it has become common practice for governments and their advisers to seek guidance on what is acceptable by examining the text of the ECHR and its relevant protocols. Such an examination reveals that the Convention is not hostile to the needs of law enforcement. As Duffy has remarked:

> Throughout the text of the Convention, provision is made for the legitimate policing and security needs of states. Powers of arrest, necessary interferences with privacy for investigative purposes, use of force – all were expressly recognised in the Convention's drafting.[84]

The outer limits of such provisions have been tested on a number of occasions with the result that there is also a fairly extensive jurisprudence from both the Court and the Commission to assist the legislative drafter. For example, of relevance in the present context are past decisions relating to Convention requirements in respect of such issues as the conduct of the criminal investigation, the use of preliminary or preventative measures, and the conduct of the eventual trial.[85] One area which has generated case-law of undoubted practical significance is the increasing resort to special investigative measures such as telephone interception and the use of undercover police agents. Cases emerging from the use of such techniques have required an examination of their consistency with various Convention provisions including respect for privacy (Article 8) and the right to a fair trial (Article 6). In the 1992 case of *Ludi* v. *Switzerland* the Court held that the use of telephone tapping in conjunction with the involvement of an undercover law enforcement agent was, in the circumstances before it, consistent with the right to privacy.[86] However, in its June 1998 judgment in *Teixeira de Castro* v. *Portugal* the Court set further limits on covert techniques. In holding that the deployment of police officers as *agents provocateurs* had resulted in a violation of the right to a fair trial, it remarked: "The use of undercover agents must be restricted and safeguards put in place even in cases concerning the fight against drug trafficking. While the rise in organised crime undoubtedly requires that appropriate measures be taken, the right to a fair administration of justice nevertheless holds such a prominent place (...) that it cannot be sacrificed for the sake of expediency. (...) The public interest cannot justify the use of evidence obtained as a result of police incitement".[87]

Increasingly the body of precedents is being enriched by individual petitions arising directly out of money laundering investigations or confiscation actions. This is well illustrated by the September 1991 decision of the Commission on the admissibility of an application against the United Kingdom made by one Mr Nazir Chinoy.[88]

Mr Chinoy was wanted in the United States on a variety of criminal charges including drugs-related money laundering and a warrant was subsequently issued in England for his arrest with a view to his extradition. A vital element of the evidence adduced by the Government of the United States in the subsequent extradition proceedings took the form of tape-recordings of telephone conversations made by US agents while Mr Chinoy was in France. It was alleged that these recordings had been made in violation of French law. Before the English courts it was argued, without success, that the evidence in question should be excluded.[89] Mr Chinoy then complained to the Commission alleging a violation of Article 8 of the Convention (respect for his private life, home, family and correspondence). He also contended that "although his extradition was not unlawful under English law, the lawfulness of his detention under Article 5, paragraph 1 (f), of the Convention pending extradition was fundamentally tainted by virtue of the unlawfulness of the tape-recordings under French law".[90]

The Commission, by a majority, disagreed and found the application to be manifestly ill-founded and hence inadmissible. In the course of its decision the Commission remarked:

The purpose of the extradition proceedings in which the United Kingdom authorities were involved was to further the international campaign against the drugs trade and the laundering of the proceeds of drug trafficking, and those proceedings were pursuant to the United Kingdom's international treaty obligations (in this case to the United States of America). Moreover, while the unlawfulness alleged in respect of the recordings in the present case is, at least, in some doubt, the domestic courts clearly considered the evidence of the tapes and transcripts to be relevant. In these circumstances, the Commission finds that the use made by the United Kingdom authorities in the present case of the recordings of the applicant's conversations does not disclose any lack of respect for his private and family life, his home or his correspondence.[91]

Given its relative novelty, the jurisprudence under the ECHR relating to the confiscation of the proceeds of crime is, in contrast to the investigative restraints on law enforcement agencies, still at a fairly early stage of evolution. However, decisions of both the Commission[92] and the Court[93] relating to Italian confiscation measures have upheld their consistency with the right to property enshrined in Article 1 of Protocol No. 1. For example, in 1991 the Commission held "that the confiscation of nearly all the property of a suspected member of the Camorra (including the property of his wife and children) pending his trial on mafia charges was compatible with the right to property".[94] In its 1994 judgment in the case of Raimondo, which is likely to prove to be highly influential, the Court addressed a number of relevant issues in the area of both seizure and confiscation. In the latter context it made the following revealing statement:

> The Court is fully aware of the difficulties encountered by the Italian State in the fight against the Mafia. As a result of its unlawful activities, in particular drug trafficking, and its international connections, this "organisation" has an enormous turnover that is subsequently invested, *inter alia*, in the real property sector. Confiscation, which is designed to block these movements of suspect capital, is an effective and necessary weapon in the combat of this cancer. It therefore appears proportionate to the aim pursued (...).[95]

A range of other Convention issues is also raised by some of the draconian confiscation legislation enacted by European states. For example, the case of *Welch* v. *United Kingdom* related to a submission that a confiscation order imposed under the Drug Trafficking Offences Act of 1986 was retroactive in nature and thus violated Article 7 of the Convention. This provides, *inter alia*, that no "heavier penalty be imposed than the one that was applicable at the time the criminal offence was committed". In its report of 15 October 1993 the Commission, which was evenly split, decided on the casting vote of the Acting President that the United Kingdom had not exceeded its competence in this regard.[96] However, in its 1995 judgment the Court unanimously disagreed.[97] It concluded that such a confiscation order was properly classifiable as a penalty for the purposes of

Article 7 and that its retroactive application must, therefore, be regarded as a breach of that fundamental obligation.[98]

It should be stressed that the Welch judgment did not directly call into question the compatibility of the rebuttable post-conviction presumption, contained in the same enactment, that property currently held or acquired in the previous six years was the proceeds of drug trafficking. This issue was, however, central to the subsequent application of one Bryan Leslie Elton against the United Kingdom.

The applicant had been convicted of drug offences in 1993 and a confiscation order had been made pursuant to the provisions of the 1986 Act. Having exhausted his domestic remedies in the United Kingdom, he invoked the Strasbourg machinery of protection. In particular, he complained that the making of the confiscation order had violated his rights under Article 6 (2) which provides thus: "Everyone charged with a criminal offence shall be presumed innocent until proved guilty according to law". In September 1997 the Commission held, unanimously, that the complaint was manifestly ill-founded and that the application was thus inadmissible.

In arriving at this determination the Commission, citing the 1988 judgment of the Court in *Salabiaku* v. *France*,[99] stressed that the ECHR did not prohibit recourse to presumptions in the sphere of criminal law so long as they were confined within reasonable limits which took into account the importance of what was at stake and maintained the rights of the defence. It also recalled that in the Welch case the Court had stated, in paragraph 36, that its judgment "does not call into question in any respect the powers of confiscation conferred on the courts as a weapon in the fight against the scourge of drug trafficking".[100]

Although the great majority of issues arising before the control mechanisms in Strasbourg relate to the consistency of domestic law and practice with the requirements of the Convention, it is of relevance to recall that both the Commission and the Court have also revealed a willingness to subject arrangements for international co-operation in criminal matters to critical scrutiny. For example, "[i]n the Soering case the European Court has held that both Article 3 (prohibition of torture or inhuman or degrading treatment or punishment) and 6 (right to a fair trial) of the European Convention can be applicable to extradition. This decision is of crucial importance: it indicates that, in the future, extradition relations, at least for the member states of the Council of Europe, may in part be governed by general human rights instruments".[101] This case, which arose out of extradition proceedings involving the United Kingdom and the United States, also underlines the fact that the ECHR remains relevant, in certain circumstances, even when the violation would take place in a state which has not become formally subject to its obligations.

The potential of the ECHR to have an impact on the co-operative relation-ships between states which are and those which are not parties to it is of obvious relevance in the context of the 1990 money laundering convention which, as we have seen, is open to non-Council of Europe countries. The jurisprudence on the extraterritorial application of the ECHR is by no means fully developed and it continues to emerge from time to time.[102] For exam-ple, the 1992 case of *Drozd and Janousek* v. *France and Spain*[103] dealt, in part, with prisoner transfer arrangements between Andorra and France. The former, in which the proceedings subject to challenge had taken place, was not then a member of the Council of Europe or a party to the ECHR. These facts did not, however, make the ECHR irrelevant. In the view of the Court:

> As the Convention does not require the Contracting Parties to impose its stan-dards on third States or territories, France was not obliged to verify whether the proceedings which resulted in the conviction were compatible with all the requirements of Article 6 of the Convention. To require such a review of the manner in which a court not bound by the Convention has applied the principles enshrined in Article 6 would also thwart the current trend towards strengthen-ing international co-operation in the administration of justice. (...) The Contracting States are, however, obliged to refuse their co-operation if it emerges that the conviction is the result of a flagrant denial of justice (...).[104]

This brief discussion of the ECHR will, it is hoped, have provided a timely reminder that those charged with elaborating measures to counter money laundering and other forms of serious crime do not, and should not, have a completely free hand. They must balance the law enforcement goals which they wish to pursue against the need for all members of society to be protected against the use of arbitrary state power. At least for the mem-ber states of the Council of Europe there exists a relatively effective mech-anism to ensure that the proper balance is, in fact, struck.

Notes: V

1. Benyon, J., *et al*, *Police Co-operation in Europe: An Investigation*, Leicester, 1993, p. 177.

2. Tarschys, D., "The Council of Europe: strengthening European security by civilian means", Nato Review, 1997, p. 4, at p. 8.

3. See, e.g., Muller-Rappard, E., "The European System", in Bassiouni, M.C., (ed.), *International Criminal Law*, Dobbs Ferry, New York, 1989, Vol. II, at pp. 95-119.

4. Also of significance in this context is Resolution (97) 24 on the twenty Guiding Principles for the Fight against Corruption which was adopted by the Committee of Ministers on 6 November 1997.

5. Csonka, P., "Organised and Economic Crime (An Overview of the Relevant Council of Europe Activities)" in Cullen, P. and Gilmore, W., (eds.), *Crime sans Frontières: International and European Legal Approaches*, Edinburgh, 1998, p. 93, at p. 97.

6. "Outline of the OCTOPUS II Programme". Council of Europe doc. Octopus (98) 59, 27 October 1998, p. 1.

7. See Anderson, M., et. al., *Policing the European Union*, Cambridge, 1995, Chapter 7.

8. Wilkitzki, P., "Development of an Effective International Crime and Justice Programme – A European View", in Eser, A., and Lagodny, O., (eds.), *Principles and Procedures for a New Transnational Criminal Law*, Freiburg, 1992, p. 267, at p. 291.

9. "Measures Against the Transfer and Safekeeping of Funds of Criminal Origin: Recommendation No. R. (80) 10 adopted by the Committee of Ministers of the Council of Europe on 27 June 1980 and Explanatory Memorandum". Reproduced in Gilmore, W., (ed.), *International Efforts to Combat Money Laundering*, Cambridge, 1992, p. 169, at p. 171.

10. Id., p. 169.

11. Id., p. 170.

12. Nilsson, H., "The Council of Europe Laundering Convention: A Recent Example of a Developing International Criminal Law", *Criminal Law Forum*, 1992, p. 419, at p. 423.

13. See, e.g., Carlson, S., and Zagaris, B., "International Co-operation in Criminal Matters: Western Europe's International Approach to International Crime", *Nova Law Review*, 1991, p. 551, at pp. 565-567. See also, "Origin, Functioning and Achievements of the Pompidou Group", Council of Europe, Strasbourg, 1997. A Political Declaration and work programme for the period to 2000 were adopted by a Pompidou Group Ministerial Conference in Norway in May 1997.

14. "Explanatory Report on the Convention on Laundering, Search, Seizure and Confiscation of the Proceeds from Crime". Reproduced in Gilmore, W., (ed.), op. cit., p. 192, at p. 192. (hereafter E.R.).

15. Nilsson, op. cit., p. 423.

16. E.R., p. 195.

17. Id., p. 197.

18. Id., p. 193.

19. Id., p. 204.

20. See generally, Organised and International Crime Directorate, Home Office, *Confiscation and Money Laundering: Law and Practice – A Guide for Enforcement Authorities*, London, 1997.

21. See the Law of the Republic of Latvia on Laundering of Proceeds from Crime, adopted on 18 December 1997.

22. See Art. 13.

23. "Money Laundering and Associated Issues: The Need for International Co-operation". UN Doc. E/CN.15/1992/4/Add. 5; 23 March 1992, pp. 22-23. See also, Levi, M., "Regulating Money Laundering: The Death of Bank Secrecy in the UK", *British Journal of Criminology*, 1991, p. 109 *et seq.*

24. *Supra*, note 20, p. 69.

25. E.R., p. 103.

26. See Scottish Law Commission, *Confiscation and Forfeiture*, Edinburgh, 1994 (Scot. Law Com. No. 147).

27. For the position in Scots law, see generally, Brown, A.N., *Proceeds of Crime: Money Laundering, Confiscation and Forfeiture*, Edinburgh, 1996.

28. See 1998 Criminal Law Convention on Corruption, Art. 19 (3).

29. See 1998 Convention on the Protection of the Environment through Criminal Law, Art. 7.

30. E.R. p. 205.

31. *International Legal Materials*, 1987, p. 1637, at p. 1690.

32. Reproduced as Appendix A to Gilmore, W., "Police Co-operation and the European Communities: Current Trends and Recent Developments", in *Action Against Transnational Criminality: Papers from the 1993 Oxford Conference on International and White Collar Crime*, London, 1994, p. 147, at pp. 154-156.

33. "Financial Action Task Force on Money Laundering: Annual Report 1995-96", p. 8.

34. Nilsson, op. cit., p. 434.

35. See, id., at p. 435. But see, to the same general effect Art. 12 of the 1971 UN Convention for the Suppression of Unlawful Acts against the Safety of Civil Aviation.

36. Id., p. 433.

37. See, e.g., Art. 13 (4). But see, Art. 18 (4) (b).

38. See E.R., at p. 198.

39. See Art. 13 (1).

40. See E.R., at pp. 217-218.

41. See id., at pp. 218-219.

42. See, e.g., Zander, M., *Confiscation and Forfeiture Law: English and American Comparisons*, London, 1989.

43. See, *Re JL: the Drug Trafficking Offences Act (Designated Countries and Territories) Order 1990, The Times*, 4 May 1994 (Q.B.D.).

44. E.R., p. 214.

45. "Action Plan to Combat Organised Crime", *Official Journal of the European Communities*, No. C 251/1. 15.8.97, Part III, Ch.III, Rec. 13. Reproduced in full as Appendix VII of this study.

46. See "Conclusions and Recommendations" of the Council of Europe Conference on Money Laundering in States in Transition, Strasbourg, 29 November-1 December 1994 (hereafter the Transition Conference), (typescript), p. 2.

47. "Financial Action Task Force on Money Laundering: Annual Report 1996-97", Annex A, p. 11.

48. See *Select Committee of Experts on the Evaluation of Anti-Money Laundering Measures (PC-R-EV): Annual Report 1997-98*, Strasbourg, 1998, Appendix E, pp. 38-40.

49. See Council of Europe doc. M-MINT (98) 8, 6 November 1998, p. 2.

50. See, e.g., Nadelmann, E., *Cops Across Borders: The Internationalisation of US Criminal Law Enforcement*, University Park, Pennsylvania, 1993, p. 389; and Zagaris, B., and Kingma, E., "Asset Forfeiture International and Foreign Law: An Emerging Regime", *Emory International Law Review*, 1991, p. 445, at p. 467.

51. "Financial Action Task Force on Money Laundering: Annual Report 1991-92", p. 20.

52. See, id.

53. "Financial Action Task Force on Money Laundering: Annual Report 1992-93", p. 22.

54. "Financial Action Task Force on Money Laundering: Annual Report 1993-94", at p. 26.

55. See, *supra*, note 47, at p. 24.

56. "Second Commission Report to the European Parliament and the Council on the implementation of the Money Laundering Directive", Commission of the European Communities, COM (1998) 401 final, Brussels, 1 July 1998, p. 6.

57. *Supra*, note 47, Annex A, p. 11.

58. Id., p. 12.

59. Id., p. 25.

60. *Supra*, note 48, p. 3.

61. See, id., at pp. 3-4.

62. See, id., pp. 10-21.

63. Id., p. 3.

64. See, *id.*, Appendix D, p. 37.

65. For the composition and functioning of the Bureau, see, *id.*, p. 5.

66. Id., p. 1.

67. Id., p. 22.

68. Dolle, S., "The Potential Impact of the European Convention on Human Rights". Paper presented to the Council of Europe Money Laundering Conference, Strasbourg, 28-30 September 1992, (typescript), p. 2.

69. Gomien, D., *Short Guide to the European Convention on Human Rights*, Strasbourg, 2nd ed., 1998, p. 5.

70. E.R., p. 231.

71. Id., pp. 206-207.

72. Id., p. 222.

73. See, e.g., Wilson, R., "Human Rights and Money Laundering: The Prospect of International Seizure of Defence Attorney Fees", *Criminal Law Forum*, 1991, at p. 85-103.

74. E.R., p. 208.

75. See, id., at p. 207.

76. See generally, Harris, D.J., O'Boyle, M., and Warbrick, C., *Law of the European Convention on Human Rights*, London, 1995.

77. Shaw, M., *International Law*, Cambridge, 4th ed., 1997, p. 260.

78. See, e.g., Finnie, W., "Rewriting the European Convention on Human Rights", *Scots Law Times*, 1994, p. 389, at p. 389.

79. Id., p. 390.

80. "The European Court of Human Rights: Historical background, organisation and procedure". Information document issued by the Registrar of the Court and dated 4 January 1999, p. 2.

81. *Supra*, note 69, p. 140.

82. Schermers, H., "Human Rights in Europe", *Legal Studies*, 1986, p. 170, at p. 171.

83. Id., pp. 174-175. This is not to say, however, that the ECHR was regarded as entirely irrelevant in judicial proceedings. For example a significant jurisprudence was developed in relation to the impact of the ECHR in the area of statutory interpretation. See generally, Dickson, B., (ed.), *Human Rights and the European Convention: The Effects of the Convention on the United Kingdom and Ireland*, London, 1997.

84. Duffy, P., "The Police and the European Convention on Human Rights" (Directorate of Human Rights, Council of Europe, Strasbourg, 1992), p. 2.

85. See generally, Dolle, op. cit.

86. Case No. 17/1991/269/340.

87. Case No. 44/1997/828/1034, para. 36.

88. See, Decision of the Commission as to the Admissibility of Application No. 15199/89 by Nazir Chinoy against the United Kingdom.

89. See, e.g., *R. v. Governor of Pentonville Prison, ex parte Chinoy*, [1992] 1 All E.R. 317.

90. Dolle, op. cit., p.7.

91. *Supra*, note 88, p. 9.

92. See, *M. v. Italy* (No. 12386/86; Dec. 15/4/91).

93. Case of *Raimondo v. Italy* (1/1993/396/474), Judgment of 22 February 1994.

94. Dolle, op. cit., p. 8.

95. *Supra*, note 93, p. 13.

96. See, *Welch v. United Kingdom* (No. 17440/90; 15/10/93).

97. Reproduced at 20 E.H.R.R. 247. See also, Andrew, J., and Sherlock, A., "Council of Europe: European Court of Human Rights", *European Law Review*, 1996, pp. 83-86.

98. The apparent scope and severity of the limitation on state action so imposed was somewhat limited by the 10 September 1997 decision of the Commission as to the admissibility of Application No. 31209/96 by Ronald J. M. Taylor against the United Kingdom.

99. Series A, No. 141, p. 16, para. 28.

100. Decision of the Commission as to the admissibility of Application No. 32344/96 by Bryan Leslie Elton against the United Kingdom.

101. Van den Wyngaert, C., "Applying the European Convention on Human Rights to Extradition: Opening Pandora's Box?", *International and Comparative Law Quarterly*, 1990, p. 757, at p. 759.

102. See, e.g., Lush, C., "The Territorial Application of the European Convention on Human Rights: Recent Case Law", *International and Comparative Law Quarterly*, 1993, at pp. 897-906.

103. (21/1991/273/344), Judgment of 26 June 1992.

104. Id., p. 32.

CHAPTER VI – ACTION WITHIN THE EUROPEAN UNION

The context

Since the 1970s the members of the European Union[1] (as it is now known) have sought to promote closer co-operation among themselves in order to combat criminal activities with a transfrontier dimension. Prior to the entry into force of the Treaty on European Union, commonly known as the Maastricht Treaty, on 1 November 1993, discussions relating to such matters took place primarily within the framework of European Political Co-operation. As will be seen in greater detail below, Title VI of the Maastricht Treaty took this process further by making extensive provision for inter-governmental co-operation in the key fields of justice and home affairs.[2] Among the matters formally deemed to be of "common interest", Article K.1 mentions judicial and customs co-operation, combating fraud and drug addiction, and "police co-operation for the purposes of preventing and combating terrorism, unlawful drug trafficking and other serious forms of international crime, including if necessary certain aspects of customs co-operation, in connection with the organisation of a Union-wide system for exchanging information within a European Police Office (Europol)". Pursuant to Article K.2, such matters are to be dealt with in compliance with the European Convention on Human Rights (ECHR) and the 1951 Geneva Convention relating to the Status of Refugees.

However, these arrangements continue to rely primarily on the traditional intergovernmental mechanism rather than on Community initiatives and legislation to secure progress.[3] The competence of the Community in this respect remains limited. As the relevant commissioner was to note in an address to the World Ministerial Conference on Organised Transnational Crime, held in Naples in November 1994: "The Treaty on European Union does not attribute to the European Community, and thus not to its Commission either, any direct role in the field of judicial co-operation in criminal matters or in the field of police co-operation. We do not have our own police force, nor any of the other traditional law enforcement instruments".[4]

It should be noted that a further element of complexity in this general context arises out of the Treaty of Amsterdam which was signed on 2 October 1997 but has yet to enter into force. As Walker has put it, "this latest amendment to the constitutional architecture of the European Union responds to a general chorus of criticism to the effect that lack of involvement of Community institutions in the Third Pillar has compromised its effectiveness. It does so by announcing a new chapter on the so-called "area of freedom, security and justice'. Within this chapter are to be found both a new EC treaty title on visas, asylum, immigration and other matters related to free movement of persons, most of which competences have been transferred from the Maastricht Third Pillar, and also a revised and truncated version of the Third Pillar restricted to police and customs co-operation and judicial co-operation in criminal matters".[5] A further notable feature concerns the decision to incorporate the so-called Schengen *acquis*.[6] The changes agreed to in the Treaty of Amsterdam are, in the present context, relevant primarily to the evolving mandate of Europol and will be returned to when that matter is addressed at a later stage of this chapter.

While the emphasis to date has been on securing incremental advances in the justice and home affairs sphere through intergovernmental co-operation, on occasion the constituent agreements have provided a basis on which the unification of the law of the member states through regulations, or its approximation through the use of directives, could be achieved. Such competences have provided the basis for Community action in a number of areas ranging from insider trading to the control of the trade in precursor and essential chemicals to prevent diversion for the production of illicit drugs. Of more immediate relevance, Articles 57 and 100a of the EEC Treaty provided the necessary legal basis for the Council directive of 10 June 1991 on Prevention of the Use of the Financial System for the Purpose of Money Laundering. It is to that important anti-money laundering initiative, the text of which is reproduced in Appendix VI, that this study now turns.

The 1991 directive

Background and development

Although the 1991 directive was the first legislative measure to be adopted by the EC in this area, it had been actively involved in earlier international initiatives. As we have seen at earlier stages of this work, the Commission participated in the negotiation of both the 1988 UN Convention Against Illicit Traffic in Narcotic drugs and Psychotropic Substances, which the EC has since ratified, and the Council of Europe 1990 Convention on Laundering, Search, Seizure and Confiscation of the Proceeds from Crime. Furthermore, along with all fifteen member states, it is an active participant in the FATF process. For this reason the drafters of the directive were well positioned to ensure that it reinforced rather than undermined the achievements which had been recorded in those other fora.

The directive, in contrast to the 1988 and 1990 precedents, fully embraces the preventative approach to money laundering. As a then leading official of the Directorate of Legal Affairs of the Council of Europe was to explain to the House of Lords Select Committee on the European Communities in late 1990, the two approaches are complementary: "In principle, the directive ends where the [1990] convention begins (with the criminal investigations)".[7] Thus, while the UN and the Council of Europe initiatives were directed to articulating a repressive approach towards this issue, the directive "is primarily addressed to credit and financial institutions and imposes obligations on them which are designed to ensure that laundering is detected before the stage of criminal investigation is reached".[8]

The trigger for Community action in this area was the perceived need to ensure "the integrity and cleanliness of the financial system"[9] in the light of moves towards the creation of the single market. As the House of Lords committee noted, the free movement of capital and financial services "offers great scope for organised crime as well as for legitimate enterprises".[10] Similarly, it was felt that "lack of Community action against money laundering could lead member states, for the purpose of protecting their financial systems, to adopt measures which could be inconsistent with completion of the single market".[11]

Before examining the actual requirements of the directive three points of general interest should be made. First, and, as was to be expected, its content has been heavily influenced by the countermeasures elaborated within the FATF context and, in particular, by the 1990 recommendations. This fact is recalled in the recitals to the directive and also finds specific mention in the domestic implementing legislation of certain member states such as the Netherlands.[12] Second, the intention has not been to create a system of "complete uniformity" in relation to the treatment of this issue at the national level.[13] As Dine has remarked, "directives are supposed to leave a measure of discretion to the member states as to the exact way to achieve the object described".[14] Indeed, Article 15 permits each country to adopt even stricter measures in this field if so wished. Finally, it was intended that the directive would have an impact beyond the internal borders of EU member countries. Of particular importance for present purposes is the fact that those European Free Trade Association (EFTA) countries which ratified the Agreement for a European Economic Space were obliged to give effect to its terms in domestic law. Thus, Austria, Finland and Sweden were not faced with the need to address this issue anew upon entry to the EU in January 1995. Similarly, in spite of the fact that the people of Norway rejected the possibility of EU membership in a referendum in late 1994, the need for compliance with the directive remained unaffected.

Requirements of the directive and their implementation

As with the 1990 Council of Europe convention, the directive recognises the fact that "since money laundering occurs not only in relation to the proceeds of drug-related offences but also in relation to the proceeds of other criminal activities (such as organised crime and terrorism), the member states should, within the meaning of their legislation, extend the effects of the directive to include the proceeds of such activities, to the extent that they are likely to result in laundering operations justifying sanctions on that basis". Thus, whilst the definition of laundering contained in Article 1 is derived from that used in the 1988 UN convention, it relates to "criminal activity" rather than merely serious drug trafficking offences. The term "criminal activity" is defined as "a crime specified in Article 3 (1) (a) of the Vienna Convention and any other criminal activity designated as such for the purposes of this directive by each member state".[15] Article 2 then requires all member states to ensure that laundering, as so defined, "is prohibited". As a result of differences of view as to the competence of an EC measure of this kind to require the imposition of a criminal penalty it was left to the members acting outside the Community framework to issue a statement on the same day in which they undertook: "to take all necessary steps by 31 December 1992 at the latest to enact criminal legislation enabling them to comply with their obligations".

While there was significant slippage in the time-frame for meeting this commitment, all members now comply with the minimum requirements. Furthermore, EU members have progressively accepted the invitation to extend money laundering beyond the drug trafficking sphere. Some countries, such as Greece, have done so in relation to other specified forms of serious crime while others, including Ireland, have legislated on an all crimes basis. The clear trend of moving away from a drug-specific focus in this area is well illustrated by the French law of 13 May 1996.[16] Indeed, such has been the extent of this transformation of governmental perception that in December 1998 it proved possible to reach agreement on a significant measure of harmonisation of approach. Acting within the framework of Title VI, a joint action has been adopted which seeks to ensure that no member state makes or upholds a reservation in respect of Article 6 of the 1990 Council of Europe convention in relation to serious offences. It provides that "[s]uch offences should in any event include offences which are punishable by deprivation of liberty or a detention order of a maximum of more than one year or, as regards those states which have a minimum threshold for offences in their legal system, offences punishable by deprivation of liberty or a detention order of a minimum of more than six months".

Following an examination of a 1995 Commission report on the implementation of the directive, the European Parliament in 1996 called on member states to extend the scope of their money laundering legislation to embrace "all money acquired from professional and organised crime".[17] Concern was also expressed in the course of the review that the directive did not "explicitly cover the proceeds of fraud against the budget of the European Union".[18] This matter was subsequently addressed in the second Protocol to the 1995 Convention on the Protection of the European Communities' Financial Interests. This protocol, adopted in June 1997, requires the criminalisation of laundering of the proceeds of such fraud, at least in serious cases, and of active and passive corruption.[19] Interestingly, this initiative also requires the states concerned to take measures to ensure that legal persons can be held liable when a variety of offences, including money laundering, are committed for their benefit in this context.[20]

Closely related to the question of the scope of the prohibition on money laundering is that of sanctions. In this area also there is no attempt to harmonise the penalties to be imposed for the infringement of any of the measures contained in the directive, including Article 2.[21] Consequently individual national practices differ considerably.[22] Notwithstanding this fact the Commission has indicated that it will monitor the practice of member countries in order to ensure that they comply with the principles of effectiveness, proportionality and dissuasion as articulated in the jurisprudence of the European Court of Justice.[23]

It is important to note that the decision has been taken to ensure that the directive applies to the whole financial system. This reflects the feeling that "partial coverage (...) could provoke a shift in money laundering from one to another kind of financial institutions".[24] So broad are the definitions of credit and financial institutions used in Article 1 that "virtually any financial intermediary such as credit institutions, life insurance companies, credit card issuers, leasing and factoring companies, bureaux de change etc. fall under the scope of the money laundering legislation".[25] It is appreciated that in some member states not all of these institutions are subject to supervision on a prudential basis and that this poses particular problems in ensuring effective implementation. The Commission has followed developments in this regard with particular care.[26] This concern is also shared by the wider membership of the FATF as reflected in the strengthened wording contained in Recommendation 8 agreed to during the recent stocktaking exercise.

Given the understandable focus of money laundering countermeasures on banks and other financial and credit institutions, it was inevitable that launderers would increasingly seek to utilise non-financial businesses and professions in an effort to avoid detection. This migration of funds has, in turn, been facilitated by the emergence of professional money launderers including "solicitors, attorneys, accountants, financial advisers, notaries and other fiduciaries whose services are employed to assist in the disposal of criminal profits".[27] Mindful of this possibility, Article 12 of the directive obliges member states to extend its provisions, in whole or in part, "to include those professions and undertakings whose activities are particularly likely to be used for money laundering purposes". National implementation practices differ considerably in this regard.[28]

Given the open-textured nature of this obligation the directive created, in the form of a contact committee, a mechanism through which an element of co-ordination and harmonisation of policy could be achieved in this area. Under the terms of Article 13 (d), one of the functions of this body is "to examine whether a profession or category of undertaking should be included in the scope of Article 12 where it has been established that such profession or category of undertaking has been used in a member state for money laundering". Discussions within the committee in this sphere have been guided by the need to "keep the balance between the burdens to be imposed and the real risk of money laundering".[29] Although it has had the possibility of formulating a common list of such professions and undertakings under consideration for some time, it has proved to be difficult to fashion a consensus. While there is broad agreement in principle on the need to extend coverage to the gaming industry (including casinos and bookmakers) and to dealers in high value items (such as real estate agents and jewellers) "the main sticking point remains the obligations to be imposed on certain professions and in particular the legal professions".[30] However, developments in other fora such as the European Parliament and the European Council have been such that it is likely that action on this point will be taken in the near future. The prospects for such changes to be embodied in a revised and extended directive are examined at a later stage of this chapter.

The first specific obligations imposed upon institutions covered by the directive relate to identification of customers and record keeping. As has been pointed out elsewhere: "Keeping records of customers and their transactions is an essential part of the audit trail procedures which the authorities require to assist them in tracking down the criminals and the illicit proceeds of their money laundering activities".[31] These measures are also designed to enable suspicious customers and transactions to be identified and reported to the appropriate national authorities for action to be taken. To these ends, Article 3 requires the identification of customers and beneficial owners when entering into business relations "particularly when opening an account or savings accounts or when offering safe custody facilities".[32] As was seen in Chapter IV, Austria has declined to abolish anonymous passbooks for Austrian residents – a stance deemed to be in conflict with FATF Recommendation 10. Not surprisingly this has also been regarded as being inconsistent with the obligations of that country under

Article 3 of the directive. Consequently the Commission has initiated infringement proceedings against Austria before the European Court of Justice.[33]

The identification requirement also applies to those engaging in one-off transactions at or above a threshold of 15000 ecus "whether the transaction is carried out in a single operation or in several operations which seem to be linked".[34] The latter is specifically designed to discourage the structuring of transactions, or "smurfing", in an effort to evade the identification obligation. Special derogation provisions have, however, been agreed in respect of the identification requirement in certain categories of insurance policy transactions.[35] As the European Commission has explained: "The exoneration from the identification requirements in small insurance operations and occupational pension schemes under certain conditions, as provided for in Article 3 (3) and (4) of the directive, were introduced by the Council following an amendment proposed by the European Parliament which was aimed at facilitating insurance operations involving very low risk of money laundering".[36] While a majority of EU members have taken full advantage of these exceptions, several have elected not to do so and, to that extent, have instituted policies stricter than those required by the directive.[37] However, it is specified in Article 3 (6) that: "Credit and financial institutions shall carry out such identification even where the amount of the transaction is lower than the thresholds laid down, wherever there is suspicion of money laundering".

While concrete expression is given by the directive to the "know your customer" principle it does not impose a standard method through which such identification requirements are to be satisfied. The decision as to the most appropriate way of making the procedure effective is left to each member country. This approach, which mirrors that taken by the FATF in its 1990 recommendations, was necessary given the diverse range of factual situations which are presented in practice. For example identification procedures for personal customers when opening accounts may need to be varied depending on whether the individual is resident or non-resident. Different considerations may apply in relation to the opening of "trust" accounts. An even greater range of possibilities will need to be catered for in the opening of accounts for legal persons. The resulting practice has been far from uniform. For example, in relation to personal customers the German Act of 25 October 1993 on the Detection of Proceeds from Serious Crimes provides, in section 1 (5), as follows:

> For the purposes of this Act, identification shall be the establishment of a person's name by means of an identity card or passport as well as the date of birth and the address to the extent that they are contained therein, and the determination of the type, number and issuing authority of the official identity document.

In contrast is the open textured approach adopted in the United Kingdom, a country where there is no compulsory official identity card and where many persons do not possess a passport. The 1993 Money Laundering Regulations therefore had to adopt a flexible position. This was done by requiring the production of "satisfactory evidence" of identity or "the taking of such measures (...) as will produce satisfactory evidence of (...) identity".[38] Regulation 11 (1) goes on to provide that "evidence of identity is satisfactory if (a) it is reasonably capable of establishing that the applicant is the person he claims to be; and, (b) the person who obtains the evidence is satisfied, in accordance with the procedures maintained under these regulations in relation to the relevant financial business concerned, that it does establish that fact". Extensive advice of a more practical nature is, however, provided as to what is deemed to constitute "good industry practice" in official guidance notes designed to cater for different parts of the private sector.[39] Also of relevance in this context is the obligation, contained in Article 3 (5) of the directive, to "take reasonable measures to obtain information as to the real identity of the persons on whose behalf" customers are acting when it is known or suspected that beneficial ownership rests elsewhere.

In the period since the directive was promulgated, there has been increasing concern within the FATF that its 1990 recommendations were not sufficiently robust in ensuring that corporations and other legal persons could not be utilised by individuals as a means of operating what were, in effect, anonymous accounts. Further consideration of this matter resulted in a strengthening of what had been Recommendation 12 by incorporating specific steps which should be taken in the identification of legal persons. The new recommendation (now Recommendation 10), agreed to in June 1996, reads in relevant part thus:

> In order to fulfil identification requirements concerning legal entities, financial institutions should, when necessary, take measures:
>
> i. to verify the legal existence and structure of the customer by obtaining either from a public register or from the customer or both, proof of incorporation, including information concerning the customer's name, legal form, address, directors and provisions regulating the power to bind the entity;
>
> ii. to verify that any person purporting to act on behalf of the customer is so authorised and identify that person.

As was seen in Chapter IV, the recommendations of the FATF are to be read in conjunction with the various "interpretative notes" which have been formulated to clarify their application. One such note is directed towards the identification of beneficial owners of legal entities. In this context "financial institutions should, if the information is not otherwise available through public registers or other reliable sources, request information – and update that information – from the customer concerning principal owners and ben-eficiaries. If the customer does not have such information, the financial institution should request information from the customer on whoever has actual control. If adequate information is not obtainable, financial institu-tions should give special attention to business relations and transactions with the customer". It will be of interest to see if an initiative is taken by the European Commission to achieve a further harmonisation of approach in this area. It would appear to be more likely, however, that it will leave the issue of compliance to be monitored through the self-assessment and mutual evaluation procedures of the Task Force.

In other areas covered by Article 3, national implementation practices dif-fer – sometimes considerably. Indeed, on occasion elements of flexibility have been introduced which appear to go beyond that permitted by the text. One example is provided by Article 3 (7) which creates an exemption "where the customer is also a credit or financial institution covered by this directive". It is clear from the wording used that this only extends to insti-tutions "covered by this directive"; namely, those located in the fifteen member states of the EU and, as will be seen below, in those European Free Trade Association (EFTA) countries which are part of the European Economic Area. However, the 1995 Commission report on implementation identified a minority practice of expanding the scope of this exemption. In its words: "Three member states have (...) opened the possibility of exon-erating under certain conditions third country credit and financial institu-tions: Luxembourg and the United Kingdom require these institutions to be subject to equivalent obligations to the directive; the Netherlands have empowered their Government to exonerate other categories of institu-tions".[40] Leaving aside the question of the legal justification (if any) for such initiatives, the wisdom of this approach is open to serious question. Take the issue of the identification of states with "equivalent" countermeasures. Clearly the mere utilisation of the list of FATF members would present con-siderable difficulties since not all of those countries have fully implemented the recommended countermeasures. The possibility of the EU reaching agreement on a common list of countries whose money laundering coun-termeasures could be regarded as being equivalent to those contained in the directive has been regarded thus far as being remote. It has also been felt that, even if such a consensus did emerge, it would have to be revisit-ed with some frequency to take account of developments in terms of implementation in many countries throughout the globe.[41] That being said the success of the external relations programme of the FATF has been such that it may, in time, offer a solution to this difficulty. The most recent ver-sion of the approach adopted in the UK may offer a way forward. Here the process of identifying those with equivalent legislation incorporates FATF members and third countries which have undergone successful mutual evaluations which have been validated by the Task Force. Such countries are listed in an annex to the guidance notes which is updated on a regular basis.[42] That listing is, in turn, supplemented by the identification of jurisdictions where the mutual evaluation procedures have indicated major issues of non-compliance as well as those where extreme caution should be exercised. In the June 1997 version, for instance, Austria and Turkey, both FATF members, were placed in the first category while the Seychelles was the sole entry in the latter.

Another area in which certain member states have resorted to a questionably excessive degree of flexibility is that of remote or non-face-to-face financial transactions such as those conducted by postal, telephonic or electronic means. In this regard Article 3 (8) of the directive contains only a very limited exemption from the general identification requirements. As the Commission has recalled: "This article allows member states to presume that the identification requirements regarding insurance operations have been fulfilled "when it is established that the payment for the transaction is to be debited from an account opened in the customer's name with a credit institution subject to this directive'. The rationale of this provision is that insurance companies should not be obliged to follow the identification procedures when the customer has already been identified by a credit institution holding the account through which the payment must be carried out".[43]

The contact committee has examined the adequacy of this exemption within the context of the practical issues posed in the sphere of customer identification in the case of remote financial operations more generally. The 1998 Commission report indicated that the committee "has agreed a number of principles to be applied to ensure that customers are adequately identified".[44] While the Commission appears to regard the overall customer identification regime as being generally satisfactory, it has acknowledged that it will have "to be kept under review with particular reference to the development of electronic transactions and financial services through new technologies".[45]

Closely allied to the requirements concerning identification is the obligation to retain certain records for specified periods of time in order to preserve the "audit trail" for use in any subsequent investigation. For example, pursuant to Article 4 credit and financial institutions must, in the case of transactions, keep "the supporting evidence and records, consisting of the original documents or copies admissible in court proceedings under the applicable national legislation for a period of at least five years following execution of the transactions". Though a new burden for some private sector concerns it was felt that, in the wider interest, such a step was essential.

Provisions were also inserted to ensure the due diligence of credit and financial institutions. In particular, they are obliged by Article 5 to "examine with special attention any transaction which they regard as particularly likely, by its nature, to be related to money laundering". It is clear from the drafting history of this measure, and from an examination of the text as a whole, that the intention was to give effect to Recommendation 21 of the FATF programme. In doing so it reaches two somewhat different sets of circumstances. First, it promotes a particular sensitivity to transactions involving third countries which apply no or insufficient anti-money laundering procedures. Second, it encourages the paying of special attention to unusual transactions having no apparent economic or visible lawful purpose. Given the extremely open-textured nature of the wording of Article 5, it was to be expected that its implementation would vary considerably among member states. France, Belgium and Portugal have, for example, introduced fairly exacting systems. By way of contrast a number of other member states "have not explicitly transposed this article apparently because the principle of enhanced diligence is implicitly encompassed in the implementation of other provisions of the directive, in particular Article 11 (1)".[46]

Articles 6, 7 and 10, considered by many to form the "cornerstone" of the directive, seek to ensure that the authorities responsible for combating laundering operations obtain the necessary level of co-operation in their work from both the institutions concerned and the relevant supervisory bodies. In so far as the former is concerned the directive embraces the view that the most effective means to accomplish this goal is through a system of mandatory reporting of suspicious transactions. To that end Article 6 requires credit and financial institutions to inform the authorities "on their own initiative, of any fact which might be an indication of money laundering".

The directive itself does not seek either to define or to give examples of suspicious transactions and the task of making the system both operational and effective is left to member governments. In this area, practice also differs considerably from country to country. In the United Kingdom the effort to give substance to the concept takes place in official guidance notes rather than in the body of the primary or secondary legislation. A broadly similar approach is followed in Germany. In the Netherlands the reporting obligation is keyed to the somewhat wider, but arguably more user-friendly, concept of unusual transactions. The question of whether or not a transaction should be regarded as unusual is assessed on the basis of established objective and subjective indicators. As has been noted elsewhere, these are "formulated and, where necessary, amended in close consultation with the relevant sectors".[47] When these reports are received by the relevant agency, the MOT, they are, in conjunction with information from a variety of other sources, subject to a process of investigation and analysis. Those then deemed to be suspicious are passed on to the police and judicial authorities for further action.[48] A further significant distinction in the approach to implementation relates to the use of the criminal law in this sphere. Thus, while the majority of member states have resorted to administrative law as the basis for giving effect to this obligation, the United Kingdom, Ireland and Denmark have adopted the view that failure to report should constitute a criminal offence.[49]

The directive also provides that institutions must, upon request, furnish the relevant authorities with all necessary information. The fact that such information has been transmitted must not, in order to safeguard the integrity of any subsequent investigation, be brought to the attention of the customer concerned or to that of any other third parties; an activity commonly known as "tipping off".[50] In respect of such disclosures by institutions, Article 9 provides them with an essential form of legal immunity from suit for breach of contract or other legal obligations such as customer confidentiality. The information itself may, under Article 6, "be used only in connection with the combating of money laundering. However, member states may provide that such information may also be used for other purposes".

The final element in the system of co-operation is contained in Article 7. This requires the relevant institutions to refrain from carrying out suspicious transactions until they have brought the matter to the attention of the appropriate authorities. It is up to such authorities to give instructions whether or not to execute the transaction. However, "[w]here such a transaction is suspected of giving rise to money laundering and where to refrain in such manner is impossible or is likely to frustrate efforts to pursue the beneficiaries of a suspected money laundering operation, the institutions concerned shall apprise the authorities immediately afterwards". The flexibility of Article 7 and its sensitivity to the needs of investigators is in contrast to the original Commission proposal which would have required institutions, in all circumstances, to refrain from executing suspect transactions.

It was recognised that in reaching out to and involving the private sector to such an unprecedented extent it would be necessary to ensure that those whose participation was required would, in fact, be in a position to play their role fully and effectively. To that end, the directive in Article 11 (1) obliges the institutions concerned to establish adequate internal control and communications systems. It is, however, silent on such fundamental practical issues as the type of system to be introduced and the responsibilities of those within it. In addition, and of the utmost importance, credit and financial institutions must, pursuant to paragraph 2 thereof: "take appropriate measures so that their employees are aware of the provisions contained in this directive. These measures shall include participation of their relevant employees in special training programmes to help them recognise operations which may be related to money laundering as well as to instruct them as to how to proceed in such cases". By way of illustration, the United Kingdom regulations concentrate the mind in this context by providing for a maximum penalty for failure to comply of two years imprisonment or a fine or both.[51] The importance of the need to foster staff awareness through training is, in turn, emphasised by the guidance notes and is increasingly being facilitated by the production by relevant institutions, industry associations, and others of specific training packages. The intended audiences range from senior management to bank clerks; the programmes from computer-assisted learning to videos.

Extraterritorial issues

The directive, though elaborated within the confines of the EU, was intended to have a broader geographic impact and for this reason certain of its provisions contain an extraterritorial dimension. Of special importance here is the definition of money laundering contained in Article 1. This is deliberately sensitive to the increasingly international character of the problem. It provides that "[m]oney laundering shall be regarded as such even where the activities which generated the property to be laundered were perpetrated in the territory of another member state or in that of a third country". The wider geographic relevance of the measure is also ensured by the decision, reflected in the same article, to subject Community-based branch offices of non-Community financial and credit institutions to its obligations. This stance was reflected in the German legislation of 1993 which simply stated: "A locally resident branch office of a foreign credit institution shall be deemed to be a credit institution. A locally resident branch office of a foreign financial institution shall be deemed to be a financial institution".[52]

Though not specifically required by the directive, some member states, including Germany, have subjected the branches of their financial institutions located abroad to home country rules to the extent that such rules are not inconsistent with the laws of the host state.[53] This stance, is consistent with FATF Recommendation 20 (formerly Recommendation 22).

Of greater importance is the fact that the directive applies to those European Free Trade Association (EFTA) countries which ratified the Agreement for a European Economic Area (EEA). Consequently, Austria, Finland and Sweden were not faced with the need to address this issue *de novo* upon entry to the EU in January 1995. Similarly the fact that Norway, Liechtenstein and Iceland are not EU members does not affect the need for them to comply with this measure. The eastward expansion of the influence of the directive has also been a feature of the strategy of the Commission in this sphere. This has been most obvious in the negotiation of "Europe Agreements" – association arrangements of the most advanced form – with various of the new democratic states of central Europe. In each of those concluded to date the Commission has insisted upon the inclusion of specific clauses on money laundering. For example, Article 86 of the 1993 agreement with the Czech Republic reads:

> 1. The parties agree on the necessity of making every effort and co-operation in order to prevent the use of their financial systems for laundering of proceeds from criminal activities in general and drug offences in particular.

> 2. Co-operation in this area shall include administrative and technical assistance with the purpose of establishing suitable standards against money laundering equivalent to those adopted by the Community and international fora in this field including the Financial Action Task Force (FATF).

Following upon the decision in principle to broaden the membership of the EU, the directive has taken on an even deeper significance for applicants. As the Commission has recently stated: "The money laundering directive is an integral part of the *acquis communautaire* and all candidate countries will be required to implement it. Efforts to assist in this process form part of the pre-accession strategy".[54] This emphasis has been strengthened and deepened by the 1998 Pre-Accession Pact on Organised Crime between the applicant countries and the member states of the EU. Principle 13 thereof expresses agreement that there should be not only full implementation of the directive but also of the FATF recommendations and the 1990 Council of Europe convention. In this manner, as Cullen has pointed out, the directive is gradually coming to provide "the basis for a comprehensive code of anti-laundering legislation throughout the continent of Europe".[55]

While the primary focus of the European Commission is on the countries of Europe, these are not its sole concern. It is convinced that "[t]he fight against money laundering has to be seen in global terms" and that "the anti-money laundering message be delivered and be heard in every country of the world".[56] To this end it has been involved in the financing of anti-laundering initiatives, the provision of technical assistance, and other anti-laundering efforts on an ever widening geographic basis. The Commission also seeks "to incorporate an anti-money laundering clause in all the agreements, of whatever type, it concludes with non-member countries. The standard clause refers to efforts and co-operation to avoid money laundering and to the establishment of suitable standards against money laundering equivalent to those adopted in the EU and in international fora such as the FATF".[57]

The future of the directive

There is, both within the Commission and in the FATF, a fairly high degree of satisfaction concerning formal compliance with the obligations of the directive by the fifteen member states of the EU. In its 1998 report to the European Parliament the Commission concluded that "this legislation has been applied conscientiously in all the member states".[58] The position regarding actual effectiveness, however, required more guarded wording. In its view:

> Despite the relative lack of statistics it can be concluded that while the financial sector's response has generally been good in terms of the number of suspicious transaction reports made to the competent authorities, it does not seem that this effort is at present being translated into large numbers of prosecutions, convictions or asset confiscations. The Commission would stress once again that the directive has an important preventative role and believes that the directive has been successful in making access to the EU's financial system more difficult for criminal money. At the same time it is clear that money laundering is going on and that suspicious transaction reports must be pinpointing a proportion of that criminal money. That being the case it has to be noted that the results beyond the directive in the police and judicial spheres appear to be limited, even if on the increase.[59]

Although further efforts by national authorities will be required in the future in order to seek to improve upon this somewhat mixed and incomplete picture, it has also come to be generally recognised that the directive itself is in need of updating. In this regard Financial Services Commissioner Mario Monti announced, on 13 July 1998, the intention to come forward with "proposals to extend and improve the current rules".[60] It is anticipated that the text, which is due after consultation with member states during 1999, will focus on three major issues.

The first of these is the perceived need for a wider prohibition of money laundering. As was seen at an earlier stage of this chapter, this is a matter on which member states have moved significantly beyond the minimum requirements of the directive. Here the issue is one of perception rather than a desire to impose significant new obligations. As the Commission has stated, the question arises "as to whether it is acceptable that the directive, which remains one of the basic international texts in this area, should fail so clearly now to reflect the current reality".[61]

The second area likely to receive treatment is the extension of the obligation to specific non-financial activities and professions which are considered to pose a serious risk of money laundering. A Commission press release of July 1998 indicated that it was examining, *inter alia*, "casinos, auditors, real estate agents and the legal professions when carrying out financial transactions on behalf of their clients".[62] An initiative in this area would have the advantage of bringing a degree of harmonisation of approach to national practices and would be of particular utility if it came to embody an agreed policy on the controversial issue of the application of anti-laundering measures to lawyers and notaries.

Finally, it is expected that the Commission will propose amendments which seek to enhance the exchange of information and co-operation between national bodies set up to receive suspicious transaction reports. As was seen in Chapter III, the 1991 directive was not alone in failing to include detailed treatment of Financial Intelligence Units (FIUs). As has been pointed out elsewhere, it "does not specify what form those bodies should take and, in contrast to other Community financial services legislation, does not contain provisions on professional secrecy and on the exchange of information".[63] As things stand at present, for example, the differing legal status enjoyed by FIUs in domestic law has had a negative impact on the ability to exchange information with counterpart agencies in other member states.[64] While it is acknowledged that it is not realistic, for technical and other reasons, for a comprehensive solution to this problem to be reflected in a new directive there is a growing perception that it could make a substantive contribution towards an overall solution. It could "perhaps set out some provisions for relations between the administrative FIUs while encouraging co-operation with and between those of a different type".[65]

Other relevant EU initiatives

As was mentioned earlier in this chapter, the member states of the EU have a longstanding tradition of co-operation in the criminal justice area. While some of this effort was directed to judicial co-operation issues, such as extradition, other initiatives had a far more immediate impact on practical law enforcement concerns. Of these, the creation in 1975 of the Trevi Group was of particular significance. As has been pointed out elsewhere: "Trevi's initial objective was to provide a basis for greater European co-operation to combat terrorism, but its role has developed to include co-operation over policing, drugs trafficking and other types of serious organised crime. Subsequently, consideration of the implications of the single European market and Europol were added to the Trevi Group's agenda".[66]

This effort, which took place on an intergovernmental basis outside the formal EC structure, involved ministers, senior officials and working groups. Working Group III on Serious Organised International Crime, established in 1975, is of interest in this context as its remit extends to both drug trafficking and money laundering. That these areas were afforded high priority within this grouping was underlined by a formal declaration issued by Trevi ministers meeting in Paris in December 1989.[67]

With the entry into force of the Maastricht Treaty, Trevi was absorbed by the new "Third Pillar" arrangements contained in Title VI. This, as we have seen, makes extensive provision for co-operation in a broad range of justice and home affairs issues. The specific tasks undertaken within the Trevi framework have thus been integrated into the new structure in which the so-called "K4 Committee" of senior officials plays a pivotal role.

While the processes of facilitating consultation and improving co-ordination under Title VI are directed to achieving the objectives of the EU, particularly the free movement of persons, it should be stressed that this takes place primarily on an intergovernmental basis. As has been stated elsewhere: "the general legal acts of the EC as laid down in Article 189 EC – regulation, directive and decision – cannot be used to enforce a policy in the framework of Title VI. Consequently, the provisions of Title VI basically do not automatically fall within the jurisdiction of the Court of Justice of the European Communities".[68] The manner in which progress is achieved continues to rely heavily on traditional diplomatic practices and to be governed primarily by international rather than EC law. This is of some importance in considering the moves in the 1990s towards the creation of a central European criminal intelligence office (Europol) – a development specifically contemplated in Article K.1 (9) of the Maastricht Treaty.

Although the background to this initiative is a complex one, it can be fairly said that it gained both momentum and political credibility as a consequence of the public support afforded to it by Germany. In May 1991 Chancellor Kohl, speaking in Edinburgh, argued strongly and publicly for a European police force "that would be able to operate without let or hindrance in all the Community countries in important matters such as the fight against drug barons or organised international crime".[69] This was followed by the discussion of a detailed German paper on the subject at the Luxembourg summit of EC heads of state and government on 28 and 29 June. Somewhat surprisingly the underlying thrust of the German paper was favourably received by the European Council which "mandated the Trevi group of ministers to report to the European Council in Maastricht in December 1991 with their proposals on how "Europol" should be set up and what preparatory or interim steps were required. This report was adopted by the Trevi Group which met at the same time as the European Council in Maastricht".[70]

Formal acceptance of the Europol concept was, as noted above, contained in the resulting Maastricht Treaty on European Union. It should be stressed, however, that the treaty provisions were less extensive and ambitious than those contained in the original German proposals. In particular, the treaty whilst embracing "a Union-wide system for exchanging information" made no provision for the exercise of executive policing powers on a supranational basis. This limitation, which was seen by many as necessary given the perceived absence of adequate political, legal and procedural structures needed for operational policing, was reinforced by the associated political declaration on police co-operation which indicated a willingness to adopt practical measures "in the exchange of information and experience".

Subsequent years have witnessed the phased, and often halting, process of making the Europol concept a practical reality. It commenced operations in February 1994 and its restricted initial mandate was "to act as a non-operational team for the exchange and analysis of intelligence in relation to illicit drug trafficking, the criminal organisations involved and associated money laundering activities affecting two or more member states".[71]

Following the Essen European Council in December 1994 it was decided to extend the Europol mandate to include illicit trafficking in radioactive and nuclear substances, illicit vehicle trafficking, and crimes involving clandestine immigration networks along with associated money laundering activities.[72] In 1996 its competence was extended to include trafficking in human beings.[73]

The most important objective, that of placing Europol on a firm and formal legal footing, was finally achieved with the conclusion, in July 1995, of a convention on the establishment of Europol, though the associated process of bringing it into full force and effect was not completed until October 1998. While a comprehensive analysis of this lengthy and complex text, along with its associated protocols, lies beyond the scope of this work, some of its more significant features should be noted.

First, the convention paves the way for a further broadening of its mandate. In this regard, it is specifically provided that within two years of entry into force of the convention Europol will start to "deal with crimes committed in the course of terrorist activities against life, limb, personal freedom or property".[74] An annex also contains an extensive list of additional forms of serious crime, ranging from fraud to environmental offences, which the member states, acting unanimously, can instruct Europol to deal with. It is of particular importance to note that its competence extends to "illegal money laundering activities in connection with these forms of crime or specific manifestations thereof".[75] Money laundering is, in turn, defined in its annex by reference to Article 6 of the 1990 Council of Europe convention.

The objective set by the convention is for Europol to improve the effectiveness of co-operation among member states in both preventing and combating crimes falling within its mandate "where there are factual indications that an organised criminal structure is involved and two or more member states are affected by the forms of crime in question in such a way as to require a common approach by the member states owing to the scale, significance and consequences of the offences concerned".[76] To this end, it has been given various tasks including facilitating the exchange of information and obtaining, collating and analysing information and intelligence.[77] In addition, as Mackarel has noted, "[a]lthough the Convention primarily establishes a basis for police co-operation between member states of the EU, it also contains limited provision for co-operation with 'outside' parties".[78] On this basis Europol has ambitious plans to develop an extensive network of relationships with non-member countries, Interpol and other relevant bodies.

The policy process in relation to police co-operation is, however, a dynamic one; a fact well illustrated by the conclusion of the Amsterdam Treaty which is expected to enter into force during 1999. As Walker has noted: "For its part, Europol is allocated a range of new functions, including authority to establish joint operational teams to support national investigations, the power to ask the competent authorities of the member states to conduct and co-ordinate investigations in specific cases, and the capacity to develop specific expertise which may be put at the disposal of member states to assist them in investigating organised crime ...".[79] In a money laundering specific context, the new Article K.2 of the Treaty on European Union which is provided for in the Amsterdam Treaty of 1997 seeks to promote more effective co-operation. Among other matters, its effort to develop common action in the area of police co-operation includes "the collection, storage, processing, analysis and exchange of relevant information, including information held by law enforcement services on reports on suspicious financial transactions, in particular through Europol, subject to appropriate provisions on the protection of personal data".[80]

While action under the Third Pillar has thus resulted in significant developments in the sphere of police co-operation, it has by no means been restricted to that area.[81] For example, it has been actively engaged in initiatives to improve various aspects of judicial co-operation and has achieved notable progress in the critical area of extradition.[82] Here the innovative convention of September 1996 has attracted considerable attention. As Hans Nilsson, the Head of the Division of Judicial Co-operation in the Council of the EU, has pointed out:

That convention (...) largely does away with principles of extradition law hitherto considered sacred by a number of member states. Extradition of nationals, renunciation of double criminality requirements for organised crime offences and of the political offence exception are all laid down as principles in the text of the most modern convention on extradition to date. The fact that these principles (which allow for certain exceptions) have been laid down in an instrument adopted by the European Union, demonstrates that it is possible among the like-minded member states of the Union to conclude far-reaching agreements even when negotiating under rules of unanimity.[83]

In so far as money laundering is concerned, much of the progress achieved in recent years has emerged out of the increasing concentration by the EU on the threat posed by organised crime. Various initiatives have been taken designed, directly or indirectly, to address this important issue. In so far as the latter is concerned one might mention, in addition to extradition, the Convention on the Protection of the European Communities' Financial Interests with its two protocols, and the 1997 Convention on the Fight against Corruption involving Officials of the European Communities or Officials of Member States of the European Union. Measures more specifically focused on organised crime as such include the 1995 and 1996 Council resolutions on witness protection and on individuals who co-operate with the judicial process in the fight against organised crime.

At the December 1996 Dublin European Council, the decisions were taken both to step up EU efforts to counter organised crime and to alter its strategy from one of reliance on *ad hoc* measures to co-ordinated action within the framework of a coherent and multifaceted programme. To these ends the Council "decided to create a high-level group to draw up a comprehensive action plan containing specific recommendations, including realistic timetables for carrying out the work"[84] The group was mandated to complete its work no later than April 1997.

To the surprise of many, its report, consisting of fifteen political guidelines and thirty detailed recommendations, was completed on time and the Action Plan to Combat Organised Crime was eventually approved by the Amsterdam European Council in mid-June. As the European Parliament was later to lament: "It is worth noting how the action plan originated, as it was developed for the Third Pillar, but outside its structures. No Council working group, not the K4 Committee or COREPER, not even the Justice and Home Affairs Council itself were able to change the content of the guidelines and recommendations drawn up by the high-level group. Even the European Council declined to make any changes. In these remarkable circumstances it is hardly surprising that Parliament was not included in drawing up the action plan either".[85]

Acting on the premise that "[i]f Europe is to develop into an area of freedom, security and justice, it needs to organise itself better, and to provide strategic and tactical responses to the challenge facing it"[86], the group decided to base its approach on a number of agreed factors. Within that context it then elaborated a series of political guidelines restricted to matters which it considered "appropriate to be drawn to the particular attention of heads of state and government, as they require commitment at the highest level".[87] The final element in the package was a detailed action plan; in essence a work programme which includes an ambitious timetable along with specific indications of the *locus* of responsibility for their implementation.

The detailed action plan is sub-divided as follows: an approach to the phenomenon of organised crime; prevention of organised crime; legal instruments, scope, implementation; practical co-operation between police, judicial authorities and customs in the fight against organised crime; development of a fully-fledged Europol and extension of Europol's mandate and tasks; and organised crime and money. As the European Parliament noted in the resolution which welcomed "in principle" the action plan, "it sets out, for the first time in the existence of the Third Pillar, the political guidelines underlying the Council's action in an important subject area and contains numerous comprehensive, coherent and concrete recommendations for the fight against organised crime together with a realistic timetable for their implementation".[88] However, the support given was far from unqualified.[89]

A comprehensive analysis of this initiative and of the criticisms of it lies beyond the scope of this work. For present purposes it will suffice to examine certain of those guidelines falling under the headings of "legal instruments, scope, implementation" and "organised crime and money".

Central to the approach adopted in the former is the identification of an extensive list of EU, Council of Europe and other multilateral conventions as "essential for the common fight against organised crime".[90] Target dates for ratification have been set with the added requirement that in the event of failure to comply the state concerned "shall report to the Council in writing on the reasons therefor every six months until the convention has been ratified". One such instrument is the 1990 Council of Europe money laundering convention. All EU members save Greece and Luxembourg met the target date of ratification; namely, the end of 1998. Emphasis is also placed on seeking to ensure the speedy completion of the negotiation of certain draft instruments, particularly a convention on mutual assistance in criminal matters, and in a manner which is sensitive to the difficulties encountered in the investigation and prosecution of transnational organised crime cases. It has also been agreed that in respect of such new conventions the Council should set a target date for their adoption and implementation.

To their credit the high-level group recognised that, while formal participation in such treaty regimes was a necessary condition for the provision of specific forms of international co-operation, it was not, in itself, sufficient to ensure effective and co-ordinated action. For this reason Political Guideline 3 requests the Council "to establish a mechanism, based on the experience with the model developed in the FATF for mutually evaluating the manner in which instruments concerning international co-operation in criminal matters are applied and implemented in each of the member states". Elsewhere in the action plan the principles on which this "peer evaluation" process are to be based are set out in summary form.

Following consultations with the European Parliament a joint action was adopted by the Council on 5 December 1997 establishing a mechanism for evaluating the application and implementation at national level of international undertakings in the fight against organised crime. This sets out in some detail the procedures which are to be followed at each stage of the process from the selection of evaluation subjects, through the nomination of the evaluation team and the discharge of its functions, to the discussion and adoption of the country reports and follow-up activity by the Council. In all of this the new Multidisciplinary Working Party on Organised Crime (MDW) – itself a creature of the action plan – is given a key role. The FATF precedent has been closely followed although it has been diverged from in certain respects. For instance while in both the FATF and EU processes the country reports are to remain confidential, in the former early agreement was reached that executive summaries were to be made public. These are contained in the annual reports of the group and can now, as noted in Chapter IV, be accessed through the Internet. By way of contrast, Article 9 (2) of the joint action provides that "the member state evaluated may publish the report on its own responsibility. It must obtain the Council's consent if it wishes to publish only parts of it".[91]

The action plan identified the general area of judicial co-operation as the priority focus for the mutual evaluation process. Following the entry into force of the formal mechanism, it was decided to commence with the important and highly practical issue of delays in mutual assistance, asset tracing and seizure of property. The first country mission ('on-the-spot evaluation') was due to take place in 1998. At least five evaluations are to be undertaken each year and provision has been made for the Council to review the process after the first full cycle of evaluations has been completed.[92]

The report of the high-level group anticipated that if the experience of mutual evaluation in relation to judicial co-operation proved to be positive it could "be extended to other areas of implementation".[93] It may be of interest to note that by the time that this review process takes place many of the members of the European Union are likely to have had further experience of such processes through participation in a Council of Europe initiative designed "to improve the capacity of its members to fight corruption by following up, through a dynamic process of mutual evaluation and peer pressure, compliance with their undertakings in this field". An agreement to establish the Group of States Against Corruption (Greco) – one which acknowledges the links between corruption, organised crime and money laundering – was finalised in 1998 and is expected to enter into force during 1999. One of the first formal arrangements to fall within the purview of this planned evaluation body will be the 1999 Council of Europe Criminal Law Convention on Corruption.

The final major element of that part of the action plan dealing with legal instruments takes the form of an undertaking "to adopt a joint action aiming at making it an offence under the laws of each member state for a person, present in its territory, to participate in a criminal organisation, irrespective of the location in the Union where the organisation is concentrated or is carrying out its criminal activity".[94] The intention here was to build upon the progress secured in this sphere by Article 3 of the September 1996 EU Extradition Convention. As the official explanatory report to that convention notes "the domestic laws of the member states lack homogeneous provisions criminalising the aggregation of two or more persons with a view to committing crimes. This is due to different legal traditions but does not amount to differences in criminal policy. These differences may make judicial co-operation more difficult".[95]

As an integral element of any such joint action would be common agreement on what constitutes a "criminal organisation", this would go some way towards meeting the criticism of the European Parliament that the action plan contained no definition of organised crime as such. Given the different legal and law enforcement traditions in this area it was anticipated that difficulties might be encountered in giving effect to this element of the programme. For that reason the action plan expressly provides that it would be "acceptable, for a limited period of time, that not all member states will be able to sign up immediately to the agreed definition".[96] Notwithstanding this element of flexibility, consensus proved to be elusive and the target date of the end of 1997 was not met. However, on 21 December 1998, agreement on this important and complex issue was finally achieved.[97] Progress has also been recorded in a number of other areas. For example, in late May 1998 – and some seven months within the deadline – the EU and the applicant countries concluded a pre-accession pact on organised crime.

The action plan also gives extensive expression to the importance of attacking the financial base of organised crime through the more effective use of confiscation of criminal proceeds and enhancing anti-money laundering systems. Several of the political guidelines are relevant in this context, as is Chapter VI of the detailed action plan entitled "organised crime and money".

Some of the developments envisaged in that chapter relate to the strengthening of the 1991 directive which was discussed in detail above. Similarly, a recommendation to enhance the role of Europol in the international exchange of information derived from suspicious transaction reports found expression, as we have seen, in the 1997 Treaty of Amsterdam. However, a range of issues remain within the ambit of the Third Pillar. Here again progress has been recorded.

Of particular significance in this regard is the joint action of 3 December 1998 on money laundering, the identification, trading, freezing, seizing and confiscation of instrumentalities and the proceeds from crime.[98] This seeks to build upon the anticipated participation of all fifteen member countries in the 1990 Council of Europe convention. As noted earlier, it seeks to ensure that no reservations are made or upheld by its members in relation to Article 6 of the convention "in so far as serious offences are concerned". It extends the same philosophy to Article 2 on the scope of domestic confiscation legislation (though there is an exception in respect of proceeds from tax offences).[99] A number of practical steps are also to be taken to enhance the effectiveness of co-operation. These range from the preparation of "user friendly" guides to national laws and practices to a requirement that the same priority be afforded to requests for assistance in this area as is given in domestic proceedings.[100]

A strategy to implement various other aspects of the action plan is being elaborated within the Third Pillar. Among the matters under consideration are the improvement of co-operation between tax authorities and those responsible for law enforcement, and the elaboration of measures to deal with the perceived abuse of offshore centres. Both of these issues, it will be recalled, also find reflection in concerns articulated by G-7 finance ministers in 1998 and have since found their way onto the work agenda of the FATF. Given the priority which has been afforded to such issues to date, as well as the highly constructive analysis carried out during 1998 by an informal group of experts on money laundering, it is to be anticipated that further concrete proposals for improving the effectiveness of anti-money laundering and related measures will emerge with some frequency in the months and years ahead.

Notes: VI

1. As of January 1998 the fifteen members were: Austria, Belgium, Denmark, Finland, France, Germany, Greece, Ireland, Italy, Luxembourg, the Netherlands, Portugal, Spain, Sweden, and the United Kingdom.

2. For a detailed discussion see, Anderson, M., et al., *Policing the European Union*, Oxford, 1995; and, Benyon, J., *et al.*, *Police Co-operation in Europe: An Investigation*, Leicester, 1993.

3. See, e.g., Dine, J., "European Community Criminal Law?" *Criminal Law Review*, 1993, pp. 246-354. See also, Schutte, J., "The European Market of 1993: Test for a Regional Model of Supranational Criminal Justice or of Interregional Co-operation in Criminal Law", *Criminal Law Forum*, 1991, pp. 5-83.

4. Speech of 21 November 1994. Text kindly supplied by the European Commission.

5. Walker, N., "European Policing and the Politics of Regulation" in Gilmore, W., and Cullen, P., (eds.), *Crime sans Frontières: International and European Legal Approaches*, Edinburgh, 1998, p. 141, at p. 144. See also, "Action Plan of the Council and the Commission on how best to implement the provisions of the Treaty of Amsterdam on an Area of Freedom, Justice and Security", *Official Journal of the European Communities*, No. C 19/1, 23.1.1999.

6. See, e.g., Schutte, J., "The Incorporation of the Schengen *Acquis* in the European Union"; and Genson, R., "The Schengen Agreements – Police Co-operation and Security Aspects", in Gilmore, W., and Cullen, P., (eds.), id., at p. 124 and p. 133 respectively.

7. Memorandum of H. Nilsson, in House of Lords, Select Committee on the European Communities, *Money Laundering*, H.L. Paper 6, 1990-91, Evidence, p. 35, at p. 37.

8. Cullen, P., "The European Community directive" in MacQueen, H.L., (eds.), *Money Laundering*, Edinburgh, 1993, p. 34, at p. 36.

9. See the 1990 Commission Proposal and Explanatory Memorandum, reproduced in Gilmore, W., (ed.), *International Efforts to Combat Money Laundering*, Cambridge, 1992, p. 243, at p. 244.

10. *Supra*, note 7, p. 5.

11. *Supra*, note 9, p. 251.

12. See, e.g., the Netherlands Disclosure of Unusual Transactions (Financial Services) Act of 16 December 1993.

13. See Cullen, op. cit, at p. 47.

14. Dine, op. cit., at p. 247.

15. Directive, Art. 1.

16. See also, Article 506-1 of the Luxembourg Criminal Code, inserted by the Luxembourg Act of 11 August 1998. Given the approach of the directive to the definition of money laundering it is perhaps not surprising that there has not always been an exact correspondence between the scope of the criminal offence and that of the legislation formulated to implement the directive. However, as the March 1995 report from the Commission to the European Parliament and to the Council on the implementation of the directive noted, there is evidence of increasing convergence between the two thus contributing to the elimination of "any hiatus between the member states" preventive and punitive systems as well as to facilitating interstate co-operation in this field" ("First Commission's report on the implementation of the money laundering directive (91/308/EEC) to be submitted to the European Parliament and to the Council". COM (95) 54 final, Brussels 03.03.1995, p. 6 (hereafter 1995 Commission report)).

17. "Report on the first Commission's report to be submitted to the European Parliament and to the Council on the implementation of the directive on the prevention of the use of the financial system for the purpose of money laundering". European Parliament doc. A4-0187/96 (hereafter 1996 European Parliament report), p. 5.

18. 1996 European Parliament report, p. 21.

19. See, *Official Journal of the European Communities*, No. C 221/11, Arts. 1 (e) and 2.

20. Id., Art. 3.

21. See directive, Art. 14.

22. See, e.g., Annex 7 to the 1995 Commission report.

23. See 1995 Commission report, at p. 16.

24. Reproduced in Gilmore, W., (ed.), op. cit., p. 243, at p. 244.

25. 1995 Commission report, pp. 6-7.

26. See 1995 Commission report at p. 7; and, "Second Commission Report to the European Parliament and the Council on the Implementation of the Money Laundering directive". COM (1998) 401 final, Brussels, 01.07.1998 (hereafter 1998 Commission report), at pp. 8-9.

27. FATF-VII Report on Money Laundering Typologies in "Financial Action Task Force on Money Laundering: Annual Report 1995-1996", Annex 3, p. 4.

28. See 1998 Commission report, Annex 6, pp. 39-40.

29. 1995 Commission report, p. 8.

30. 1998 Commission report, p. 10.

31. Vardon, L., "The Role of Investment Firms", in Parlour, R., (ed.), *Butterworths International Guide to Money Laundering Law and Practice*, London, 1995, p. 265, at p. 272.

32. Directive, Art. 3 (1).

33. See 1998 Commission report, at p. 7.

34. Directive, Art. 3 (2).

35. See directive, Art. 3 (3) and (4).

36. 1995 Commission report, p. 10.

37. See, 1995 Commission report, p. 10.

38. S.I. 1993, No. 1933, Reg. 7 (1).

39. For current practice and guidance, see Joint Money Laundering Steering Group, *Money Laundering Guidance Notes for the Financial Section [Revised and Consolidated June 1997]*, London, 1997, section 4.

40. 1995 Commission report, p. 10.

41. See 1995 Commission report, at pp. 10-11.

42. See *supra*, note 39, at R4.7-9, and Appendix D.

43. 1995 Commission report, p. 11.

44. 1998 Commission report, p. 12.

45. 1998 Commission report, p. 12. See also, p. 17.

46. 1995 Commission report, p. 12.

47. Westerweel, J., and Hillen, J., *Measures to Combat Money Laundering in the Netherlands*, The Hague, 1995, p. 5.

48. Ministry of Justice, Office for the Disclosure of Unusual Transactions (MOT), *The Fight Against Money Laundering*, The Hague, 1997, p. 20. See also, Schutte, J., "Police Co-operation", in Swart, B., and Klip, A., (eds.), *International Criminal Law in the Netherlands*, Freiburg im Breisgau, 1997, p. 145, at pp. 161-162.

49. See 1995 Commission report, at p. 13.

50. Directive, Art. 8.

51. See, *supra*, note 38, Regulation 5 (2).

52. Art. 1, s.1 (3) of the Money Laundering Act of 25 October 1993.

53. See 1995 Commission report, at p. 17.

54. 1998 Commission report, p. 6.

55. Cullen, op. cit., p. 49.

56. 1998 Commission report, p. 4.

57. 1998 Commission report, p. 7.

58. 1998 Commission report, p. 23.

59. 1998 Commission report, p. 25.

60. "Money Laundering: EU directive to be extended". Press Release, IP/98/654. Brussels 13 July 1998. The European Parliament also supports the need for a new directive. See generally, Committee on Legal Affairs and Citizen's Rights, "Report on the Second Commission Report to the European Parliament and the Council on the implementation of the Money Laundering Directive". European Parliament doc. A4-0093/99, 26 February 1999.

61. 1998 Commission report, p. 8.

62. *Supra*, note 60.

63. 1998 Commission report, p. 13.

64. See, e.g., 1998 Commission report, Annex 7, p. 41.

65. 1998 Commission report, p. 13.

66. Benyon, J. *et al.*, op. cit., p. 152.

67. See, id., at p. 157.

68. Muller-Graff, P.-C., "The Legal Bases of the Third Pillar and its Position in the Framework of the Union Treaty", *Common Market Law Review*, 1994, p. 493, at p. 495.

69. Kohl, H., "Our Future in Europe", Europa Institute, University of Edinburgh, 1991, p. 16.

70. Cullen, P., "The German Police and European Co-operation", Department of Politics, University of Edinburgh, 1992, p. 79.

71. Gilmore, W., "Police Co-operation and the European Communities: Current Trends and Recent Developments", in *Action Against Transnational Criminality: Papers from the 1993 Oxford Conference on International and White Collar Crime*, London, 1994, p. 147, at p. 156.

72. See joint action of 10 March 1995 concerning the Europol Drugs Unit. *Official Journal of the European Communities*, No. L62/1, 20.3.95.

73. See joint action of 16 December 1996 extending the mandate given to the Europol Drugs Unit. *Official Journal of the European Communities*, No. L342/4, 31.12.96.

74. See convention on the establishment of a European Police Office (Europol convention). *Official Journal of the European Communities*, No. C316/2, 27.11.95, Art. 2 (2).

75. Europol convention, Art. 2 (3) (1).

76. Art. 2 (1).

77. See Art. 3.

78. Mackarel, M., "Europol", *Scottish Law and Practice Quarterly*, 1996, p. 197, at p. 203.

79. Walker, op. cit., p. 145.

80. Art. K.2 (1) (b).

81. See generally, Barrett, G., (ed.), *Justice Co-operation in the European Union*, Dublin, 1997.

82. See, e.g., Vermeulen, G., and Vander Beken, T., "New Conventions on Extradition in the European Union", *Dickinson Journal of International Law*, 1997, p. 265.

83. Nilsson, H., "Co-operation in Justice and Home Affairs", in Cullen, P., and Gilmore, W., (eds.), op. cit., p. 116, at p. 120.

84. "Action Plan to Combat Organised Crime". *Official Journal of the European Communities*, No. C251/1, 15.8.97 (hereafter action plan), Part I, para. 2. Reproduced in full at Appendix VII. See also, Council Resolution of 21 December 1998 on the prevention of organised crime with reference to the establishment of a comprehensive strategy for combating it. *Official Journal of the European Communities*, No. C 408/1, 29.12.98.

85. *Report on the Action Plan to Combat Organised Crime: Committee on Civil Liberties and Internal Affairs*. European Parliament, Session doc. No. A4-0333/97, p. 18.

86. Action plan, Part I, para. 1.

87. Action plan, Part II, para. 8.

88. 1997 Resolution of the European Parliament on the Action Plan to Combat Organised Crime (7421/97-C4-0199/97), para. 9.

89. See, e.g., id., para.10.

90. Action plan, Part III, Recommendations 13 and 14.

91. Joint action of 5 December 1997 establishing a mechanism for evaluating the application and implementation at national level of international undertakings in the fight against organised crime. *Official Journal of the European Communities*, No. L344/7, 15 December 1997.

92. See, id., Art. 10.

93. Action plan, Part III, Recommendation 15.

94. Action plan, Part III, Recommendation 17.

95. *Official Journal of the European Communities*, No. C 191/13, 23 June 1997, p. 16.

96. Action plan, Part III, Recommendation 17.

97. See, joint action of 21 December 1998 on making it a criminal offence to participate in a criminal organisation in the member states of the European Union. *Official Journal of the European Communities*, No. L351/1, 29 December 1998.

98. *Official Journal of the European Communities*, No. L333/1, 9 December 1998.

99. See, id., Art. 1.

100. See, id., Arts. 2 and 3.

CHAPTER VII – WIDENING THE NET: AN OVERVIEW OF PROGRESS AND PROSPECTS IN OTHER REGIONS

The Caribbean basin

Well before the demise of the cold war and the problems of transition attracted attention to central and eastern Europe, the law enforcement community and money laundering experts had identified a number of jurisdictions and regions outside the developed financial elite represented by the members of the OECD as sources of concern. Of these, particular attention was devoted, even before the creation of the FATF, to the countries and territories of the Caribbean basin. As the Bureau of International Narcotics Matters of the US Department of State was to remark in March 1988: "The Caribbean basin is the first stop for most Latin American drug dollars moving through international channels. For both the foreign suppliers and their US distributors, the Caribbean basin has for long been a natural stop because of its proximity to the United States, high levels of corruption, and the region's many financial centres with secrecy laws and lenient taxes".[1] This latter aspect is deserving of comment. Confronted by an inadequate natural resource base and a marked decline in the viability of the agricultural sector, an increasing number of the small island states of the Caribbean have turned to the development of "offshore" financial services as part of their efforts to promote rapid economic diversification. Some of these efforts have met with spectacular success. By way of illustration: "In 1964 the Cayman Islands had two banks and no offshore business. By 1981 the Caymans had 360 branches of US and foreign banks, over 8 000 registered companies, and more telex machines per capita (...) than any other country".[2] It is now the world's fifth most significant financial centre. Other major players include Aruba, the Bahamas, the Netherlands Antilles and, in Central America, Panama.

The use of the range of facilities afforded by such emerging financial centres was of particular concern to the authorities of the United States. The absence of an established framework for co-operation and strict commercial confidentiality legislation gave rise to difficulties in efforts to secure vital evidence for use in US prosecutions. This resulted in an increasing readiness to resort to controversial unilateral measures.[3] Although such tactics not infrequently resulted in short-term success, this tended to be at the expense of creating a climate of conflict which strained international relationships.

By the mid-1980s, however, reliance on unilateral measures started to give way to an increased readiness to negotiate formal co-operative relation-ships on a bilateral basis. For example, in 1984 the US and the UK entered into an agreement which established a simple and straightforward proce-dure whereby the former could obtain assistance from the British depen-dent territory of the Cayman Islands in investigations and prosecutions involving drug trafficking. So positive was the experience of the parties with its practical operation that similar arrangements were concluded in respect of all of the remaining Caribbean dependencies of the UK. This experience of co-operation was to provide the foundations for efforts to deepen and widen the relationship; a process which was to lead to the con-clusion of a full mutual legal assistance treaty relating to the Caymans which entered into force in early 1990.[4] Somewhat similar bilateral devel-opments were recorded in respect of other jurisdictions including the Bahamas.[5]

It was within this context that the countries of the Caribbean and Central America met in Aruba in June 1990 in order to seek a common position on appropriate money laundering countermeasures. There the participants took note of the fact that trafficking networks had established a drug ser-vice industry within the region significant parts of which existed simply to facilitate the laundering of illicit proceeds. It was also acknowledged that as the United States and other highly developed industrialised countries moved to implement the recommendations of the FATF, the attractiveness of the region to criminal money managers was likely to increase. Consequently they "agreed to consider the forty recommendations of the Financial Action Task Force of the G-7 countries plus twenty-one addition-al recommendations".[6] The latter, since reduced to nineteen in number,[7] are complementary measures intended to address the problem as it has mani-fested itself in that area of the world.[8] Subsequently, the Eleventh Meeting of Heads of Government of the Caribbean Community (CARICOM), held in August 1990, discussed a number of issues relating to the financial aspects of drug trafficking and took note of the active participation of many of its members at the Aruba conference.[9] The Aruba meeting also resulted in the establishment of the Caribbean Financial Action Task Force (CFATF).[10]

This major regional precedent was reinforced by an anti-laundering region-al workshop which was hosted by the Government of Jamaica in May 1992.[11] This was then followed by a regional ministerial meeting held in Kingston, Jamaica, in November of the same year. At that meeting partici-pants "agreed that they would sign and ratify the 1988 UN Convention Against Illicit Traffic in Narcotic Drugs and Psychotropic Substances and fur-ther agreed to endorse and implement both the forty FATF recommenda-tions and the nineteen Aruba recommendations".[12]

This gathering also recognised the need to create a structure to monitor and encourage progress towards implementation of the Kingston Declaration. Both self-assessment and mutual evaluation processes were to be utilised. To further this aim and to facilitate the provision of training and technical assistance in the region, the meeting proposed the creation of a small CFATF secretariat to be based in Trinidad and Tobago.[13] With the financial support of a number of FATF "sponsoring countries" (Canada, France, the Netherlands, the United Kingdom, and the United States) this step was taken in early 1994.[14]

The membership of the CFATF, now in excess of twenty, is drawn from the independent states of the Commonwealth Caribbean, United Kingdom dependencies (known as Overseas Territories), the Dutch associated states and Spanish-speaking states from the Caribbean, and Central and South America. After a somewhat hesitant start this regional initiative has become firmly entrenched and has made significant progress in giving effect to an extensive programme of work. In particular, it is on course to complete its first round of mutual evaluations in the year 2000 at which stage it intends to commence a further round. It has, in addition, undertaken several typologies exercises.

In October 1996 the CFATF, following the expression of concern by some participants over its informal nature, adopted a memorandum of understanding (MOU).[15] This codifies its objectives and formalises its structures and procedures. The text of this instrument is reproduced in full at Appendix VIII. Article I addresses its objectives in the following terms:

> Members agree to adopt and implement effectively the 1988 UN Convention Against Illicit Traffic in Narcotic Drugs and Psychotropic Substances, endorse and implement the recommendations, fulfil the obligations expressed in the Kingston Declaration and, where applicable, the Plan of Action of the Summit of the Americas, and to adopt and implement any other measures for the prevention and control of the laundering of the proceeds of all serious crimes as defined by the laws of each member.

The MOU can be amended by the unanimous vote of a meeting of the CFATF Council.[16] The Council, which consists of one ministerial representative from each member, is the "supreme authority".[17] It includes among its functions the adoption of mutual evaluation reports, taking decisions on policy matters (including the adoption of revised recommendations)[18] and taking appropriate action with respect to members which fail to meet the organisation's standards.[19]

As noted above, the CFATF secretariat has from the outset been charged with responsibility for the identification of the training and technical assistance needs of participating countries and for facilitating and co-ordinating their provision. This aspect of its work is due to be substantially strengthened when it assumes the leading role in the implementation of an ambitious four-year joint US-EU anti-money laundering training and technical assistance initiative for the region.[20]

These developments have been assisted and reinforced by initiatives taking place under the auspices of the Organisation of American States (OAS) which includes among its members the independent states of the Caribbean basin. The OAS, it should be stressed, has for many years identified action to counter money laundering and to confiscate proceeds as critical to the fight against drug trafficking in the Americas. Thus, the April 1986 Inter-American Program of Action of Rio de Janeiro Against the Illicit Use and Production of Narcotic Drugs and Psychotropic Substances and Traffic Therein recommended the study of draft legislation designed: to strengthen the ability of the appropriate authorities to trace the origin of the funds; to criminalise drug-related laundering; and, "to forfeit assets derived from or used to facilitate drug trafficking, irrespective of where such trafficking occurred".[21] It also called for, among other measures, the creation of a regional Inter-American Drug Abuse Control Commission (CICAD).

In April 1990 a meeting of the ministers of member states responsible for the control of drug trafficking issued the Declaration and Program of Action of Ixtapa.[22] This both underlined the continuing importance attached to these law enforcement strategies and called upon CICAD to convene a group of regional experts to draft model regulations in this area which were in conformity with the 1988 UN Convention. Out of this process there emerged the Model Regulations Concerning Laundering Offences Connected to Illicit Drug Trafficking and Related Offences which were approved by the OAS General Assembly in 1992.

Both influenced by and compatible with the 1988 convention and the FATF recommendations, the original text consisted of some nineteen articles which addressed all of the key elements of a modern counter-strategy including the enhancement of the preventative role of the private sector.[23] In doing so they reached out to cover a broad range of financial institutions and activities in addition to banks. These included, among others, securities brokers, currency dealers and persons carrying out "any other activity subject to supervision by government bank or other financial institution authorities" (Article 9). The regulations can, when deemed advisable by the competent domestic authorities, be extended to encompass any other type of economic activity "when a transaction is carried out in cash and in excess of an amount specified" by such authorities (Article 16). Furthermore, the financial sector provisions, drafted with the 1990 FATF recommendations in mind, gave expression to familiar principles including those relating to customer identification, compliance with laws, co-operation with law enforcement agencies, and the introduction of internal compliance and training programmes by the institutions concerned. Finally, it should be noted that unlike the 1991 European directive and the Council of Europe convention, the 1992 model regulations were limited in their scope to drug trafficking and related offences. This was due, in the main, to the nature of the mandate given to the group of experts charged with elaborating them. However, the experts recommended that member states of the OAS consider applying them to laundering connected with other serious offences.

CICAD has actively promoted the adoption of these regulations by member countries of the OAS including those which are participants in the CFATF process.[24] Indeed, in the Kingston Declaration, Caribbean basin participants specifically agreed to consider adopting the OAS model regulations "as soon as possible". In this regard progress towards implementation has been recorded both by CFATF participants and within the wider OAS context. Indeed, by mid-1998 the OAS secretariat was able to report that the model regulations had been adopted by in excess of half of the CICAD membership.

Recent years have also witnessed significant developments at the policy level which have, in turn, found reflection in amendments to the model regulations and the commencement of discussions concerning, *inter alia*, the implementation within the region of a mutual evaluation procedure. These developments owe much to the Declaration of Principles and Plan of Action adopted by the December 1994 Summit of the Americas. Among other matters the action plan committed participating states to criminalise the laundering of the proceeds of all serious crimes and to work towards adopting the model regulations. In addition, they agreed to "[h]old a working-level conference, to be followed by a ministerial conference, to study and agree on a co-ordinated hemispheric response (...) to combat money laundering".[25]

Following working-level meetings held in Washington, D.C., ministers with responsibility for the money laundering issue drawn from thirty-four countries met in Buenos Aires in late 1995. They endorsed a declaration of principles and agreed to recommend a detailed and ambitious plan of action. The latter called for, among other matters, the criminalisation of the laundering of the proceeds of serious offences, the conclusion of asset-sharing agreements, the creation of national forfeiture funds to administer forfeited property, and the establishment of national FIUs. It also recorded the intention "to institute ongoing assessments of the implementation of this plan of action within the OAS framework".

In June of 1996 the CICAD Group of Experts to Control Money Laundering was reconvened to assist in the implementation of the December 1995 action plan. One matter to receive early attention was whether or not to amend the model regulations. Having concluded that such a modernising effort was called for, the group first turned its attention to the formulation of a new provision (Article 8 *bis*) which requires the establishment of FIUs in accordance with the Egmont Group definition. This initiative, approved in the course of 1997, has been followed by further updating efforts which have focused on a range of issues trailed by the ministerial meeting of December 1995 which were noted above.

Agreement has also been reached on the institution of an ongoing self-assessment procedure the results of which are subject to analysis by the group of experts. Perhaps more surprisingly the Second Summit of the Americas, held in Santiago in April 1998, agreed to move towards adopting a system of mutual evaluation in connection with drug trafficking and other related crimes. In the words of the action plan, governments will "with the intention of strengthening mutual confidence, dialogue and hemispheric co-operation (...) develop (...) a singular and objective process of multilateral governmental evaluation in order to monitor the progress of their individual and collective efforts (...)". It is understood that the possibility of taking such an initiative was subject to detailed discussion prior to the summit and that related matters have been considered since. The final outcome is still awaited. However, it is clear that the envisaged procedure will not be confined to – but will include – money laundering. It is the hope of many that "this multilateral approach will prove effective enough to win repeal of the United States' law requiring yearly, unilateral "certification" (...) of its neighbours' drug-fighting zeal".[26]

Within the context provided by CICAD, an annual money laundering typologies exercise is now carried out and a training and technical assistance plan is ongoing. This latter aspect has recently attracted the potentially significant support of the Inter-American Development Bank.[27] In addition, the OAS has projected the philosophy of taking the profit out of crime into new areas. Of particular relevance in this regard is the fact that the 1996 Inter-American Convention against Corruption acknowledges the links between the profit generated by drug trafficking and corruption. Article XV consequently requires the provision of "assistance in the identification, tracing, freezing, seizure and forfeiture of property or proceeds obtained, derived from or used in the commission of offences established in accordance with this convention".

Selected developments elsewhere

Another early priority area for the FATF's outreach programme was Asia. This regional concentration was primarily due to its pivotal role in the world trade in heroin based on the "Golden Crescent" and "Golden Triangle" production areas. It is also in the drugs sphere where progress has been most evident. A significant cross section of states, from Afghanistan in the west to the Peoples Republic of China in the east, have become parties to the 1988 UN Convention. These countries have either fully implemented their obligations to criminalise drug-related money laundering and provide for extensive international co-operation in relation to serious drug trafficking offences or claim to be in the process of doing so.

Less well entrenched thus far is a commitment towards enhancing the role of the financial sector in the effort to combat laundering or to broaden the agenda to include non-drug specific crimes. Part of the explanation lies in the vastness of the geographic area, the diversity which exists among its members in terms of socio-economic development, and the initial absence of a regional institution to promote and facilitate progress. To this must be added the level of complexity which results from the ready availability of extensive and efficient underground and parallel banking systems, of the types discussed in Chapter II, capable of acting either as a substitute for or as complement to the orthodox financial sector in international money laundering operations.

In these circumstances the FATF concentrated its efforts, as was seen in Chapter IV, on raising the level of awareness of regional policy makers and seeking to promote a momentum towards acceptance of its package of countermeasures which might eventually become self-sustaining. In this it was greatly assisted by the fact that it counts Hong Kong, Japan and Singapore among its own members. Of these, Hong Kong has the longest experience, has been the most innovative and effective, and the least conservative. However, its capacity to act as a regional catalyst was circumscribed by its status as a UK dependent territory and by its return to Chinese rule in 1997. Australia, and to a lesser extent New Zealand, also have special interests in securing progress in a region which is geographically proximate and of considerable economic and political importance to them. Recently, Japan has adopted a more positive and dynamic position.

As was noted in Chapter IV, in April 1993 the FATF combined with the Commercial Crime Unit of the Commonwealth secretariat to organise a major regional conference in Singapore. Subsequently the decision was taken to establish a small Asian money laundering secretariat to support the work of the FATF in the region. Throughout this early phase of development it was also recognised that the small island states of the Pacific faced many of the same challenges. Indeed, political leaders from those countries had collectively acknowledged the threat which they faced as a consequence of the growth of transnational criminal activity. Of particular significance in this regard was a declaration on law enforcement co-operation adopted by the South Pacific Forum in July 1992.

In this declaration they accepted that "there is a risk the South Pacific region may be targeted for such activities". Accordingly, they recommended that members consider the recommendations of the FATF and move towards the implementation of those which were deemed to be applicable to their individual circumstances. Significantly, for present purposes, the forum leaders also specifically "accepted the need to strengthen national and international legal provisions to enable the proceeds and instrumentalities of crime to be traced, frozen and seized, and acknowledged the need to regulate banking and other financial services to reduce the possible manipulation of these services to "launder" the proceeds of crime. The forum recognised that bank secrecy laws can be used as a shield for the laundering of criminal profits and determined that it should not be permitted to obstruct the operation of mutual assistance arrangements". Elsewhere in this document progress was urged in the modernisation of extradition legislation and in making appropriate statutory provision for mutual assistance in criminal matters. Furthermore, members agreed to afford priority to the ratification and implementation of the 1988 UN Convention Against Illicit Traffic in Narcotic Drugs and Psychotropic Substances – a step which Fiji, very much the regional leader, took in early 1993.

Eventually these two regions became fully linked for the purpose of anti-money laundering developments with the formal creation of the Asia/Pacific Group on Money Laundering (APG). It currently consists of sixteen members drawn from South, Southeast and East Asia and the South Pacific. As has been pointed out elsewhere: "In March 1998, the first annual meeting of the APG was held in Tokyo and attended by twenty-five jurisdictions from the region. A revised terms of reference was agreed, as well as an action plan for the future. The Tokyo meeting represented the full establishment of the APG as a cohesive regional group following on from the earlier awareness-raising efforts".[28] The terms of reference are reproduced in full at Appendix IX of this study.

Efforts to promote greater international co-operation in the administration of justice and an acceptance of the need for comprehensive anti-money laundering measures have also been undertaken by non-regional bodies. Of particular interest in this regard is the Commonwealth – an extensive grouping of states with close ties of history, language and legal tradition. Significantly for present purposes this body includes several Task Force participants (Australia, Canada, New Zealand, Singapore and the UK) in a membership dominated by developing countries many of which, as with the English-speaking states of Africa, are from regions where the FATF has to date had no representation.

The Commonwealth has for many years afforded priority to encouraging close co-operation in criminal matters and has elaborated arrangements dealing with extradition, the transfer of convicted offenders and like matters.[29] Of special relevance in this context is the 1986 Scheme Relating to Mutual Assistance in Criminal Matters (as amended in 1990).[30] Not only did this have a major impact in promoting an important mechanism of co-operation which had for long been neglected by the common law world, it also took the significant, and at the time innovative, step of making extensive provision for international action in tracing, seizing and confiscating proceeds on an all crimes basis.[31] Another highly relevant initiative was taken by Commonwealth heads of government, meeting in Malaysia in 1989 and again in Zimbabwe in 1991, when they welcomed the conclusion of the 1988 UN convention and urged its early ratification and implementation.[32]

Such actions have had a positive impact as an ever growing number of countries take the necessary steps to modernise their legislation. Take, for example, the southern African Republic of Botswana which is not considered to be either a money laundering centre or to be of any significance from a money laundering perspective.[33] It has none-the-less put in place legislation which creates the criminal offence of money laundering, provides for mutual assistance in the investigation and prosecution of money laundering, permits the confiscation of the proceeds of crime, and recognises money laundering as an extraditable offence.[34] Other illustrations of such responsible international conduct can be found among Commonwealth countries in southern Africa and elsewhere.

It is, however, also recognised that some of its developing country members – and in particular the small island states of the Caribbean and the Pacific – face particular difficulties in elaborating policy and modernising legislation in such a complex area. Accordingly the Commercial Crime Unit of the Legal and Constitutional Affairs Division of the Commonwealth secretariat has prepared a comprehensive model law for the prohibition of money laundering on which such countries can draw. It also provides a range of other forms of technical assistance to these and other members. All Commonwealth countries also benefit from the provision of constantly updated information on legislative, case-law and other relevant developments.[35]

The issue of money laundering has been considered with some frequency at the highest level. For instance, in October 1993 Commonwealth heads of government, at their meeting in Cyprus "commended" the forty FATF recommendations, "urged steps for their early implementation" and mandated law and finance ministers to examine the matter further.[36] The first opportunity to do so was provided by the meeting of Commonwealth law ministers which took place in Mauritius in November 1993. In the final communiqué ministers: "expressed their desire that this issue be addressed as a matter of urgency and their resolve, individually and collectively, to put in place comprehensive provisions criminalising money laundering in respect of the proceeds of all serious crimes, facilitating the disclosure by financial institutions of information giving rise to suspicion of money laundering activities, enabling confiscation of the proceeds of crime, making money laundering extraditable, and promoting international co-operation in the investigation and prosecution of money laundering and in confiscation proceedings".[37] They also collectively agreed to initiate a process of self-evaluation and mandated their senior officials to monitor, with the assistance of the London-based Commonwealth secretariat, the implementation of these measures. In September 1994 Commonwealth finance ministers, meeting in Malta, also instructed their senior officials to identify appropriate strategies and to review progress towards implementation. Since that time one round of self-evaluation has taken place in relation to legal issues while Commonwealth finance ministers have mandated two rounds in areas falling under their responsibility. As a May 1998 secretariat paper has noted: "These evaluations use exactly the same methods as those which are employed by the FATF and CFATF, first because they have proved successful and second to save work for these Commonwealth countries which are members of these other bodies".[38]

In June of 1998, a joint meeting of Commonwealth law and finance officials was convened in London to ensure that a co-ordinated approach to the money laundering issue was followed and to consider further measures which could be taken by members. Among the major issues discussed in the latter context was the strengthening of regional initiatives; a matter of particular significance given the decision, announced later the same month, of the FATF to emphasise this as a central feature of its new mandate. Importantly, as early as October 1996 the Commonwealth secretariat had joined with the FATF to sponsor the first Southern and Eastern African Money Laundering Conference. Convened in Cape Town and attended by thirteen African states, representatives agreed in principle to move towards the formation of a sub-regional task force. The Commonwealth has continued to facilitate discussion of this possibility which, even should it come to fruition, would leave much to be done in other parts of the continent. For example, in West Africa there has been little opportunity thus far for countries to work together on this issue in a structured and co-ordinated way.[39]

Conclusions

The primary focus for action beyond the confines of the restricted membership of the FATF was initially on the laundering of the proceeds of drug trafficking as represented by the ever-increasing spread of participation in the 1988 UN convention regime and the resulting implementation of its criminal justice obligations. However, more recently there has been a growing awareness that a broader multifaceted approach is required. As this selective overview has demonstrated, the extent to which this more comprehensive agenda has been embraced at the political and policy levels differs greatly both between and within the regions of the developing world. It is apparent from the western hemisphere experience that the encouragement of sophisticated market economy jurisdictions needs to be reinforced by enhanced and targeted provision of technical and other forms of assistance if the promise afforded by the current momentum is to be translated into reality.

Notes: VII

1. Bureau of International Narcotics Matters, US Department of State, *International Narcotics Control Strategy Report*, Washington, D.C., 1988, p. 45.

2. Nadelmann, E., "Negotiations in Criminal Law Assistance Treaties", *American Journal of Comparative Law*, 1985, p. 467, at p. 499.

3. See, eg, Gilmore, W., "International Action Against Drug Trafficking: Trends in United Kingdom Law and Practice", *International Lawyer*, 1990, p. 365, at pp. 380-381.

4. See id., at pp. 381-388.

5. This process continues. For example in mid-1998 the US Government submitted nineteen new MLATs to the Senate for approval. Of these eight were with Caribbean island states.

6. Zagaris, B., "Caribbean Financial Action Task Force Aruba Meeting Presages Co-operation by Caribbean Jurisdictions", *International Enforcement Law Reporter*, 1990, at pp. 217-218.

7. Recommendations 11 and 17 have been deleted.

8. Reproduced in Gilmore, W., (ed.), *International Efforts to Combat Money Laundering*, Cambridge, 1992, at pp. 25-30.

9. See Zagaris, B., and Kingma, E., "Asset Forfeiture International and Foreign Law: An Emerging Regime", *Emory International Law Review*, 1991, p. 445, at p. 477.

10. See Smellie, A., "The Work of the Caribbean Regional Division of the Financial Action Task Force", in *Action Against Transnational Criminality: Papers from the 1993 Oxford Conference on International and White Collar Crime*, London, 1994, at pp. 17-38.

11. See Gilmore, W., "Money Laundering: The International Aspect", in MacQueen, H.L., (ed.), *Money Laundering*, Edinburgh, 1993, p. 1, at p. 10.

12. The Kingston Declaration is reproduced in full by Smellie, op. cit., at pp. 34-37.

13. See, "Financial Action Task Force on Money Laundering: Annual Report 1992-93", p. 21.

14. See "Caribbean Financial Action Task Force: Annual Report 1994-95", p. 5.

15. See "Caribbean Financial Action Task Force: Annual Report 1995-96", at p. 4.

16. See Art. XIX.

17. See Art. VII (1).

18. The CFATF has had under consideration for some time the implications arising from the 1996 revisions to the FATF recommendations and, in particular, whether it would be necessary to formulate any interpretative notes to ensure that they could be applied within the region in an appropriate manner. See,

e.g., paper presented by the Chairman Designate of the CFATF to the Joint Meeting of Commonwealth Finance and Law Officials on Money Laundering, London 1-2 June 1998, Commonwealth Secretariat doc. SOMML (98) INF.3, at p. 8, and p. 12. At its November 1998 plenary meeting held in the Cayman Islands, the CFATF Council resolved to endorse the 1996 revisions to the FATF recommendations. It was also determined that the revised recommendations would be the benchmark for the second round of mutual evaluations.

19. See Art. VII (4) (x). See also, id., at p. 7.

20. See "Caribbean Prepares for New Anti-Laundering Program", *International Enforcement Law Reporter*, 1999, at pp. 49-50. This in turn gives practical effect to one element of the May 1996 Plan of Action for Drug Control Co-ordination and Co-operation in the Caribbean adopted in Barbados at a conference convened under UNDCP sponsorship.

21. Gilmore, W., (ed.), op. cit., p. 271.

22. Reproduced in relevant part in id., at pp. 290-295.

23. See, e.g., Jiminez, H., "Inter-American Measures to Combat Money Laundering", *International Enforcement Law Reporter*, 1992, at pp. 165-169; and, Solomon, P., "Are Money Launderers All Washed Up in the Western Hemisphere? The OAS Model Regulations", *Hastings International and Comparative Law Review*, 1994, pp. 433-455.

24. See "Presentation of the Executive Secretary of CICAD". Paper presented at the International Conference on Preventing and Controlling Money Laundering and the Use of the Proceeds of Crime, Courmayeur Mont Blanc, Italy, 18-20 June 1994 (hereafter the 1994 conference), (typescript).

25. See, Vol. 34, *International Legal Materials*, 1995, p. 808, at p. 820.

26. *The Economist*, London, 25 April 1998, p. 61, at p. 62.

27. See "Financial Action Task Force on Money Laundering: Annual Report 1997-98", at p. 33.

28. Id., p. 31.

29. See, e.g., Gilmore, W., "International Co-operation in the Administration of Justice: Developments and Prospects", in *Action Against Transnational Criminality: Papers from the 1992 Oxford Conference on International and White Collar Crime*, London, 1993, at pp. 147-154.

30. See McClean, J.D., *International Judicial Assistance*, Oxford, 1992, at pp. 149-164.

31. See id., at pp. 234-235.

32. See, e.g., Brown, A., "Money Laundering: International Law and the Commonwealth", *Commonwealth Judicial Journal*, 1994, p. 23, at p. 23.

33. See US Department of State, *International Narcotics Control Strategy Report*, Washington, D.C., 1998.

34. See Segopolo, S.M., "Mutual Assistance in Criminal Matters – Developing Country Perspectives", in *Action Against Transnational Criminality, supra*, note 29, at pp. 135-140.

35. See generally, Stafford, D., "Combating Transnational Crime: The Role of the Commonwealth", in Cullen, P., and Gilmore, W., (eds.), *Crimes Sans Frontières: International and European Legal Approaches*, Edinburgh, 1998, pp. 44-49.

36. Reproduced in *Commonwealth Law Bulletin*, 1993, p. 2003, at p. 2004. See also, p. 2006.

37. Id., p. 2009.

38. "The Promotion of Regional Groupings to Help Member Countries Accelerate Progress in Implementing Anti-Money Laundering Measures". Paper presented to the Joint Meeting of Commonwealth Finance and Law Officials on Money Laundering, London, 1-2 June 1998. Commonwealth Secretariat doc. SOMML (98) 8, p. 3.

39. See id., at p. 7.

CHAPTER VIII – CONCLUSIONS

In the course of the last decade there has been unprecedented action by the world community to combat what is perceived to be a significant and increasing threat from drug trafficking and other forms of serious crime. Those activities which generate significant profits and possess transnational features have been singled out for especially aggressive treatment. Furthermore, a broad consensus has emerged that both domestic and international strategies should be directed towards undermining the economic power of the criminals and organised crime groups involved.

In order to achieve this goal, three closely interconnected ingredients have been identified as essential. The first, and most orthodox, is based on enhancing domestic criminal justice systems in order to increase the "law enforcement risk". In addition to the traditional threat posed by prosecution and conviction for the underlying profit-generating offence this element of the strategy has come to emphasise the need to criminalise money laundering and to provide for the tracing and confiscation of the profits accumulated through involvement in illicit activities. These criminal justice measures are essentially offensive in nature and intent. Thanks to the innovative work of the Basle Committee, the Council of Europe, and the FATF, among others, they have come to be supplemented and complemented by a series of defensive or preventative measures which reach out to involve private sector actors to an extent never before attempted. Here, as we have seen, the policy seeks "to reduce the opportunities for accumulating profits through illicit activities, and to reduce the vulnerability of societies and governments to infiltration by organised crime".[1]

The final element of the strategy stems from the recognition that such is the ingenuity, sophistication and flexibility of modern money launderers, and of the organised crime groups whose needs they service, that domestic initiatives are, in and of themselves, necessary but insufficient preconditions for effective action. Greatly enhanced levels of international co-operation are essential if the "seizure risk" is not be rendered illusory when launderers make use, as they frequently do in practice, of the facilities of the global financial system in their efforts to disguise and break the money trail.

Progress towards the formulation and implementation of this multifaceted strategy has been greatly assisted by the importance which has been afforded to the issues of laundering and the confiscation of criminal proceeds at the highest political levels. They are matters which, far from remaining in the secretive confines of law enforcement discussions, now arise with considerable frequency at the meetings of heads of state or government and those of their ministerial colleagues. Such political support has produced the environment and created the momentum out of which concrete achievements have been recorded.

Progress at the global level has, as we have seen, been particularly impressive in the area of international drug trafficking. Here the 1988 UN convention deserves pride of place. Its requirement that drug-related money laundering be criminalised, its approach to the problem of bank secrecy, and the range of the obligations imposed in relation to the provision of international assistance have laid the foundations on which others, including the Council of Europe, have sought to build. The centrality of this UN precedent has been recognised, both explicitly and implicitly, by the highly influential package of countermeasures elaborated by the FATF.

The 1990 report of that specialised group was, of course, much more ambitious than the 1988 convention in its scope. Drawing upon earlier work undertaken by the Council of Europe and the Basle Committee, it contributed decisively to the broad acceptance which the preventative aspects of the strategy now enjoy. In this regard the relevant FATF recommendations have exercised a considerable influence on subsequent supportive initiatives undertaken by the EU, the OAS, the CFATF and others. Furthermore, the FATF has, in spite of its limited advanced financial centre jurisdiction membership, played a highly significant role in the continuing process of policy formulation, best illustrated by the 1996 revisions to its package of countermeasures, and in the equally important task of generating a much greater awareness of the complex issues involved.

With the advent of the second round of the mutual evaluation process, the Task Force entered into a phase in which the major concern has been with the effectiveness of the strategies put in place by its members rather than, as had previously been the case, with formal legislative, administrative and regulatory compliance therewith. In the course of the next few years, the Task Force will continue to emphasise this important aspect of its work. No further major alterations to its recommendations are expected to be considered prior to 2003. This should, in turn, ensure that its members can, individually and collectively, focus on how best to improve the somewhat disappointing results achieved thus far. As has been noted on various occasions throughout this study, when viewed in terms of activity measures, such as the total value of criminal funds confiscated or the number of money launderers convicted, it is clear that the actual results achieved to date have been, at best, mixed.

Such apparent defects in the operation of the anti-money laundering strategy continue to be regarded by governments and specialist inter-governmental bodies as being due to "implementation failure" rather than a more fundamental underlying "theory failure".[2] Consequently it is to be anticipated that the major emphasis in the short to medium term will fall on how best to improve its operation.[3] It is, for example, likely that further consideration will be given to the perceived benefits of following the example of countries such as the United States and Ireland in supplementing post-conviction confiscation with civil or *in rem* forfeiture.[4]

The issue of effectiveness cannot, however, be addressed solely within the confines of the world's leading financial centre jurisdictions. As *The Economist* noted in a leading article in July 1997: "Fighting money laundering is rather like tackling global warming: unless everybody joins in, there is little hope of curbing the problem".[5] To its credit the FATF has, from the outset, fully recognised this fact. Working in conjunction with other leading organisations and bodies with a mandate in the area of money laundering, it has actively promoted the greatest possible geographic spread of the anti-money laundering message. Largely as a consequence of these efforts, there are clear indications of an ever growing acceptance of the contention that "[e]very corner of the globe is affected by money laundering".[6] Although at its most advanced state in western Europe, substantial progress has also been achieved in central and eastern Europe, in the Caribbean and elsewhere. However, much remains to be done if the remaining gaps in the anti-money laundering net are to be closed. By way of illustration of the magnitude of this task, Pino Arlacchi, the Executive Director of the UN Office for Drug Control and Crime Prevention, proffered the view in mid-1998 that fewer than forty members of the international community had fully complied with the relevant obligations contained in the 1988 convention and other international anti-money laundering standards.[7] The highly ambitious regional strategy announced by the FATF in June 1998, which was examined in Chapter IV, is the major element of its plan to address this critical issue.

The execution of this strategy will not be without difficulty. For example, even when the political will to take action is present many nations face very real problems and constraints in enacting the complex domestic legislation and adapting administrative and regulatory systems in order to reflect best international practice. Making such a structure effective in operational terms will be even more demanding. Some appreciation of the nature and extent of the challenge faced by the states of central and eastern Europe will have been gleaned from this study. Great as those problems are they are of a different and lesser order of magnitude than those which confront many of the world's least developed countries, for which the complexity and sophistication of the countermeasures which have been elaborated sometimes seem to sit uneasily with domestic realities. Some of these diffi-culties can be tackled on the basis of a substantial programme of technical assistance and support. Others are essentially issues of social and econom-ic development and can be addressed properly only in the longer term and in that wider context. It is essential that the OECD and financial centre jurisdictions, individually and collectively, remain fully sensitive to such issues as they press for progress. A continued willingness to admit that, in spite of their best efforts, many of the major money laundering centres continue to be located in FATF jurisdictions will assist in the formulation of a balanced attitude.

These leading nations must also be prepared to adopt a flexible and con-structive stance when presented with initiatives from developing countries and states in transition which are intended to increase the relevance or improve the functioning of the strategy in the light of particular local or regional circumstances. Here the track record is not particularly encourag-ing. One example is provided by the debate within the UN on proposals to create an international criminal court. Although the idea that the interna-tional community should establish a judicial body to exercise criminal juris-diction over individuals, as opposed to states, has a lengthy history, it was not until it was revived by the Prime Minister of Trinidad and Tobago in the late 1980s that it came to gather substantial political momentum.[8] In tak-ing this step, the Trinidadian leader was responding to the magnitude of the problem posed by the international drugs trade for countries such as his own. As the Commonwealth Secretary General subsequently remarked, "small countries cannot often handle the complex, expensive and some-times dangerous consequences of a major trial involving international crim-inals".[9]

In spite of the considerable technical problems which arise as a conse-quence of moving beyond crimes under general international law,[10] the International Law Commission, to which the issues were remitted for expert study, suggested that the proposed international criminal court be given jurisdiction, under certain circumstances, over serious drug trafficking offences, including money laundering, which possess an international dimension. However, leading industrialised nations, including the United States and the United Kingdom, resisted this concession with the result that the Statute of the International Criminal Court, as approved in mid-1998, excludes such matters from its jurisdiction.

While the great majority of countries have indicated a willingness to adopt a positive approach to the notion of participation in the global fight against money laundering, a small minority has stood aside, at least in some mea-sure because of a desire to attract criminal money. Many would agree with Savona and De Feo that this group of countries "is inviting sanctions from the responsible elements of the world financial and law enforcement community, and deserve them".[11]

The question of sanctions and inducements has been discussed on occasion within the FATF. This was especially the case during the 1990-91 round of meetings. Among the options discussed at that time were the production of a "black list" of non-co-operative jurisdictions and, alternatively, the production of a "white list" of countries which had satisfactorily implemented its forty recommendations.[12] It was felt at that time that it was too early in the process to arrive at common and definitive assessments. Consequently, in its report of May 1991 it was decided to continue to rely on peer and public pressure to achieve the desired results. It was agreed, however, that should this approach not bear fruit "additional measures might be envisaged in the future".[13]

In subsequent years the emphasis has remained on providing help, assistance and encouragement. However, there appears to be growing sympathy for the view that the time has come to reconsider this position – to examine, with much increased seriousness, the benefits to be derived from the imposition of practical and progressive financial or political sanctions to reinforce efforts to effectively combat this form of serious transnational criminality. Various suggestions have been made as to the best strategy to adopt. These range from recourse to forms of economic warfare against the most delinquent states, as recommended by US Senator John Kerry,[14] to the formulation and enforcement "of a set of rules which will form the basis for full participation by any country in the international financial market", as proposed by Vito Tanzi of the IMF.[15] While, at the time of writing, no consensus on how to proceed in this difficult area had emerged within the Task Force, it has found its way back onto the agenda as a consequence of the unprecedented decision of G-7 finance ministers in May 1998 to refer to it for consideration aspects of the question of action to counter financial crime. It will be of interest to see if the work now being done within the FATF on non-co-operative countries and territories in this context paves the way for agreement on the identification of such jurisdictions and the imposition of countermeasures against them.

It is to be hoped, of course, that action of this kind will not have to be resorted to and that the widespread and increasing commitment of governments to participate as fully and effectively as possible in the fight against this form of serious criminality will eventually become, to all intents and purposes, universal. Even now the international community is in a position to take co-ordinated action against the financial power of drug trafficking networks and other criminal organisations of a kind to an extent which seemed hardly possible a decade ago. It should not be thought, however, that action against money laundering and the confiscation of proceeds constitutes, even potentially, some form of panacea of crime control. The strategy will not eradicate international drug trafficking or transnational organised crime. It will, however, create an increasingly hostile and inhospitable environment for the money launderer and others involved in highly lucrative forms of criminal behaviour and afford new elements of protection to economic and political systems. To achieve this is to achieve something of real and lasting value.

Notes: VIII

1. "National Legislation and its Adequacy to Deal with the Various Forms of Organised Transnational Crime: Appropriate Guidelines for Legislative and Other Measures to be Taken at the National Level". UN Doc. E/CONF.88/3; 25 August 1994, p. 2.

2. See, e.g., Gold, M., and Levi, M., *Money Laundering in the UK: an appraisal of suspicion-based reporting*, London, 1994, p. 91.

3. This is well illustrated by the nature and scope of the November 1998 draft report of the informal EU Money Laundering Experts Group submitted to the Multidisciplinary Working Group on Organised Crime.

4. See, e.g., "Financial Action Task Force on Money Laundering: Annual Report 1996-97", Annex B, at p. 12. See also, Organised and International Crime Directorate, Home Office, *Home Office Working Group on Confiscation: Third Report – Criminal Assets*, London, 1998, Ch. 4.

5. "Cleaning up dirty money", *The Economist*, London, 26 July 1997.

6. Sherman, T., "International Efforts to Combat Money Laundering: The Role of the Financial Action Task Force", in MacQueen, H.L., (ed.), *Money Laundering*, Edinburgh, 1993, p. 12, at p. 13.

7. UN Global Programme Against Money Laundering, *Attacking the Profits of Crime: Drugs, Money and Laundering*, Vienna, 1998, p. 10.

8. See, e.g., Patel, F., "Crime Without Frontiers: A Proposal For an International Narcotics Court", *New York University Journal of International Law and Politics*, 1990, at pp. 709-747.

9. Speech of the Commonwealth Secretary General to the September 1993 Oxford Conference on International and White Collar Crime, (typescript), p. 8.

10. See, e.g., Crawford, J., "The ILC's Draft Statute for an International Criminal Tribunal", *American Journal of International Law*, 1994, p. 140, at pp. 145-146; and, Gilmore, W., "The Proposed International Criminal Court: Recent Developments", *Transnational Law and Contemporary Problems*, 1995, p. 264.

11. Savona, E., and De Feo, M., "Money Trails: International Money Laundering Trends and Prevention/Control Policies". Paper presented to the International Conference on Preventing and Controlling Money Laundering and the Use of the Proceeds of Crime, Courmayeur Mont Blanc, Italy, 18-20 June 1994 (hereafter the 1994 Conference), (typescript), p. 101.

12. See "Proposals for the Future of the Financial Action Task Force: Report to the FATF from Working Group 3", in "Financial Action Task Force on Money Laundering: Annexes to the Report, 1990-91", at p. 6.

13. Reproduced in Gilmore, W., (ed.), *International Efforts to Combat Money Laundering*, Cambridge, 1992, p. 31, at p. 49.

14. See generally, Kerry, J., *The New War*, New York, 1997.

15. Tanzi, V., "Money Laundering and the International Financial System", IMF Working Paper, WP/96/55. May 1996, p. 12.

Notes VIII.

APPENDICES

APPENDIX 1 – THE 1998 UNITED NATIONS CONVENTION AGAINST ILLICIT TRAFFIC IN NARCOTIC DRUGS AND PSYCHOTROPIC SUBSTANCES

(Adopted by the Conference at its 6th plenary meeting, on 19 December 1988)

The Parties to this Convention,

Deeply concerned by the magnitude of and rising trend in the illicit production of, demand for and traffic in narcotic drugs and psychotropic substances, which pose a serious threat to the health and welfare of human beings and adversely affect the economic, cultural and political foundations of society,

Deeply concerned also by the steadily increasing inroads into various social groups made by illicit traffic in narcotic drugs and psychotropic substances, and particularly by the fact that children are used in many parts of the world as an illicit drug consumers market and for purposes of illicit production, distribution and trade in narcotic drugs and psychotropic substances, which entails a danger of incalculable gravity,

Recognising the links between illicit traffic and other related organised criminal activities which undermine the legitimate economies and threaten the stability, security and sovereignty of States,

Recognising also that illicit traffic is an international criminal activity, the suppression of which demands urgent attention and the highest priority,

Aware that illicit traffic generates large financial profits and wealth enabling transnational criminal organisations to penetrate, contaminate and corrupt the structures of government, legitimate commercial and financial business, and society at all its levels,

Determined to deprive persons engaged in illicit traffic of the proceeds of their criminal activities and thereby eliminate their main incentive for so doing,

Desiring to eliminate the root causes of the problem of abuse of narcotic drugs and psychotropic substances, including the illicit demand for such drugs and substances and the enormous profits derived from illicit traffic,

Considering that measures are necessary to monitor certain substances, including precursors, chemicals and solvents, which are used in the manufacture of narcotic drugs and psychotropic substances, the ready availability of which has led to an increase in the clandestine manufacture of such drugs and substances,

Determined to improve international co-operation in the suppression of illicit traffic by sea,

Recognising that eradication of illicit traffic is a collective responsibility of all States and that, to that end, co-ordinated action within the framework of international co-operation is necessary,

Acknowledging the competence of the United Nations in the field of control of narcotic drugs and psychotropic substances and desirous that the international organs concerned with such control should be within the framework of that Organisation,

Reaffirming the guiding principles of existing treaties in the field of narcotic drugs and psychotropic substances and the system of control which they embody,

Recognising the need to reinforce and supplement the measures provided in the Single Convention on Narcotic Drugs, 1961, that Convention as amended by the 1972 Protocol Amending the Single Convention on Narcotic Drugs, 1961, and the 1971 Convention on Psychotropic Substances, in order to counter the magnitude and extent of illicit traffic and its grave consequences,

Recognising also the importance of strengthening and enhancing effective legal means for international co-operation in criminal matters for suppressing the international criminal activities of illicit traffic,

Desiring to conclude a comprehensive, effective and operative international convention that is directed specifically against illicit traffic and that considers the various aspects of the problem as a whole, in particular those aspects not envisaged in the existing treaties in the field of narcotic drugs and psychotropic substances,

Hereby agree as follows:

Article 1

Definitions

Except where otherwise expressly indicated or where the context otherwise requires, the following definitions shall apply throughout this Convention:

    a. "Board" means the International Narcotics Control Board established by the Single Convention on Narcotic Drugs, 1961, and that

Convention as amended by the 1972 Protocol Amending the Single Convention on Narcotic Drugs, 1961;

b. "Cannabis plant" means any plant of the genus Cannabis;

c. "Coca bush" means the plant of any species of the genus Erythroxylon;

d. "Commercial carrier" means any person or any public, private or other entity engaged in transporting persons, goods or mails for remuneration, hire or any other benefit;

e. "Commission" means the Commission on Narcotic Drugs of the Economic and Social Council of the United nations;

f. "Confiscation", which includes forfeiture where applicable, means the permanent deprivation of property by order of a court or other competent authority;

g. "Controlled delivery" means the technique of allowing illicit or suspect consignments of narcotic drugs, psychotropic substances, substances in Table I and Table II annexed to this Convention, or substances substituted for them, to pass out of, through or into the territory of one or more countries, with the knowledge and under the supervision of their competent authorities, with a view to identifying persons involved in the commission of offences established in accordance with Article 3, paragraph 1 of the Convention;

h. "1961 Convention" means the Single Convention on Narcotic Drugs, 1961;

i. "1961 Convention as amended" means the Single Convention on Narcotic Drugs, 1961, as amended by the 1972 Protocol Amending the Single Convention on Narcotic Drugs, 1961;

j. "1971 Convention" means the Convention on Psychotropic Substances, 1971;

k. "Council" means the Economic and Social Council of the United Nations;

l. "Freezing" or "seizure" means temporarily prohibiting the transfer, conversion, disposition or movement of property or temporarily assuming custody or control of property on the basis of an order issued by a court or a competent authority;

m. "Illicit traffic" means the offences set forth in Article 3, paragraphs 1 and 2, of this Convention;

n. "Narcotic drug" means any of the substances, natural or synthetic, in Schedules I and II of the Single Convention on Narcotic Drugs, 1961, and that Convention as amended by the 1972 Protocol Amending the Single Convention on Narcotic Drugs, 1961;

o. "Opium poppy" means the plant of the species Papaver somniferum L;

p. "Proceeds" means any property derived from or obtained, directly or indirectly, through the commission of an offence established in accordance with Article 3, paragraph 1;

q. "Property" means assets of every kind, whether corporeal or incorporeal, movable or immovable, tangible or intangible, and legal documents or instruments evidencing title to, or interest in, such assets;

r. "Psychotropic substance" means any substance, natural or synthetic, or any natural material in Schedules I, II, III and IV of the Convention on Psychotropic Substances, 1971;

s. "Secretary-General" means the Secretary-General of the United Nations;

t. "Table I" and "Table II" mean the correspondingly numbered lists of substances annexed to this Convention, as amended from time to time in accordance with Article 12;

u. "Transit State" means a State through the territory of which illicit narcotic drugs, psychotropic substances and substances in Table I and Table II are being moved, which is neither the place of origin nor the place of ultimate destination thereof.

Article 2

Scope of the Convention

1. The purpose of this Convention is to promote co-operation among the Parties so that they may address more effectively the various aspects of illicit traffic in narcotic drugs and psychotropic substances having an international dimension. In carrying out their obligations under the Convention, the Parties shall take necessary measures, including legislative and administrative measures, in conformity with the fundamental provisions of their respective domestic legislative systems.

2. The Parties shall carry out their obligations under this Convention in a manner consistent with the principles of sovereign equality and territorial integrity of States and that of non-intervention in the domestic affairs of other States.

3. A Party shall not undertake in the territory of another Party the exercise of jurisdiction and performance of functions which are exclusively reserved for the authorities of that other Party by its domestic law.

Article 3

Offences and sanctions

1. Each Party shall adopt such measures as may be necessary to establish as criminal offences under its domestic law, when committed intentionally:

    a. i. The production, manufacture, extraction, preparation, offering, offering for sale, distribution, sale, delivery on any terms whatsoever, brokerage, dispatch, dispatch in transit, transport, importation or exportation of any narcotic drug or any psychotropic substance contrary to the provisions of the 1961 Convention, the 1961 Convention as amended or the 1971 Convention;

        ii. The cultivation of opium poppy, coca bush or cannabis plant for the purpose of the production of narcotic drugs contrary to the provisions of the 1961 Convention and the 1961 Convention as amended;

        iii. The possession or purchase of any narcotic drug or psychotropic substance for the purpose of any of the activities enumerated in i. above;

        iv. The manufacture, transport or distribution of equipment, materials or of substances listed in Table I and Table II, knowing that they are to be used in or for the illicit cultivation, production or manufacture of narcotic drugs or psychotropic substances;

        v. The organisation, management or financing of any of the offences enumerated in i., ii., iii. or iv. above;

    b. i. The conversion or transfer of property, knowing that such property is derived from any offence or offences established in accordance with subparagraph a. of this paragraph, or from an act of participation in such offence or offences, for the purpose of concealing or disguising the illicit origin of the property or of assisting any person who is involved in the commission of such an offence or offences to evade the legal consequences of his actions;

        ii. The concealment or disguise of the true nature, source, location, disposition, movement, rights with respect to, or ownership of property, knowing that such property is derived from an offence or offences established in accordance with subparagraph a. of this paragraph or from an act of participation in such an offence or offences;

   c. Subject to its constitutional principles and the basic concepts of its legal system:

     i. The acquisition, possession or use of property, knowing, at the time of receipt, that such property was derived from an offence or offences established in accordance with subparagraph *a.* of this paragraph or from an act of participation in such offence or offences;

     ii. The possession of equipment or materials or substances listed in Table I and Table II, knowing that they are being or are to be used in or for the illicit cultivation, production or manufacture of narcotic drugs or psychotropic substances;

     iii. Publicly inciting or inducing others, by any means, to commit any of the offences established in accordance with this article or to use narcotic drugs or psychotropic substances illicitly;

     iv. Participation in, association or conspiracy to commit, attempts to commit and aiding, abetting, facilitating and counselling the commission of any of the offences established in accordance with this article.

2. Subject to its constitutional principles and the basic concepts of its legal system, each Party shall adopt such measures as may be necessary to establish as a criminal offence under its domestic law, when committed intentionally, the possession, purchase or cultivation of narcotic drugs or psychotropic substances for personal consumption contrary to the provisions of the 1961 Convention, the 1961 Convention as amended or the 1971 Convention.

3. Knowledge, intent or purpose required as an element of an offence set forth in paragraph 1 of this article may be inferred from objective factual circumstances.

4. *a.* Each Party shall make the commission of the offences established in accordance with paragraph 1 of this article liable to sanctions which take into account the grave nature of these offences, such as imprisonment or other forms of deprivation of liberty, pecuniary sanctions and confiscation.

   b. The Parties may provide, in addition to conviction or punishment, for an offence established in accordance with paragraph 1 of this article, that the offender shall undergo measures such as treatment, education, aftercare, rehabilitation or social reintegration.

   c. Notwithstanding the preceding subparagraphs, in appropriate cases of a minor nature, the Parties may provide, as alternatives to conviction or punishment, measures such as education, rehabilitation or social reintegration, as well as, when the offender is a drug abuser, treatment and aftercare.

 d. The Parties may provide, either as an alternative to conviction or punishment, or in addition to conviction or punishment of an offence established in accordance with paragraph 2 of this article, measures for the treatment, education, aftercare, rehabilitation or social reintegration of the offender.

5. The Parties shall ensure that their courts and other competent authorities having jurisdiction can take into account factual circumstances which make the commission of the offences established in accordance with paragraph 1 of this article particularly serious, such as:

 a. The involvement in the offence of an organised criminal group to which the offender belongs;
 b. The involvement of the offender in other international organised criminal activities;
 c. The involvement of the offender in other illegal activities facilitated by commission of the offence;
 d. The use of violence or arms by the offender;
 e. The fact that the offender holds a public office and that the offence is connected with the office in question;
 f. The victimisation or use of minors;
 g. The fact that the offence is committed in a penal institution or in an educational institution or social service facility or in their immediate vicinity or in other places to which school children and students resort for educational, sports and social activities;
 h. Prior conviction, particularly for similar offences, whether foreign or domestic, to the extent permitted under the domestic law of a Party.

6. The Parties shall endeavour to ensure that any discretionary legal powers under their domestic law relating to the prosecution of persons for offences established in accordance with this article are exercised to maximise the effectiveness of law enforcement measures in respect of those offences and with due regard to the need to deter the commission of such offences.

7. The Parties shall ensure that their courts or other competent authorities bear in mind the serious nature of the offences enumerated in paragraph 1 of this article and the circumstances enumerated in paragraph 5 of this article when considering the eventuality of early release or parole of persons convicted of such offences.

8. Each Party shall, where appropriate, establish under its domestic law a long statute of limitations period in which to commence proceedings for

any offence established in accordance with paragraph 1 of this article, and a longer period where the alleged offender has evaded the administration of justice.

9. Each Party shall take appropriate measures, consistent with its legal system, to ensure that a person charged with or convicted of an offence established in accordance with paragraph 1 of this article, who is found within its territory, is present at the necessary criminal proceedings.

10. For the purpose of co-operation among the Parties under this Convention, including, in particular, co-operation under Articles 5, 6, 7 and 9, offences established in accordance with this article shall not be considered as fiscal offences or as political offences or regarded as politically motivated, without prejudice to the constitutional limitations and the fundamental domestic law of the Parties.

11. Nothing contained in this article shall affect the principle that the description of the offences to which it refers and of legal defences thereto is reserved to the domestic law of a Party and that such offences shall be prosecuted and punished in conformity with that law.

Article 4

Jurisdiction

1. Each Party:
   a. Shall take such measures as may be necessary to establish its jurisdiction over the offences it has established in accordance with Article 3, paragraph 1, when:
      i. The offence is committed in its territory;
      ii. The offence is committed on board a vessel flying its flag or an aircraft which is registered under its laws at the time the offence is committed;
   b. May take such measures as may be necessary to establish its jurisdiction over the offences it has established in accordance with article 3, paragraph 1, when:
      i. The offence is committed by one of its nationals or by a person who has his habitual residence in its territory;
      ii. The offence is committed on board a vessel concerning which that Party has been authorised to take appropriate action pursuant to Article 17, provided that such jurisdiction shall be exercised only on the basis of agreements or arrangements referred to in paragraphs 4 and 9 of that article;

iii. The offence is one of those established in accordance with Article 3, paragraph 1, subparagraph *c.*iv., and is committed outside its territory with a view to the commission, within its territory, of an offence established in accordance with Article 3, paragraph 1.

2. Each Party:

a. Shall also take such measures as may be necessary to establish its jurisdiction over the offences it has established in accordance with Article 3, paragraph 1, when the alleged offender is present in its territory and it does not extradite him to another Party on the ground:

i That the offence has been committed in its territory or on board a vessel flying its flag or an aircraft which was registered under its law at the time the offence was committed; or

ii. That the offence has been committed by one of its nationals;

b. May also take such measures as may be necessary to establish its jurisdiction over the offences it has established in accordance with Article 3, paragraph 1, when the alleged offender is present in its territory and it does not extradite him to another Party.

3. This Convention does not exclude the exercise of any criminal jurisdiction established by a Party in accordance with its domestic law.

Article 5

Confiscation

1. Each Party shall adopt such measures as may be necessary to enable confiscation of:

a. Proceeds derived from offences established in accordance with Article 3, paragraph 1, or property the value of which corresponds to that of such proceeds;

b. Narcotic drugs and psychotropic substances, materials and equipment or other instrumentalities used in or intended for use in any manner in offences established in accordance with Article 3, paragraph 1.

2. Each Party shall also adopt such measures as may be necessary to enable its competent authorities to identify, trace, and freeze or seize proceeds, property, instrumentalities or any other things referred to in paragraph 1 of this article, for the purpose of eventual confiscation.

3. In order to carry out the measures referred to in this article, each Party shall empower its courts or other competent authorities to order that bank, financial or commercial records be made available or be seized. A Party shall

not decline to act under the provisions of this paragraph on the ground of bank secrecy.

4. a. Following a request made pursuant to this article by another Party having jurisdiction over an offence established in accordance with Article 3, paragraph 1, the Party in whose territory proceeds, property, instrumentalities or any other things referred to in paragraph 1 of this article are situated shall:

   i. Submit the request to its competent authorities for the purpose of obtaining an order of confiscation and, if such order is granted, give effect to it; or

   ii. Submit to its competent authorities, with a view to giving effect to it to the extent requested, an order of confiscation issued by the requesting Party in accordance with paragraph I of this article, in so far as it relates to proceeds, property, instrumentalities or any other things referred to in paragraph I situated in the territory of the requested Party.

   b. Following a request made pursuant to this article by another Party having jurisdiction over an offence established in accordance with Article 3, paragraph I, the requested Party shall take measures to identify, trace, and freeze or seize proceeds, property, instrumentalities or any other things referred to in paragraph I of this article for the purpose of eventual confiscation to be ordered either by the requesting Party or, pursuant to a request under subparagraph a. of this paragraph, by the requested Party.

   c. The decisions or actions provided for in subparagraphs a. and b. of this paragraph shall be taken by the requested Party, in accordance with and subject to the provisions of its domestic law and its procedural rules or any bilateral or multilateral treaty, agreement or arrangement to which it may be bound in relation to the requesting Party.

   d. The provisions of Article 7, paragraphs 6 to 19 are applicable *mutatis mutandis*. In addition to the information specified in Article 7, paragraph 10, requests made pursuant to this article shall contain the following:

   i. In the case of a request pertaining to subparagraph a.i. of this paragraph, a description of the property to be confiscated and a statement of the facts relied upon by the requesting Party sufficient to enable the requested Party to seek the order under its domestic law;

   ii. In the case of a request pertaining to subparagraph a.ii., a legally admissible copy of an order of confiscation issued by the requesting Party upon which the request is based, a statement of the facts and information as to the extent to which the execution of the order is requested;

  iii. In the case of a request pertaining to subparagraph b., a statement of the facts relied upon by the requesting Party and a description of the actions requested.

e. Each Party shall furnish to the Secretary-General the text of any of its laws and regulations which give effect to this paragraph and the text of any subsequent changes to such laws and regulations.

f. If a Party elects to make the taking of the measures referred to in subparagraphs a. and b. of this paragraph conditional on the existence of a relevant treaty, that Party shall consider this Convention as the necessary and sufficient treaty basis.

g. The Parties shall seek to conclude bilateral and multilateral treaties, agreements or arrangements to enhance the effectiveness of international co-operation pursuant to this article.

5. a. Proceeds or property confiscated by a Party pursuant to paragraph 1 or paragraph 4 of this article shall be disposed of by that Party according to its domestic law and administrative procedures.

b. When acting on the request of another Party in accordance with this article, a Party may give special consideration to concluding agreements on:

  i. Contributing the value of such proceeds and property, or funds derived from the sale of such proceeds or property, or a substantial part thereof, to intergovernmental bodies specialising in the fight against illicit traffic in and abuse of narcotic drugs and psychotropic substances;

  ii. Sharing with other Parties, on a regular or case-by-case basis, such proceeds or property, or funds derived from the sale of such proceeds or property, in accordance with its domestic law, administrative procedures or bilateral or multilateral agreements entered into for this purpose.

6. a. If proceeds have been transformed or converted into other property, such property shall be liable to the measures referred to in this article instead of the proceeds.

b. If proceeds have been intermingled with property acquired from legitimate sources, such property shall, without prejudice to any powers relating to seizure or freezing, be liable to confiscation up to the assessed value of the intermingled proceeds.

c. Income or other benefits derived from:

  i. Proceeds;

    ii. Property into which proceeds have been transformed or convert-
       ed; or

    iii. Property with which proceeds have been intermingled

shall also be liable to the measures referred to in this article, in the same manner and to the same extent as proceeds.

7. Each Party may consider ensuring that the onus of proof be reversed regarding the lawful origin of alleged proceeds or other property liable to confiscation, to the extent that such action is consistent with the principles of its domestic law and with the nature of the judicial and other proceedings.

8. The provisions of this article shall not be construed as prejudicing the rights of bona fide third parties.

9. Nothing contained in this article shall affect the principle that the measures to which it refers shall be defined and implemented in accordance with and subject to the provisions of the domestic law of a Party.

Article 6

Extradition

1. This article shall apply to the offences established by the Parties in accordance with Article 3, paragraph 1.

2. Each of the offences to which this article applies shall be deemed to be included as an extraditable offence in any extradition treaty existing between Parties. The Parties undertake to include such offences as extraditable offences in every extradition treaty to be concluded between them.

3. If a Party which makes extradition conditional on the existence of a treaty receives a request for extradition from another Party with which it has no extradition treaty, it may consider this Convention as the legal basis for extradition in respect of any offence to which this article applies. The Parties which require detailed legislation in order to use this Convention as a legal basis for extradition shall consider enacting such legislation as may be necessary.

4. The Parties which do not make extradition conditional on the existence of a treaty shall recognise offences to which this article applies as extraditable offences between themselves.

5. Extradition shall be subject to the conditions provided for by the law of the requested Party or by applicable extradition treaties, including the grounds upon which the requested Party may refuse extradition.

6. In considering requests received pursuant to this article, the requested State may refuse to comply with such requests where there are substantial grounds leading its judicial or other competent authorities to believe that compliance would facilitate the prosecution or punishment of any person on account of his race, religion, nationality or political opinions, or would cause prejudice for any of those reasons to any person affected by the request.

7. The Parties shall endeavour to expedite extradition procedures and to simplify evidentiary requirements relating thereto in respect of any offence to which this article applies.

8. Subject to the provisions of its domestic law and its extradition treaties, the requested Party may, upon being satisfied that the circumstances so warrant and are urgent, and at the request of the requesting Party, take a person whose extradition is sought and who is present in its territory into custody or take other appropriate measures to ensure his presence at extradition proceedings.

9. Without prejudice to the exercise of any criminal jurisdiction established in accordance with its domestic law, a Party in whose territory an alleged offender is found shall:

a. If it does not extradite him in respect of an offence established in accordance with Article 3, paragraph 1, on the grounds set forth in Article 4, paragraph 2, subparagraph a., submit the case to its competent authorities for the purpose of prosecution, unless otherwise agreed with the requesting Party;

b. If it does not extradite him in respect of such an offence and has established its jurisdiction in relation to that offence in accordance with Article 4, paragraph 2, subparagraph b., submit the case to its competent authorities for the purpose of prosecution, unless otherwise requested by the requesting Party for the purposes of preserving its legitimate jurisdiction.

10. If extradition, sought for purposes of enforcing a sentence, is refused because the person sought is a national of the requested Party, the requested Party shall, if its law so permits and in conformity with the requirements of such law, upon application of the requesting Party, consider the enforcement of the sentence which has been imposed under the law of the requesting Party, or the remainder thereof.

11. The Parties shall seek to conclude bilateral and multilateral agreements to carry out or to enhance the effectiveness of extradition.

12. The Parties may consider entering into bilateral or multilateral agreements, whether *ad hoc* or general, on the transfer to their country of persons sentenced to imprisonment and other forms of deprivation of liberty for offences to which this article applies, in order that they may complete their sentences there.

Article 7

Mutual legal assistance

1. The Parties shall afford one another, pursuant to this article, the widest measure of mutual legal assistance in investigations, prosecutions and judicial proceedings in relation to criminal offences established in accordance with Article 3, paragraph 1.

2. Mutual legal assistance to be afforded in accordance with this article may be requested for any of the following purposes:

  a. Taking evidence or statements from persons;

  b. Effecting service of judicial documents;

  c. Executing searches and seizures;

  d. Examining objects and sites;

  e. Providing information and evidentiary items;

  f. Providing originals or certified copies of relevant documents and records, including bank, financial, corporate or business records;

  g. Identifying or tracing proceeds, property, instrumentalities or other things for evidentiary purposes.

3. The Parties may afford one another any other forms of mutual legal assistance allowed by the domestic law of the requested Party.

4. Upon request, the Parties shall facilitate or encourage, to the extent consistent with their domestic law and practice, the presence or availability of persons, including persons in custody, who consent to assist in investigations or participate in proceedings.

5. A Party shall not decline to render mutual legal assistance under this article on the ground of bank secrecy.

6. The provisions of this article shall not affect the obligations under any other treaty, bilateral or multilateral, which governs or will govern, in whole or in part, mutual legal assistance in criminal matters.

7.   Paragraphs 8 to 19 of this article shall apply to requests made pursuant to this article if the Parties in question are not bound by a treaty of mutual legal assistance. If these Parties are bound by such a treaty, the corresponding provisions of that treaty shall apply unless the Parties agree to apply paragraphs 8 to 19 of this article in lieu thereof.

8.   Parties shall designate an authority, or when necessary authorities, which shall have the responsibility and power to execute requests for mutual legal assistance or to transmit them to the competent authorities for execution. The authority or the authorities designated for this purpose shall be notified to the Secretary-General. Transmission of requests for mutual legal assistance and any communication related thereto shall be effected between the authorities designated by the Parties; this requirement shall be without prejudice to the right of a Party to require that such requests and communications be addressed to it through the diplomatic channel and, in urgent circumstances, where the Parties agree, through channels of the International Criminal Police Organisation, if possible.

9.   Requests shall be made in writing in a language acceptable to the requested Party. The language or languages acceptable to each Party shall be notified to the Secretary-General. In urgent circumstances, and where agreed by the Parties, requests may be made orally, but shall be confirmed in writing forthwith.

10.   A request for mutual legal assistance shall contain:

   a. The identity of the authority making the request;
   b. The subject matter and nature of the investigation, prosecution or proceeding to which the request relates, and the name and the functions of the authority conducting such investigation, prosecution or proceeding;
   c. A summary of the relevant facts, except in respect of requests for the purpose of service of judicial documents;
   d. A description of the assistance sought and details of any particular procedure the requesting Party wishes to be followed;
   e. Where possible, the identity, location and nationality of any person concerned;
   f. The purpose for which the evidence, information or action is sought.

11. The requested Party may request additional information when it appears necessary for the execution of the request in accordance with its domestic law or when it can facilitate such execution.

12. A request shall be executed in accordance with the domestic law of the requested Party and, to the extent not contrary to the domestic law of the

requested Party and where possible, in accordance with the procedures specified in the request.

13. The requesting Party shall not transmit nor use information or evidence furnished by the requested Party for investigations, prosecutions or proceedings other than those stated in the request without the prior consent of the requested Party.

14. The requesting Party may require that the requested Party keep confidential the fact and substance of the request, except to the extent necessary to execute the request. If the requested Party cannot comply with the requirement of confidentiality, it shall promptly inform the requesting Party.

15. Mutual legal assistance may be refused:

    a. If the request is not made in conformity with the provisions of this article;

    b. If the requested Party considers that execution of the request is likely to prejudice its sovereignty, security, *ordre public* or other essential interests;

    c. If the authorities of the requested Party would be prohibited by its domestic law from carrying out the action requested with regard to any similar offence, had it been subject to investigation, prosecution or proceedings under their own jurisdiction;

    d. If it would be contrary to the legal system of the requested Party relating to mutual legal assistance for the request to be granted.

16. Reasons shall be given for any refusal of mutual legal assistance.

17. Mutual legal assistance may be postponed by the requested Party on the ground that it interferes with an ongoing investigation, prosecution or proceeding. In such a case, the requested Party shall consult with the requesting Party to determine if the assistance can still be given subject to such terms and conditions as the requested Party deems necessary.

18. A witness, expert or other person who consents to give evidence in a proceeding or to assist in an investigation, prosecution or judicial proceeding in the territory of the requesting Party, shall not be prosecuted, detained, punished or subjected to any other restriction of his personal liberty in that territory in respect of acts, omissions or convictions prior to his departure from the territory of the requested Party. Such safe conduct shall cease when the witness, expert or other person having had, for a period of fifteen consecutive days, or for any period agreed upon by the Parties, from the date on which he has been officially informed that his presence is no longer required by the judicial authorities, an opportunity of leaving, has

nevertheless remained voluntarily in the territory or, having left it, has returned of his own free will.

19. The ordinary costs of executing a request shall be borne by the requested Party, unless otherwise agreed by the Parties concerned. If expenses of a substantial or extraordinary nature are or will be required to fulfil the request, the Parties shall consult to determine the terms and conditions under which the request will be executed as well as the manner in which the costs shall be borne.

20. The Parties shall consider, as may be necessary, the possibility of concluding bilateral or multilateral agreements or arrangements that would serve the purposes of, give practical effect to, or enhance the provisions of this article.

Article 8

Transfer of proceedings

The Parties shall give consideration to the possibility of transferring to one another proceedings for criminal prosecution of offences established in accordance with Article 3, paragraph 1, in cases where such transfer is considered to be in the interests of a proper administration of justice.

Article 9

Other forms of co-operation and training

1. The Parties shall co-operate closely with one another, consistent with their respective domestic legal and administrative systems, with a view to enhancing the effectiveness of law enforcement action to suppress the commission of offences established in accordance with Article 3, paragraph 1. They shall, in particular, on the basis of bilateral or multilateral agreements or arrangements:

   a. Establish and maintain channels of communication between their competent agencies and services to facilitate the secure and rapid exchange of information concerning all aspects of offences established in accordance with Article 3, paragraph 1, including, if the Parties concerned deem it appropriate, links with other criminal activities;

   b. Co-operate with one another in conducting enquiries, with respect to offences established in accordance with Article 3, paragraph 1, having an international character, concerning:

i. The identity, whereabouts and activities of persons suspected of being involved in offences established in accordance with Article 3, paragraph 1;

ii. The movement of proceeds or property derived from the commission of such offences;

iii. The movement of narcotic drugs, psychotropic substances, substances in Table I and Table II of this Convention and instrumentalities used or intended for use in the commission of such offences;

c. In appropriate cases and if not contrary to domestic law, establish joint teams, taking into account the need to protect the security of persons and of operations, to carry out the provisions of this paragraph. Officials of any Party taking part in such teams shall act as authorised by the appropriate authorities of the Party in whose territory the operation is to take place; in all such cases, the Parties involved shall ensure that the sovereignty of the Party on whose territory the operation is to take place is fully respected;

d. Provide, when appropriate, necessary quantities of substances for analytical or investigative purposes;

e. Facilitate effective co-ordination between their competent agencies and services and promote the exchange of personnel and other experts, including the posting of liaison officers.

2. Each Party shall, to the extent necessary, initiate, develop or improve specific training programmes for its law enforcement and other personnel, including customs, charged with the suppression of offences established in accordance with Article 3, paragraph 1. Such programmes shall deal, in particular, with the following:

a. Methods used in the detection and suppression of offences established in accordance with Article 3, paragraph 1;

b. Routes and techniques used by persons suspected of being involved in offences established in accordance with Article 3, paragraph 1, particularly in transit States, and appropriate countermeasures;

c. Monitoring of the import and export of narcotic drugs, psychotropic substances and substances in Table I and Table II;

d. Detection and monitoring of the movement of proceeds and property derived from, and narcotic drugs, psychotropic substances and substances in Table I and Table II, and instrumentalities used or intended for use in, the commission of offences established in accordance with Article 3, paragraph 1;

e. Methods used for the transfer, concealment or disguise of such proceeds, property and instrumentalities;

f. Collection of evidence;

g. Control techniques in free trade zones and free ports;

h. Modern law enforcement techniques.

3. The Parties shall assist one another to plan and implement research and training programmes designed to share expertise in the areas referred to in paragraph 2 of this article and, to this end, shall also, when appropriate, use regional and international conferences and seminars to promote co-operation and stimulate discussion on problems of mutual concern, including the special problems and needs of transit States.

Article 10

International co-operation and assistance for transit states

1. The Parties shall co-operate, directly or through competent international or regional organisations, to assist and support transit States and, in particular, developing countries in need of such assistance and support, to the extent possible, through programmes of technical co-operation on interdiction and other related activities.

2. The Parties may undertake, directly or through competent international or regional organisations, to provide financial assistance to such transit States for the purpose of augmenting and strengthening the infrastructure needed for effective control and prevention of illicit traffic.

3. The Parties may conclude bilateral or multilateral agreements or arrangements to enhance the effectiveness of international co-operation pursuant to this article and may take into consideration financial arrangements in this regard.

Article 11

Controlled delivery

1. If permitted by the basic principles of their respective domestic legal systems, the Parties shall take the necessary measures, within their possibilities, to allow for the appropriate use of controlled delivery at the international level, on the basis of agreements or arrangements mutually consented to, with a view to identifying persons involved in offences established in accordance with Article 3, paragraph 1, and to taking legal action against them.

2. Decisions to use controlled delivery shall be made on a case-by-case basis and may, when necessary, take into consideration financial arrangements and understandings with respect to the exercise of jurisdiction by the Parties concerned.

3. Illicit consignments whose controlled delivery is agreed to may, with the consent of the Parties concerned, be intercepted and allowed to continue with the narcotic drugs or psychotropic substances intact or removed or replaced in whole or in part.

Article 12

Substances frequently used in the illicit manufacture of narcotic drugs or psychotropic substances

1. The Parties shall take the measures they deem appropriate to prevent diversion of substances in Table I and Table II used for the purpose of illicit manufacture of narcotic drugs or psychotropic substances, and shall cooperate with one another to this end.

2. If a Party or the Board has information which in its opinion may require the inclusion of a substance in Table I or Table II, it shall notify the Secretary-General and furnish him with the information in support of that notification. The procedure described in paragraphs 2 to 7 of this article shall also apply when a Party or the Board has information justifying the deletion of a substance from Table I or Table II, or the transfer of a substance from one Table to the other.

3. The Secretary-General shall transmit such notification, and any information which he considers relevant, to the Parties, to the Commission, and, where notification is made by a Party, to the Board. The Parties shall communicate their comments concerning the notification to the Secretary-General, together with all supplementary information which may assist the Board in establishing an assessment and the Commission in reaching a decision.

4. If the Board, taking into account the extent, importance and diversity of the licit use of the substance, and the possibility and ease of using alternate substances both for licit purposes and for the illicit manufacture of narcotic drugs or psychotropic substances, finds:

    a. That the substance is frequently used in the illicit manufacture of a narcotic drug or psychotropic substance;

    b. That the volume and extent of the illicit manufacture of a narcotic drug or psychotropic substance creates serious public health or social problems, so as to warrant international action, it shall communicate to the Commission an assessment of the substance, including the likely effect of adding the substance to either Table I or Table II on both licit use and illicit manufacture, together with recommendations of monitoring measures, if any, that would be appropriate in the light of its assessment.

5. The Commission, taking into account the comments submitted by the Parties and the comments and recommendations of the Board, whose assessment shall be determinative as to scientific matters, and also taking into due consideration any other relevant factors, may decide by a two-thirds majority of its members to place a substance in Table I or Table II.

6. Any decision of the Commission taken pursuant to this article shall be communicated by the Secretary-General to all States and other entities which are, or which are entitled to become, Parties to this Convention, and to the Board. Such decision shall become fully effective with respect to each Party one hundred and eighty days after the date of such communication.

7. a. The decisions of the Commission taken under this article shall be subject to review by the Council upon the request of any Party filed within one hundred and eighty days after the date of notification of the decision. The request for review shall be sent to the Secretary-General, together with all relevant information upon which the request for review is based.

b. The Secretary-General shall transmit copies of the request for review and the relevant information to the Commission, to the Board and to all the Parties, inviting them to submit their comments within ninety days. All comments received shall be submitted to the Council for consideration.

c. The Council may confirm or reverse the decision of the Commission. Notification of the Council's decision shall be transmitted to all States and other entities which are, or which are entitled to become, Parties to this Convention, to the Commission and to the Board.

8. a. Without prejudice to the generality of the provisions contained in paragraph 1 of this article and the provisions of the 1961 Convention, the 1961 Convention as amended and the 1971 Convention, the Parties shall take the measures they deem appropriate to monitor the manufacture and distribution of substances in Table I and Table II which are carried out within their territory.

b. To this end, the Parties may:

i. Control all persons and enterprises engaged in the manufacture and distribution of such substances;

ii. Control under licence the establishment and premises in which such manufacture or distribution may take place;

iii. Require that licensees obtain a permit for conducting the aforesaid operations

iv. Prevent the accumulation of such substances in the possession of manufacturers and distributors, in excess of the quantities required for the normal conduct of business and the prevailing market conditions.

9. Each Party shall, with respect to substances in Table I and Table II, take the following measures:

a. Establish and maintain a system to monitor international trade in substances in Table I and Table II in order to facilitate the identification of suspicious transactions. Such monitoring systems shall be applied in close co-operation with manufacturers, importers, exporters, wholesalers and retailers, who shall inform the competent authorities of suspicious orders and transactions.

b. Provide for the seizure of any substance in Table I or Table II if there is sufficient evidence that it is for use in the illicit manufacture of a narcotic drug or psychotropic substance.

c. Notify, as soon as possible, the competent authorities and services of the Parties concerned if there is reason to believe that the import, export or transit of a substance in Table I or Table II is destined for the illicit manufacture of narcotic drugs or psychotropic substances, including in particular information about the means of payment and any other essential elements which led to that belief.

d. Require that imports and exports be properly labelled and documented. Commercial documents such as invoices, cargo manifests, customs, transport and other shipping documents shall include the names, as stated in Table I or Table II, of the substances being imported or exported, the quantity being imported or exported, and the name and address of the exporter, the importer and, when available, the consignee.

e. Ensure that documents referred to in subparagraph d. of this paragraph are maintained for a period of not less than two years and may be made available for inspection by the competent authorities.

10. a. In addition to the provisions of paragraph 9, and upon request to the Secretary-General by the interested Party, each Party from whose territory a substance in Table I is to be exported shall ensure that, prior to such export, the following information is supplied by its competent authorities of the competent authorities of the importing country:

    i Name and address of the exporter and importer and, when available, the consignee;

    ii. Name of the substance in Table I;

    iii. Quantity of the substance to be exported;

    iv. Expected point of entry and expected date of dispatch;

    v. Any other information which is mutually agreed upon by the Parties.

  b. A Party may adopt more strict or severe measures of control than those provided by this paragraph if, in its opinion, such measures are desirable or necessary.

11. Where a Party furnishes information to another Party in accordance with paragraphs 9 and 10 of this article, the Party furnishing such information may require that the Party receiving it keep confidential any trade, business, commercial or professional secret or trade process.

12. Each Party shall furnish annually to the Board, in the form and manner provided for by it and on forms made available by it, information on:

  a. The amounts seized of substances in Table I and Table II and, when known, their origin;

  b. Any substance not included in Table I or Table II which is identified as having been used in illicit manufacture of narcotic drugs or psychotropic substances, and which is deemed by the Party to be sufficiently significant to be brought to the attention of the Board;

  c. Methods of diversion and illicit manufacture.

13. The Board shall report annually to the Commission on the implementation of this article and the Commission shall periodically review the adequacy and propriety of Table I and Table II.

14. The provisions of this article shall not apply to pharmaceutical preparations, nor to other preparations containing substances in Table I or Table II that are compounded in such a way that such substances cannot be easily used or recovered by readily applicable means.

Article 13

Materials and equipment

The Parties shall take such measures as they deem appropriate to prevent trade in and the diversion of materials and equipment for illicit production or manufacture of narcotic drugs and psychotropic substances and shall cooperate to this end.

Article 14

Measures to eradicate illicit cultivation of narcotic plants and to eliminate illicit demand for narcotic drugs and psychotropic substances

1. Any measures taken pursuant to this Convention by Parties shall not be less stringent than the provisions applicable to the eradication of illicit cultivation of plants containing narcotic and psychotropic substances and to the elimination of illicit demand for narcotic drugs and psychotropic substances under the provisions of the 1961 Convention, the 1961 Convention as amended and the 1971 Convention.

2. Each Party shall take appropriate measures to prevent illicit cultivation of and to eradicate plants containing narcotic or psychotropic substances, such as opium poppy, coca bush and cannabis plants, cultivated illicitly in its territory. The measures adopted shall respect fundamental human rights and shall take due account of traditional licit uses, where there is historic evidence of such use, as well as the protection of the environment.

3. *a.* The Parties may co-operate to increase the effectiveness of eradication efforts. Such co-operation may, inter alia, include support, when appropriate, for integrated rural development leading to economically viable alternatives to illicit cultivation. Factors such as access to markets, the availability of resources and prevailing socio-economic conditions should be taken into account before such rural development programmes are implemented. The Parties may agree on any other appropriate measures of co-operation.

   b. The Parties shall also facilitate the exchange of scientific and technical information and the conduct of research concerning eradication.

   c. Whenever they have common frontiers, the Parties shall seek to co-operate in eradication programmes in their respective areas along those frontiers.

4. The Parties shall adopt appropriate measures aimed at eliminating or reducing illicit demand for narcotic drugs and psychotropic substances, with a view to reducing human suffering and eliminating financial incentives for illicit traffic. These measures may be based, *inter alia*, on the recommendations of the United Nations, specialised agencies of the United Nations such as the World Health Organisation, and other competent international organisations, and on the Comprehensive Multidisciplinary Outline adopted by the International Conference on Drug Abuse and Illicit Trafficking, held in 1987, as it pertains to governmental and non-governmental agencies and private efforts in the fields of prevention, treatment and rehabilitation. The Parties may enter into bilateral or multilateral agreements or arrangements aimed at eliminating or reducing illicit demand for narcotic drugs and psychotropic substances.

5. The Parties may also take necessary measures for early destruction or lawful disposal of the narcotic drugs, psychotropic substances and substances in Table I and Table II which have been seized or confiscated and for the admissibility as evidence of duly certified necessary quantities of such substances.

Article 15

Commercial carriers

1. The Parties shall take appropriate measures to ensure that means of transport operated by commercial carriers are not used in the commission of offences established in accordance with Article 3, paragraph 1; such measures may include special arrangements with commercial carriers.

2. Each Party shall require commercial carriers to take reasonable precautions to prevent the use of their means of transport for the commission of offences established in accordance with Article 3, paragraph 1. Such precautions may include:

   a. If the principal place of business of a commercial carrier is within the territory of the Party:
      i. Training of personnel to identify suspicious consignments or persons;
      ii. Promotion of integrity of personnel;
   b. If a commercial carrier is operating within the territory of the Party:
      i. Submission of cargo manifests in advance, whenever possible;
      ii. Use of tamper-resistant, individually verifiable seals on containers;
      iii. Reporting to the appropriate authorities at the earliest opportunity all suspicious circumstances that may be related to the commission of offences established in accordance with Article 3, paragraph 1.

3. Each Party shall seek to ensure that commercial carriers and the appropriate authorities at points of entry and exit and other customs control areas co-operate, with a view to preventing unauthorised access to means of transport and cargo and to implementing appropriate security measures.

Article 16

Commercial documents and labelling of exports

1. Each Party shall require that lawful exports of narcotic drugs and psychotropic substances be properly documented. In addition to the

requirements for documentation under Article 31 of the 1961 Convention, Article 31 of the 1961 Convention as amended and Article 12 of the 1971 Convention, commercial documents such as invoices, cargo manifests, customs, transport and other shipping documents shall include the names of the narcotic drugs and psychotropic substances being exported as set out in the respective Schedules of the 1961 Convention, the 1961 Convention as amended and the 1971 Convention, the quantity being exported, and the name and address of the exporter, the importer and, when available, the consignee.

2. Each Party shall require that consignments of narcotic drugs and psychotropic substances being exported be not mislabelled.

Article 17

Illicit traffic by sea

1. The Parties shall co-operate to the fullest extent possible to suppress illicit traffic by sea, in conformity with the international law of the sea.

2. A Party which has reasonable grounds to suspect that a vessel flying its flag or not displaying a flag or marks of registry is engaged in illicit traffic may request the assistance of other Parties in suppressing its use for that purpose. The Parties so requested shall render such assistance within the means available to them.

3. A Party which has reasonable grounds to suspect that a vessel exercising freedom of navigation in accordance with international law and flying the flag or displaying marks of registry of another Party is engaged in illicit traffic may so notify the flag State, request confirmation of registry and, if confirmed, request authorisation from the flag State to take appropriate measures in regard to that vessel.

4. In accordance with paragraph 3 or in accordance with treaties in force between them or in accordance with any agreement or arrangement otherwise reached between those Parties, the flag State may authorise the requesting State to, inter alia:

   a. Board the vessel;

   b. Search the vessel;

   c. If evidence of involvement in illicit traffic is found, take appropriate action with respect to the vessel, persons and cargo on board.

5. Where action is taken pursuant to this article, the Parties concerned shall take due account of the need not to endanger the safety of life at sea,

the security of the vessel and the cargo or to prejudice the commercial and legal interests of the flag State or any other interested State.

6. The flag State may, consistent with its obligations in paragraph 1 of this article, subject its authorisation to conditions to be mutually agreed between it and the requesting Party, including conditions relating to responsibility.

7. For the purposes of paragraphs 3 and 4 of this article, a Party shall respond expeditiously to a request from another Party to determine whether a vessel that is flying its flag is entitled to do so, and to requests for authorisation made pursuant to paragraph 3. At the time of becoming a Party to this Convention, each Party shall designate an authority or, when necessary, authorities to receive and respond to such requests. Such designation shall be notified through the Secretary-General to all other Parties within one month of the designation.

8. A Party which has taken any action in accordance with this article shall promptly inform the flag State concerned of the results of that action.

9. The Parties shall consider entering into bilateral or regional agreements or arrangements to carry out, or to enhance the effectiveness of, the provisions of this article.

10. Action pursuant to paragraph 4 of this article shall be carried out only by warships or military aircraft, or other ships or aircraft clearly marked and identifiable as being on government service and authorised to that effect.

11. Any action taken in accordance with this article shall take due account of the need not to interfere with or affect the rights and obligations and the exercise of jurisdiction of coastal States in accordance with the international law of the sea.

Article 18

Free trade zones and free ports

1. The Parties shall apply measures to suppress illicit traffic in narcotic drugs, psychotropic substances and substances in Table I and Table II in free trade zones and in free ports that are no less stringent than those applied in other parts of their territories.

2. The Parties shall endeavour:

   a. To monitor the movement of goods and persons in free trade zones and free ports, and, to that end, shall empower the competent authorities to search cargoes and incoming and outgoing vessels, including pleasure craft and fishing vessels, as well as aircraft and vehicles and, when appropriate, to search crew members, passengers and their baggage;

b. To establish and maintain a system to detect consignments suspected of containing narcotic drugs, psychotropic substances and substances in Table I and Table II passing into or out of free trade zones and free ports;

c. To establish and maintain surveillance systems in harbour and dock areas and at airports and border control points in free trade zones and free ports.

Article 19

The use of the mails

1. In conformity with their obligations under the Conventions of the Universal Postal Union, and in accordance with the basic principles of their domestic legal systems, the Parties shall adopt measures to suppress the use of the mails for illicit traffic and shall co-operate with one another to that end.

2. The measures referred to in paragraph 1 of this article shall include, in particular:

a. Co-ordinated action for the prevention and repression of the use of the mails for illicit traffic;

b. Introduction and maintenance by authorised law enforcement personnel of investigative and control techniques designed to detect illicit consignments of narcotic drugs, psychotropic substances and substances in Table I and Table II in the mails;

c. Legislative measures to enable the use of appropriate means to secure evidence required for judicial proceedings.

Article 20

Information to be furnished by the Parties

1. The Parties shall furnish, through the Secretary-General, information to the Commission on the working of this Convention in their territories and, in particular:

a. The text of laws and regulations promulgated in order to give effect to the Convention;

b. Particulars of cases of illicit traffic within their jurisdiction which they consider important because of new trends disclosed, the quantities involved, the sources from which the substances are obtained, or the methods employed by persons so engaged.

2. The Parties shall furnish such information in such a manner and by such dates as the Commission may request.

Article 21

Functions of the Commission

The Commission is authorised to consider all matters pertaining to the aims of this Convention and, in particular:

a. The Commission shall, on the basis of the information submitted by the Parties in accordance with Article 20, review the operation of this Convention;

b. The Commission may make suggestions and general recommendations based on the examination of the information received from the Parties;

c. The Commission may call the attention of the Board to any matters which may be relevant to the functions of the Board;

d. The Commission shall, on any matter referred to it by the Board under Article 22, paragraph 1.*b*, take such action as it deems appropriate;

e. The Commission may, in conformity with the procedures laid down in Article 12, amend Table I and Table II;

f. The Commission may draw the attention of non-Parties to decisions and recommendations which it adopts under this Convention, with a view to their considering taking action in accordance therewith.

Article 22

Functions of the Board

1. Without prejudice to the functions of the Commission under Article 21, and without prejudice to the functions of the Board and the Commission under the 1961 Convention, the 1961 Convention as amended and the 1971 Convention:

a. If, on the basis of its examination of information available to it, to the Secretary-General or to the Commission, or of information communicated by United Nations organs, the Board has reason to

237

believe that the aims of this Convention in matters related to its competence are not being met, the Board may invite a Party or Parties to furnish any relevant information;

b. With respect to Articles 12, 13 and 16:

   i. After taking action under subparagraph a. of this article, the Board, if satisfied that it is necessary to do so, may call upon the Party concerned to adopt such remedial measures as shall seem under the circumstances to be necessary for the execution of the provisions of Articles 12, 13 and 16;

   ii. Prior to taking action under iii. below, the Board shall treat as confidential its communications with the Party concerned under the preceding subparagraphs;

   iii. If the Board finds that the Party concerned has not taken remedial measures which it has been called upon to take under this subparagraph, it may call the attention of the Parties, the Council and the Commission to the matter. Any report published by the Board under this subparagraph shall also contain the views of the Party concerned if the latter so requests.

2. Any Party shall be invited to be represented at a meeting of the Board at which a question of direct interest to it is to be considered under this article.

3. If in any case a decision of the Board which is adopted under this article is not unanimous, the views of the minority shall be stated.

4. Decisions of the Board under this article shall be taken by a two-thirds majority of the whole number of the Board.

5. In carrying out its functions pursuant to subparagraph 1.a of this article, the Board shall ensure the confidentiality of all information which may come into its possession.

6. The Board's responsibility under this article shall not apply to the implementation of treaties or agreements entered into between Parties in accordance with the provisions of this Convention.

7. The provisions of this article shall not be applicable to disputes between Parties falling under the provisions of Article 32.

Article 23

Reports of the Board

1. The Board shall prepare an annual report on its work containing an analysis of the information at its disposal and, in appropriate cases, an

account of the explanations, if any, given by or required of Parties, together with any observations and recommendations which the Board desires to make. The Board may make such additional reports as it considers necessary. The reports shall be submitted to the Council through the Commission which may make such comments as it sees fit.

2. The reports of the Board shall be communicated to the Parties and subsequently published by the Secretary-General. The Parties shall permit their unrestricted distribution.

Article 24

Application of stricter measures than those required by this Convention

A Party may adopt more strict or severe measures than those provided by this Convention if, in its opinion, such measures are desirable or necessary for the prevention or suppression of illicit traffic.

Article 25

Non-derogation from earlier treaty rights and obligations

The provisions of this Convention shall not derogate from any rights enjoyed or obligations undertaken by Parties to this Convention under the 1961 Convention, the 1961 Convention as amended and the 1971 Convention.

Article 26

Signature

This Convention shall be open for signature at the United Nations Office at Vienna, from 20 December 1988 to 28 February 1989, and thereafter at the Headquarters of the United Nations at New York, until 20 December 1989, by:

a. All States;

b. Namibia, represented by the United Nations Council for Namibia;

c. Regional economic integration organisations which have competence in respect of the negotiation, conclusion and application of international agreements in matters covered by this Convention, references under the Convention to Parties, States or national services being applicable to these organisations within the limits of their competence.

Article 27

Ratification, acceptance, approval or act of formal confirmation

1. This Convention is subject to ratification, acceptance or approval by States and by Namibia, represented by the United Nations Council for Namibia, and to acts of formal confirmation by regional economic integration organisations referred to in Article 26, subparagraph c. The instruments of ratification, acceptance or approval and those relating to acts of formal confirmation shall be deposited with the Secretary-General.

2. In their instruments of formal confirmation, regional economic integration organisations shall declare the extent of their competence with respect to the matters governed by this Convention. These organisations shall also inform the Secretary-General of any modification in the extent of their competence with respect to the matters governed by the Convention.

Article 28

Accession

1. This Convention shall remain open for accession by any State, by Namibia, represented by the United Nations Council for Namibia, and by regional economic integration organisations referred to in Article 26, subparagraph c. Accession shall be effected by the deposit of an instrument of accession with the Secretary-General.

2. In their instruments of accession, regional economic integration organisations shall declare the extent of their competence with respect to the matters governed by this Convention. These organisations shall also inform the Secretary-General of any modification in the extent of their competence with respect to the matters governed by the Convention.

Article 29

Entry into force

1. This Convention shall enter into force on the ninetieth day after the date of the deposit with the Secretary-General of the twentieth instrument of

ratification, acceptance, approval or accession by States or by Namibia, represented by the Council for Namibia.

2. For each State or for Namibia, represented by the Council for Namibia, ratifying, accepting, approving or acceding to this Convention after the deposit of the twentieth instrument of ratification, acceptance, approval or accession, the Convention shall enter into force on the ninetieth day after the date of the deposit of its instrument of ratification, acceptance, approval or accession.

3. For each regional economic integration organisation referred to in Article 26, subparagraph *c.* depositing an instrument relating to an act of formal confirmation or an instrument of accession, this Convention shall enter into force on the ninetieth day after such deposit, or at the date the Convention enters into force pursuant to paragraph 1 of this article, whichever is later.

Article 30

Denunciation

1. A Party may denounce this Convention at any time by a written notification addressed to the Secretary-General.

2. Such denunciation shall take effect for the Party concerned one year after the date of receipt of the notification by the Secretary-General.

Article 31

Amendments

1. Any Party may propose an amendment to this Convention. The text of any such amendment and the reasons therefor shall be communicated by that Party to the Secretary-General, who shall communicate it to the other Parties and shall ask them whether they accept the proposed amendment. If a proposed amendment so circulated has not been rejected by any Party within twenty-four months after it has been circulated, it shall be deemed to have been accepted and shall enter into force in respect of a Party ninety days after that Party has deposited with the Secretary-General an instrument expressing its consent to be bound by that amendment.

2. If a proposed amendment has been rejected by any Party, the Secretary-General shall consult with the Parties and, if a majority so requests, he shall bring the matter, together with any comments made by the Parties, before the Council which may decide to call a conference in accordance with

Article 62, paragraph 4, of the Charter of the United Nations. Any amendment resulting from such a conference shall be embodied in a Protocol of Amendment. Consent to be bound by such a Protocol shall be required to be expressed specifically to the Secretary-General.

Article 32

Settlement of disputes

1. If there should arise between two or more Parties a dispute relating to the interpretation or application of this Convention, the Parties shall consult together with a view to the settlement of the dispute by negotiation, enquiry, mediation, conciliation, arbitration, recourse to regional bodies, judicial process or other peaceful means of their own choice.

2. Any such dispute which cannot be settled in the manner prescribed in paragraph 1 of this article shall be referred, at the request of any one of the States Parties to the dispute, to the International Court of Justice for decision.

3. If a regional economic integration organisation referred to in Article 26, subparagraph c. is a Party to a dispute which cannot be settled in the manner prescribed in paragraph 1 of this article, it may, through a State Member of the United Nations, request the Council to request an advisory opinion of the International Court of Justice in accordance with Article 65 of the Statute of the Court, which opinion shall be regarded as decisive.

4. Each State, at the time of signature or ratification, acceptance or approval of this Convention or accession thereto, or each regional economic integration organisation, at the time of signature or deposit of an act of formal confirmation or accession, may declare that it does not consider itself bound by paragraphs 2 and 3 of this article. The other Parties shall not be bound by paragraphs 2 and 3 with respect to any Party having made such a declaration.

5. Any Party having made a declaration in accordance with paragraph 4 of this article may at any time withdraw the declaration by notification to the Secretary-General.

Article 33

Authentic texts

The Arabic, Chinese, English, French, Russian and Spanish texts of this Convention are equally authentic.

Article 34

Depositary

The Secretary-General shall be the depositary of this Convention.

In witness whereof the undersigned, being duly authorised thereto, have signed this Convention.

Done at Vienna, in one original, this twentieth day of December one thousand nine hundred and eighty-eight.

Annex – Revised Tables including the amendments made by the Commission on Narcotic Drugs in force as of 23 November 1992

Table I	Table II
N-acetylanthranilic acid	Acetic anhydride
Ephedrine	Acetone
Ergometrine	Anthranilic acid
Ergotamine	Ethyl ether
Isosafrole	Hydrochloric acid
Lysergic acid	Methyl ethyl ketone
3,4-methylenedioxyphenyl-2-propanone	Phenylacetic acid
1-phenyl-2-propanone	Piperidine
Piperonal	Potassium permanganate
Pseudoephedrine	Sulphuric acid
Safrole	Toluene

The salts of the substances listed in this Table whenever the existence of such salts is possible.

The salts of the substances listed in this Table whenever the existence of such salts is possible. The salts of hydrochloric acid and sulphuric acid are specifically excluded.

APPENDIX II – THE 1990 RECOMMENDATIONS OF THE FATF

A. General framework of the recommendations

1.   Each country should, without further delay, take steps to fully implement the Vienna Convention, and proceed to ratify it.

2.   Financial institution secrecy laws should be conceived so as not to inhibit implementation of the recommendations of this group.

3.   An effective money laundering enforcement programme should include increased multilateral co-operation and mutual legal assistance in money laundering investigations and prosecutions and extradition in money laundering cases, where possible.

B. Improvement of national legal systems to combat money laundering

Definition of the criminal offence of money laundering

4.   Each country should take such measures as may be necessary, including legislative ones, to enable it to criminalise drug money laundering as set forth in the Vienna Convention.

5.   Each country should consider extending the offence of drug money laundering to any other crimes for which there is a link to narcotics; an alternative approach is to criminalise money laundering based on all serious offences, and/or on all offences that generate a significant amount of proceeds, or on certain serious offences.

6.   As provided in the Vienna Convention, the offence of money laundering should apply at least to knowing money laundering activity, including the concept that knowledge may be inferred from objective factual circumstances.

7.   Where possible, corporations themselves – not only their employees – should be subject to criminal liability.

Provisional measures and confiscation

8.   Countries should adopt measures similar to those set forth in the Vienna Convention, as may be necessary, including legislative ones, to enable their competent authorities to confiscate property laundered, pro-

ceeds from, instrumentalities used in or intended for use in the commission of any money laundering offence, or property of corresponding value.

Such measures should include the authority to: (1) identify, trace and evaluate property which is subject to confiscation; (2) carry out provisional measures, such as freezing and seizing, to prevent any dealing, transfer or disposal of such property; and (3) take any appropriate investigative measures.

In addition to confiscation and criminal sanctions, countries also should consider monetary and civil penalties, and/or proceedings including civil proceedings, to void contracts entered by parties, where parties knew or should have known that as a result of the contract, the State would be prejudiced in its ability to recover financial claims, e.g. through confiscation or collection of fines and penalties.

C. Enhancement of the role of the financial system

Scope of the following recommendations

9. Recommendations 12 to 29 of this paper should apply not only to banks, but also to non-bank financial institutions.

10. The appropriate national authorities should take steps to ensure that these Recommendations are implemented on as broad a front as is practically possible.

11. A working group should further examine the possibility of establishing a common minimal list of non-bank financial institutions and other professions dealing with cash subject to these recommendations.

Customer identification and record-keeping rules

12. Financial institutions should not keep anonymous accounts or accounts in obviously fictitious names: they should be required (by law, by regulations, by agreements between supervisory authorities and financial institutions or by self-regulatory agreements among financial institutions) to identify, on the basis of an official or other reliable identifying document, and record the identity of their clients, either occasional or usual, when establishing business relations or conducting transactions (in particular opening of accounts or passbooks, entering into fiduciary transactions, renting of safe deposit boxes, performing large cash transactions).

13. Financial institutions should take reasonable measures to obtain information about the true identity of the persons on whose behalf an account is opened or a transaction conducted if there are any doubts as to whether these clients or customers are not acting on their own behalf, in particular,

in the case of domiciliary companies (i.e. institutions, corporations, foundations, trusts, etc. that do not conduct any commercial or manufacturing business or any other form of commercial operation in the country where their registered office is located).

14. Financial institutions should maintain, for at least five years, all necessary records on transactions, both domestic or international, to enable them to comply swiftly with information requests from the competent authorities. Such records must be sufficient to permit reconstruction of individual transactions (including the amounts and types of currency involved if any) so as to provide, if necessary, evidence for prosecution of criminal behaviour.

Financial institutions should keep records on customer identification (e.g. copies or records of official identification documents like passports, identity cards, driving licences or similar documents), account files and business correspondence for at least five years after the account is closed.

These documents should be available to domestic competent authorities in the context of relevant criminal prosecutions and investigations.

Increased diligence of financial institutions

15. Financial institutions should pay special attention to all complex, unusual large transactions, and all unusual patterns of transactions, which have no apparent economic or visible lawful purpose. The background and purpose of such transactions should, as far as possible, be examined, the findings established in writing, and be available to help supervisors, auditors and law enforcement agencies.

16. If financial institutions suspect that funds stem from a criminal activity, they should be permitted or required to report promptly their suspicions to the competent authorities. Accordingly, there should be legal provisions to protect financial institutions and their employees from criminal or civil liability for breach of any restriction on disclosure of information imposed by contract or by any legislative, regulatory or administrative provision, if they report in good faith, in disclosing suspected criminal activity to the competent authorities, even if they did not know precisely what the underlying criminal activity was, and regardless of whether illegal activity actually occurred.

17. Financial institutions, their directors and employees, should not, or, where appropriate, should not be allowed, to warn their customers when information relating to them is being reported to the competent authorities.

18. In the case of a mandatory reporting system, or in the case of a voluntary reporting system where appropriate, financial institutions reporting

their suspicions should comply with instructions from the competent authorities.

19. When a financial institution develops suspicions about the operations of a customer, and when no obligation of reporting these suspicions exists, makes no report to the competent authorities, it should deny assistance to this customer, sever relations with him and close his accounts.

20. Financial institutions should develop programmes against money laundering. These programmes should include, as a minimum:

a.   the development of internal policies, procedures and controls, including the designation of compliance officers at management level, and adequate screening procedures to ensure high standards when hiring employees;

b.   an ongoing employee training programme;

c.   an audit function to test the system.

Measures to cope with the problem of countries with no or insufficient anti-money laundering measures

21. Financial institutions should give special attention to business relations and transactions with persons, including companies and financial institutions, from countries which do not or insufficiently apply these recommendations. Whenever these transactions have no apparent economic or visible lawful purpose, their background and purpose should, as far as possible, be examined, the findings established in writing, and be available to help supervisors, auditors and law enforcement agencies.

22. Financial institutions should ensure that the principles mentioned above are also applied to branches and majority owned subsidiaries located abroad, especially in countries which do not or insufficiently apply these recommendations, to the extent that local applicable laws and regulations permit. When local applicable laws and regulations prohibit this implementation, competent authorities in the country of the mother institution should be informed by the financial institutions that they cannot apply these recommendations.

Other measures to avoid currency laundering

23. The feasibility of measures to detect or monitor cash at the border should be studied, subject to strict safeguards to ensure proper use of information and without impeding in any way the freedom of capital movements.

24. Countries should consider the feasibility and utility of a system where banks and other financial institutions and intermediaries would report all domestic and international currency transactions above a fixed amount, to

a national central agency with a computerised data base, available to competent authorities for use in money laundering cases, subject to strict safeguards to ensure proper use of the information.

25. Countries should further encourage in general the development of modern and secure techniques of money management, including increased use of cheques, payment cards, direct deposit of salary cheques, and book entry recording of securities, as a means to encourage the replacement of cash transfers.

Implementation, and role of regulatory and other administrative authorities

26. The competent authorities supervising banks or other financial institutions or intermediaries, or other competent authorities, should ensure that the supervised institutions have adequate programmes to guard against money laundering. These authorities should co-operate and lend expertise spontaneously or on request with other domestic judicial or law enforcement authorities in money laundering investigations and prosecutions.

27. Competent authorities should be designated to ensure an effective implementation of all these recommendations, through administrative supervision and regulation, in other professions dealing with cash as defined by each country.

28. The competent authorities should establish guidelines which will assist financial institutions in detecting suspicious patterns of behaviour by their customers. It is understood that such guidelines must develop over time, and will never be exhaustive. It is further understood that such guidelines will primarily serve as an educational tool for financial institutions' personnel.

29. The competent authorities regulating or supervising financial institutions should take the necessary legal or regulatory measures to guard against control or acquisition of a significant participation in financial institutions by criminals or their confederates.

D. Strengthening of international co-operation

Administrative co-operation

a. *Exchange of general information*

30. National administrations should consider recording, at least in the aggregate, international flows of cash in whatever currency, so that estimates can be made of cash flows and reflows from various sources abroad, when this is

combined with central bank information. Such information should be made available to the IMF and BIS to facilitate international studies.

31. International competent authorities, perhaps Interpol and the Customs Co-operation Council, should be given responsibility for gathering and disseminating information to competent authorities about the latest developments in money laundering and money laundering techniques. Central banks and bank regulators could do the same on their network. National authorities in various spheres, in consultation with trade associations, could then disseminate this to financial institutions in individual countries.

b. Exchange of information relating to suspicious transactions

32. Each country should make efforts to improve a spontaneous or "upon request" international information exchange relating to suspicious transactions, persons and corporations involved in those transactions between competent authorities. Strict safeguards should be established to ensure that this exchange of information is consistent with national and international provisions on privacy and data protection.

Co-operation between legal authorities

a. Basis and means for co-operation in confiscation, mutual assistance and extradition

33. Countries should try to ensure, on a bilateral or multilateral basis, that different knowledge standards in national definitions – i.e. different standards concerning the intentional element of the infraction – do not affect the ability or willingness of countries to provide each other with mutual legal assistance.

34. International co-operation should be supported by a network of bilateral and multilateral agreements and arrangements based on generally shared legal concepts with the aim of providing practical measures to affect the widest possible range of mutual assistance.

35. Countries should encourage international Conventions such as the draft Convention of the Council of Europe on Confiscation of the Proceeds from Offences.

b. Focus of improved mutual assistance on money laundering issues

36. Co-operative investigations among appropriate competent authorities of countries should be encouraged.

37. There should be procedures for mutual assistance in criminal matters regarding the use of compulsory measures including the production of

records by financial institutions and other persons, the search of persons and premises, seizure and obtaining of evidence for use in money laundering investigations and prosecutions and in related actions in foreign jurisdictions.

38. There should be authority to take expeditious action in response to requests by foreign countries to identify, freeze, seize and confiscate proceeds or other property of corresponding value to such proceeds, based on money laundering or the crimes underlying the laundering activity. There should also be arrangements for co-ordinating seizure and confiscation proceedings which may include the sharing of confiscated assets.

39. To avoid conflicts of jurisdiction, consideration should be given to devising and applying mechanisms for determining the best venue for prosecution of defendants in the interests of justice in cases that are subject to prosecution in more than one country. Similarly, there should be arrangements for co-ordinating seizure and confiscation proceedings which may include the sharing of confiscated assets.

40. Countries should have procedures in place to extradite, where possible, individuals charged with a money laundering offence or related offences. With respect to its national legal system, each country should recognise money laundering as an extraditable offence. Subject to their legal frameworks, countries may consider simplifying extradition by allowing direct transmission of extradition requests between appropriate ministries, extraditing persons based only on warrants of arrests or judgements, extraditing their nationals, and/or introducing a simplified extradition of consenting persons who waive formal extradition proceedings.

APPENDIX III – THE 1996 REVISED RECOMMENDATIONS OF THE FATF

Introduction

1.   The Financial Action Task Force on Money Laundering (FATF) is an intergovernmental body whose purpose is the development and promotion of policies to combat money laundering – the processing of criminal proceeds in order to disguise their illegal origin. These policies aim to prevent such proceeds from being utilised in future criminal activities and from affecting legitimate economic activities.

2.   The FATF currently consists of twenty-six countries[1] and two international organisations.[2] Its membership includes the major financial centre countries of Europe, North America and Asia. It is a multidisciplinary body – as is essential in dealing with money laundering – bringing together the policy-making power of legal, financial and law enforcement experts.

3.   This need to cover all relevant aspects of the fight against money laundering is reflected in the scope of the forty FATF recommendations – the measures which the Task Force have agreed to implement and which all countries are encouraged to adopt. The recommendations were originally drawn up in 1990. In 1996 the forty recommendations were revised to take into account the experience gained over the last six years and to reflect the changes which have occurred in the money laundering problem.[3]

4.   These forty recommendations set out the basic framework for anti-money laundering efforts and they are designed to be of universal application. They cover the criminal justice system and law enforcement; the financial system and its regulation, and international co-operation.

5.   It was recognised from the outset of the FATF that countries have diverse legal and financial systems and so all cannot take identical measures. The recommendations are therefore the principles for action in this

---

1.   Reference in this document to "countries" should be taken to apply equally to "territories" or "jurisdictions". The twenty-six FATF member countries and governments are: Australia, Austria, Belgium, Canada, Denmark, Finland, France, Germany, Greece, Hong Kong, Iceland, Ireland, Italy, Japan, Luxembourg, the Kingdom of the Netherlands, New Zealand, Norway, Portugal, Singapore, Spain, Sweden, Switzerland, Turkey, United Kingdom, and the United States.
2.   The two international organisations are: the European Commission and the Gulf Co-operation Council.
3.   During the period 1990 to 1995, the FATF also elaborated various interpretative notes which are designed to clarify the application of specific recommendations. Some of these interpretative notes have been updated in the Stocktaking Review to reflect changes in the recommendations.

field, for countries to implement according to their particular circumstances and constitutional frameworks allowing countries a measure of flexibility rather than prescribing every detail. The measures are not particularly complex or difficult, provided there is the political will to act. Nor do they compromise the freedom to engage in legitimate transactions or threaten economic development.

6. FATF countries are clearly committed to accept the discipline of being subjected to multilateral surveillance and peer review. All member countries have their implementation of the forty recommendations monitored through a two-pronged approach: an annual self-assessment exercise and the more detailed mutual evaluation process under which each member country is subject to an on-site examination. In addition, the FATF carries out cross-country reviews of measures taken to implement particular recommendations.

7. These measures are essential for the creation of an effective anti-money laundering framework.

The forty recommendations of the Financial Action Task Force on Money Laundering

A. General framework of the recommendations

1. Each country should take immediate steps to ratify and to implement fully, the 1988 United Nations Convention against Illicit Traffic in Narcotic Drugs and Psychotropic Substances (the Vienna Convention).

2. Financial institution secrecy laws should be conceived so as not to inhibit implementation of these recommendations.

3. An effective money laundering enforcement programme should include increased multilateral co-operation and mutual legal assistance in money laundering investigations and prosecutions and extradition in money laundering cases, where possible.

B. Role of national legal systems in combating money laundering

Scope of the criminal offence of money laundering

4. Each country should take such measures as may be necessary, including legislative ones, to enable it to criminalise money laundering as set forth in the Vienna Convention. Each country should extend the offence of drug

money laundering to one based on serious offences. Each country would determine which serious crimes would be designated as money laundering predicate offences.

5.   As provided in the Vienna Convention, the offence of money laundering should apply at least to knowing money laundering activity, including the concept that knowledge may be inferred from objective factual circumstances.

6.   Where possible, corporations themselves – not only their employees – should be subject to criminal liability.

Provisional measures and confiscation

7.   Countries should adopt measures similar to those set forth in the Vienna Convention, as may be necessary, including legislative ones, to enable their competent authorities to confiscate property laundered, proceeds from, instrumentalities used in or intended for use in the commission of any money laundering offence, or property of corresponding value, without prejudicing the rights of bona fide third parties.

Such measures should include the authority to: (1) identify, trace and evaluate property which is subject to confiscation; (2) carry out provisional measures, such as freezing and seizing, to prevent any dealing, transfer or disposal of such property; and (3) take any appropriate investigative measures.

In addition to confiscation and criminal sanctions, countries also should consider monetary and civil penalties, and/or proceedings including civil proceedings, to void contracts entered into by parties, where parties knew or should have known that as a result of the contract, the State would be prejudiced in its ability to recover financial claims, e.g. through confiscation or collection of fines and penalties.

C. Role of the financial system in combating money laundering

8.   Recommendations 10 to 29 should apply not only to banks, but also to non-bank financial institutions. Even for those non-bank financial institutions which are not subject to a formal prudential supervisory regime in all countries, for example bureaux de change, governments should ensure that these institutions are subject to the same anti-money laundering laws or regulations as all other financial institutions and that these laws or regulations are implemented effectively.

9. The appropriate national authorities should consider applying Recommendations 10 to 21 and 23 to the conduct of financial activities as a commercial undertaking by businesses or professions which are not financial institutions, where such conduct is allowed or not prohibited. Financial activities include, but are not limited to, those listed in the attached annex. It is left to each country to decide whether special situations should be defined where the application of anti-money laundering measures is not necessary, for example, when a financial activity is carried out on an occasional or limited basis.

Customer identification and record-keeping rules

10. Financial institutions should not keep anonymous accounts or accounts in obviously fictitious names: they should be required (by law, by regulations, by agreements between supervisory authorities and financial institutions or by self-regulatory agreements among financial institutions) to identify, on the basis of an official or other reliable identifying document, and record the identity of their clients, either occasional or usual, when establishing business relations or conducting transactions (in particular opening of accounts or passbooks, entering into fiduciary transactions, renting of safe deposit boxes, performing large cash transactions).

In order to fulfil identification requirements concerning legal entities, financial institutions should, when necessary, take measures:

i.   to verify the legal existence and structure of the customer by obtaining either from a public register or from the customer or both, proof of incorporation, including information concerning the customer's name, legal form, address, directors and provisions regulating the power to bind the entity;

ii.   to verify that any person purporting to act on behalf of the customer is so authorised and identify that person.

11. Financial institutions should take reasonable measures to obtain information about the true identity of the persons on whose behalf an account is opened or a transaction conducted if there are any doubts as to whether these clients or customers are acting on their own behalf, for example, in the case of domiciliary companies (i.e. institutions, corporations, foundations, trusts, etc. that do not conduct any commercial or manufacturing business or any other form of commercial operation in the country where their registered office is located).

12. Financial institutions should maintain, for at least five years, all necessary records on transactions, both domestic or international, to enable them to comply swiftly with information requests from the competent authorities. Such records must be sufficient to permit reconstruction of individual

transactions (including the amounts and types of currency involved if any) so as to provide, if necessary, evidence for prosecution of criminal behaviour.

Financial institutions should keep records on customer identification (e.g. copies or records of official identification documents like passports, identity cards, driving licences or similar documents), account files and business correspondence for at least five years after the account is closed.

These documents should be available to domestic competent authorities in the context of relevant criminal prosecutions and investigations.

13. Countries should pay special attention to money laundering threats inherent in new or developing technologies that might favour anonymity, and take measures, if needed, to prevent their use in money laundering schemes.

Increased diligence of financial institutions

14. Financial institutions should pay special attention to all complex, unusual large transactions, and all unusual patterns of transactions, which have no apparent economic or visible lawful purpose. The background and purpose of such transactions should, as far as possible, be examined, the findings established in writing, and be available to help supervisors, auditors and law enforcement agencies.

15. If financial institutions suspect that funds stem from a criminal activity, they should be required to report promptly their suspicions to the competent authorities.

16. Financial institutions, their directors, officers and employees should be protected by legal provisions from criminal or civil liability for breach of any restriction on disclosure of information imposed by contract or by any legislative, regulatory or administrative provision, if they report their suspicions in good faith to the competent authorities, even if they did not know precisely what the underlying criminal activity was, and regardless of whether illegal activity actually occurred.

17. Financial institutions, their directors, officers and employees, should not, or, where appropriate, should not be allowed to, warn their customers when information relating to them is being reported to the competent authorities.

18. Financial institutions reporting their suspicions should comply with instructions from the competent authorities.

19. Financial institutions should develop programmes against money laundering. These programmes should include, as a minimum :

i.   the development of internal policies, procedures and controls, including the designation of compliance officers at management level, and adequate screening procedures to ensure high standards when hiring employees;

ii. an ongoing employee training programme;

iii. an audit function to test the system.

Measures to cope with the problem of countries with no or insufficient anti-money laundering measures

20. Financial institutions should ensure that the principles mentioned above are also applied to branches and majority owned subsidiaries located abroad, especially in countries which do not or insufficiently apply these recommendations, to the extent that local applicable laws and regulations permit. When local applicable laws and regulations prohibit this implementation, competent authorities in the country of the mother institution should be informed by the financial institutions that they cannot apply these recommendations.

21. Financial institutions should give special attention to business relations and transactions with persons, including companies and financial institutions, from countries which do not or insufficiently apply these recommendations. Whenever these transactions have no apparent economic or visible lawful purpose, their background and purpose should, as far as possible, be examined, the findings established in writing, and be available to help supervisors, auditors and law enforcement agencies.

Other measures to avoid money laundering

22. Countries should consider implementing feasible measures to detect or monitor the physical cross-border transportation of cash and bearer negotiable instruments, subject to strict safeguards to ensure proper use of information and without impeding in any way the freedom of capital movements.

23. Countries should consider the feasibility and utility of a system where banks and other financial institutions and intermediaries would report all domestic and international currency transactions above a fixed amount, to a national central agency with a computerised data base, available to competent authorities for use in money laundering cases, subject to strict safeguards to ensure proper use of the information.

24. Countries should further encourage in general the development of modern and secure techniques of money management, including increased use of cheques, payment cards, direct deposit of salary cheques, and book entry recording of securities, as a means to encourage the replacement of cash transfers.

25. Countries should take notice of the potential for abuse of shell corporations by money launderers and should consider whether additional measures are required to prevent unlawful use of such entities.

Implementation and role of regulatory and other administrative authorities

26. The competent authorities supervising banks or other financial institutions or intermediaries, or other competent authorities, should ensure that the supervised institutions have adequate programmes to guard against money laundering. These authorities should co-operate and lend expertise spontaneously or on request with other domestic judicial or law enforcement authorities in money laundering investigations and prosecutions.

27. Competent authorities should be designated to ensure an effective implementation of all these recommendations, through administrative supervision and regulation, in other professions dealing with cash as defined by each country.

28. The competent authorities should establish guidelines which will assist financial institutions in detecting suspicious patterns of behaviour by their customers. It is understood that such guidelines must develop over time, and will never be exhaustive. It is further understood that such guidelines will primarily serve as an educational tool for financial institutions' personnel.

29. The competent authorities regulating or supervising financial institutions should take the necessary legal or regulatory measures to guard against control or acquisition of a significant participation in financial institutions by criminals or their confederates.

D. Strengthening of international co-operation

Administrative co-operation

Exchange of general information

30. National administrations should consider recording, at least in the aggregate, international flows of cash in whatever currency, so that estimates can be made of cash flows and reflows from various sources abroad,

when this is combined with central bank information. Such information should be made available to the International Monetary Fund and the Bank for International Settlements to facilitate international studies.

31. International competent authorities, perhaps Interpol and the World Customs Organisation, should be given responsibility for gathering and disseminating information to competent authorities about the latest developments in money laundering and money laundering techniques. Central banks and bank regulators could do the same on their network. National authorities in various spheres, in consultation with trade associations, could then disseminate this to financial institutions in individual countries.

Exchange of information relating to suspicious transactions

32. Each country should make efforts to improve a spontaneous or 'upon request' international information exchange relating to suspicious transactions, persons and corporations involved in those transactions between competent authorities. Strict safeguards should be established to ensure that this exchange of information is consistent with national and international provisions on privacy and data protection.

Other forms of co-operation

Basis and means for co-operation in confiscation, mutual assistance and extradition

33. Countries should try to ensure, on a bilateral or multilateral basis, that different knowledge standards in national definitions – i.e. different standards concerning the intentional element of the infraction – do not affect the ability or willingness of countries to provide each other with mutual legal assistance.

34. International co-operation should be supported by a network of bilateral and multilateral agreements and arrangements based on generally shared legal concepts with the aim of providing practical measures to affect the widest possible range of mutual assistance.

35. Countries should be encouraged to ratify and implement relevant international conventions on money laundering such as the 1990 Council of Europe Convention on Laundering, Search, Seizure and Confiscation of the Proceeds from Crime.

Focus of improved mutual assistance on money laundering issues

36. Co-operative investigations among countries' appropriate competent authorities should be encouraged. One valid and effective investigative technique in this respect is controlled delivery related to assets known or

suspected to be the proceeds of crime. Countries are encouraged to support this technique, where possible.

37. There should be procedures for mutual assistance in criminal matters regarding the use of compulsory measures including the production of records by financial institutions and other persons, the search of persons and premises, seizure and obtaining of evidence for use in money laundering investigations and prosecutions and in related actions in foreign jurisdictions.

38. There should be authority to take expeditious action in response to requests by foreign countries to identify, freeze, seize and confiscate proceeds or other property of corresponding value to such proceeds, based on money laundering or the crimes underlying the laundering activity. There should also be arrangements for co-ordinating seizure and confiscation proceedings which may include the sharing of confiscated assets.

39. To avoid conflicts of jurisdiction, consideration should be given to devising and applying mechanisms for determining the best venue for prosecution of defendants in the interests of justice in cases that are subject to prosecution in more than one country. Similarly, there should be arrangements for co-ordinating seizure and confiscation proceedings which may include the sharing of confiscated assets.

40. Countries should have procedures in place to extradite, where possible, individuals charged with a money laundering offence or related offences. With respect to its national legal system, each country should recognise money laundering as an extraditable offence. Subject to their legal frameworks, countries may consider simplifying extradition by allowing direct transmission of extradition requests between appropriate ministries, extraditing persons based only on warrants of arrests or judgements, extraditing their nationals, and/or introducing a simplified extradition of consenting persons who waive formal extradition proceedings.

Annex to Recommendation 9: List of financial activities undertaken by businesses or professions which are not financial institutions

1. Acceptance of deposits and other repayable funds from the public.

2. Lending.[1]

3. Financial leasing.

4. Money transmission services.

---

1. Including, *inter alia*, consumer credit, mortgage credit, factoring, with or without recourse, and finance of commercial transactions (including forfeiting).

5. Issuing and managing means of payment (e.g. credit and debit cards, cheques, traveller's cheques and bankers' drafts...).

6. Financial guarantees and commitments.

7. Trading for account of customers (spot, forward, swaps, futures, options...) in:
a. money market instruments (cheques, bills, CDs, etc.) ;
b. foreign exchange;
c. exchange, interest rate and index instruments;
d. transferable securities;
e. commodity futures trading.

8. Participation in securities issues and the provision of financial services related to such   issues.

9. Individual and collective portfolio management.

10. Safekeeping and administration of cash or liquid securities on behalf of clients.

11. Life insurance and other investment related insurance.

12. Money changing.

APPENDIX IV – THE INTERPRETATIVE NOTES TO THE 1996 RECOMMENDATIONS OF THE FATF

Recommendation 4

Countries should consider introducing an offence of money laundering based on all serious offences and/or on all offences that generate a significant amount of proceeds.

Recommendation 8

The FATF recommendations should be applied in particular to life insurance and other investment products offered by insurance companies, whereas Recommendation 29 applies to the whole of the insurance sector.

Recommendations 8 and 9 (Bureaux de change)

Introduction

1.   *Bureaux de change* are an important link in the money laundering chain since it is difficult to trace the origin of the money once it has been exchanged. Typologies exercises conducted by the FATF have indicated increasing use of *bureaux de change* in laundering operations. Hence it is important that there should be effective countermeasures in this area. This interpretative note clarifies the application of FATF recommendations concerning the financial sector in relation to *bureaux de change* and, where appropriate, sets out options for their implementation.

Definition of bureaux de change

2.   For the purpose of this note, *bureaux de change* are defined as institutions which carry out retail foreign exchange operations (in cash, by cheque or credit card). Money changing operations which are conducted only as an ancillary to the main activity of a business have already been covered in Recommendation 9. Such operations are therefore excluded from the scope of this note.

---

1. During the period 1990 to 1995, the FATF elaborated various interpretative notes which are designed to clarify the application of specific recommendations. Some of these interpretative notes have been updated in the Stocktaking Review to reflect changes in the recommendations.

Necessary countermeasures applicable to bureaux de change

3.   To counter the use of *bureaux de change* for money laundering purposes, the relevant authorities should take measures to know the existence of all natural and legal persons who, in a professional capacity, perform foreign exchange transactions.

4.   As a minimum requirement, FATF members should have an effective system whereby the *bureaux de change* are known or declared to the relevant authorities (whether regulatory or law enforcement). One method by which this could be achieved would be a requirement on *bureaux de change* to submit to a designated authority a simple declaration containing adequate information on the institution itself and its management. The authority could either issue a receipt or give a tacit authorisation: failure to voice an objection being considered as approval.

5.   FATF members could also consider the introduction of a formal authorisation procedure. Those wishing to establish *bureaux de change* would have to submit an application to a designated authority empowered to grant authorisation on a case-by-case basis. The request for authorisation would need to contain such information as laid down by the authorities but should at least provide details of the applicant institution and its management. Authorisation would be granted, subject to the bureau de change meeting the specified conditions relating to its management and the shareholders, including the application of a "fit and proper test".

6.   Another option which could be considered would be a combination of declaration and authorisation procedures. *bureaux de change* would have to notify their existence to a designated authority but would not need to be authorised before they could start business. It would be open to the authority to apply a "fit and proper" test to the management of *bureaux de change* after the *bureau* had commenced its activity, and to prohibit the bureau de change from continuing its business, if appropriate.

7.   Where *bureaux* are required to submit a declaration of activity or an application for registration, the designated authority (which could be either a public body or a self-regulatory organisation) could be empowered to publish the list of registered *bureaux de change*. As a minimum, it should maintain a (computerised) file of *bureaux de change*. There should also be powers to take action against *bureaux de change* conducting business without having made a declaration of activity or having been registered.

8.   As envisaged under FATF Recommendations 8 and 9, *bureaux de change* should be subject to the same anti-money laundering regulations as any other financial institution. The FATF recommendations on financial matters should therefore be applied to *bureaux de change*. Of particular

importance are those on identification requirements, suspicious transactions reporting, due diligence and record-keeping.

9.   To ensure effective implementation of anti-money laundering requirements by *bureaux de change*, compliance monitoring mechanisms should be established and maintained. Where there is a registration authority for *bureaux de change* or a body which receives declarations of activity by *bureaux de change*, it could carry out this function. But the monitoring could also be done by other designated authorities (whether directly or through the agency of third parties such as private audit firms). Appropriate steps would need to be taken against *bureaux de change* which failed to comply with the anti-laundering requirements.

10.   The *bureaux de change* sector tends to be an unstructured one without (unlike banks) national representative bodies which can act as a channel of communication with the authorities. Hence it is important that FATF members should establish effective means to ensure that *bureaux de change* are aware of their anti-money laundering responsibilities and to relay information, such as guidelines on suspicious transactions, to the profession. In this respect it would be useful to encourage the development of professional associations.

Recommendations 11, 15 through 18

Whenever it is necessary in order to know the true identity of the customer and to ensure that legal entities cannot be used by natural persons as a method of operating in reality anonymous accounts, financial institutions should, if the information is not otherwise available through public registers or other reliable sources, request information – and update that information – from the customer concerning principal owners and beneficiaries. If the customer does not have such information, the financial institution should request information from the customer on whoever has actual control.

If adequate information is not obtainable, financial institutions should give special attention to business relations and transactions with the customer.

If, based on information supplied from the customer or from other sources, the financial institution has reason to believe that the customer's account is being utilised in money laundering transactions, the financial institution must comply with the relevant legislation, regulations, directives or agreements concerning reporting of suspicious transactions or termination of business with such customers.

Recommendation 11

A bank or other financial institution should know the identity of its own customers, even if these are represented by lawyers, in order to detect and prevent suspicious transactions as well as to enable it to comply swiftly to information or seizure requests by the competent authorities. Accordingly Recommendation 11 also applies to the situation where an attorney is acting as an intermediary for financial services.

Recommendation 14

a.   In the interpretation of this requirement, special attention is required not only to transactions between financial institutions and their clients, but also to transactions and/or shipments especially of currency and equivalent instruments between financial institutions themselves or even to transactions within financial groups. As the wording of Recommendation 14 suggests that indeed 'all' transactions are covered, it must be read to incorporate these interbank transactions.

b.   The word "transactions" should be understood to refer to the insurance product itself, the premium payment and the benefits.

Recommendation 22

a.   To facilitate detection and monitoring of cash transactions, without impeding in any way the freedom of capital movements, members could consider the feasibility of subjecting all cross-border transfers, above a given threshold, to verification, administrative monitoring, declaration or record-keeping requirements.

b.   If a country discovers an unusual international shipment of currency, monetary instruments, precious metals, or gems, etc., it should consider notifying, as appropriate, the customs service or other competent authorities of the countries from which the shipment originated and/or to which it is destined, and should co-operate with a view toward establishing the source, destination, and purpose of such shipment and toward the taking of appropriate action.

Recommendation 26

In respect of this requirement, it should be noted that it would be useful to actively detect money laundering if the competent authorities make relevant statistical information available to the investigative authorities, especially if this information contains specific indicators of money laundering activity. For instance, if the competent authorities' statistics show an imbalance between the development of the financial services industry in a certain geographical area within a country and the development of the local economy, this imbalance might be indicative of money laundering activity in the region. Another example would be manifest changes in domestic currency flows without an apparent legitimate economic cause. However, prudent analysis of these statistical data is warranted, especially as there is not necessarily a direct relationship between financial flows and economic activity (e.g. the financial flows in an international financial centre with a high proportion of investment management services provided for foreign customers or a large interbank market not linked with local economic activity).

Recommendation 29

Recommendation 29 should not be read as to require the introduction of a system of regular review of licensing of controlling interests in financial institutions merely for anti-money laundering purposes, but as to stress the desirability of suitability review for controlling shareholders in financial institutions (banks and non-banks in particular) from a FATF point of view. Hence, where shareholder suitability (or "fit and proper") tests exist, the attention of supervisors should be drawn to their relevance for anti-money laundering purposes.

Recommendation 33

Subject to principles of domestic law, countries should endeavour to ensure that differences in the national definitions of the money laundering offences – e.g., different standards concerning the intentional element of the infraction, differences in the predicate offences, differences with regard to charging the perpetrator of the underlying offence with money laundering – do not affect the ability or willingness of countries to provide each other with mutual legal assistance.

Recommendation 36 (Controlled delivery)

The controlled delivery of funds known or suspected to be the proceeds of crime is a valid and effective law enforcement technique for obtaining information and evidence in particular on international money laundering operations. In certain countries, controlled delivery techniques may also include the monitoring of funds. It can be of great value in pursuing particular criminal investigations and can also help in obtaining more general intelligence on money laundering activities. The use of these techniques should be strongly encouraged. The appropriate steps should therefore be taken so that no obstacles exist in legal systems preventing the use of controlled delivery techniques, subject to any legal requisites, including judicial authorisation for the conduct of such operations. The FATF welcomes and supports the undertakings by the World Customs Organisation and Interpol to encourage their members to take all appropriate steps to further the use of these techniques.

Recommendation 38

a. Each country shall consider, when possible, establishing an asset forfeiture fund in its respective country into which all or a portion of confiscated property will be deposited for law enforcement, health, education, or other appropriate purposes.

b. Each country should consider, when possible, taking such measures as may be necessary to enable it to share among or between other countries confiscated property, in particular, when confiscation is directly or indirectly a result of co-ordinated law enforcement actions.

Deferred arrest and seizure

Countries should consider taking measures, including legislative ones, at the national level, to allow their competent authorities investigating money laundering cases to postpone or waive the arrest of suspected persons and/or the seizure of the money for the purpose of identifying persons involved in such activities or for evidence gathering. Without such measures the use of procedures such as controlled deliveries and undercover operations are precluded.

Appendix V – The 1990 Council of Europe Convention on Laundering, Search, Seizure and Confiscation of the Proceeds from Crime

Preamble

The member States of the Council of Europe and the other States signatory hereto,

Considering that the aim of the Council of Europe is to achieve a greater unity between its members;

Convinced of the need to pursue a common criminal policy aimed at the protection of society;

Considering that the fight against serious crime, which has become an increasingly international problem, calls for the use of modern and effective methods on an international scale;

Believing that one of these methods consists in depriving criminals of the proceeds from crime;

Considering that for the attainment of this aim a well-functioning system of international co-operation also must be established,

Have agreed as follows:

Chapter I – Use of terms

Article 1 – Use of terms

For the purposes of this Convention:

a.   "proceeds" means any economic advantage from criminal offences. It may consist of any property as defined in sub-paragraph b. of this article;

b.   "property" includes property of any description, whether corporeal or incorporeal, movable or immovable, and legal documents or instruments evidencing title to, or interest in such property;

c.   "instrumentalities" means any property used or intended to be used, in any manner, wholly or in part, to commit a criminal offence or criminal offences;

d.   "confiscation" means a penalty or a measure, ordered by a court following proceedings in relation to a criminal offence or criminal offences resulting in the final deprivation of property;

e. "predicate offence" means any criminal offence as a result of which proceeds were generated that may become the subject of an offence as defined in Article 6 of this Convention.

Chapter II – Measures to be taken at national level

Article 2 – Confiscation measures

1. Each Party shall adopt such legislative and other measures as may be necessary to enable it to confiscate instrumentalities and proceeds or property the value of which corresponds to such proceeds.

2. Each Party may, at the time of signature or when depositing its instrument of ratification, acceptance, approval or accession, by a declaration addressed to the Secretary General of the Council of Europe, declare that paragraph 1 of this article applies only to offences or categories of offences specified in such declaration.

Article 3 – Investigative and provisional measures

Each Party shall adopt such legislative and other measures as may be necessary to enable it to identify and trace property which is liable to confiscation pursuant to Article 2, paragraph 1, and to prevent any dealing in, transfer or disposal of such property.

Article 4 – Special investigative powers and techniques

1. Each Party shall adopt such legislative and other measures as may be necessary to empower its courts or other competent authorities to order that bank, financial or commercial records be made available or be seized in order to carry out the actions referred to in Articles 2 and 3. A Party shall not decline to act under the provisions of this article on grounds of bank secrecy.

2. Each Party shall consider adopting such legislative and other measures as may be necessary to enable it to use special investigative techniques facilitating the identification and tracing of proceeds and the gathering of evidence related thereto. Such techniques may include monitoring orders, observation, interception of telecommunications, access to computer systems and orders to produce specific documents.

Article 5 – Legal remedies

Each Party shall adopt such legislative and other measures as may be necessary to ensure that interested parties affected by measures under Articles 2 and 3 shall have effective legal remedies in order to preserve their rights.

Article 6 – Laundering offences

1.   Each Party shall adopt such legislative and other measures as may be necessary to establish as offences under its domestic law, when committed intentionally:

a.   the conversion or transfer of property, knowing that such property is proceeds, for the purpose of concealing or disguising the illicit origin of the property or of assisting any person who is involved in the commission of the predicate offence to evade the legal consequences of his actions;

b.   the concealment or disguise of the true nature, source, location, disposition, movement, rights with respect to, or ownership of, property, knowing that such property is proceeds; and, subject to its constitutional principles and the basic concepts of its legal system;

c.   the acquisition, possession or use of property, knowing, at the time of receipt, that such property was proceeds;

d.   participation in, association or conspiracy to commit, attempts to commit and aiding, abetting, facilitating and counselling the commission of any of the offences established in accordance with this article.

2.   For the purposes of implementing or applying paragraph 1 of this article:

a.   it shall not matter whether the predicate offence was subject to the criminal jurisdiction of the Party;

b.   it may be provided that the offences set forth in that paragraph do not apply to the persons who committed the predicate offence;

c.   knowledge, intent or purpose required as an element of an offence set forth in that paragraph may be inferred from objective, factual circumstances.

3.   Each Party may adopt such measures as it considers necessary to establish also as offences under its domestic law all or some of the acts referred to in paragraph 1 of this article, in any or all of the following cases where the offender:

a.   ought to have assumed that the property was proceeds;

b.   acted for the purpose of making profit;

c.   acted for the purpose of promoting the carrying on of further criminal activity.

4.   Each Party may, at the time of signature or when depositing its instrument of ratification, acceptance, approval or accession, by declaration addressed to the Secretary General of the Council of Europe declare that paragraph 1 of this article applies only to predicate offences or categories of such offences specified in such declaration.

Chapter III – International co-operation

Section 1 – Principles of international co-operation

Article 7 – General principles and measures for international co-operation

1.   The Parties shall co-operate with each other to the widest extent possible for the purposes of investigations and proceedings aiming at the confiscation of instrumentalities and proceeds.

2.   Each Party shall adopt such legislative or other measures as may be necessary to enable it to comply, under the conditions provided for in this chapter, with requests:

a.   for confiscation of specific items of property representing proceeds or instrumentalities, as well as for confiscation of proceeds consisting in a requirement to pay a sum of money corresponding to the value of proceeds;

b.   for investigative assistance and provisional measures with a view to either form of confiscation referred to under a above.

Section 2 – Investigative assistance

Article 8 – Obligation to assist

The Parties shall afford each other, upon request, the widest possible measure of assistance in the identification and tracing of instrumentalities, proceeds and other property liable to confiscation. Such assistance shall include any measure providing and securing evidence as to the existence, location or movement, nature, legal status or value of the aforementioned property.

Article 9 – Execution of assistance

The assistance pursuant to Article 8 shall be carried out as permitted by and in accordance with the domestic law of the requested Party and, to the extent not incompatible with such law, in accordance with the procedures specified in the request.

Article 10 – Spontaneous information

Without prejudice to its own investigations or proceedings, a Party may without prior request forward to another Party information on instrumentalities and proceeds, when it considers that the disclosure of such information might assist the receiving Party in initiating or carrying out investigations or proceedings or might lead to a request by that Party under this chapter.

Section 3 – Provisional measures

Article 11 – Obligation to take provisional measures

1.   At the request of another Party which has instituted criminal proceedings or proceedings for the purpose of confiscation, a Party shall take the necessary provisional measures, such as freezing or seizing, to prevent any dealing in, transfer or disposal of property which, at a later stage, may be the subject of a request for confiscation or which might be such as to satisfy the request.

2.   A Party which has received a request for confiscation pursuant to Article 13 shall, if so requested, take the measures mentioned in paragraph 1 of this article in respect of any property which is the subject of the request or which might be such as to satisfy the request.

Article 12 – Execution of provisional measures

1.   The provisional measures mentioned in Article 11 shall be carried out as permitted by and in accordance with the domestic law of the requested Party and, to the extent not incompatible with such law, in accordance with the procedures specified in the request.

2.   Before lifting any provisional measure taken pursuant to this article, the requested Party shall, wherever possible, give the requesting Party an opportunity to present its reasons in favour of continuing the measure.

Section 4 – Confiscation

Article 13 – Obligation to confiscate

1.   A Party, which has received a request made by another Party for confiscation concerning instrumentalities or proceeds, situated in its territory, shall:

a.   enforce a confiscation order made by a court of a requesting Party in relation to such instrumentalities or proceeds; or

b.   submit the request to its competent authorities for the purpose of obtaining an order of confiscation and, if such order is granted, enforce it.

2.   For the purposes of applying paragraph 1.*b* of this article, any Party shall whenever necessary have competence to institute confiscation proceedings under its own law.

3.   The provisions of paragraph 1 of this article shall also apply to confiscation consisting in a requirement to pay a sum of money corresponding to the value of proceeds, if property on which the confiscation can be enforced is located in the requested Party. In such cases, when enforcing confiscation pursuant to paragraph 1, the requested Party shall, if payment is not obtained, realise the claim on any property available for that purpose.

4.   If a request for confiscation concerns a specific item of property, the Parties may agree that the requested Party may enforce the confiscation in the form of a requirement to pay a sum of money corresponding to the value of the property.

Article 14 – Execution of confiscation

1.   The procedures for obtaining and enforcing the confiscation under Article 13 shall be governed by the law of the requested Party.

2.   The requested Party shall be bound by the findings as to the facts in so far as they are stated in a conviction or judicial decision of the requesting Party or in so far as such conviction or judicial decision is implicitly based on them.

3.   Each Party may, at the time of signature or when depositing its instrument of ratification, acceptance, approval or accession, by a declaration addressed to the Secretary General of the Council of Europe, declare that paragraph 2 of this article applies only subject to its constitutional principles and the basic concepts of its legal system.

4.   If the confiscation consists in the requirement to pay a sum of money, the competent authority of the requested Party shall convert the amount thereof into the currency of that Party at the rate of exchange ruling at the time when the decision to enforce the confiscation is taken.

5.   In the case of Article 13, paragraph 1.*a*, the requesting Party alone shall have the right to decide on any application for review of the confiscation order.

Article 15 – Confiscated property

Any property confiscated by the requested Party shall be disposed of by that Party in accordance with its domestic law, unless otherwise agreed by the Parties concerned.

Article 16 – Right of enforcement and maximum amount of confiscation

1.   A request for confiscation made under Article 13 does not affect the right of the requesting Party to enforce itself the confiscation order.

2.   Nothing in this Convention shall be so interpreted as to permit the total value of the confiscation to exceed the amount of the sum of money specified in the confiscation order. If a Party finds that this might occur, the Parties concerned shall enter into consultations to avoid such an effect.

Article 17 – Imprisonment in default

The requested Party shall not impose imprisonment in default or any other measure restricting the liberty of a person as a result of a request under Article 13, if the requesting Party has so specified in the request.

Section 5 – Refusal and postponement of co-operation

Article 18 – Grounds for refusal

1.   Co-operation under this chapter may be refused if:

a.   the action sought would be contrary to the fundamental principles of the legal system of the requested Party; or

b.   the execution of the request is likely to prejudice the sovereignty, security, ordre public or other essential interests of the requested Party; or

c.   in the opinion of the requested Party, the importance of the case to which the request relates does not justify the taking of the action sought; or

d.   the offence to which the request relates is a political or fiscal offence; or

e.   the requested Party considers that compliance with the action sought would be contrary to the principle of *ne bis in idem*; or

f.   the offence to which the request relates would not be an offence under the law of the requested Party if committed within its jurisdiction. However, this ground for refusal applies to co-operation under Section 2 only in so far as the assistance sought involves coercive action.

2. Co-operation under Section 2, in so far as the assistance sought involves coercive action, and under Section 3 of this chapter, may also be refused if the measures sought could not be taken under the domestic law of the requested Party for the purposes of investigations or proceedings, had it been a similar domestic case.

3. Where the law of the requested Party so requires, co-operation under Section 2, in so far as the assistance sought involves coercive action, and under Section 3 of this chapter may also be refused if the measures sought or any other measures having similar effects would not be permitted under the law of the requesting Party, or, as regards the competent authorities of the requesting Party, if the request is not authorised by either a judge or another judicial authority, including public prosecutors, any of these authorities acting in relation to criminal offences.

4. Co-operation under Section 4 of this chapter may also be refused if:

a. under the law of the requested Party confiscation is not provided for in respect of the type of offence to which the request relates; or

b. without prejudice to the obligation pursuant to Article 13, paragraph 3, it would be contrary to the principles of the domestic laws of the requested Party concerning the limits of confiscation in respect of the relationship between an offence and:

    i. an economic advantage that might be qualified as its proceeds; or

    ii. property that might be qualified as its instrumentalities; or

c. under the law of the requested Party confiscation may no longer be imposed or enforced because of the lapse of time; or

d. the request does not relate to a previous conviction, or a decision of a judicial nature or a statement in such a decision that an offence or several offences have been committed, on the basis of which the confiscation has been ordered or is sought; or

e. confiscation is either not enforceable in the requesting Party, or it is still subject to ordinary means of appeal; or

f. the request relates to a confiscation order resulting from a decision rendered *in absentia* of the person against whom the order was issued and, in the opinion of the requested Party, the proceedings conducted by the requesting Party leading to such decision did not satisfy the minimum rights of defence recognised as due to everyone against whom a criminal charge is made.

5. For the purpose of paragraph 4.*f* of this article a decision is not considered to have been rendered *in absentia* if:

a. it has been confirmed or pronounced after opposition by the person concerned; or

b.   it has been rendered on appeal, provided that the appeal was lodged by the person concerned.

6.   When considering, for the purposes of paragraph 4.f of this article if the minimum rights of defence have been satisfied, the requested Party shall take into account the fact that the person concerned has deliberately sought to evade justice or the fact that that person, having had the possibility of lodging a legal remedy against the decision made *in absentia*, elected not to do so. The same will apply when the person concerned, having been duly served with the summons to appear, elected not to do so nor to ask for adjournment.

7.   A Party shall not invoke bank secrecy as a ground to refuse any co-operation under this chapter. Where its domestic law so requires, a Party may require that a request for co-operation which would involve the lifting of bank secrecy be authorised by either a judge or another judicial authority, including public prosecutors, any of these authorities acting in relation to criminal offences.

8.   Without prejudice to the ground for refusal provided for in paragraph 1.a of this article:

a.   the fact that the person under investigation or subjected to a confiscation order by the authorities of the requesting Party is a legal person shall not be invoked by the requested Party as an obstacle to affording any co-operation under this chapter;

b.   the fact that the natural person against whom an order of confiscation of proceeds has been issued has subsequently died or the fact that a legal person against whom an order of confiscation of proceeds has been issued has subsequently been dissolved shall not be invoked as an obstacle to render assistance in accordance with Article 13, paragraph 1.*a*.

Article 19 – Postponement

The requested Party may postpone action on a request if such action would prejudice investigations or proceedings by its authorities.

Article 20 – Partial or conditional granting of a request

Before refusing or postponing co-operation under this chapter, the requested Party shall, where appropriate after having consulted the requesting Party, consider whether the request may be granted partially or subject to such conditions as it deems necessary.

Section 6 – Notification and protection of third parties' rights

Article 21 – Notification of documents

1.   The Parties shall afford each other the widest measure of mutual assistance in the serving of judicial documents to persons affected by provisional measures and confiscation.

2.   Nothing in this article is intended to interfere with:

a.   the possibility of sending judicial documents, by postal channels, directly to persons abroad;

b.   the possibility for judicial officers, officials or other competent authorities of the Party of origin to effect service of judicial documents directly through the consular authorities of that Party or through judicial officers, officials or other competent authorities of the Party of destination,

unless the Party of destination makes a declaration to the contrary to the Secretary General of the Council of Europe at the time of signature or when depositing its instrument of ratification, acceptance, approval or accession.

3.   When serving judicial documents to persons abroad affected by provisional measures or confiscation orders issued in the sending Party, this Party shall indicate what legal remedies are available under its law to such persons.

Article 22 – Recognition of foreign decisions

1.   When dealing with a request for co-operation under Sections 3 and 4, the requested Party shall recognise any judicial decision taken in the requesting Party regarding rights claimed by third parties.

2.   Recognition may be refused if:

a.   third parties did not have adequate opportunity to assert their rights; or

b.   the decision is incompatible with a decision already taken in the requested Party on the same matter; or

c.   it is incompatible with the *ordre public* of the requested Party; or

d.   the decision was taken contrary to provisions on exclusive jurisdiction provided for by the law of the requested Party.

Section 7 – Procedural and other general rules

Article 23 – Central authority

1. The Parties shall designate a central authority or, if necessary, authorities, which shall be responsible for sending and answering requests made under this chapter, the execution of such requests or the transmission of them to the authorities competent for their execution.

2. Each Party shall, at the time of signature or when depositing its instrument of ratification, acceptance, approval or accession, communicate to the Secretary General of the Council of Europe the names and addresses of the authorities designated in pursuance of paragraph 1 of this article.

Article 24 – Direct communication

1. The central authorities shall communicate directly with one another.

2. In the event of urgency, requests or communications under this chapter may be sent directly by the judicial authorities, including public prosecutors, of the requesting Party to such authorities of the requested Party. In such cases a copy shall be sent at the same time to the central authority of the requested Party through the central authority of the requesting Party.

3. Any request or communication under paragraphs 1 and 2 of this article may be made through the International Criminal Police Organisation (Interpol).

4. Where a request is made pursuant to paragraph 2 of this article and the authority is not competent to deal with the request, it shall refer the request to the competent national authority and inform directly the requesting Party that it has done so.

5. Requests or communications under Section 2 of this chapter, which do not involve coercive action, may be directly transmitted by the competent authorities of the requesting Party to the competent authorities of the requested Party.

Article 25 – Form of request and languages

1. All requests under this chapter shall be made in writing. Modern means of telecommunications, such as telefax, may be used.

2. Subject to the provisions of paragraph 3 of this article, translations of the requests or supporting documents shall not be required.

3.　At the time of signature or when depositing its instrument of ratification, acceptance, approval or accession, any Party may communicate to the Secretary General of the Council of Europe a declaration that it reserves the right to require that requests made to it and documents supporting such requests be accompanied by a translation into its own language or into one of the official languages of the Council of Europe or into such one of these languages as it shall indicate. It may on that occasion declare its readiness to accept translations in any other language as it may specify. The other Parties may apply the reciprocity rule.

Article 26 – Legalisation

Documents transmitted in application of this chapter shall be exempt from all legalisation formalities.

Article 27 – Content of request

1.　Any request for co-operation under this chapter shall specify:

a.　the authority making the request and the authority carrying out the investigations or proceedings;

b.　the object of and the reason for the request;

c.　the matters, including the relevant facts (such as date, place and circumstances of the offence) to which the investigations or proceedings relate, except in the case of a request for notification;

d.　in so far as the co-operation involves coercive action:

　　i.　the text of the statutory provisions or, where this is not possible, a statement of the relevant law applicable; and

　　ii.　an indication that the measure sought or any other measures having similar effects could be taken in the territory of the requesting Party under its own law;

e.　where necessary and in so far as possible:

　　i.　details of the person or persons concerned, including name, date and place of birth, nationality and location, and, in the case of a legal person, its seat; and

　　ii.　the property in relation to which co-operation is sought, its location, its connection with the person or persons concerned, any connection with the offence, as well as any available information about other persons, interests in the property; and

f.　any particular procedure the requesting Party wishes to be followed.

2.　A request for provisional measures under Section 3 in relation to seizure of property on which a confiscation order consisting in the requirement to pay a sum of money may be realised shall also indicate a maximum amount for which recovery is sought in that property.

3. In addition to the indications mentioned in paragraph 1, any request under Section 4 shall contain:

a. in the case of Article 13, paragraph 1.a:

i. a certified true copy of the confiscation order made by the court in the requesting Party and a statement of the grounds on the basis of which the order was made, if they are not indicated in the order itself;

ii. an attestation by the competent authority of the requesting Party that the confiscation order is enforceable and not subject to ordinary means of appeal;

iii. information as to the extent to which the enforcement of the order is requested; and

iv. information as to the necessity of taking any provisional measures;

b. in the case of Article 13, paragraph 1.b, a statement of the facts relied upon by the requesting Party sufficient to enable the requested Party to seek the order under its domestic law;

c. when third parties have had the opportunity to claim rights, documents demonstrating that this has been the case.

Article 28 – Defective requests

1. If a request does not comply with the provisions of this chapter or the information supplied is not sufficient to enable the requested Party to deal with the request, that Party may ask the requesting Party to amend the request or to complete it with additional information.

2. The requested Party may set a time-limit for the receipt of such amendments or information.

3. Pending receipt of the requested amendments or information in relation to a request under Section 4 of this chapter, the requested Party may take any of the measures referred to in Sections 2 or 3 of this chapter.

Article 29 – Plurality of requests

1. Where the requested Party receives more than one request under Sections 3 or 4 of this chapter in respect of the same person or property, the plurality of requests shall not prevent that Party from dealing with the requests involving the taking of provisional measures.

2. In the case of plurality of requests under Section 4 of this chapter, the requested Party shall consider consulting the requesting Parties.

Article 30 – Obligation to give reasons

The requested Party shall give reasons for any decision to refuse, postpone or make conditional any co-operation under this chapter.

Article 31 – Information

1.   The requested Party shall promptly inform the requesting Party of:

a.   the action initiated on a request under this chapter;

b.   the final result of the action carried out on the basis of the request;

c.   a decision to refuse, postpone or make conditional, in whole or in part, any co-operation under this chapter;

d.   any circumstances which render impossible the carrying out of the action sought or are likely to delay it significantly; and

e.   in the event of provisional measures taken pursuant to a request under Sections 2 or 3 of this chapter, such provisions of its domestic law as would automatically lead to the lifting of the provisional measure.

2.   The requesting Party shall promptly inform the requested Party of:

a.   any review, decision or any other fact by reason of which the confiscation order ceases to be wholly or partially enforceable; and

b.   any development, factual or legal, by reason of which any action under this chapter is no longer justified.

3.   Where a Party, on the basis of the same confiscation order, requests confiscation in more than one Party, it shall inform all Parties which are affected by an enforcement of the order about the request.

Article 32 – Restriction of use

1.   The requested Party may make the execution of a request dependent on the condition that the information or evidence obtained will not, without its prior consent, be used or transmitted by the authorities of the requesting Party for investigations or proceedings other than those specified in the request.

2.   Each Party may, at the time of signature or when depositing its instrument of ratification, acceptance, approval or accession, by declaration addressed to the Secretary General of the Council of Europe, declare that, without its prior consent, information or evidence provided by it under this chapter may not be used or transmitted by the authorities of the requesting Party in investigations or proceedings other than those specified in the request.

Article 33 – Confidentiality

1.   The requesting Party may require that the requested Party keep confidential the facts and substance of the request, except to the extent necessary to execute the request. If the requested Party cannot comply with the requirement of confidentiality, it shall promptly inform the requesting Party.

2.   The requesting Party shall, if not contrary to basic principles of its national law and if so requested, keep confidential any evidence and information provided by the requested Party, except to the extent that its disclosure is necessary for the investigations or proceedings described in the request.

3.   Subject to the provisions of its domestic law, a Party which has received spontaneous information under Article 10 shall comply with any requirement of confidentiality as required by the Party which supplies the information. If the other Party cannot comply with such requirement, it shall promptly inform the transmitting Party.

Article 34 – Costs

The ordinary costs of complying with a request shall be borne by the requested Party. Where costs of a substantial or extraordinary nature are necessary to comply with a request, the Parties shall consult in order to agree the conditions on which the request is to be executed and how the costs shall be borne.

Article 35 – Damages

1.   When legal action on liability for damages resulting from an act or omission in relation to co-operation under this chapter has been initiated by a person, the Parties concerned shall consider consulting each other, where appropriate, to determine how to apportion any sum of damages due.

2.   A Party which has become subject of a litigation for damages shall endeavour to inform the other Party of such litigation if that Party might have an interest in the case.

Chapter IV – Final provisions

Article 36 – Signature and entry into force

1.   This Convention shall be open for signature by the member States of the Council of Europe and non-member States which have participated in its elaboration. Such States may express their consent to be bound by:

a.   signature without reservation as to ratification, acceptance or approval; or

b.   signature subject to ratification, acceptance or approval, followed by ratification, acceptance or approval.

2.   Instruments of ratification, acceptance or approval shall be deposited with the Secretary General of the Council of Europe.

3.   This Convention shall enter into force on the first day of the month following the expiration of a period of three months after the date on which three States, of which at least two are member States of the Council of Europe, have expressed their consent to be bound by the Convention in accordance with the provisions of paragraph 1.

4.   In respect of any signatory State which subsequently expresses its consent to be bound by it, the Convention shall enter into force on the first day of the month following the expiration of a period of three months after the date of the expression of its consent to be bound by the Convention in accordance with the provisions of paragraph 1.

Article 37 – Accession to the Convention

1.   After the entry into force of this Convention, the Committee of Ministers of the Council of Europe, after consulting the Contracting States to the Convention, may invite any State not a member of the Council and not having participated in its elaboration to accede to this Convention, by a decision taken by the majority provided for in Article 20.*d* of the Statute of the Council of Europe and by the unanimous vote of the representatives of the Contracting States entitled to sit on the Committee.

2.   In respect of any acceding State the Convention shall enter into force on the first day of the month following the expiration of a period of three months after the date of deposit of the instrument of accession with the Secretary General of the Council of Europe.

Article 38 – Territorial application

1.   Any State may, at the time of signature or when depositing its instrument of ratification, acceptance, approval or accession, specify the territory or territories to which this Convention shall apply.

2.   Any State may, at any later date, by a declaration addressed to the Secretary General of the Council of Europe, extend the application of this Convention to any other territory specified in the declaration. In respect of such territory the Convention shall enter into force on the first day of the month following the expiration of a period of three months after the date of receipt of such declaration by the Secretary General.

3. Any declaration made under the two preceding paragraphs may, in respect of any territory specified in such declaration, be withdrawn by a notification addressed to the Secretary General. The withdrawal shall become effective on the first day of the month following the expiration of a period of three months after the date of receipt of such notification by the Secretary General.

Article 39 – Relationship to other conventions and agreements

1. This Convention does not affect the rights and undertakings derived from international multilateral conventions concerning special matters.

2. The Parties to the Convention may conclude bilateral or multilateral agreements with one another on the matters dealt with in this Convention, for purposes of supplementing or strengthening its provisions or facilitating the application of the principles embodied in it.

3. If two or more Parties have already concluded an agreement or treaty in respect of a subject which is dealt with in this Convention or otherwise have established their relations in respect of that subject, they shall be entitled to apply that agreement or treaty or to regulate those relations accordingly, in lieu of the present Convention, if it facilitates international co-operation.

Article 40 – Reservations

1. Any State may, at the time of signature or when depositing its instrument of ratification, acceptance, approval or accession, declare that it avails itself of one or more of the reservations provided for in Article 2, paragraph 2, Article 6, paragraph 4, Article 14, paragraph 3, Article 21, paragraph 2, Article 25, paragraph 3 and Article 32, paragraph 2. No other reservation may be made.

2. Any State which has made a reservation under the preceding paragraph may wholly or partly withdraw it by means of a notification addressed to the Secretary General of the Council of Europe. The withdrawal shall take effect on the date of receipt of such notification by the Secretary General.

3. A Party which has made a reservation in respect of a provision of this Convention may not claim the application of that provision by any other Party; it may, however, if its reservation is partial or conditional, claim the application of that provision in so far as it has itself accepted it.

Article 41 – Amendments

1.   Amendments to this Convention may be proposed by any Party, and shall be communicated by the Secretary General of the Council of Europe to the member States of the Council of Europe and to every non-member State which has acceded to or has been invited to accede to this Convention in accordance with the provisions of Article 37.

2.   Any amendment proposed by a Party shall be communicated to the European Committee on Crime Problems which shall submit to the Committee of Ministers its opinion on that proposed amendment.

3.   The Committee of Ministers shall consider the proposed amendment and the opinion submitted by the European Committee on Crime Problems and may adopt the amendment.

4.   The text of any amendment adopted by the Committee of Ministers in accordance with paragraph 3 of this article shall be forwarded to the Parties for acceptance.

5.   Any amendment adopted in accordance with paragraph 3 of this article shall come into force on the thirtieth day after all Parties have informed the Secretary General of their acceptance thereof.

Article 42 – Settlement of disputes

1.   The European Committee on Crime Problems of the Council of Europe shall be kept informed regarding the interpretation and application of this Convention.

2.   In case of a dispute between Parties as to the interpretation or application of this Convention, they shall seek a settlement of the dispute through negotiation or any other peaceful means of their choice, including submission of the dispute to the European Committee on Crime Problems, to an arbitral tribunal whose decisions shall be binding upon the Parties, or to the International Court of Justice, as agreed upon by the Parties concerned.

Article 43 – Denunciation

1.   Any Party may, at any time, denounce this Convention by means of a notification addressed to the Secretary General of the Council of Europe.

2.   Such denunciation shall become effective on the first day of the month following the expiration of a period of three months after the date of receipt of the notification by the Secretary General.

3. The present Convention shall, however, continue to apply to the enforcement under Article 14 of confiscation for which a request has been made in conformity with the provisions of this Convention before the date on which such a denunciation takes effect.

Article 44 – Notifications

The Secretary General of the Council of Europe shall notify the member States of the Council and any State which has acceded to this Convention of:

a. any signature;

b. the deposit of any instrument of ratification, acceptance, approval or accession;

c. any date of entry into force of this Convention in accordance with Articles 36 and 37;

d. any reservation made under Article 40, paragraph 1;

e. any other act, notification or communication relating to this Convention.

In witness whereof the undersigned, being duly authorised thereto, have signed this Convention.

Done at Strasbourg, the 8th day of November 1990, in English and in French, both texts being equally authentic, in a single copy which shall be deposited in the archives of the Council of Europe. The Secretary General of the Council of Europe shall transmit certified copies to each member State of the Council of Europe, to the non-member States which have participated in the elaboration of this Convention, and to any State invited to accede to it.

Appendix VI – The 1991 European Communities Directive

Council Directive of 10 June 1991 on Prevention of the use of the Financial System for the Purpose of Money Laundering (91/308/EEC)

The Council of the European Communities,

Having regard to the Treaty establishing the European Economic Community, and in particular Article 57 (2), first and third sentences, and Article 100a thereof,

Having regard to the proposal from the Commission,[1]

In co-operation with the European Parliament,[2]

Having regard to the opinion of the Economic and Social Committee,[3]

Whereas when credit and financial institutions are used to launder proceeds from criminal activities (hereinafter referred to as "money laundering"), the soundness and stability of the institution concerned and confidence in the financial system as a whole could be seriously jeopardised, thereby losing the trust of the public;

Whereas lack of Community action against money laundering could lead member states, for the purpose of protecting their financial systems, to adopt measures which could be inconsistent with completion of the single market; whereas, in order to facilitate their criminal activities, launderers could try to take advantage of the freedom of capital movement and freedom to supply financial services which the integrated financial area involves, if certain co-ordinating measures are not adopted at Community level;

Whereas money laundering has an evident influence on the rise of organised crime in general and drug trafficking in particular; whereas there is more and more awareness that combating money laundering is one of the most effective means of opposing this form of criminal activity, which constitutes a particular threat to member states' societies;

Whereas money laundering must be combated mainly by penal means and within the framework of international co-operation among judicial and law

---

1. OJ No. C 106, 28.4.1990, p. 6; and OJ No. C 319, 19.12.1990, p. 9.
2. OJ No. C 324, 24.12.1990, p. 264; and OJ No. C 129, 20.5.1991.
3. OJ No. C 332, 31.12.1990, p. 86.

enforcement authorities, as has been undertaken, in the field of drugs, by the United Nations Convention against Illicit Traffic in Narcotic Drugs and Psychotropic Substances, adopted on 19 December 1988 in Vienna (hereinafter referred to as the "Vienna Convention") and more generally in relation to all criminal activities, by the Council of Europe Convention on Laundering, Tracing, Seizure and Confiscation of the Proceeds from Crime, opened for signature on 8 November 1990 in Strasbourg;

Whereas a penal approach should, however, not be the only way to combat money laundering, since the financial system can play a highly effective role; whereas reference must be made in this context to the recommendation of the Council of Europe of 27 June 1980 and to the declaration of principles adopted in December 1988 in Basle by the banking supervisory authorities of the Group of Ten, both of which constitute major steps towards preventing the use of the financial system for money laundering;

Whereas money laundering is usually carried out in an international context so that the criminal origin of the funds can be better disguised; whereas measures exclusively adopted at a national level, without taking account of international co-ordination and co-operation, would have very limited effects;

Whereas any measures adopted by the Community in this field should be consistent with other action undertaken in other international fora; whereas in this respect any Community action should take particular account of the recommendations adopted by the Financial Action Task Force on Money Laundering, set up in July 1989 by the Paris summit of the seven most developed countries;

Whereas the European Parliament has requested, in several resolutions, the establishment of a global Community programme to combat drug trafficking, including provisions on prevention of money laundering;

Whereas for the purposes of this Directive the definition of money laundering is taken from that adopted in the Vienna Convention; whereas, however, since money laundering occurs not only in relation to the proceeds of drug-related offences but also in relation to the proceeds of other criminal activities (such as organised crime and terrorism), the member states should, within the meaning of their legislation, extend the effects of the Directive to include the proceeds of such activities, to the extent that they are likely to result in laundering operations justifying sanctions on that basis;

Whereas prohibition of money laundering in member states' legislation backed by appropriate measures and penalties is a necessary condition for combating this phenomenon;

Whereas ensuring that credit and financial institutions require identification of their customers when entering into business relations or conducting transactions, exceeding certain thresholds, are necessary to avoid launderers' taking advantage of anonymity to carry out their criminal activities; whereas such provisions must also be extended, as far as possible, to any beneficial owners;

Whereas credit and financial institutions must keep for at least five years copies or references of the identification documents required as well as supporting evidence and records consisting of documents relating to transactions or copies thereof similarly admissible in court proceedings under the applicable national legislation for use as evidence in any investigation into money laundering;

Whereas ensuring that credit and financial institutions examine with special attention any transaction which they regard as particularly likely, by its nature, to be related to money laundering is necessary in order to preserve the soundness and integrity of the financial system as well as to contribute to combating this phenomenon; whereas to this end they should pay special attention to transactions with third countries which do not apply comparable standards against money laundering to those established by the Community or to other equivalent standards set out by international fora and endorsed by the Community;

Whereas, for those purposes, member states may ask credit and financial institutions to record in writing the results of the examination they are required to carry out and to ensure that those results are available to the authorities responsible for efforts to eliminate money laundering;

Whereas preventing the financial system from being used for money laundering is a task which cannot be carried out by the authorities responsible for combating this phenomenon without the co-operation of credit and financial institutions and their supervisory authorities; whereas banking secrecy must be lifted in such cases; whereas a mandatory system of reporting suspicious transactions which ensures that information is transmitted to the above-mentioned authorities without alerting the customers concerned, is the most effective way to accomplish such co-operation; whereas a special protection clause is necessary to exempt credit and financial institutions, their employees and their directors from responsibility for breaching restrictions on disclosure of information;

Whereas the information received by the authorities pursuant to this Directive may be used only in connection with combating money laundering; whereas member states may nevertheless provide that this information may be used for other purposes;

Whereas establishment by credit and financial institutions of procedures of internal control and training programmes in this field are complementary provisions without which the other measures contained in this Directive could become ineffective;

Whereas, since money laundering can be carried out not only through credit and financial institutions but also through other types of professions and categories of undertakings, member states must extend the provisions of this Directive in whole or in part, to include those professions and undertakings whose activities are particularly likely to be used for money laundering purposes;

Whereas it is important that the member states should take particular care to ensure that co-ordinated action is taken in the Community where there are strong grounds for believing that professions or activities the conditions governing the pursuit of which have been harmonised at Community level are being used for laundering money;

Whereas the effectiveness of efforts to eliminate money laundering is particularly dependent on the close co-ordination and harmonisation of national implementing measures; whereas such co-ordination and harmonisation which is being carried out in various international bodies requires, in the Community context, co-operation between member states and the Commission in the framework of a contact committee;

Whereas it is for each member state to adopt appropriate measures and to penalise infringement of such measures in an appropriate manner to ensure full application of this Directive,

Has adopted this Directive:

Article 1

For the purpose of this Directive:

• "credit institution" means a credit institution, as defined as in the first indent of Article 1 of Directive 77/780/EEC,[1] as last amended by Directive 89/646/EEC,[2] and includes branches within the meaning of the third indent of that article and located in the Community, of credit institutions having their head offices outside the Community,

• "financial institution" means an undertaking other than a credit institution whose principal activity is to carry out one or more of the operations included in numbers 2 to 12 and number 14 of the list annexed to Directive 89/646/EEC, or an insurance company duly authorised in accordance with Directive 79/267/EEC,[3] as last amended by Directive 90/619/EEC,[4] in so far

---

1. OJ No. L 322, 17.12.1997, p. 30.
2. OJ No. L 386, 30.12.1989, p. 1.
3. OJ No. L 63, 13.3.1979, p. 1.
4. OJ No. L 330, 29.11.1990, p. 50.

as it carries out activities covered by that Directive; this definition includes branches located in the Community of financial institutions whose head offices are outside the Community,

- "money laundering" means the following conduct when committed intentionally:

    – the conversion or transfer of property, knowing that such property is derived from criminal activity or from an act of participation in such activity, for the purpose of concealing or disguising the illicit origin of the property or of assisting any person who is involved in the commission of such activity to evade the legal consequences of his action;

    – the concealment or disguise of the true nature, source, location, disposition, movement, rights with respect to, or ownership of property, knowing that such property is derived from criminal activity or from an act of participation in such activity;

    – the acquisition, possession or use of property, knowing, at the time of receipt, that such property was derived from criminal activity or from an act of participation in such activity;

    – participation in, association to commit, attempts to commit and aiding, abetting, facilitating and counselling the commission of any of the actions mentioned in the foregoing paragraphs.

Knowledge, intent or purpose required as an element of the above mentioned activities may be inferred from objective factual circumstances.

Money laundering shall be regarded as such even where the activities which generated the property to be laundered were perpetrated in the territory of another member state or in that of a third country.

- "Property" means assets of every kind, whether corporeal or incorporeal, movable or immovable, tangible or intangible, and legal documents or instruments evidencing title to or interests in such assets.

- "Criminal activity" means a crime specified in Article 3 (1) (a) of the Vienna Convention and any other criminal activity designated as such for the purposes of this Directive by each member state.

- "Competent authorities" means the national authorities empowered by law or regulation to supervise credit or financial institutions.

Article 2

Member states shall ensure that money laundering as defined in this Directive is prohibited.

Article 3

1.   Member states shall ensure that credit and financial institutions require identification of their customers by means of supporting evidence when entering into business relations, particularly when opening an account or savings accounts, or when offering safe custody facilities.

2.   The identification requirement shall also apply for any transaction with customers other than those referred to in paragraph 1, involving a sum amounting to ecu 15 000 or more, whether the transaction is carried out in a single operation or in several operations which seem to be linked. Where the sum is not known at the time when the transaction is undertaken, the institution concerned shall proceed with identification as soon as it is apprised of the sum and establishes that the threshold has been reached.

3.   By way of derogation from paragraphs 1 and 2, the identification requirements with regard to insurance policies written by insurance undertakings within the meaning of Directive 79/267/EEC, where they perform activities which fall within the scope of that Directive shall not be required where the periodic premium amount or amounts to be paid in any given year does or do not exceed ecu 1 000 or where a single premium is paid amounting to ecu 2 500 or less. If the periodic premium amount or amounts to be paid in any given year is or are increased so as to exceed the ecu 1 000 threshold, identification shall be required.

4.   Member states may provide that the identification requirement is not compulsory for insurance policies in respect of pension schemes taken out by virtue of a contract of employment or the insured's occupation, provided that such policies contain no surrender clause and may not be used as collateral for a loan.

5.   In the event of doubt as to whether the customers referred to in the above paragraphs are acting on their own behalf, or where it is certain that they are not acting on their own behalf, the credit and financial institutions shall take reasonable measures to obtain information as to the real identity of the persons on whose behalf those customers are acting.

6.   Credit and financial institutions shall carry out such identification, even where the amount of the transaction is lower than the threshold laid down, wherever there is suspicion of money laundering.

7.   Credit and financial institutions shall not be subject to the identification requirements provided for in this article where the customer is also a credit or financial institution covered by this Directive.

8.   Member states may provide that the identification requirements regarding transactions referred to in paragraphs 3 and 4 are fulfilled when

it is established that the payment for the transaction is to be debited from an account opened in the customer's name with a credit institution subject to this Directive according to the requirements of paragraph 1.

Article 4

Member states shall ensure that credit and financial institutions keep the following for use as evidence in any investigation into money laundering:

• in the case of identification, a copy or the references of the evidence required, for a period of at least five years after the relationship with their customer has ended,

• in the case of transactions, the supporting evidence and records, consisting of the original documents or copies admissible in court proceedings under the applicable national legislation for a period of at least five years following execution of the transactions.

Article 5

Member states shall ensure that credit and financial institutions examine with special attention any transaction which they regard as particularly likely, by its nature, to be related to money laundering.

Article 6

Member states shall ensure that credit and financial institutions and their directors and employees co-operate fully with the authorities responsible for combating money laundering:

• by informing those authorities, on their own initiative, of any fact which might be an indication of money laundering,

• by furnishing those authorities, at their request, with all necessary information, in accordance with the procedures established by the applicable legislation.

The information referred to in the first paragraph shall be forwarded to the authorities responsible for combating money laundering of the member state in whose territory the institution forwarding the information is situated. The person or persons designated by the credit and financial institutions in accordance with the procedures provided for in Article 11 (1) shall normally forward the information.

Information supplied to the authorities in accordance with the first paragraph may be used only in connection with the combating of money laundering. However, member states may provide that such information may also be used for other purposes.

Article 7

Member states shall ensure that credit and financial institutions refrain from carrying out transactions which they know or suspect to be related to money laundering until they have apprised the authorities referred to in Article 6. Those authorities may, under conditions determined by their national legislation, give instructions not to execute the operation. Where such a transaction is suspected of giving rise to money laundering and where to refrain in such manner is impossible or is likely to frustrate efforts to pursue the beneficiaries of a suspected money laundering operation, the institutions concerned shall apprise the authorities immediately afterwards.

Article 8

Credit and financial institutions and their directors and employees shall not disclose to the customer concerned nor to other third persons that information has been transmitted to the authorities in accordance with Articles 6 and 7 or that a money laundering investigation is being carried out.

Article 9

The disclosure in good faith to the authorities responsible for combating money laundering by an employee or director of a credit or financial institution of the information referred to in Articles 6 and 7 shall not constitute a breach of any restriction on disclosure of information imposed by contract or by any legislative, regulatory or administrative provision, and shall not involve the credit or financial institution, its directors or employees in liability of any kind.

Article 10

Member states shall ensure that if, in the course of inspections carried out in credit or financial institutions by the competent authorities, or in any other way, those authorities discover facts that could constitute evidence of money laundering, they inform the authorities responsible for combating money laundering.

Article 11

Member states shall ensure that credit and financial institutions:

1.   establish adequate procedures of internal control and communication in order to forestall and prevent operations related to money laundering,

2.   take appropriate measures so that their employees are aware of the provisions contained in this Directive. These measures shall include participation of their relevant employees in special training programmes to help

them recognise operations which may be related to money laundering as well as to instruct them as to how to proceed in such cases.

Article 12

Member states shall ensure that the provisions of this Directive are extended in whole or in part to professions and to categories of undertakings, other than the credit and financial institutions referred to in Article 1, which engage in activities which are particularly likely to be used for money laundering purposes.

Article 13

1.   A contact committee (hereinafter referred to as "the Committee") shall be set up under the aegis of the Commission. Its function shall be:

a.   without prejudice to Articles 169 and 170 of the Treaty, to facilitate harmonised implementation of this Directive through regular consultation on any practical problems arising from its application and on which exchanges of view are deemed useful;

b.   to facilitate consultation between the member states on the more stringent or additional conditions and obligations which they may lay down at national level;

c.   to advise the Commission, if necessary, on any supplements or amendments to be made to this Directive or on any adjustments deemed necessary, in particular to harmonise the effects of Article 12;

d.   to examine whether a profession or a category of undertaking should be included in the scope of Article 12 where it has been established that such profession or category of undertaking has been used in a member state for money laundering.

2.   It shall not be the function of the Committee to appraise the merits of decisions taken by the competent authorities in individual cases.

3.   The Committee shall be composed of persons appointed by the member states and of representatives of the Commission. The Secretariat shall be provided by the Commission. The chairman shall be a representative of the Commission. It shall be convened by its chairman, either on his own initiative or at the request of the delegation of a member state.

Article 14

Each member state shall take appropriate measures to ensure full application of all the provisions of this Directive and shall in particular determine the penalties to be applied for infringement of the measures adopted pursuant to this Directive.

Article 15

The member states may adopt or retain in force stricter provisions in the field covered by this Directive to prevent money laundering.

Article 16

1. Member states shall bring into force the laws, regulations and administrative decisions necessary to comply with this Directive before 1 January 1993 at the latest.

2. Where member states adopt these measures, they shall contain a reference to this Directive or shall be accompanied by such reference on the occasion of their official publication. The methods of making such a reference shall be laid down by the member states.

3. Member states shall communicate to the Commission the text of the main provisions of national law which they adopt in the field governed by this Directive.

Article 17

One year after 1 January 1993, whenever necessary and at least at three yearly intervals thereafter, the Commission shall draw up a report on the implementation of this Directive and submit it to the European Parliament and the Council.

Article 18

This Directive is addressed to the member states.

Done at Luxembourg, 10 June 1991.

For the Council
The President
J.-C. Juncker

Statement by the representatives of the governments of the member states meeting within the Council

The representatives of the governments of the member states, meeting within the Council,

Recalling that the member states signed the United Nations Convention against Illicit Traffic in Narcotic Drugs and Psychotropic Substances, adopted on 19 December 1988 in Vienna;

Recalling also that most member states have already signed the Council of Europe Convention on Laundering, Tracing, Seizure and Confiscation of the Proceeds from Crime on 8 November 1990 in Strasbourg;

Conscious of the fact that the description of money laundering contained in Article 1 of Council Directive 91/308/EEC derives its wording from the relevant provisions of the aforementioned Conventions;

Hereby undertake to take all necessary steps by 31 December 1992 at the latest to enact criminal legislation enabling them to comply with their obligations under the aforementioned instruments.

APPENDIX VII – THE 1997 EUROPEAN UNION ACTION PLAN TO COMBAT ORGANISED CRIME

(Adopted by the European Council on 28 April 1997)

(97/C 251/01)

Part I – Introduction

Chapter I – Background

1.   Organised crime is increasingly becoming a threat to society as we know it and want to preserve it. Criminal behaviour no longer is the domain of individuals only, but also of organisations that pervade the various structures of civil society, and indeed society as a whole. Crime is increasingly organising itself across national borders, also taking advantage of the free movement of goods, capital, services and persons. Technological innovations such as Internet and electronic banking turn out to be extremely convenient vehicles either for committing crimes or for transferring the resulting profits into seemingly licit activities. Fraud and corruption take on massive proportions, defrauding citizens and civic institutions alike.

In comparison, effective means of preventing and repressing these criminal activities are developing only at a slow pace, almost always one step behind. If Europe is to develop into an area of freedom, security and justice, it needs to organise itself better, and to provide strategic and tactical responses to the challenge facing it. This requires a political commitment at the highest level.

2.   The European Council (Dublin 13 and 14 December 1996) underlined its absolute determination to fight organised crime and stressed the need for a coherent and co-ordinated approach by the Union. It decided to create a High Level Group to draw up a comprehensive Action Plan containing specific recommendations, including realistic timetables for carrying out the work. The Group was requested to examine the fight against organised crime in all its aspects on the clear understanding that it would refer any issues involving Treaty change to the Intergovernmental Conference (IGC) which is addressing Treaty changes in this area as a priority. The Group should complete its work by March/April 1997.[1] The letter of the Chairman of the High Level Group to the Chairman of the IGC containing the results of this examination is set out in an Annex to this report.

---

1. It is recalled that the European Council also welcomed the report made by the Irish Presidency on stepping up the fight against organised crime (see 11564/4/96 CK4 53, REV 4) and asked the Council to reinforce its Secretariat, in order to implement rapidly the measures proposed in the report.

3.   The High Level Group has held six meetings in pursuance of this mandate. Its findings have led to the drawing up of fifteen Political Guidelines and thirty Specific Recommendations, together with a proposed timetable and an indication of where the responsibility for implementation of each recommendation might be considered to lie. These are set out in Part III of this report in the form of a detailed Action Plan.

4.   In submitting this Action Plan to the Heads of State and Government, the High Level Group underlines its conviction that the fight against organised crime and terrorism is a never-ending endeavour. The fight must be uncompromising but must always use legitimate means and pay full respect to the principles of the Rule of Law, democracy and human rights, not losing sight of the fact that it is the protection of those values which is the *raison d'être* for fighting organised crime.

Chapter II – General approach of the High Level Group

5.   In seeking to respond to the high level of urgency and political importance attached by Heads of State and Government to the problem of combating organised crime, as reflected in the Dublin European Council conclusions, the Group has based its approach on the following elements:

a.   full account should be taken of the work already being pursued on this same question nationally, within the European Union itself and in a number of international fora. This has been particularly relevant since some of the most significant of these international fora, notably the P-8 and the Visby Group, involve several European Union member states. It also means working closely with the countries that are candidates for membership of the Union, with the Union's transatlantic partners, with other countries such as Russia and the Ukraine and with the major international players active in the fight against organised crime (Interpol, United Nations bodies such as the United Nations International Drug Control Programme (UNDCP) and the Commission on Crime Prevention and Criminal Justice, Council of Europe, the Financial Action Task Force (FATF), etc.);

b.   the Group's recommendations should, however, focus on the particular strengths and objectives of the European Union as such, as set out in the Treaty. This provides its member states with a range of instruments, resources (including budgetary resources), institutions and mutual commitments not available to any other group of nations seeking to address a problem of this magnitude;

c.   the right balance should be sought between the respective contributions that can be mobilised by practical co-operation on the one hand and approximation or harmonisation of laws on the other. The extent to which approximation or harmonisation should be a long-term objective of the Union will remain the subject of ongoing study. In the meantime, the

Group has sought to establish the degree of approximation or harmonisation necessary to ensure the most effective possible framework for practical co-operation;

d.   judicial co-operation needs to be brought up to a comparable level to police co-operation. Otherwise, it will not, in the long run, be possible to enhance further police co-operation without distortions in the system. Therefore, it is necessary to seek to achieve maximum synergy in co-operation between law enforcement[1] and the judiciary;

e.   when it comes to the collection and analysis of data to fight organised crime, the relevant data protection rules have to be taken into account;

f.   prevention is no less important than repression in any integrated approach to organised crime, to the extent that it aims at reducing the circumstances in which organised crime can operate. The Union should have the instruments to confront organised crime at each step on the continuum from prevention to repression and prosecution. It is particularly important that legislation does not invite fraud and other undue exploitation. The member states and, where applicable, the institution issuing such rules should ensure that this is not the case;

g.   the major driving force behind organised crime is the pursuit of financial gain. This both attracts it into an ever-increasing number of areas of activity where it sees possibilities for economic crime (corruption, counterfeiting, VAT and other fiscal fraud, piracy, fraud against the Community's financial interests) and also faces it with a need to launder the profits thereafter;

h.   organised crime has shown itself well able to turn to its advantage the speed and anonymity offered by modern forms of communication. This is a vast and fast-moving area, deserving of the sustained attention of legislators and law enforcement authorities alike.

Chapter III – Means to combat organised crime

6.   Taking into account this general approach, the Group has identified the use of the following means, available to the Union, to ensure that the fight against organised crime is carried out in an effective and co-ordinated manner and that a new impetus is given to the protection of the citizens of the Union:

a.   the Union and its member states must mobilise its full potential by introducing a maximum level of two-way involvement between those who draw up the initial legislation, often at Community level, and those whose task it is to enforce it in the police, the customs and the judiciary. This

---

1. Where this Action Plan mentions law enforcement agencies, it includes, where appropriate, its financial regulators as well as customs agencies even if in a particular member state they are not considered to be a law enforcement agency.

implies the full involvement of the member states as well as the European Commission and a co-ordinated effort between the First and Third Pillars of the Union, including a full and reciprocal exchange of relevant information;

b.   in combating organised crime, there is a clear need to "know your enemy" and to agree on the characteristics which make it both dangerous and, it is hoped, vulnerable. This in turn requires the building up and pooling of analytical expertise, including support from the scientific community, from all member states and, where appropriate, the European Institutions and Europol. So far as possible, this should be done according to common definitions, common standards and a common methodology with a view to facilitating the recognition of the phenomenon when it appears and the formulation of an effective policy to counter it, including its repression at the level of law enforcement and prosecution;

c.   the adoption, ratification and effective implementation of all instruments directly or indirectly relevant to the fight against organised crime will continue to be an essential part of the Union's armoury. Political input from the European Council is needed to ensure:

    –   that any remaining obstacles to the finalising of the texts of unfinished instruments (for example, the draft Conventions on Mutual Legal Assistance and on Corruption as well as the draft Third Protocol to the Convention on the Protection of the European Communities' Financial Interests and the Naples II Convention concerning customs co-operation) are quickly overcome;

    –   that any necessary ratification procedures are urgently put on the agenda of national parliaments;

    –   that the necessary implementing measures are rapidly and fully introduced;

d.   there is a need for an effective system to be introduced to monitor the implementation by member states of all the relevant instruments adopted by the Union to combat organised crime. As far as instruments adopted under Community law are concerned, such a system to some extent exists in the form of the Article 169 procedure which the Commission is responsible for initiating. No comparable system exists under the existing provisions of the Third Pillar. This gap could be filled by drawing on the experiences of, for instance, the FATF;

e.   the problem of imperfect co-operation between the various authorities responsible for law enforcement and prosecution has to be addressed both within and among member states. Centralised national points are recommended as an addition to, but not a replacement for, existing networks to facilitate exchanges of information between member states;

f.   it is important to optimise the role Europol might play at each stage of the fight against organised crime. The Europol Convention, as presently drafted, provides scope for a considerable role, and priority must continue to be attached to the rapid ratification and implementation of the Convention, without prejudice to the need to enable the Europol Drugs Unit (EDU) to fully fulfil its mandate. However, following the ratification of the Europol Convention, the Group sees an enhanced role for Europol which is set out in the detailed recommendations and could be seen to go beyond that provided for in the Convention;

g.   To counter money laundering in particular the international community has drawn up a number of conventions, agreements and recommendations (Strasbourg, Vienna, the FATF) which are applied with varying degrees of rigour. The Union and its member states must be totally rigorous, both in the implementation of the various international instruments to combat money laundering, as well as its own legislation (including the 1991 Directive), and in ensuring the maximum level of co-operation and two-way information exchange between its financial and fiscal institutions and its law enforcement and judicial authorities. This can in turn require adjustments in national procedures and a higher level of specialised training than is currently undertaken.

Part II – Political guidelines

7.   The High Level Group recommends the European Council to approve this Action Plan and the time-frame indicated for its realisation.

8.   Among the recommendations set out in the Action Plan are a certain number which the Group considers appropriate to be drawn to the particular attention of Heads of State and Government, as they require a commitment at the highest level. The High Level Group recommends that the European Council adopts the following recommendations as its own political guidelines:

(1)   The Council is requested rapidly to adopt a joint action aiming at making it an offence under the laws of each member state for a person, present in its territory, to participate in a criminal organisation, irrespective of the location in the Union where the organisation is concentrated or is carrying out its criminal activity.

Moreover, the European Council calls upon the Council to examine to what extent, and within which priority areas, a possible approximation or harmonisation of member states' laws could contribute to the fight against organised crime.

(2)   The European Council urges the early adoption of the Conventions, as listed in Recommendations 13 and 14 in Part III and within the time-frame indicated there, which are considered essential for the common fight against organised crime.

In order to further an effective implementation of the European Union conventions on extradition already drawn up, the European Council asks the member states to take, at national level, the necessary measures to ensure that extradition requests can be dealt with in the most simple and expeditious manner.

In this context, the Council should also examine, taking into account the member states' undertakings under international treaties, the means to ensure that the right of asylum is not abused to avoid justice by offenders involved in serious crime.

(3) The Council is requested to establish a mechanism, based on the experience with the model developed in the FATF, for mutually evaluating the manner in which instruments concerning international co-operation in criminal matters, are applied and implemented in each of the member states.

(4) The European Council reiterates that it attaches the greatest importance to an early agreement on the draft Convention on Mutual Assistance in Criminal Matters between the member states of the European Union. The draft should include, among other matters, provisions which aim at rendering reservations made to the Council of Europe Convention on Mutual Assistance in Criminal Matters and its Protocol superfluous in the relations between the member states. In this context, special attention should be given to the reconsideration of the requirement of double criminality.

(5) The European Council encourages the Council and the Commission to define in common with the candidate countries of central and eastern Europe, including the Baltic states, a pre-accession pact on co-operation against crime, which shall be based on the *acquis* of the Union and may include provisions for close co-operation between those countries and Europol and undertakings by those countries to rapid ratification and full implementation of the Council of Europe instruments which are essential to the fight against organised crime.

The European Council stresses the need to develop closer co-operation in the fight against organised crime with other countries such as Russia and Ukraine and asks the Council and the Commission to develop proposals to that end.

(6) The European Council stresses the importance for each member state to have competent law enforcement agencies co-ordinate their action, at national level, in the fight against organised crime as well as share information and act in a concerted manner.

(7) Each member state shall ensure that, in order to facilitate contacts with other member states, with Europol and with the Commission, it shall have a single contact point providing access to all the law enforcement agencies having a responsibility to fight organised crime.

(8) Similarly, and without prejudice to the need to foster direct contacts between judicial authorities of the member states, a network for judicial co-operation should be established at the European level. In order to develop this network, each member state shall set up, where this does not already exist, in accordance with its constitutional structure, a central contact point permitting the exchange of information between national judicial authorities.

(9) Within the Council a permanent multidisciplinary Working Party on organised crime shall be established, consisting of competent authorities, to develop policies to co-ordinate the fight against organised crime. The setting up in each member state of comparable multidisciplinary teams with the same tasks and their input into the Council Working Party would facilitate a co-ordinated approach at a European level.

(10) The European Council reiterates its view that Europol should be given operative powers working together with national authorities. To that end, and without prejudice to the outcome of the IGC, Europol should, as soon as possible, be enabled to:

i.   facilitate and support the preparation, co-ordination and carrying out of specific investigative actions by the competent authorities of member states, including operational actions of joint teams comprising representatives of Europol in a support capacity;

ii.   ask the competent authorities of the member states to conduct investigations into specific cases and develop specific expertise which may be put at the disposal of member states to assist them in investigating cases of organised crime;

iii.   be instrumental in the collation and exchange of information by the law enforcement agencies of reave actions by the competent authorities of member states, including operational actions of joint teams comprising representatives of Europol in a support capacity;

iv.   ask the competent authorities of the member states to conduct investigations into specific cases and develop specific expertise which may be put at the disposal of member states to assist them in investigating cases of organised crime;

v.   be instrumental in the collation and exchange of information by the law enforcement agencies of reports on suspicious financial transactions.

In so far as the legal instruments of the Union have to be changed in order to enable Europol to carry out this mandate, the European Council requests the Council to take the necessary steps rapidly to do so. In the meantime, the European Council stresses the need to enable the EDU to fully fulfil its mandate.

An in-depth study should be carried out with a view to examining the place and the role of judicial authorities in their relations with Europol, in step with the enlargement of Europol's competences.

(11) The European Council stresses the importance for each member state of having well-developed and wide-ranging legislation in the field of confiscation of the proceeds from crime and the laundering of such proceeds. The Council, and the Commission, are requested to develop proposals aiming at a further enhancement of such legislation bearing in mind the importance of:

– introducing special procedures for tracing, seizure and confiscation of proceeds from crime;

– preventing an excessive use of cash payments and cash currency exchanges by natural and legal persons from serving to cover up the conversion of the proceeds from crime into other property;

– extending the scope of the laundering provisions to the proceeds from all forms of serious crime, and making a failure to comply with the obligation to report suspicious financial transactions liable to dissuasive sanctions;

– addressing the issue of money laundering on the Internet and via electronic money products.

(12) The European Council stresses the need for developing closer co-operation at the national level, between fiscal and law enforcement authorities in the fight against organised crime. Rules should be examined so that:

– financial centres and offshore facilities, subject to the jurisdiction of member states, shall have adequate defences against being used by organised crime;

– in cases linked with organised crime, there is no legal bar to allowing or obliging the fiscal authorities to exchange information with the competent authorities of the member states concerned, and in particular with the judiciary, while fully respecting fundamental rights;

– fiscal fraud linked with organised crime is treated as any other form of organised crime, notwithstanding that fiscal laws may contain special rules on recovering the proceeds of fiscal fraud;

– disbursements for criminal purposes such as corruption, are not tax-deductible.

Moreover, the prevention and the suppression of organised fiscal fraud such as VAT and excise fraud, including in particular its transnational aspects, should be considerably improved at both national and European level.

(13) The European Council stresses the importance of enhancing transparency in public administration and in businesses and preventing the use by organised crime of corrupt practices. In this context, the member states, the Council and the Commission, should:

– develop, while taking account of work carried out in other international fora, a comprehensive policy to tackle corruption, including appropriate and efficient sanctions, but also tackling all aspects linked with the proper functioning of the internal market and other internal policies, as well as external assistance and co-operation;

– develop rules allowing the exchange of information between member states with respect to legal persons registered in each member state and the physical persons involved in their creation, direction and funding, with a view to preventing the penetration of organised crime in the public and legitimate private sector;

– taking necessary steps to allow the exclusion of criminal organisations or their members from participation in tendering procedures, receiving subsidies or governmental licences. Specific attention should be paid to the illicit origin of funds as a possible reason for exclusion from tendering procedures.

Moreover,

– standards should be studied and developed, where necessary, at the European level aimed at preventing the liberal professions and other professions particularly exposed to influences of organised crime, from being involved in such crime or being exploited by criminals. The active assistance of the professional organisations involved should be sought to that end,

– the Union institutions as well as the member states should, when drawing up legal instruments, emphasise crime prevention aspects in order to ensure that the rules do not invite fraud or other undue exploitation, or in other ways may be used to commit or conceal crime.

(14) The possibilities offered by the structural funds, notably the European Social Fund and the Urban programme, should be mobilised to prevent large cities in the Union from becoming breeding grounds for organised crime. Particular attention should be given to the circumstances in which socially weak groups become vulnerable to the prospect of a criminal career. The exchange of information on projects which proved successful in this field should be enhanced.

(15) A cross-pillar study on high-technology crime should be carried out. This study should pave the way for a policy ensuring that law enforcement and judicial authorities have the possibility to prevent and combat the abuse of these new technologies. Special attention should be given to both illegal practices and illegal content.

Moreover, the Council and the Commission should address the issue of fraud and counterfeiting relating to all payment instruments, including electronic payment instruments.

The High Level Group recommends that the European Council should ask the Council to report to it in June 1998 on the progress made in the carrying out of the measures proposed in the Action Plan.

The High Level Group recommends that the European Council should instruct the Council to monitor at regular intervals, for instance through the meetings of the K.4 Committee, progress made in the carrying out of this Action Plan.

Part III – Detailed Action Plan

This Detailed Action Plan translates in operational terms the Political Guidelines in Part II and adds some technical elements to ensure a coherent approach to the fight against organised crime. The recommendations made in the Detailed Action Plan should be seen as a work programme, indicating the direction which further work by the various Union institutions and bodies shall take, rather than as a legal instrument.

Chapter I – An approach to the phenomenon of organised crime

This chapter draws inspiration from political guidelines Nos. 5-7 and 15 set by the European Council.

Recommendations:

1.   It is for each member state to decide on the organisation of its own structures to fight organised crime. Nevertheless, the High Level Group considered it appropriate that the European Council should stress the importance of an appropriate co-ordination between competent agencies at national level (see political guideline No. 6). Such a co-ordination might in particular enable law enforcement agencies better to share information and act in a concerted manner. Therefore, each member state should examine whether it would be appropriate, in accordance with its constitutional law or practice, to designate a body at national level which would have an overall responsibility for the co-ordination of the fight against organised crime. It will be for the authorities of the member state – and for them alone – to draw the consequences of such an examination.

Target date: end of 1997.

Responsible:[1] Member states.

---

1. Each recommendation given an indication of the body or bodies to be considered responsible for implementation. In each case it is clearly understood that the body or bodies concerned will exercise that responsibility within its competences as laid down in the Treaty on European Union.

2. The member states, and the Commission, should, where it does not already exist, set up or identify a mechanism for the collection and analysis of data which is so construed that it can provide a picture of the organised crime situation in the member state and which can assist law enforcement authorities in fighting organised crime. member states shall use common standards for the collection and analysis of data. The information so collected and analysed shall be organised in such a way that it is readily accessible for investigations and prosecutions at national level and can be effectively used and exchanged with other member states.

To that end, the member states and the Commission shall set up a Contact and Support Network to serve as advising mechanism for the collection of data and the analysis at European level. Europol shall be integrated in this work and produce annual reports on the basis of the information from the member states. The academic and scientific world should be further encouraged to contribute by their studies and research to the understanding of the phenomenon of organised crime.

Target date: mid-1998.

Responsible: Member states/Council/Europol/Commission.

3. The European Council encourages the Council and the Commission to define in common with the candidate countries of central and eastern Europe, including the Baltic states, a pre-accession pact on co-operation against crime, which may include provisions for close co-operation between these countries and Europol and undertakings for the rapid ratification and full implementation of the Council of Europe instruments which are essential to the fight against organised crime (see political guideline No. 5). The pact should be based on the *acquis* of the Union in the field of organised crime and form part of the pre-accession strategy in which the potential of the existing instruments such as the Phare programme should be fully explored. In the discussions with the candidate countries, the need should be underlined for them to reach a standard which is comparable to that of the member states of the Union, in particular as regards undertakings contained in international instruments such as those relating to terrorism. In this context, it should be examined whether these countries could be associated with some of the activities of the Multidisciplinary Party on Organised Crime.

Target date: end 1998.

Responsible: Council/Commission.

4. Separate from the discussions on a pre-accession pact, it is necessary to develop closer co-operation with other countries and international organisations and bodies involved in the fight against organised crime. In

particular relations with the Union's transatlantic partners as well as with Russia and Ukraine need to be developed, the latter two for instance through the Tacis programme. Concrete proposals for closer co-operation, for instance through the intermediary of Europol, should be developed by the Council and the Commission (see political guideline No. 5).

Target date: end 1998.

Responsible: Council/Commission.

5.   A cross-pillar study on high-technology crime and its use and links with organised crime should be carried out within the Union (see political guideline No. 15). This study should pave the way for a policy ensuring an efficient public protection. While avoiding undue restrictions, law enforcement and judicial authorities should have the means, as a complement to the specific responsibilities incumbent on the technology and service-providers, to prevent and combat the misuse of these new technologies. Attention should be paid both to illegal practices (such as the use of these technologies by criminal organisations to facilitate their activities) or illegal contents (such as child pornography or dissemination of synthetic drug recipes).

Target date: end 1998.

Responsible: Commission/Europol/Council.

Chapter II – Prevention of organised crime

This chapter draws inspiration from political guidelines Nos. 13-14 set by the European Council.

Recommendations:

6.   A comprehensive policy against corruption should be developed, taking into account the work already carried out in other international fora, in order to enhance the transparency in public administration, at the level of both the member states and the Communities (see political guideline No. 13). This policy should primarily focus on elements of prevention, addressing such issues as the impact of defective legislation, public-private relationships, transparency of financial management, rules on participation in public procurement, and criteria for appointments to positions of public responsibility, etc. It should also cover the area of sanctions, be they of a penal, administrative or civil character, as well as the impact of the Union's policy on relations with third states.

Target date: mid-1998.

Responsible: Commission/Council/member states.

7.   The member states and the European Commission should ensure that the applicable legislation provides for the possibility for an applicant in a public tender procedure who has committed offences connected with organised crime to be excluded from the participation in tender procedures conducted by member states and by the Community. In this context it should be studied whether and under what conditions persons who are currently under investigation or prosecution for involvement in organised crime could also be excluded. Specific attention should be paid to the illicit origin of funds as a possible reason for exclusion. The decision to exclude the person from participation in the tender procedure should be capable of being challenged in court.

Similarly, the member states and the Commission should ensure that the applicable legislation provides for the possibility of rejecting, on the basis of the same criteria, applications for subsidies or governmental licences (see political guideline No. 13).

Appropriate Community instruments and instruments of the European Union, enabling *inter alia* exchange of information among member states and between member states and the Commission, and containing specific provisions relating to the role of the Commission both in administrative co-operation and the setting up of black-lists, should be drawn up to ensure that these commitments can be carried out, while ensuring conformity with the relevant rules relating to data protection.

Target date: end 1998.

Responsible: Member states/Commission.

8.   Member states shall, with respect to legal persons registered in their territory, seek to collect information, in compliance with the relevant rules relating to data protection, with respect to the physical persons involved in their creation and direction, as well as their funding, as a means to prevent the penetration of organised crime in the public and legitimate private sector. It should be studied how such data could be systematically compiled and analysed and be available for exchange with other member states and, where appropriate, with bodies responsible at Union level for the fight against organised crime, on the basis of appropriate rules to be developed by the Council (see political guideline No. 13).

Target date: end 1998.

Responsible: Member states/Council/Commission.

9.   The possibilities offered by structural funds, notably the European Social Fund in the context of action to assist the labour market, and the Urban programme, should be mobilised to prevent large cities in the Union

from becoming breeding grounds for organised crime. Those funds can help those most at risk of exclusion from the labour market and thus alleviate the circumstances that could contribute to the development of organised crime. Particular attention should be given to groups not fully integrated in society, since these may be vulnerable targets for criminal organisations. The exchange of information on projects which proved successful in this field should be enhanced. The results of the annual consultations of Chiefs of police from the capitals of member states should be taken into account in this context (see political guideline No. 14).

Target date: end 1998.

Responsible: Commission/member states.

10. The member states should consult regularly the competent services of the Commission with a view to analysing cases of fraud affecting the financial interests of the Community, and deepening the knowledge and understanding of the complexities of these phenomena within existing mechanisms and frameworks. If necessary, additional mechanisms shall be put in place with a view to arranging such consultations on a regular basis. In this context, future relations between Europol and the Commission's anti-fraud unit (Uclaf) should be taken into account.

Target date: end 1997

Responsible: Member states/Commission/Europol.

11. The Council should adopt a joint action establishing a specific multi-annual programme to combat organised crime, including fraud affecting the financial interests of the Communities, permitting specific actions in the fields of training for key players responsible for preventive policies, exchanges of information, research, and other forms of improving skills and operational methods.

Target date: end 1997.

Responsible: Council/Commission.

12. Measures to shield certain vulnerable professions from influences of organised crime should be developed, for instance through the adoption of codes of conduct. A study should propose specific measures, including legislative action, to prevent notaries, lawyers, accountants and auditors from being exploited or getting involved in organised crime and ensure that their professional organisations are engaged in the establishment and enforcement of such codes of conduct at the European level (see political guideline No. 2)

Target date: mid 1998 and, possibly, joint action mid 1999.

Responsible: Council/Commission/member states (in co-operation with the professional organisations concerned, e.g. the Council of the Bars and Law Societies of the European community (CCBE)).

Chapter III – Legal instruments, scope, implementation

This Chapter draws inspiration from political guidelines Nos. 1-5 and 15 set by the European Council.

Recommendations:

13. Member states consider that the conventions mentioned below and in Recommendation 14 are essential to the fight against organised crime (see political guideline No. 2). Those states which have not yet ratified them should make proposals to their parliaments with a view to a speedy ratification within the given timetable. Should any convention not have been ratified by the set target date, they shall report to the Council in writing on the reasons therefor every six months until the convention has been ratified.

If a member state has not ratified a convention within a reasonable time for any given reason, the Council shall assess the situation with a view to solving it. As part of the pre-accession pact (see political guideline No. 5) to be defined with the candidate countries of central and eastern Europe, including the Baltic States, undertakings should be sought from these countries of a similar character.

(1) European Convention on Extradition, Paris 1957.

(2) Second Protocol to the European Convention on Extradition, Strasbourg 1978.

(3) Protocol to the European Convention on Mutual Assistance in Criminal Matters, Strasbourg 1978.

(4) Convention on Laundering, Search, Seizure and Confiscation of the Proceeds from Crime, Strasbourg 1990.

(5) Convention on Mutual Assistance between Customs Administrations and Protocol thereto, Naples 1967.

(6) Agreement on Illicit Traffic by Sea, implementing Article 17 of the United Nations Convention against Illicit Traffic in Narcotic Drugs and Psychotropic Substances, Strasbourg 1995.

(7) Convention on the Fight against Illicit Traffic in Narcotic Drugs and Psychotropic Substances, Vienna 1988.

(8) European Convention on the Suppression of Terrorism, Strasbourg 1977.

Target date: end 1998.

Responsible: Member states.

14. The following European Union conventions should each be ratified (see political guideline No 2) by the target dates set out below, while taking into account availability of explanatory reports, where applicable. When drawing up new conventions, the Council should set a target date for their adoption and implementation in accordance with the constitutional requirements of the member states.

(1) Convention on simplified extradition procedure between the member states of the European Union – end 1998.

(2) Europol Convention – end 1997 as an absolute latest date.

(3) Convention on the Protection of the European Communities' Financial Interests – mid 1998.

(4) Convention on the Use of Information Technology for Customs Purposes – end 1998.

(5) Convention relating to Extradition between the member states of the European Union – end 1998.

(6) Protocols to the Convention on the Protection of the European Communities' Financial Interests – mid 1998.

Responsible: Member states/Council.

Moreover, all efforts should be made to ensure that current discussions on draft instruments, and in particular those relating to the draft Third Protocol to the Convention on the Protection of the European Communities' Financial Interests, the draft Convention on Corruption and the so-called Naples II draft convention on customs co-operation are finalised by the end of 1997.

Responsible: Council.

15. A mechanism should be established, based on the experience with the model developed in the FATF, to mutually evaluate the application and implementation at national level of the European Union and other international instruments and undertakings in criminal matters as well as ensuing national law, policies and practices (see political guideline No. 3). Such a mutual "peer-evaluation" should as a priority be carried out in respect of

judicial co-operation and, could, if the experience proves positive, be extended to other areas of implementation.

The evaluation should be based on the following principles: parity of the member states, mutual trust, pre-established scope and criteria for the evaluation in the form of a self-evaluation and, in respect of the mutual evaluation procedure, check-lists and an assurance that experts from all member states will participate, at some stage, in the evaluation process. The results of the evaluation shall remain confidential unless the member state concerned wishes to make them public.

Target date: end 1997/mid-1998.

Responsible: Council/member states/Commission.

16. In order to render judicial co-operation in the fight against organised crime more efficient, the ongoing work on a draft Convention on Mutual Assistance in Criminal Matters should be finalised before the end of 1997 (see political guideline No. 4). As soon as possible, the content of the Convention should be enlarged, while taking into account the necessity to accelerate procedures for judicial co-operation in matters relating to organised crime and considerably reducing delay in transmission and responses to requests.

Instruments adopted by the Council regarding individuals who co-operate with the judicial process and on the protection of witnesses as well as the specific needs of police co-operation connected with pre-trial investigations and judicial co-operation in certain countries should be considered.

Specific consideration to the needs to fight organised crime should be given in the ongoing work on a draft Convention. To this end, the competent working party should examine how:

a. reservations entered with regard to the 1959 European Convention on Mutual Assistance and its Protocol can be rendered superfluous among member states of the European Union, for instance by including provisions in the draft providing for the safeguarding of principles of *non bis in idem*, by reconsidering requirements of double criminality or by making use of the right of refusal under the Convention only in cases where the request is likely to prejudice the sovereignty, security, public order. or other essential interests of the member state;

b. a legal basis could be created for the transboundary application of certain modern investigative methods, such as controlled delivery, deployment of undercover agents and the interception of various forms of telecommunications.

Target date: end 1997/mid-1998.

Responsible: Member states/Council.

17. The Council is requested rapidly to adopt a joint action aiming at making it an offence under the laws of each member state for a person, present in its territory, to participate in a criminal organisation irrespective of the location in the Union where the organisation is concentrated or is carrying out its criminal activity (see political guideline No. 1). Such an offence could consist in the behaviour described in Article 3 (4) of the Extradition Convention adopted by the Council on 27 September 1996. Since legal traditions differ among member states, it could be considered acceptable, for a limited period of time that not all member states will be able to sign up immediately to the agreed definition.

Target date: end 1997.

Responsible: Council.

Moreover, the Council should examine to what extent, and within which priority areas, a possible approximation or harmonisation of member states' laws could contribute to the fight against organised crime. The study should in particular make concrete proposals as to the areas which could be considered as priority areas and assess the practical effects in the fight against organised crime of an approximation or harmonisation of the laws of the member states in those areas.

Target date: end 1999.

Responsible: Council.

18. Furthermore, the following specific starting points for future discussions on organised crime, most of them agreed by the Council in the 1993 report on organised crime should be established, while taking account of the rights of individuals and in particular the alleged offender and bona fide third parties:

a.   combating those forms of crime which affect the Communities' financial interests in close co-operation between the member states and the Commission;

b.   liability of legal persons should be introduced where the legal person has been involved in organised crime;

c.   fairly long time limits for prosecution of serious offences connected with organised crime should be provided for;

d.   addressing the issue of fraud and counterfeiting relating to all payment instruments including electronic payment instruments (see political guideline No. 15).

Target date: end 1998.

Responsible: Council/member states/Commission.

Chapter IV – Practical co-operation between police, judicial authorities and customs in the fight against organised crime

This Chapter draws inspiration from political guidelines Nos. 6-9 set by the European Council.

Recommendations:

19. Central national contact points, where they do not already exist, should be designated, while fully respecting the constitutional structure of each member state, in order to speed up the exchange of information and the completion of application procedures for law enforcement co-operation, wherever a national authority in a member state considers that it would be more efficient to direct itself to a central contact point instead of making direct contact with the authority in another member state (see political guideline No. 7). With regard to the Europol Convention, the central national unit referred to therein should be the contact point on behalf of all law enforcement authorities in the member states. It is advisable that existing contact points, such as the Interpol NCB, Sirene bureaux, etc. should be brought together in this central contact point, or at least, that close relations between such units should be established.

These contact points should serve as an interface in bringing the competent authorities in the member states and the Commission into contact with each other rapidly. A second function of these contact points might be to act as a national focus point for information to law enforcement agencies on national legislation, jurisdiction and procedures. The relevant information concerning these central contact points shall be kept by the General Secretariat of the Council and shall be regularly updated.

Target date: end 1997.

Responsible: Member states/Council/Commission.

20. Political guideline No. 6 underlines the importance of co-ordination between competent law enforcement authorities at national level. Therefore, while taking into account constitutional structures and national traditions, and taking into account the fact that each member state decides on its own internal structures, it is advisable that multidisciplinary integrated teams should be set up at national level, if they do not already exist, specifically in the area of organised crime (see political guideline Nos. 6 and 9). Unlike the contact points referred to in Recommendation No. 19, the primary function of which is to facilitate contacts and to relay information to other member states, these co-ordinating teams should have sufficient insight into national criminal investigations to be able to contribute to the development of national policies in the fight against organised crime.

These teams could discuss the results of Europol's analyses with a view to initiating large-scale joint multidisciplinary investigations involving two or more member states. Given the broad range of tasks involved, it is necessary to ensure an efficient co-ordination between the investigating authorities and the judicial authorities. In the interests of smooth co-operation, it is advisable that the national contact points and the multidisciplinary integrated team co-operate very closely with one another.

Target date: mid-1998.

Responsible: Member states/Europol/Commission.

21. While taking into account national legal systems, safeguarding judicial independence and taking into account the fact that each member state decides on its own internal structures, the member states should seek to pool their resources at European level by setting up a network for judicial co-operation. The network should be given a special mandate and consist of practitioners having extensive practical experience in fighting organised crime. In this context, the study being conducted by the Belgian authorities under the Grotius programme in the setting up of a judicial contact network may be examined (see political guideline No. 8).

In order to develop this network, each member state should designate a central contact point permitting the exchange of information between national judicial authorities, while fully respecting safeguards provided for by national law.

This network shall be given the appropriate logistical support by the Third Pillar structures to discuss questions of practical judicial co-operation and it shall act as a clearing house, problem-solver and contact maker between judicial authorities at national level.[1]

An in-depth study should be carried out with a view to examining the place and the role of judicial authorities in their relations with Europol, in step with the enlargement of Europol's competences (see political guideline No. 10). In that context, and if the experience of the network proves to be positive, it could in the future be examined whether it should in the long term be transformed into a more permanent structure, which could become an important interlocutor of Europol.

Target date: mid-1998.

Responsible: Council.

---

1. See the document approved by the Dublin European Council, CK4 53, REV 4.

22. Within the Council, a Multidisciplinary Working Party on Organised Crime, should be established within the Third Pillar structures, consisting of competent high level authorities, for the purpose of developing policy orientations to co-ordinate the fight against organised crime. At the same time, the Working Group on International Organised Crime, set up under Steering Group III, should be abolished and the Working Group on Drugs and Organised crime should either limit its remit to drugs issues relevant to tasks performed in accordance with Article K of the Treaty or be abolished. Coreper is requested to examine the matter with a view to taking a decision.

The fact that the multidisciplinary working party has been established should not hinder items relating for instance purely to police co-operation against organised crime being dealt with by other Council working groups. It is a matter for the K4 Committee to decide on the appropriate co-ordination between working groups under its responsibility.

The new Working Party on Organised Crime, to be attended by competent authorities such as representatives of comparable co-ordination teams wherever such teams have been designated, or at least with the input of such teams, together with officials involved in policy-making and representatives of Europol, could be assigned the task of pinpointing, on the basis of assessment of practical co-operation, difficulties resolvable only by means of political decision-making, and design the strategies and policies of the Union in the fight against organised crime and prepare matters which require decisions at a high level. Examples that come to mind are decisions on new instruments (for instance relating to practical police co-operation), priorities in tackling organised crime and other forms of agreements needed for the efficient fight against organised crime.

Target date: end 1997.

Responsible: Council/Coreper.

Chapter V – Development of a fully-fledged Europol and extension of Europol's mandate and tasks

This chapter draws inspiration from political guidelines Nos. 5 and 10 by the European Council.

Recommendations:

23. The member states and the Council should take all necessary preparatory and budgetary measures with a view to enable Europol to take up its activities at the latest by mid-1998.

Responsible: Member states/Council.

24. The possibilities for Europol to co-operate and liaise with third countries and international organisations should be elaborated. To that end, the Council should draw up one or more suitable legal instruments which ensure that contacts may be entertained with the Commission and third countries which are the most important partners for the member states in the fight against organised crime, with relevant international organisations such as Interpol and the World Customs Organisation (WCO).

Target date: end 1999.

Responsible: Member states/Council/Europol.

25. Without prejudice to the outcome of the IGC, Europol's mandate and tasks will, as soon as possible, be further developed, taking into account the decision of the heads of state and government at the Dublin Summit, to include the following:

a.   Europol should be enabled to facilitate and support the preparation, co-ordination and carrying out of specific investigative actions by the competent authorities of the member states, including operational actions of joint teams comprising representatives of Europol in a support capacity. The legislation of each member state will determine which authority is competent, be they police, customs or judicial authorities;

b.   Europol should be allowed to ask member states to conduct investigations in specific cases. Europol could in this respect take the initiative of drawing the attention of the competent authorities of one or more member states to the importance of having certain matters investigated, although such an initiative would not oblige the member state(s) concerned to take action as requested;

c.   Europol should develop specific expertise which may be put at the disposal of member states to assist them in investigating cases of organised cross-border crime (see political guideline No. 10);

d.   Full use should be made of possibilities of Europol in fields of operational techniques and support, analysis and data analyses files (for instance registers on stolen cars or other property). The development of operational techniques could take the form of studies of practices at national and Union level and their effectiveness, and the development of common strategies, policies and tactics. The development of operational support could, *inter alia*, take the form of the organisation of meetings, the development of common action plans and their implementation, strategic analyses, facilitating information and intelligence exchange, analytical support for multilateral national investigations, technical and tactical support, legal support, offering technical facilities, development of common manuals, facilitating training, evaluation of results and giving advice to the competent authorities of the member states;

e. Access by Europol may be sought to the Schengen Information System or its European successor.

The Council will need to assess, without prejudice to the rapid ratification and implementation of the Europol Convention, whether the development of the role of Europol requires amendment to the Convention, and, if so, immediate steps should be taken. In the meantime, the EDU should be able to fully fulfil its mandate.

An in-depth study should be carried out with a view to examining the place and the role of judicial authorities in their relations with Europol, in step with the enlargement of Europol's competences.

Target date: end 1998.

Responsible: Member states/Council/Europol.

Chapter VI – Organised crime and money

This chapter draws inspiration from political guidelines Nos. 5, 10-12 set by the European Council.

Recommendations:

26. In the field of money laundering and confiscation of the proceeds from crime, the following measures should be envisaged:

a. to improve the international exchange of police data, it is necessary to set up a system for exchanging information concerning suspected money laundering at the European level, in conformity with the relevant rules relating to data protection. To this end, the Europol Convention should be supplemented with a provision permitting Europol to be instrumental therein (see political guideline No. 10);

b. criminalisation of laundering of the proceeds of crime should be made as general as possible, and a legal basis should be created for as broad as possible a range of powers of investigation into it. The opportunity of extending laundering to negligent behaviour should be examined. A study should be undertaken with a view to strengthening the tracing and seizure of illegal assets and of the enforcement of court decisions on the confiscation of assets of organised crime (see political guideline No. 11);

c. confiscation rules should be introduced which enable confiscation regardless of the presence of the offender, such as when the offender has died or absconded (see political guideline No. 11);

d. there should be a study of the possibility to share, at the level of member states, assets confiscated following international co-operation (see political guideline No. 11);

e.   the reporting obligation in Article 6 of the Money Laundering Directive should be extended to all offences connected with serious crime and to persons and professions other than the financial institutions mentioned in the Directive. Member states should examine the opportunity of making the failure to report suspicious transactions liable to dissuasive sanctions (see political guideline No. 11). At the same time, fiscal authorities should be subjected in the national law to a similar reporting obligation for trans-actions connected with organised crime, at least for transactions relating to VAT and excise. Co-operation between contact points under the Directive needs to be improved;

f.   addressing the issue of money laundering on the Internet and via elec-tronic money products and requiring, in electronic payment and message systems, that the messages sent give details of the originator and the ben-eficiary (see political guideline No. 11);

g.   preventing an excessive use of cash payments and cash exchanges by natural and legal persons from serving to cover up the conversion of the proceeds from crime into other property (see political guideline No. 11).

Moreover, the Council and the Commission should consider in the light of existing national and international instruments the need to put in place common provisions to combat organised crime in the fields of economic and commercial counterfeiting as well as counterfeiting and falsification of banknotes and coins in view of the introduction of the single currency.

Target date: end 1998.

Responsible: Council/Europol/Commission.

27.   Adequate legislation, and public awareness, particularly in the financial sector, to combat money laundering and other forms of financial crime is necessary for potential members of the Union. This subject should be given high priority in the structured dialogue and programmes such as Phare. The need for the countries concerned to join international commitments in this field, and in particular the Council of Europe Convention on Laundering, Search, Seizure and Confiscation of Proceeds from Crime, should also be addressed in the Pre-accession Pact on co-operation against crime (see political guideline No. 5).

Target date: end 1999.

Responsible: Council/Commission.

28.   A study should be undertaken on the basis of practical experiences as to what extent legislation of the member states relating to criminal pro-ceedings and procedures for international co-operation in the tracing,

seizure and confiscation of assets from crime, and financial investigations for that purpose, should be further developed.

Target date: end of 1999.

Responsible: Member states/Commission.

29. Legislation to combat organised crime in connection with fiscal fraud should be developed in conformity with the relevant rules relating to data protection (see political guideline No. 12). To this end the following should be examined so that:

− in cases linked with organised crime, there should be no legal bar to allowing or obliging the fiscal authorities to exchange, at the national level, information with the competent authorities of the member state concerned, and in particular not with the judiciary, while fully respecting fundamental rights,

− fiscal fraud linked with organised crime should be treated as any other form of organised crime, notwithstanding that fiscal laws may contain special rules on recovering the proceeds of fiscal fraud,

− disbursements for criminal purposes such as corruption, should not be tax deductible,

− the prevention and suppression of organised fiscal fraud such as VAT and excise fraud, including its transnational aspects, should be improved at both the national and the European level.

Target date: end of 1998.

Responsible: Member states/Council/Commission.

30. member states should examine how to take action and provide adequate defences against the use by organised crime of financial centres and off-shore facilities, in particular where these are located in places subject to their jurisdiction. With respect to those located elsewhere, the Council should develop a common policy, consistent with the policy conducted by member states internally with a view to prevent the use thereof by criminal organisations operating within the Union (see political guideline No. 12).

Target date: 1998.

Responsible: Member states/Council/Commission.

Annex

Letter from the High Level Group to the IGC

The High Level Group, created by the European Council (Dublin, 13 and 14 December 1996), and tasked to examine the fight against organised crime in all its aspects, has also been requested to refer any issues involving Treaty change to the Intergovernmental Conference.

The High Level Group has, at its meeting on 9 April 1997, adopted an Action Plan containing political guidelines to be endorsed by the European Council (Amsterdam, 16 and 17 June 1997), as well as a detailed action plan which, as necessary, translates the political guidelines into a work programme to be implemented by the Union and its member states. The Action Plan is in an Annex to this letter.

In adopting the report, sometimes after lengthy discussions on certain points, the High Level Group agreed that the consensus reached was without prejudice to any positions delegations might take in the Intergovernmental Conference. This is true in particular with a view to certain proposals already on the table in the Intergovernmental Conference.

First of all, it was felt that a distinction should be made between recommendations of the Group to the European Council that could require Treaty change, and recommendations which might be implemented on the basis of the present Treaty, but might be translated into provisions of the new Treaty, in order for the Treaty to better reflect the priority that the Union is to give to the fight against organised crime.

Secondly, whilst the Group on a number of occasions touched upon the question of improving the effectiveness of European co-operation in the field of justice and home affairs, it felt that it should not focus on questions of a primarily institutional character, such as decision-making and instruments of the Union. While these questions are of considerable importance also for the Union's ability to fight against organised crime, the Group abstained from taking a position since these questions are under consideration in the IGC anyway.

In the political guidelines presented by the Group, it is recommended that Europol be granted operative powers as defined in political guideline No. 10. The Group invites the Intergovernmental Conference to consider whether this requires a change of Article K.1.9 of the Treaty and to act accordingly.

Some other recommendations, whilst not necessarily leading to Treaty change, might still be even better implemented if the future Treaty were to provide for a legal and institutional basis. This is the case for political guideline No. 3, which calls for a mutual evaluation mechanism of the application and implementation of instruments concerning international co-operation in criminal matters. Moreover, political guideline No. 5 stresses the need for closer co-operation in the fight against organised crime with relevant third countries. Such co-operation might equally merit a reflection in the Treaty.

The deliberations of the Group as reflected in Chapters II and III might provide even further material for consideration by the IGC. This is particularly the case with regard to the need to bring practical judicial co-operation to a comparable level with police co-operation.

The Group has spent some time discussing the contribution that legislative approximation or harmonisation might offer to the fight against organised crime. It limited itself to a political guideline related to criminal organisations (namely political guideline No. 1), with a view to ensuring the most effective possible framework for practical co-operation. The Intergovernmental Conference will note that in the opinion of the Group, the question whether approximation or harmonisation of member states' laws could contribute to the fight against organised crime, is a matter to be examined (namely political guideline No. 1).

Close co-ordination, both at the national and the Union level, between the various agencies (police, justice, customs) that take part in the fight against organised crime is considered by the Group to be of paramount importance. Although such co-ordination is primarily to be achieved through organisational measures, it might merit to be reflected in the Treaty as a matter of principle.

The same applies to the notion of prevention as a necessary corollary to repression. As the report states at various places (namely political guideline No. 13), prevention (notably in the area of corruption, fraud and money laundering) requires not only increased efforts by member states and closer co-operation between them at European Union level but also full exercise of the Union's possibilities in the First Pillar.

Finally, given the overall need for the Union to organise itself better in the fight against organised crime in all its forms, the phenomenon should be mentioned as such among the objectives of the Union's co-operation in the Third Pillar.

(as set out in *Official Journal of the European Communities* No. C 251/1, 15 August 1997)

APPENDIX VIII – 1996 MEMORANDUM OF UNDERSTANDING AMONG MEMBER GOVERNMENTS OF THE CARIBBEAN FINANCIAL ACTION TASK FORCE

Considering the threat posed by the activities of money launderers;

Determined to preserve and maintain social, economic and political stability in the Caribbean Region;

Considering the work since 1990 of the Caribbean Financial Action Task Force (CFATF) and taking into account the interest of Caribbean countries and territories in formalising this organisation and securing the participation of other countries and territories in the study, formulation and implementation of recommendations to improve the prevention and control of money laundering;

Conscious of the benefit to countries and territories of the Caribbean region of continued work in the study and the effective implementation of mechanisms to prevent and control money laundering;

Acknowledging the need for expertise and training to ensure the effective implementation of money laundering counter-measures and the support of the FATF members and international organisations in sustaining such training programmes; and,

Acknowledging that international co-operation is critical in the fight against money laundering and reaffirming their commitment given in various fora to adopt and implement effectively the 1988 UN Convention Against Illicit Traffic in Narcotic Drugs and Psychotropic Substances, the forty FATF and nineteen CFATF recommendations, adopted in 1990 and 1992 respectively (the Recommendations), the obligations expressed in the Kingston Declaration and, where applicable, the Plan of Action of the Summit of the Americas,

The governments party to this memorandum have reached the following understanding:

I – Objectives

Members agree to adopt and implement effectively the 1988 UN Convention Against Illicit Traffic in Narcotic Drugs and Psychotropic Substances, endorse and implement the Recommendations, fulfil the obligations expressed in the Kingston Declaration and, where applicable, the Plan of Action of the Summit of the Americas, and to adopt and implement any other measures for the prevention and control of the laundering of the proceeds of all serious crimes as defined by the laws of each Member.

II – Members

1.   Members are those countries or territories within the Caribbean region which have agreed to subscribe to this Memorandum.

2.   Such countries or territories become Members:

i.   by signing this Memorandum at the meeting of the Council in Costa Rica in October 1996; or,

ii.   upon approval of an application by the Council.

3.   Applications shall be made in writing to the Secretariat.

4.   Upon receipt of an application, the Secretariat shall promptly transmit it to the Chair.

5.   Applications will be considered by the Council within twelve months of receipt. Countries or territories will be admitted as Members upon approval of their application by two-thirds of the members and their subscription to this Memorandum.

III – Co-operating and Supporting Nations

1.   Co-operating and Supporting Nations are countries or territories which have expressed their support for the objectives of the CFATF. Initial Co-operating and Supporting Nations are Canada, the Kingdom of the Netherlands, France, the United Kingdom and the United States of America.

2.   Co-operating and Supporting Nations are committed to the mutual evaluation of their progress in implementing the forty Recommendations of the FATF and will make such contributions to the work and/or resources of the CFATF as are permitted by their respective national laws and policies.

3.   Other nations that are not Members of the CFATF may become Co-operating and Supporting Nations. All future Co-operating and Supporting Nations must express their commitment to the support of the CFATF and have undergone a positive mutual evaluation by the FATF or an FATF-approved regional body.

4.   Countries or territories may apply in writing to the Secretariat to become Co-operating and Supporting Nations. Applications will be considered by the Council within twelve months of receipt. A country or territory will be considered a Co-operating and Supporting Nation upon approval of their application by three-fourths of the Members.

IV – Observers

1. Observers are:

i. organisations which actively support or otherwise are interested in the objectives of the CFATF;

ii. countries or territories which are considering Membership or becoming Co-operating and Supporting Nations;

iii. any other country or organisation invited by the Chair and to which no Member objects.

2. Initial observers to the CFATF are the CARICOM Secretariat, the FATF Secretariat, OAS/CICAD, and UNDCP.

3. An organisation, country, or territory may apply in writing to the Secretariat to become an Observer. Applications will be considered by the Council within twelve months of receipt. Organisations, countries, or territories will be admitted as Observers upon the unanimous approval of the Members present at a meeting of the Council.

V – Funding

1. The activities of the CFATF are funded by annual contributions from Members as decided by the Council and by contributions from Co-operating and Supporting Nations or any other source approved by the Council.

2. Members will bear the cost of their participation in the activities of the CFATF.

VI – Structure

The Caribbean Financial Action Task Force comprises:

i. The Council of Ministers (the Council);

ii. The Plenary of Senior Officials (the Plenary);

iii. The Secretariat.

VII – The Council

1. The Council is the Supreme authority within the CFATF and consists of one ministerial representative or duly authorised alternate from each Member.

2. The Council will meet at least once annually.

3. The Council shall elect the Deputy Chair by two-thirds majority.

4. The Council will:

i.   consider and adopt the agenda;

ii.   approve the Annual Report;

iii. approve the Financial Reports for the previous financial year;

iv.   approve the Work Programme for the following year;

v.   approve the budget for the following year;

vi.   appoint an Accountant and an Auditor;

vii. consider and adopt Mutual Evaluation Reports on Members;

viii. decide on policy matters, including the adoption of any revised Recommendations;

ix.   approve the admission of new Members, Co-operating and Supporting Nations, and Observers;

x.   take appropriate action with respect to Members that do not comply with this Memorandum;

xi.   appoint the Executive Director and the Deputy Executive Director of the Secretariat;

xii. determine the location of the Secretariat;

xiii. discuss any other business of which written notice has been given to the Secretariat at least three months prior to the meeting of the Council; and

xiv. agree on the date and venue of the next meeting of the Council.

VIII – The Chair

1.   The Chair will hold office until the next annual meeting of the Council.

2.   The Member holding the Chair will appoint a Minister who will:

i.   represent the CFATF at FATF meetings and other occasions determined by the Council;

ii.   preside over meetings of the Council and the Plenary;

iii. carry out activities assigned by the Council and any other activities consistent with his mandate; and

iv.   be regularly briefed regarding the activities of the Secretariat and supervise its Work Programme.

3.   In the event that the Chair is unable to perform any official function, the Deputy Chair will assume the Chair.

IX – The Deputy Chair

1.   The Deputy Chair will assume the Chair at the next annual meeting of the Council.

2.   The Deputy Chair will undertake such functions as may be delegated by the Chair.

X – The Plenary

1.   Each Member will be represented by one senior official in the Plenary.

2.   The Plenary will meet at least twice annually.

3.   The Chair and Deputy Chair of the Council will be respectively Chair and Deputy Chair of the Plenary.

4.   For submission to the Council, the Plenary will:

i.   prepare the draft agenda;

ii.   consider the draft Annual Report;

iii.   consider the Financial Reports;

iv.   review progress in the implementation of the approved Work Programme;

v.   consider the draft Work Programme for the following year;

vi.   consider a budget for the following year;

vii.   make recommendations for the appointment of the Accountant and an independent Auditor;

viii.   develop, consider and recommend proposals for funding;

ix.   consider Mutual Evaluation Reports on Members;

x.   make recommendations on policy matters, including the adoption of any revised Recommendations;

xi.   make recommendations on the admission of new Members, Co-operating and Supporting Nations, and Observers; and

xii.   recommend candidates for the positions of Executive Director and Deputy Executive Director of the Secretariat.

5.   The Plenary may establish working groups to undertake specific tasks.

XI – Procedures at meetings

1.   A validly constituted quorum for a meeting will exist when at least one half of the voting Members is present.

2.   All Members, Co-operating and Supporting Nations and Observers participate in meetings.

3.   Only Members present have the right to vote.

4.   Observers may participate in the discussion of mutual evaluations unless the evaluated Member objects.

5.   Resolutions will be adopted by two-thirds majority of the Members present.

XII – The Secretariat

1.   The Secretariat will perform technical and administrative functions under the direction of the Executive Director and the Deputy Executive Director.

2.   The Secretariat will submit to the Plenary:

i.   the Annual Report;

ii.   the Financial Reports;

iii. the Work Programme for the following year;

iv.   the budget for the following year.

3.   The Secretariat will provide periodic reports to the Chair regarding its activities. The Secretariat, under supervision of the Chair, will:

i.   implement the Work Programme approved by the Council;

ii.   administer the approved budget;

iii. co-ordinate and participate in Mutual Evaluations;

iv.   co-ordinate and make technical recommendations on the self-assessment of Members, disseminate self-assessment questionnaires, and collate and analyse the responses thereto;

v.   identify training and technical assistance needs of Members and facilitate the provision thereof;

vi.   act as a liaison between the CFATF and third countries and organisations involved in countering money laundering and related matters;

vii. monitor anti-money laundering developments and on authorisation by the Chair, participate in activities not included in the Work Programme;

viii. receive applications on behalf of the Chair;

ix.   receive notices of intention to withdraw and notify Members accordingly; and

x.   discharge any other responsibility assigned by the Plenary or the Council.

XIII – National committees

Members will, in accordance with applicable domestic law, establish Standing Anti-Money Laundering Committees or similar entities, comprising senior representatives of relevant disciplines: Legal and Judicial, Financial Supervision, and Law Enforcement.

XIV – Self-assessment

Members agree to participate in an ongoing Self-Assessment Programme co-ordinated by the Secretariat.

XV – Mutual evaluation

Members agree to participate in a programme of mutual evaluation conducted in accordance with Mutual Evaluation Procedures approved by the Council.

XVI – Languages and authentic text

The official languages of the CFATF are English and Spanish. The English and Spanish texts of this Memorandum are equally valid and authentic.

XVII – Accounting period

The financial year will be from the first day of January to the 31st day of December.

XVIII – Financial reports

1.   The Accountant will prepare financial statements comprising a balance sheet, income and expenditure statement, cash flow and source of funds statements to December 31st each year.

2.   The Auditor will carry out an annual audit of the books and accounts of the CFATF, and prepare and submit a report to the Council.

XIX – Amendment of this Memorandum

This Memorandum may be amended by unanimous vote of a meeting of the Council.

XX – Entry into effect

This Memorandum will come into effect on the date when signed by seven Members. For any Member which signs subsequently, it will become effective on the date of signature by that Member.

XXI – Withdrawal

A withdrawal by a Member or a Co-operating and Supporting Nation will be effective three months after receipt by the Secretariat of written notice of intention to withdraw.

Joint statement of co-operation and support for the Caribbean Financial Action Task Force

1.   Representatives of the Governments of Canada, the Kingdom of the Netherlands, France, the United Kingdom, and the United States of America (the "Co-operating and Supporting Nations"), meeting together in San Jose, Costa Rica, 9-10 October, 1996, considered the work of the Caribbean Financial Action Task Force (the "CFATF") since 1990, the benefits of effective implementation of mechanisms to prevent and control money laundering; and the need for expertise and training, and co-operation among Nations to assure such implementation in the Caribbean region.

2.   The Co-operating and Supporting Nations are members of the Financial Action Task Force on Money Laundering (the "FATF") and as such are committed to the 1988 UN Convention Against Illicit Traffic in Narcotic Drugs and Psychotropic Substances and to the implementation of the forty FATF recommendations concerning anti-money laundering measures.

3.   The Co-operating and Supporting Nations recognise the relationship between the work and objectives of the FATF and the work and objectives of the CFATF. Those Nations will make such contributions to the work and/or resources of the CFATF as are permitted by their respective national laws and policies.

4.   As members of the FATF, the Co-operating and Supporting Nations are committed to the mutual evaluation of their progress in implementing the forty recommendations of the FATF. Other Nations that are not Members of the CFATF may become Co-operating and Supporting Nations. All future Co-operating and Supporting Nations must express their commitment to the support of the CFATF and must have undergone a positive mutual evaluation by the FATF or an FATF-approved regional body.

APPENDIX IX – THE 1998 TERMS OF REFERENCE OF THE ASIA/PACIFIC GROUP ON MONEY LAUNDERING

Terms of Reference

These Revised Terms of Reference for the Asia/Pacific Group on Money Laundering (APG) were approved by members at the First Annual Meeting of the APG held in Tokyo from 10 to 12 March 1998.

Recognising in Bangkok on 27 February 1997 that:

• Money laundering is a significant international issue which requires global action;

• The Asia/Pacific region needs to address this issue as part of the global response;

• The capacity of individual jurisdictions to deal with the issue is limited because of its nature, complexity and international scope;

• Close co-operation between jurisdictions is necessary and that much can be gained by increasing understanding of the problem and its solutions;

• There are accepted international standards (the Financial Action Task Force's forty recommendations) but the best way to apply the standards within the region needs to be reviewed;

• There is an increasing risk of vulnerability to money laundering in the Asia/Pacific region as other regions introduce anti-money laundering measures; and

• A plan of action should be developed to address regional co-operation, the adoption of standards and to provide assistance to jurisdictions in tackling the problem.

Jurisdictions established the Asia/Pacific Group on Money Laundering.

Noting that

The Working Party, established by the APG met in Beijing from 7 to 9 July 1997 and agreed that:

> The forty recommendations are the guiding principles for action for the creation of an effective anti-money laundering framework. Member jurisdictions will implement the forty recommendations according to their particular cultural values and constitutional frameworks thus allowing them a measure of flexibility rather than prescribing every detail.

The first meeting of the APG in Tokyo agreed the following:

Purpose

The APG:

1.   Provides a focus for co-operative anti-money laundering efforts in the region;

2.   Provides a forum in which:

a.   regional issues can be discussed and experience shared;

b.   through exchange of information, the study and analysis of the problems caused by money laundering can be facilitated; and

c.   the issue of illegal proceeds is handled and the criminal realities in the region can be taken into account.

3.   Encourages the adoption, throughout the region, of international anti-money laundering standards;

4.   Enables regional and jurisdictional factors to be taken into account in the implementation of international anti-money laundering measures;

5.   Encourages jurisdictions to implement anti-money laundering initiatives including more effective mutual legal assistance; and

6.   Co-ordinates and provides practical support, where possible, to jurisdictions in the region which request it.

Nature

The APG is voluntary and co-operative in nature. The APG is established by agreement among its members and is autonomous. It does not derive from an international treaty. It is not part of any international organisation. However, it will need to keep itself informed of action taken or formal agreements made by relevant international and regional organisations or bodies in order to promote a consistent global response to money laundering.

The work to be done by the APG and its procedures will be decided by agreement among its members.

Membership

Membership of the APG is open to any jurisdiction within the Asia/Pacific region which:

1.   Recognises the need for action to be taken to combat money laundering;

2.   Recognises the benefits to be obtained by sharing knowledge and experience; and

3.   Has taken or is considering taking steps to develop, pass and implement anti-money laundering legislation and other measures based on accepted international standards.

It is not a precondition for participation in the APG that anti-money laundering laws be already enacted.

Membership of the APG is Australia, Bangladesh, Chinese Taipei, Fiji, Hong Kong, China, India, Japan, New Zealand, People's Republic of China, Republic of Korea, Republic of the Philippines, Singapore, Sri Lanka, Thailand, United States of America and Vanuatu.

Each jurisdiction will decide on the particular steps it will take to combat money laundering. The response by individual jurisdictions will, however, be significantly assisted by participation in the APG.

The APG will welcome new members from the Asia/Pacific region. Smaller jurisdictions whose direct involvement may be difficult may wish to participate in the APG through an appropriate sub-regional forum.

The APG recognises that there are significant benefits for members from continuing contact with non-member jurisdictions. As such, the meetings of the APG will also serve to provide opportunities for regular consultation with non-member jurisdictions who could attend as observers.

The APG recognised that many international organisations have a strong interest in anti-money laundering initiatives. In addition to the FATF, the organisations which attended the inaugural meeting (ASEAN Secretariat, Asian Development Bank, International Monetary Fund, International Organisation of Securities Commissions, Interpol, Offshore Group of Banking Supervisors, United Nations Crime Prevention and Criminal Justice Division, United Nations International Drug Control Programme and World Customs Organisation) and any other international organisation with an interest in effectively combating money laundering will be encouraged to participate in future meetings of the APG as observers.

The APG welcomes the support and co-operation from international organisations and other, non-member jurisdictions that may be willing to provide resources to assist the work of the APG. The participation (and the nature of such participation) of non-member jurisdictions and international organisations will be determined by the APG on a case-by-case basis.

Meetings

The APG will meet at least once each year.

Meetings will normally be held in member jurisdictions. In addition to an annual meeting of the APG, meetings may be conducted to coincide with money laundering methods meetings. Some meetings may be limited to APG members only.

Invitations to the annual meeting will be extended to non-member jurisdictions to attend as observers.

While meetings will generally be open to observers some part of a meeting may be limited to members only to enable the APG to conduct formal consideration of issues which require the agreement of its members.

To ensure a global approach to anti-money laundering, members of the APG will work closely with the Financial Action Task Force (FATF). The FATF Secretariat will attend APG meetings on the same basis that the APG Secretariat attends FATF meetings.

Meetings should be held at the same time each year.

Secretariat

Secretariat services will be provided by the Asia/Pacific Group on Money Laundering Secretariat. The level (scope and extent) and location of Secretariat support will be determined by the APG in the context of the available resources and adopted work programme.

Working party

To enable the work of the APG to be addressed between meetings, a working party of representatives of members will be established. Membership of the working party will be open to all members.

Chairing of the APG

The APG will be co-chaired by representatives of member jurisdictions. Co-chairs will be agreed at the annual meeting of the APG. Co-chairs may be selected for individual meetings of the APG or of the working party as necessary.

Plan of action

A work programme will be developed, reviewed and amended as necessary by the APG at each annual meeting.

The working party, in close consultation with members, will develop for consideration and adoption by the APG a statement of principles and measures for application within the region.

Obligations

The APG recognises that the ongoing work of the APG, and in particular the capacity of the Secretariat to assist jurisdictions will depend on the resources available to it. In the future, members will need to determine the work program, priorities and available resources of the APG. It will also need to determine a fair and equitable procedure to meet the costs of undertaking APG activities.

Contact points

Each member jurisdiction will nominate a person to act as the central contact point in that jurisdiction for all APG communication. In addition, each member will identify within its jurisdiction an appropriate contact point for the three relevant money laundering sectors: legal, financial and law enforcement.

Non-member jurisdictions will be requested to nominate a person or persons who will be the first point of contact in relation to money laundering matters and the work of the APG.

Tokyo, Japan
12 March 1998

Sales agents for publications of the Council of Europe
Agents de vente des publications du Conseil de l'Europe

AUSTRALIA/AUSTRALIE
Hunter Publications, 58A, Gipps Street
AUS-3066 COLLINGWOOD, Victoria
Fax: (61) 33 9 419 7154
E-mail: Robd@mentis.com.au

AUSTRIA/AUTRICHE
Gerold und Co., Graben 31
A-1011 WIEN 1
Fax: (43) 1512 47 31 29
E-mail: buch@gerold.telecom.at

BELGIUM/BELGIQUE
La Librairie européenne SA
50, avenue A. Jonnart
B-1200 BRUXELLES 20
Fax: (32) 27 35 08 60
E-mail: info@libeurop.be

Jean de Lannoy
202, avenue du Roi
B-1060 BRUXELLES
Fax: (32) 25 38 08 41
E-mail: jean.de.lannoy@euronet.be

CANADA
Renouf Publishing Company Limited
5369 Chemin Canotek Road
CDN-OTTAWA, Ontario, K1J 9J3
Fax: (1) 613 745 76 60

CZECH REPUBLIC/RÉPUBLIQUE TCHÈQUE
USIS, Publication Service
Havelkova 22
CZ-130 00 Praha 3
Fax: (420) 2 242 21 484

DENMARK/DANEMARK
Munksgaard
Østergade 26A – Postbox 173
DK-1005 KØBENHAVN K
Fax: (45) 77 33 33 77
E-mail: direct@munksgaarddirect.dk

FINLAND/FINLANDE
Akateeminen Kirjakauppa
Keskuskatu 1, PO Box 218
FIN-00381 HELSINKI
Fax: (358) 9 121 44 50
E-mail: akatilaus@stockmann.fi

FRANCE
C.I.D.
131 boulevard Saint-Michel
F-75005 Paris
Fax: (33) 01 43 54 80 73
E-mail: lecarrer@msh-paris.fr

GERMANY/ALLEMAGNE
UNO Verlag
Proppelsdorfer Allee 55
D-53115 BONN
Fax: (49) 228 21 74 92
E-mail: unoverlag@aol.com

GREECE/GRÈCE
Librairie Kauffmann
Mavrokordatou 9
GR-ATHINAI 106 78
Fax: (30) 13 23 03 20

HUNGARY/HONGRIE
Euro Info Service/Magyarország
Margitsziget (Európa Ház),
H-1138 BUDAPEST
Fax: (361) 302 50 35
E-mail: euroinfo@mail.matav.hu

IRELAND/IRLANDE
Government Stationery Office
4-5 Harcourt Road
IRL-DUBLIN 2
Fax: (353) 14 75 27 60

ISRAEL/ISRAËL
ROY International
41 Mishmar Hayarden Street
PO Box 13056
IL-69865 TEL AVIV
Fax: (972) 3 648 60 39
E-mail: royil@netvision.net.il

ITALY/ITALIE
Libreria Commissionaria Sansoni
Via Duca di Calabria 1/1, CP 552
I-50125 FIRENZE
Fax: (39) 0 55 64 12 57
E-mail: licosa@ftbcc.it

MALTA/MALTE
L. Sapienza & Sons Ltd
26 Republic Street, PO Box 36
VALLETTA CMR 01
Fax: (356) 233 621

NETHERLANDS/PAYS-BAS
De Lindeboom Internationale Publikaties
PO Box 202
NL-7480 AE HAAKSBERGEN
Fax: (31) 53 572 92 96
E-mail: lindeboo@worldonline.nl

NORWAY/NORVÈGE
Akademika, A/S Universitetsbokhandel
PO Box 84, Blindern
N-0314 OSLO
Fax: (47) 23 12 24 10

POLAND/POLOGNE
Głowna Księgarnia Naukowa im. B. Prusa
Krakowskie Przedmiescie 7
PL-00-068 WARSZAWA
Fax: (48) 22 26 64 49

PORTUGAL
Livraria Portugal
Rua do Carmo, 70
P-1200 LISBOA
Fax: (351) 13 47 02 64

SPAIN/ESPAGNE
Mundi-Prensa Libros SA
Castelló 37
E-28001 MADRID
Fax: (34) 915 75 39 98
E-mail: libreria@mundiprensa.es

SWITZERLAND/SUISSE
Buchhandlung Heinimann & Co.
Kirchgasse 17
CH-8001 ZÜRICH
Fax: (41) 12 51 14 81

BERSY
Route d'Uvrier 15
CH-1958 LIVRIER/SION
Fax: (41) 27 203 73 32

UNITED KINGDOM/ROYAUME-UNI
TSO (formerly HMSO)
51 Nine Elms Lane
GB-LONDON SW8 5DR
Fax: (44) 171 873 82 00
E-mail: denise.perkins@theso.co.uk

**UNITED STATES and CANADA/
ÉTATS-UNIS et CANADA**
Manhattan Publishing Company
468 Albany Post Road, PO Box 850
CROTON-ON-HUDSON, NY 10520, USA
Fax: (1) 914 271 58 56
E-mail: Info@manhattanpublishing.com

STRASBOURG
Librairie Kléber
Palais de l'Europe
F-67075 STRASBOURG Cedex
Fax: +33 (0)3 88 52 91 21

Council of Europe Publishing/Editions du Conseil de l'Europe
F-67075 Strasbourg Cedex
Tel. +33 (0)3 88 41 25 81 – Fax +33 (0)3 88 41 39 10
E-mail: publishing@coe.int – Website: http://book.coe.fr